Migration and Mutation

Literatures, Cultures, Translation

Literatures, Cultures, Translation presents books that engage central issues in translation studies such as history, politics, and gender in and of literary translation, as well as books that open new avenues for study. Volumes in the series follow two main strands of inquiry: one strand brings a wider context to translation through an interdisciplinary interrogation, while the other hones in on the history and politics of the translation of seminal works in literary and intellectual history.

Series Editors

Brian James Baer, Kent State University, USA
Michelle Woods, The State University of New York, New Paltz, USA

Editorial Board

Paul Bandia, Professeur titulaire, Concordia University, Canada, and Senior Fellow, the W.E.B. Du Bois Institute for African American Research, Harvard University, USA
Susan Bassnett, Professor of Comparative Literature, Warwick University, UK
Leo Tak-hung Chan, Guangxi University, Hong Kong, China
Michael Cronin, Dublin City University, Republic of Ireland
Edwin Gentzler, University of Massachusetts Amherst, USA
Denise Merkle, Moncton University, Canada
Michaela Wolf, University of Graz, Austria

Volumes in the Series

Translation and the Making of Modern Russian Literature
Brian James Baer
Interpreting in Nazi Concentration Camps
Edited by Michaela Wolf
Exorcising Translation: Towards an Intercivilizational Turn
Douglas Robinson
Literary Translation and the Making of Originals
Karen Emmerich
The Translator on Stage
Geraldine Brodie
Transgender, Translation, Translingual Address
Douglas Robinson
Western Theory in East Asian Contexts: Translation and Translingual Writing
Leo Tak-hung Chan
The Translator's Visibility: Scenes from Contemporary Latin American Fiction
Heather Cleary
The Relocation of Culture: Translations, Migrations, Borders
Simona Bertacco and Nicoletta Vallorani
The Art of Translation in Light of Bakhtin's Re-accentuation
Edited by Slav Gratchev and Margarita Marinova
Migration and Mutation: New Perspectives on the Sonnet in Translation
Edited by Carole Birkan-Berz, Oriane Monthéard,
and Erin Cunningham
This Is a Classic: Translators on Making Writers Global
Edited by Regina Galasso (forthcoming)

Migration and Mutation

New Perspectives on the Sonnet in Translation

Edited by
Carole Birkan-Berz, Oriane Monthéard,
and Erin Cunningham

BLOOMSBURY ACADEMIC
NEW YORK • LONDON • OXFORD • NEW DELHI • SYDNEY

BLOOMSBURY ACADEMIC
Bloomsbury Publishing Inc
1385 Broadway, New York, NY 10018, USA
50 Bedford Square, London, WC1B 3DP, UK
29 Earlsfort Terrace, Dublin 2, Ireland

BLOOMSBURY, BLOOMSBURY ACADEMIC and the Diana logo
are trademarks of Bloomsbury Publishing Plc

First published in the United States of America 2023
This paperback edition published 2024

Copyright © Carole Birkan-Berz, Oriane Monthéard,
and Erin Cunningham, 2023
Each chapter © Contributors, 2023

For legal purposes the Acknowledgements on pp. xviii–xix constitute
an extension of this copyright page.

Cover design by Daniel Benneworth-Gray
Cover image reproduced by permission of the British Library

All rights reserved. No part of this publication may be reproduced or transmitted in any form or by any means, electronic or mechanical, including photocopying, recording, or any information storage or retrieval system, without prior permission in writing from the publishers.

Bloomsbury Publishing Inc does not have any control over, or responsibility for, any third-party websites referred to or in this book. All internet addresses given in this book were correct at the time of going to press. The author and publisher regret any inconvenience caused if addresses have changed or sites have ceased to exist, but can accept no responsibility for any such changes.

Whilst every effort has been made to locate copyright holders the publishers would be grateful to hear from any person(s) not here acknowledged.

Library of Congress Cataloging-in-Publication Data
Names: Birkan-Berz, Carole, editor. | Monthéard, Oriane, editor. |
Cunningham, Erin, editor.
Title: Migration and mutation : new perspectives on the sonnet in translation / edited by Carole Birkan-Berz, Oriane Monthéard, and Erin Cunningham.
Description: New York : Bloomsbury Academic, 2023. | Series: Literatures, cultures, translation | Includes bibliographical references and index. |
Summary: "Explores how the sonnet has travelled through a striking range of European and other languages and cultures, from its early modern origins to the present day"– Provided by publisher.
Identifiers: LCCN 2022025448 (print) | LCCN 2022025449 (ebook) |
ISBN 9781501380464 (hardback) | ISBN 9781501380501 (paperback) | ISBN 9781501380471 (epub) | ISBN 9781501380488 (pdf) | ISBN 9781501380495
Subjects: LCSH: Poetry–Translating. | Sonnet. | Translating and interpreting. | LCGFT: Essays.
Classification: LCC PN1059.T7 M54 2023 (print) | LCC PN1059.T7 (ebook) |
DDC 809.1/42–dc23/eng/20220822
LC record available at https://lccn.loc.gov/2022025448
LC ebook record available at https://lccn.loc.gov/2022025449

ISBN: HB: 978-1-5013-8046-4
       PB: 978-1-5013-8050-1
       ePDF: 978-1-5013-8048-8
       eBook: 978-1-5013-8047-1

Typeset by Integra Software Services Pvt. Ltd.

To find out more about our authors and books visit www.bloomsbury.com and sign up for our newsletters.

Contents

List of figures	ix
List of contributors	x
Foreword *David Duff*	xv
Acknowledgements	xviii
Introduction *Carole Birkan-Berz*	1

Part 1 Revisiting early modern circulations

1. Poetic furor in translation: Spenser's and Sylvester's sonnet collections *Pádraic Lamb* — 17
2. The fashioning of English anti-Petrarchism: Spenser and Shakespeare remembering Du Bellay *Line Cottegnies* — 35
3. 'Translated out of Ronsard'?: A misattributed translation of Petrarch's *RVF* 48 by Sir John Borough *Guillaume Coatalen* — 53
4. Paving the way for Opitz: The first German sonnets at the crossroads of European circulation networks, 1556–1604 *Elisabeth Rothmund* — 69

Part 2 Sonnet translation as a space for poetic imagination

5. Keats's sonnets and the translation process: Mediation, conversion and response *Oriane Monthéard* — 89
6. On translating *Les Chimères* by Gérard de Nerval *Peter Valente* — 105
7. Reshaping Rilke: A comparative approach to the latest translations of *Die Sonette an Orpheus* into English *Frédéric Weinmann* — 115
8. Fernando Pessoa's sonnets – dislocations in form, persona and language *Carlos A. Pittella* — 131
9. English sonnet spaces in Jacques Roubaud's *Churchill 40* *Thea Petrou* — 155

10 Lyrical gestures: The essence of the form and the spirit of
    the translated text in Don Paterson's 'versions' of sonnets
    Bastien Goursaud   175

Part 3 Sonnet migrations across and outside Europe: Translating as
        a political act

11 Translation and transnationalism: Reframing the contemporary
    Irish sonnet *Erin Cunningham*   193
12 Sonnet translation and imitation during the Second World War:
    Maintaining the idea of Europe? *Thomas Vuong*   209
13 Translating Genrikh Sapgir's *Sonnets on Shirts* *Dmitri Manin*   229
14 The vulgar eloquence of Singaporean sonnets *Tse Hao Guang*   243

Part 4 Cross-media adaptations and beyond

15 On the theatricality of the *Canzoniere*, from medieval to
    modern times *Jean-Luc Nardone*   263
16 Raymond Queneau's *Cent mille milliards de poèmes*: An attempt
    to exhaust the sonnet *Natalie Berkman*   283
17 *The Four Seasons* in flux: Translating the sonnets from
    Vivaldi's score in relation to performances by Nigel Kennedy
    Paul Munden and Anouska Zummo   301
18 Debating sonnet translation in the Soviet and post-Soviet era:
    Rethinking and transforming the Russian sonnet
    Alexander Markov   315

Bibliography   333
Index   341

Figures

3.1	Harley_ms_1823_f014r. Reproduced by permission of the British Library	56
3.2	Harley_ms_1823_f014v. Reproduced by permission of the British Library	58
3.3	Harley_ms_1823_f094r. Reproduced by permission of the British Library	60
5.1	Keats, John, 1795–1821. Much have I travell'd in the realms of gold. A.MS., early draft. MS Keats 2.4. Houghton Library, Harvard University, Cambridge, MA. 49184486	91
8.1	Lima-Orpheu2-15-detail. Biblioteca Nacional de Portugal	133
8.2	BNP-E3-49A7-9v	135
8.3	BNP-E3-98(1)-2v-detail; cf. Pessoa 1918: [10]	136
8.4	BNP-E3-49B1-10r. Biblioteca Nacional de Portugal	143
8.5	BNP-E3-153-18r-detail. Biblioteca Nacional de Portugal	143
8.6	BNP-E3-49A7-3r. Biblioteca Nacional de Portugal	147
8.7	BNP-E3-49A7-3v. Biblioteca Nacional de Portugal	148
8.8	BNP-E3-49A7-8r. Biblioteca Nacional de Portugal	149
16.1	Maxime Fournier – Livre-objet Queneau. Reproduced by permission of Maxime Fournier, Programme Coordinator of the Film Department at SAE Institute Paris	289
17.1	Score by Vivaldi. Every effort has been made to trace the copyright holder	304
18.1	Empty Sonnet – Aronzon. Reproduced by permission of Felix Yacubson	320

Contributors

Natalie Berkman is a higher education specialist and award-winning scholar, currently working as Instructional Design Manager at ESSEC Business School. With almost a decade of experience in pedagogy, curriculum design, research and academic administration, she is also currently consulting with ViaX and Crimson Education. Trained as both a literary scholar and mathematician, Natalie completed her PhD in French Literature at Princeton University with a dissertation on the mathematical methods of the OuLiPo (Ouvroir de Littérature Potentielle), published under the title *OuLiPo and the Mathematics of Literature* (Peter Lang, 2022).

Carole Birkan-Berz is Associate Professor of Literary Translation at the Sorbonne nouvelle. She has published widely on the contemporary English sonnet and on poetry translation. Her last edited book is *Translating Petrarch's Poetry: L'Aura del Petrarca from the Quattrocento to the 21st Century* (Cambridge: Legenda, 2020) and she has also translated into French a selection of Jeff Hilson's *In the Assarts* (Théâtre Typographique, 2021). She teaches a wide variety of subjects, ranging from heteroglossic fiction in translation to the interlinguistic component in fiction, and the notion of world literature. She is currently at work on a monograph on the contribution of translation studies to literary criticism.

Guillaume Coatalen is Senior Lecturer in early modern English literature at CY Cergy Paris University. He has published on a variety of topics including early modern manuscripts, translation, rhetoric, Elizabeth I's French correspondence and Petrarchan sonnets. He is the author of *Two Elizabethan Treatises on Rhetoric: Richard Rainold's Foundacion of Rhetoricke (1563) and William Medley's Brief Notes in Manuscript (1575)* (Brill, 2018) and the co-editor of *Elizabeth I's Foreign Correspondence: Letters, Rhetoric, and Politics* (Palgrave Macmillan, 2014) and of *Translating Petrarch's Poetry: L'Aura del Petrarca from the Quattrocento to the 21st Century* (Legenda, 2020).

Line Cottegnies is Professor of Early Modern Literature at Sorbonne Université. Her research interests include Elizabethan drama, Caroline poetry and early modern women authors. She has worked in particular on cultural transfers and the translation and circulation of texts between England and France. She has also edited, among other works, *2 Henry IV* for

The Norton Shakespeare 3 (2016) and co-edited *Robert Garnier in Elizabethan England*, with Marie-Alice Belle (MHRA, 2017). She is currently working on an edition of three of Behn's translations from the French for the *Complete Works of Aphra Behn* to be published with Cambridge University Press.

Erin Cunningham completed a PhD on the sonnet in modern and contemporary Irish poetry at King's College London in 2021. Her research was funded by the Arts and Humanities Research Council. She is a writer and reviewer for publications including the *Times Literary Supplement, Poetry London* and *Irish Studies Review*.

Bastien Goursaud received a PhD from Sorbonne Université in 2020 and teaches English literature and translation at Université Paris Est Créteil. His thesis focused on poetry performance and/as public utterance in contemporary British poetry. His research interests also include poetry translation, close listening and sound studies, as well as poetry and popular culture.

Tse Hao Guang (謝皓光) is a Singaporean poet and editor. His first full-length poetry collection, *Deeds of Light*, was shortlisted for the 2016 Singapore Literature Prize. He co-edits the collaborative e-journal OF ZOOS, and co-edited *UnFree Verse* (2017), the anthology of Singapore poetry in received and nonce forms, as well as *Food Republic* (2020), a literary anthology of food writing. He is a 2016 fellow of the University of Iowa's International Writing Program as well as the 2018 National Writer-in-Residence at Nanyang Technological University. He edited the new edition of Windham-Campbell prize-winning poet Wong May's 1969 debut, *A Bad Girl's Book of Animals* (Ethos Books, 2023). His second poetry collection is *The International Left-Hand Calligraphy Association*, forthcoming from Tinfish Press.

Pádraic Lamb is completing his PhD thesis at the Centre des Études Supérieures de la Renaissance, Tours and teaches at Université Lumière Lyon 2. His research centres on Renaissance theories and practices of poetic inspiration, as well as Anglo-French literary relations. He has published articles on invocations in Shakespeare and Heywood, on James VI and I's French poetic models, on inspiration in Spenser and Sylvester's sonnet translations, and on Stephen Batman.

Dmitri Manin is a physicist, programmer and poetry translator. His translations from English and French into Russian have appeared in several book collections. His latest work is a complete translation of Ted Hughes's *Crow*

(Jaromír Hladík Press, 2020) and Allen Ginsberg's *Howl, Kaddish and Other Poems* (Podpisnie Izdaniya, 2021). Dmitri's Russian-to-English translations have been published in journals (*Cardinal Points, Delos, The Café Review, Metamorphoses* et al) and in Maria Stepanova's *The Voice Over* (CUP, 2021). In 2017 Dmitri won the Compass Award competition. His translation of N. Zabolotsky's collection *Columns* is slated for 2023 by Arc Publications.

Alexander Markov is Doctor of Philology, Full Professor (Art Theory) at the Russian State University for the Humanities. He is a participant in the international project *Dictionary of Untranslatables: A Philosophical Lexicon*, and author of twelve books and over 800 articles. Professor Markov's interests are primarily the history of *ekphrasis*, the interaction of the visual and verbal principles in contemporary art, the transformation of stable forms in literature and in painting in troubled eras, and the postmodern reception and processing of classical and traditional forms of art expression. In recent years, Professor Markov has been studying Soviet non-conformist art, reconstructing the communication of scholars, artists and poets in the Soviet underground communities as a pattern of general intellectual life.

Oriane Monthéard is Associate Professor of Translation and British Culture and Literature at University of Rouen-Normandie, where she teaches civilization, translation and literature. She has also translated many works of contemporary poetry, including Stephen Rodefer and Ron Padgett, as part of the collective Double Change. Her research primarily focuses on John Keats's work, and she has published articles on both his poetry and his letters. She has published a monograph on Keats's poems and letters entitled *Keats et la rencontre*. Her research interests also include graphic novels and intermediality.

Paul Munden is a poet, editor and screenwriter living in North Yorkshire. A Gregory Award winner, he has published five poetry collections, including *Chromatic* (UWA Publishing, 2017). He is editor of various poetry anthologies, most recently *Divining Dante* (RWP, 2021). For the British Council he has covered a number of scientific and humanitarian themes as conference poet and edited the anthology *Feeling the Pressure: Poetry and Science of Climate Change* (British Council, 2008). He was director of the UK's National Association of Writers in Education, 1994–2018, and is now Adjunct Associate Professor at the University of Canberra, Australia.

Jean-Luc Nardone graduated in Italian studies at Paris IV-Sorbonne and is Professor at the University of Toulouse II, France, with the chair of Italian

Literature. He is currently director of the research group of Italian studies, with a strong research focus on manuscripts, publishing practices and the story of Italian books. He is currently working on Petrarch and Petrarchism in Europe (XIV–XVIIth cent.). His most recent publications are The Spanish Match. *Le mariage manqué entre le Prince de Galles et l'Infante d'Espagne (1623)* (2020) and *Pétrarque et la poésie européenne. Anthologie pétrarquiste* (2021).

Thea Petrou is a language examiner, translator and researcher based in London. She recently graduated from UCL with a PhD in modern and contemporary French poetry. Recent and forthcoming publications include 'Octogone: Forms of Farewell' and 'Collecting, Classifying and Composing: Art and Memory in Jacques Roubaud's C'. She is currently completing her first monograph, *Form and Love in the Poetry of Jacques Roubaud*.

Carlos A. Pittella is a Latinx poet and researcher. Born on traditional lands of the Tupi, Guarani and Goitacá (Rio de Janeiro), he lives in Tiohtià:ke (Montréal), where he studies creative writing at Concordia University. Some of his poems have appeared in Brasil/Brazil, Moist, Feral and the VS Podcast. He is a researcher affiliated with the Centre for Theatre Studies of the University of Lisbon. Holding a doctorate in literary studies from PUC-Rio, he has edited several works by and about Fernando Pessoa, including Fausto (Tinta-da-China, 2018).

Elisabeth Rothmund is Full Professor of Germanic Studies at the Sorbonne and a specialist of the cultural history of the Germanic world in the sixteenth to eighteenth centuries. Her research interests include literature and music, librettology, German poetry, poetics and theatre, European cultural transfers, the representations of national identity, and confessional, political and aesthetic issues. She has published *Martin Opitz, Le livre de la poésie allemande (1624)* (Toulouse, 2009), and 'La question des modèles français dans le développement de l'écriture poétique en Allemagne: l'exemple du sonnet (XVIIe–XVIIIe siècles)'.

Peter Valente is a writer, translator and author of twelve books, including a translation of Nanni Balestrini's *Blackout* (Commune Editions, 2017), which received a starred review in Publisher's Weekly. His most recent book is *Essays on the Peripheries* (Punctum Books, 2021). Forthcoming is his translation of *Nicolas Pages* by Guillaume Dustan (Semiotext[e], 2022) and his translation of Gérard de Nerval, *The Illuminated* (Wakefield Press, 2022).

Thomas Vuong holds a doctorate from Université Sorbonne Paris-Nord. He has co-directed Translating Petrarch's Poetry (MHRA) and written papers (in French) about the sonnet and the Oulipo, Jacques Roubaud, Natasha Trethewey and P. P. Pasolini among others. His other main focus is translation studies, especially under the lens of the imaginary.

Frédéric Weinmann is a former student of the ENS, a German teacher and a Doctor of Comparative Literature. He is a historian of translation and cultural transfers. After a doctorate on the introduction of German novels into France before 1815, he was a major contributor to the *Histoire des traductions en langue française*, edited by J. Y. Masson and Y. Chevrel (Verdier). At the same time, he has written on the phenomenon of canonization and produced several articles on the notions of popular literature, classical works and national art. He is currently at work on a book on the topic of homosexuality and literature.

Anouska Zummo holds a PhD in Translation Studies from Durham University, with a thesis which addressed the rendering of Sicilian dialect poetry and representation of regional voices in English translation. She currently lives in northern France, where she works as a freelance English teacher, researcher and translator. Her research interests include translation, particularly from Italian into English, representation of minority cultures and languages, migration studies and creative writing.

Foreword

David Duff

On the spectrum of formal variability, the sonnet is a relatively fixed or 'closed' form, one that specializes in techniques of closure and in which tight constraints of length, rhyme scheme and metre are both an artistic discipline and a spur to creativity. The Tardis-like quality of the sonnet, a deceptively small poetic form in which 'one little room' can become 'an everywhere', has been frequently remarked upon by both poets and critics, and the present collection of essays provides further examples of this paradox. The emphasis of the collection, however, falls on another Tardis-like property of the sonnet: its ability to transport itself to different times and places, to play a part in literary histories far removed from its temporal and geographical origins. No poetic genre of the post-classical world has travelled further or lasted longer as an active creative presence, inspiring new efforts of composition wherever it goes. No poetic genre, moreover, is more instantly recognizable, even when it appears in improbable guises or embedded in other genres or media. Yet this is not a case of a 'literary universal' hard-wired into the human imagination and independently generated in different locations (as has been claimed for, say, romantic comedy) but, rather, of a man-made artistic form with a known point of origin transmitted from period to period and culture to culture through direct contact. This volume adds to our map of the sonnet's historical and ongoing migration, tracing its journey across cultures as far apart as Elizabethan England, Soviet Russia and modern-day Singapore.

Some of the chapters revisit the early stages of sonnet transmission, explaining in fresh detail how this thirteenth-century Sicilian form came into being, was adopted and developed by Petrarch and other Tuscan poets, then was taken up, in the centuries that followed, by a succession of writers in other languages and locations. Particular attention is paid to France, as one of the most enthusiastic importers and users of sonnet form and as a conduit for Italian Renaissance influence on England and Germany, two other countries given special emphasis in this volume. The broad contours of this history are well known but the influence of figures such as Du Bellay has been underestimated and the first section shows how French and Italian influences frequently combined with and modified one another, necessitating a comparative approach to this complex history of literary migration and adaptation. Other chapters take up later stages of the European and global history of the sonnet, pinpointing moments of contact that enabled the genre to embed itself in other cultures or to acquire a new lease of life after periods of dormancy.

In some cases, the fresh impetus is artistic – an individual author's discovery of the genre, as in the chapters on Rilke, Keats, Pessoa or Nerval, or the adoption of sonnet form as part of a collaborative poetics, as in the Oulipo group's use of sonnets in their experiments with mathematical combinatorics and 'constrained writing' techniques (fascination with the number 14 must have been part of the attraction here, the same fascination that led Robert Burns to exclaim in his 'Sonnet upon Sonnets': 'What magic myst'ries in that number lie!'). At other times, it is new historical conditions that lead to the revival or repurposing of the genre, as demonstrated by the case study of Genrikh Sapgir, the Soviet-era Russian poet who used avant-garde sonnets to test the limits of free expression before and after Perestroika, or the chapter about writers during the Second World War whose renditions of earlier European sonnets served as a symbolic resistance against totalitarianism.

Above all, though, what makes possible the extreme mobility and versatility of the sonnet – its constant crossing of temporal and cultural boundaries and its assimilation within widely different literary systems and traditions – is the act of translation, the particular focus of this volume. From the start, contributors argue, translation has been integral to the history of the sonnet, not just in the obvious sense that well-known poems by canonical authors have frequently been translated, but in the sense that the transposition into different languages or dialects has shaped the very evolution of the genre, as for example with the emergence in early-modern England of variant rhyme schemes (the 'Spenserian' and 'Shakespearean', though Shakespeare did not invent the latter) better suited to the phonology of English than that of the Italian prototype. These technical innovations arose directly out of the effort of translation, and original and translated sonnets were routinely published side by side. From the beginning translators were presented with the problem of whether to prioritize fidelity to the sound or meaning of their source texts, a dilemma that exists for all translators of poetry but one that poses itself with especial starkness in this highly compacted, densely rhymed form. One consequence of this, as several chapters reveal, is that sonnet translation has often been a focus for reflection on translation per se, by poets themselves or by critics exploring the theory of translation. Analysis of sonnet translation opens inevitably into broader questions of intertextuality, collaborative authorship and reception theory, questions directly taken up by many of the contributors.

Poems, however, do not translate themselves, and another distinctive and welcome feature of this collection is the emphasis on authorial agency. The fact that many of the contributors are translators themselves, researching texts outside their native languages and writing in a linguistic medium that is not their own, has no doubt encouraged this sensitivity to the decision-making inherent in all translation, and intellectual respect for the individuals who undertake it. That respect extends to readers and performers, including actors who translate from page to stage the interpolated sonnets that feature in many Renaissance dramas, and even musical performers such as Nigel Kennedy, whose sonic renditions of the descriptive sonnets that accompany Vivaldi's *Four Seasons* are presented in one of the chapters as an act of double translation that turns poetic text on a musical score into the wordless language of instrumental performance.

Taken as a whole, the diverse studies assembled here, and the illuminating essay that introduces them, constitute an important advance in our understanding of the history and theory of the sonnet and the role of translation and translators in shaping and perpetuating it. However notionally 'fixed' at one level, the sonnet is shown to be uniquely mobile and flexible at another, its ubiquitous presence a testimony both to its cultural adaptability and to the creative energies of those who facilitate its migration. This exciting book brings into focus a vital topic and opens new lines of inquiry which future scholars will not be able to ignore.

Acknowledgements

Mardi, 17/3/20. La France est confinée. Je n'ai toujours pas lu *Voyage autour de ma chambre* (Xavier de Maistre) et pendant que Noah fait sa leçon d'anglais dans la salle à manger	Tuesday 17/3/20. France is in lockdown. I still haven't read Xavier de Maistre's *Journey round my Room* and as Noah gets his English lesson – i-e words like *like* –
(les i-e words (*like* like)), Clémence, au canapé, télétravaille. Amaël joue sur un iPad. Et moi en attendant de retrouver mes classes, je prends de l'élan et fais mes vers sonner,	in the front-room, Clémence is remoteworking on the couch. Amaël is on an iPad gaming and I am waiting to rejoin my classes, gaining momentum sounding out
lol. Personne ne sait, à London, où tout continue (c'est *business as usual* – Christine Chia m'écrit: 'UK government is playing dice	my lines. Lol. In London it's *business as per*, Christine Chia writes to me – 'UK gov is playing dice with people's lives' – everything goes on,
with citizens' lives'), quand les autres se confineront – mais dès le CP, on sait que le mot 'dice' forme avec le mot 'hide' une unique leçon.	nobody knows when they will be confined, yet all the kids know from Year One the single lesson in the words 'dice' and 'hide'.

Pierre Vinclair. *Le Confinement du monde*.
Poem 3. Translated by Carole Birkan-Berz.

The project of this book began with a Young and Early Career Researchers project initiated at the Sorbonne Nouvelle whose first publication – *Translating Petrarch's Poetry* (Legenda, 2020) – was released the month the Covid-19 pandemic began in Europe. Slowly but surely, we began to sow the seeds of the present volume, this time devoted to *The Sonnet in Translation* in its entirety. The above sonnet provides an apt description of how we editors worked to prepare this volume, often slowed down or stressed out by a global situation that seemed to rest on the roll of a dice. In this context, we are grateful to the authors, poets and translators of the chapters for providing stimulating material in these difficult times. Our gratitude extends to our colleagues Philip Terry, Jeremy Elprin, Chris Stamatakis, JoAnn DellaNeva, Rémi Vuillemin, Carle Bonafous-Murat, Emily Merriman, Marion Naugrette-Fournier, Boris Czerny, Claire Davison, Claire Hélie, Aurélie Griffin, Madeline Delbe, Francisco José Rodríguez Mesa and Delphine Rumeau, as well as the anonymous reviewers who lent their time and expertise to review parts of our manuscript. Hearty thanks are also due to David Duff, who coined the term 'a migrant genre' with us, for writing his generous foreword. We are greatly indebted to the Sorbonne Nouvelle's research group PRISMES, particularly Alexandra Poulain and Bruno Poncharal, for providing us with generous funding for this project over the years. We also extend our gratitude to the University of Rouen's research team ERIAC for providing funding to cover the cost of translating some of the articles. As in *Translating Petrarch*, credit is due to Fanny Quément for translating two chapters in this book. Claire Létoublon, our trusted research assistant, lent her great organizational and electronic skills and provided great overall support to this project. We would like to thank Haaris Naqvi at Bloomsbury for giving this book a home and Rachel Moore, Hali Han and all at Integra for supporting us through the production process. Finally, special thanks go to our respective families and loved ones, for giving us support and encouragement, as well as the space to 'zoom' in and out of the sonnet.

We thank the British Library, Harvard Keats Collection and Biblioteca Nacional de Portugal for allowing us to reproduce images from their collection. 'Queneau' is reproduced by kind permission of Maxime Fournier. The MS image for 'Пустой Сонет' ('Empty Sonnet') is reproduced by kind permission of Felix Yacubson. 'Sonnet 3' from *Le Confinement du monde* is reproduced by kind permission of Pierre Vinclair; the translation of the extract from Nerval's 'Isis', by Bettina Knapp is reproduced courtesy of University of Alabama Press. Poems from *Sonnets on Shirts* are reproduced by kind permission of Mrs. Kira Sapgir. Poems from *Sonnets from the Singlish* are reproduced by kind permission of Joshua Ip and poems *Payday Loans* are reproduced by kind permission of Jee Leong Koh. Extracts from Jacques Roubaud's *Churchill 40* are produced by permission of Gallimard (see copyright page). Extracts from Justin Quinn's *Close Quarters* are reproduced by permission of Gallery Press. Extracts from Jean Cassou's 'Translated from Hugo von Hofmannsthal' are reproduced by kind permission of Timothy Adès. Extracts from E.C. Mason, five of Rilke's *Sonnets to Orpheus* in German Life and Letters, as well as S. Cohn, 'Introduction', in *Sonnets to Orpheus with Letters to a Young Poet*, are reprinted by kind permission of Carcanet Press, Manchester, UK. Extracts from Rainer Maria Rilke's *Sonnets to Orpheus*, translated by Christiane Marks are used with permission from Open Letter Books at the University of Rochester. Sonnet 82 from *The Complete Canzoniere* is reproduced by permission of Tony and Adam Kline.

Every effort has been made to contact rights holders prior to publication. The publishers would be happy to rectify any omissions at reprint.

Introduction

Carole Birkan-Berz

Genres travel. Although tragedy was born in Greece, the ghazal in Arabia, the sonnet in Italy, the Bildungsroman in Germany, and haiku in Japan, these and other genres, far from staying put, took flight across seas or continents, assuming new languages and local colors.
                            Jahan Ramazani, A Transnational Poetics (71)

Pasternak, for example: shestdesyat shestoy, *they shout – give us the sixty-sixth (sonnet, of Shakespeare).*
[...] Nothing true / is easy.
                            Geoffrey Hill, The Triumph of Love, CIV (53–54)

In a way [...] all the poems in this anthology are translations.
                            Jeff Hilson, The Reality Street Book of Sonnets (17)

So far no volume has dealt extensively with the subject of the sonnet in translation – perhaps because the topic seems self-evident at first. Indeed, most literary histories and studies of the sonnet start by describing the various migrations of the form, from Sicily to Italy and then to various European countries. As the authors of the *Princeton Encyclopedia of Poetry and Poetics* have it: 'in the 15th and 16th centuries, the sonnet made its way to Spain, Portugal, France, the Netherlands, Poland, and England, and later to Germany, Scandinavia, and Russia; until its use was pan-European and the number of poets not attempting it negligible'. According to these accounts, the sonnet as a lyrical genre migrated from one culture to another, and its form mutated in the process according to the constraints of the host language. Thus, various European cultures caught the 'virus' of the sonnet in succession, and 'each country seems to have produced its own sonnet form'. In this respect, the 'English' or 'Shakespearean' sonnet is a case in point, developing seven rhymes instead of five so as to ease the constraints of the form on an allegedly rhyme-poor language (Westling 41) – with the gradual dominance of an epigrammatic rhyming couplet at the end (Rush 2) and the English sonnet ultimately emerging as a 12+2 structure rather than the traditional octave and sestet characterizing its 'Italian' or 'Petrarchan' predecessors (Monferran et al., Brogan, France, Masson, Cohen 2017).[1] Because the sonnet didn't 'migrate' all by itself, most studies emphasize the key role played by certain poet-translators, thus demonstrating the decisive role of translation in the literary lineage of the sonnet. Recent works on figures such as Thomas Wyatt (Stamatakis), John Florio (Wyatt, Pfister, Iannaccone), Spenser and Du Bellay (Coldiron, Melehy), and other early translators such as Garcilaso de la Vega and Juan Boscán (Navarette, Helgerson), Francisco de Sá de Miranda (Franco) or Georg Rodolf Weckherlin (Ullrich), as well as case studies offered in the *Oxford History of Literary Translation in English* or the *Histoire des Traductions en langue française* series, show that there appears to be 'a counterpart to Wyatt in nearly every European vernacular from Portugal to Poland' (Greene 42).[2] For the early modern period, however, the line between translation and imitation of a master is a blurry one; 'sonnet translation' quickly tends to be identified with 'Petrarchism' or 'anti-Petrarchism', as opposed to the semantic translation of texts (be it line-by-line or more 'adaptive'). This trend is even more pronounced when the vernaculars – such as Spanish and Italian – are close to one another and easily understandable, so that, for instance, full translations of Petrarch's *Canzoniere* don't appear until much later than popular sonnets and sonnet sequences by Petrarchist poets such as Garcilaso in Spain or Camões in Portugal (Kennedy 2015, Mesa). Still, corpus-based studies of the first comprehensive translations of Petrarch's *Rerum Vulgarium Fragmenta* such as Vasquin Philieul's and Jacques Peletier du Mans's (Turbil) will be of great interest to scholars as these texts constituted a stock from which poets could then pick and choose in order to '*petrarchize*' (Balsamo, Hudson).

Because of the early modern identification of translation with imitation, the topic of the sonnet in translation has been examined either through studies of the genre or studies in reception and intertextuality. In addition to focusing on individual authors, these works have helped put the matter into more context, showing that the journey undertaken by the sonnet, say from Italy to England, was a complex one – moving through France, especially via the figures of Du Bellay or Desportes (Melehy, Coldiron, Prescott), occasionally through the Netherlands through the work of Jan van der Noot and Spenser (Hadfield, Melehy), or through Scotland via James VI and his coterie of Scottish poets (Jack 2007, Spiller 1998, Verweij, Steenson). Scholars have sought to uncover the reasons for this intense circulation of forms and ideas in the Renaissance (Taylor, Prescott 2007), whether through the spread of Reformist ideas (Hamrick, Hosington) or as part of a larger poetic culture of translation – one that included epic, as well as other lyric forms or modes such as psalms or madrigals (Prescott 2007, Serjeantson, Schurink) – or through a drive to assert modernity and distinctive national character (Berman, Kennedy 2003, Alduy) via the acquisition of foreign material as a means for poets to 'make it new' (Taylor 405).

Besides literary histories, the topic of the sonnet in translation has been explored by translators themselves, especially in their prefaces (Hersant), or by translation studies scholars, who have sought to evaluate the losses and gains inherent in various approaches to the translation of poetry – a question to which the genre of the sonnet aptly lends itself because of its many rules and constraints (one might also add that the sonnet's short length facilitates easy recognition, bilingual layouts and comparative analysis). One question that often occupies translators' prefaces and essays on the topic is whether to translate sonnets into verse or prose, whether to translate line for line or to compensate, and whether or not to attempt to reproduce or find an equivalent for the original rhyme scheme and canonical line (for instance, should one use the French décasyllable or the alexandrine as an equivalent for the English or Russian iambic pentameter or the Italian endecasilabo?). In the wake of historical, or 'new' formalism, a consensus seems to emerge which envisions these forms as the product of their cultural inheritance (Etkind 163, Meschonnic 95, cited by Masseau 79), which can sometimes become transnational (Ramazani 20), and sees the search for equivalence, as in other types of translation, as following an 'asymptotic' movement – coming close to the source but never meeting it.[3] Over the past few decades, scholars focusing on translating rhythm as opposed to metre (Meschonnic 1982, 297–333, Etkind 182, Scott 2000, 37) and on translating the sound of poetry (Scott 2018, 67–74, Skoulding, Birkan-Berz) have also shifted the terms of the debate, returning us poetically to the Troubadour origins of the sonnet (Spiller 24) as a spoken form in which formal aspects such as metre or rhyme could serve as 'signatures' for individual poets (Kay 12, 146).

The study of the translation and re-translation of canonical sonnets continues to occupy a significant place in the literature, as does the drive to map out various approaches to the practice, derived from the sheer amount of translations of certain classic sonnets, which can therefore be collated. Here again, the debate has been somewhat displaced to ask what, within and beyond the 'carrying over' of the genius of the author, makes a translation a poem in its own right (Paterson 74, Robinson 100), a renewed 'union of sound and sense' (Ricoeur 12, cited by Ellrodt 78), or a re-creation (Folkart 41, 123). In the wake of approaches favouring creativity – and taking their cue from the poetic works themselves – other studies have sought to expand the concept of translation to include rewritings of certain major texts (those by Robert Lowell, for instance, where the early modern term 'imitation' once again creeps in), or reinterpretations and subversions of the canon (Raimondo, Rushworth), as in Tim Atkins's versions of Petrarch. These are echoed in the variety of rewritings and performances, say, of Shakespeare's sonnets in recent years on the French stage or in anthologies such as S. Cohen and P. Legault's *The Sonnets: Translating and Rewriting Shakespeare*, featuring over 154 different takes on the original sonnets. In these studies, translations and poetic works, the concept of faithfulness to the original tends to be redefined as fidelity to an effect (Etkind 8), an imagined spirit (see Bastien Goursaud's chapter on Paterson in the present volume), or even an impression made by the original text (Reynolds 102; Robinson 31, 152).

The expansion of the concept of translation has been concomitant with the expansion of the concept of the sonnet itself, as an extremely recognizable form, a cultural icon that can become a template or identikit easily appropriated by any poet in any language or culture, keeping elements of its form while changing its meaning. Having been a vernacular poem in Italy – Petrarch was crowned Laureate for his Latin works, not for his Italian lyric poems – the sonnet was to become aristocratic elsewhere in Europe, as the language of courtiers, of aristocratic men and women, who spoke many *koinai*. No doubt this facilitated its migration across Europe, and later to other continents. Was it possible later to re-indigenize, or re-vernacularize it? There are chapters in this book devoted to the Irish or to the postcolonial sonnet, but readers are encouraged to refer to recent studies of the African-American sonnet (Westover, Müller), the American sonnet (Regan 220–285, Malech and Smith) or the challenges posed by the Hebrew and Yiddish sonnet (Finkin), as well as the 2015 conference organized by the Inalco (the National Institute for Oriental Languages and Civilizations) in Paris ('Le sonnet dans le monde') on the Chinese, Japanese, Indian and Indonesian sonnet, to name but a few. As postcolonial scholars Kwame Anthony Appiah and Jahan Ramazani have it: 'While globalization produces homogeneity […] it "is, equally, a threat to homogeneity," since people "are constantly inventing new forms of difference: new hairstyles, new slang, even, from time to time, new religions," and, we might add, new kinds of poetry' (Ramazani 10, quoting Appiah). In this respect, to paraphrase Jeff Hilson, all sonnets are translations (Hilson 2008, 17). The idea that the sonnet, which French critics such as Henri Meschonnic have called 'une forme-sens' (Meschonnic 1973, 34), already encapsulates a number of encoded meanings has fascinated all poets interested in literature as a code, including the founding members of the Oulipo such as Raymond Queneau in the 1960s, or avant-garde poets like Christian Bök today. Bök's work – storing poems into the DNA of a bacterium that could survive a nuclear apocalypse and having RNA strands of poetry 'translate' into proteins – shows how far the concept of sonnet translation can extend (Bök 150–154). But ahead of 'biological' poetry, the sonnet has become an idiom in which to couch many artistic gestures or cross-medially test the limits of the form's recognition, as in Jen Bervin's *Nets*, Sean Bonney's translations of Baudelaire (2011) or David Miller's visual sonnets (see Hilson 2008, 193–195).

All of these approaches, from the literary-historical to the more re-interpretive or subversive, are used to varying degrees in this book – we hope with a fresh twist. Editing this volume, we also hope to take translation out of its ancillary position – aiding the founding of national literatures or supporting writers' reputations – and emphasize its role as a springboard for creativity, which it continues to occupy, as testified by the contemporary work of translator-poet dyads furthering the sonnet and/in translation around the world: Pierre Vinclair, having lived in China and Singapore, translating Joshua Ip into French while writing formal sonnets in *Le Cours des choses* and *Le Confinement du monde* in turn translated by Ip; Sabine Huynh, translating Seymour Mayne's one-word sonnets and currently at work on some English *Sonnets and Contrails*; Frédéric Forte translating Oskar Pastior and writing *33 sonnets plats* (flat sonnets); my own publication of Jeff Hilson's sonnets with the publisher Bénédicte Vilgrain, also a translator of the Dutch Erik Lindner; and the list continues (see also Blakeley 141–142).

This volume revisits all of these approaches as well as some of the 'monuments' of the sonnet through a translational perspective, and interpolates scholarly essays with practice-based pieces, showing how translators, poets and artists engage with translating one or a series of sonnets. Barring one or two exceptions, the essays presented here are organized in a broadly chronological manner, from the Renaissance to the present day.

The first part of this book begins by looking at the question of translation and imitation in the early modern era. Pádraic Lamb's chapter opening the volume brings together two poets who translated political sonnets: Edmund Spenser and the lesser-known Josuah Sylvester, translator of Du Nesme; Lamb shows how these two poets appropriated the doctrine of poetic furor to justify, even exalt, poetic translation, so they might feel free to depart from the revered genius of the original French poets. In contrast to the practices of what she calls 'humanistic' imitation, Line Cottegnies in the next chapter shows how looking intertextually at Du Bellay and Shakespeare's not dissimilar attitudes in their responses to Petrarch can help us grasp how a subversive anti-Petrarchism was invented successively on both sides of the Channel. Next in the book, and reintroducing the question of authorship in early modern translation, Guillaume Coatalen's edition of a 1635 commonplace book shows how the late Renaissance man or woman could seize opportunities provided by the sonnet to translate in and out of vernacular tongues as well as into Neo-Latin, even when unsure of the translated poem's original author. Closing this early modern section, Elisabeth Rothmund offers a long retrospective look at the wide networks of sonnet circulation – in other words, of adaptations, translations, rewritings and imitations. She thus illustrates the way the French model reaches Germany and imposes itself there, either directly or via detours through the Netherlands and Scotland, thus paving the way for the German sonnet as popularized and codified by Martin Opitz in 1624.

Jumping ahead 150 years, the second part of our book is anchored in the Romantic renewal of the sonnet and explores sonnet translation as a space for the poetic imagination. Book co-editor Oriane Monthéard's chapter opens the section by looking at John Keats, as his sonnet 'On First Looking into Chapman's Homer' can be considered the first English sonnet in praise of the art of translation. Reflecting on what the practice meant to him, Keats also experimented with transposition from another language or from other types of verbal or imaginative material, sometimes resulting in a sort of self-translation. Echoing Keats in his exploration of another Romantic genius, Peter Valente offers a new translation of Nerval's mysterious and celebrated *Les Chimères*, a late revival of the sonnet form. Valente, who has also translated *The Illuminated* – Nerval's portrayal of the precursors of socialism – details the historical and biographical circumstances of this classic text and his efforts to reproduce the sounds that for him reflect these circumstances.

Moving forward towards modernism with the transitional figure of Rainer Maria Rilke – one of the most translated and retranslated sonneteers (Robinson) – the next chapter examines recent retranslations of *Die Sonette an Orpheus*, of which there have been no less than eighteen translations into English since the work fell into the public domain. Comparativist and translation studies scholar Frédéric Weinmann uses a 'prismatic' approach (Reynolds), collating all of these translations and examining them through the lens of their formal characteristics, including the rendering of particular Rilkean neologisms. The striking differences that can be witnessed between translative projects certainly underscore the various approaches to fidelity that continue to exist today.

With two of its editors rooted in twentieth-century poetics, this book would not be complete without an exploration of three central poetic figures who have accomplished in-depth work – whether as poets, critics or translators – taking the sonnet in and out of translation and/or multilingual creativity. The first is Fernando Pessoa, multilingual poet extraordinaire, who wrote in his native Portuguese as well as his quasi-native South African English and even in French. Carlos Pittella's archival work, unearthing and editing a selection of manuscripts by the multifaceted poet, shows how central certain sonnets were to Pessoa's personal and creative journey, not least Elizabeth Barrett Browning's famous 'How do I love thee? Let me count the ways' (also translated by Rilke), a pseudo-translation from the Portuguese retranslated by Pessoa and 'returned' to its imaginary source. The next figure is the French sonneteer and polymath Jacques Roubaud, studied by Thea Petrou, who takes a close look at the travel sonnets in *Churchill 40* and explores the importance of English and American echoes, in terms of language, poetic tradition, landscape and personal memory. Contrary to Roubaud's critical work, which mainly explores the Petrarchan tradition of the sonnet, his creative work is full of playful transgressions and combinations of English, French and American sonnets, showing variations or 'mutations' owed to avant-garde sonneteers such as Ted Berrigan and Jackson Mac Low, or to Gerard Manley Hopkins across the English Channel. Finally, also central to the exploration of the sonnet in – and out of – translation is the poet Don Paterson. From his detailed essays explaining the sonnets of William Shakespeare (or, as he calls him, 'WS') to a wide readership to his contemporary versioning of Antonio Machado or Rilke, Paterson often expresses his fascination with the form. Like Aragon and others before him, he envisions the sonnet as a 'thinking machine', an ideal producer of the poem's 'paraphrasable content'. Bastien Goursaud looks at Paterson's 'versioning' in terms of 'fidelity' to the spirit of the translated work expressing itself in a 'lyrical gesture'.

The third part of this book turns to preoccupations of a political nature underlying sonnet translations. Opening this section is volume co-editor Erin Cunningham's essay on twentieth-century Irish poetry, a tradition that is often examined through the perspective of Ireland's postcolonial relation to England but rarely considered in its relation to other European cultures. Examining sonnet translations by a range of contemporary Irish poets including Seamus Heaney, Ciaran Carson, Derek Mahon and Máire Mhac an tSaoi, the essay focuses most vividly on the very contemporary poets Justin Quinn and David Wheatley's poetics of transnationalism. Cunningham shows how Quinn's sonnets in 'The Months' – influenced by the Tuscan poet Folgore da San Gimignano's *Sonetti dei Mesi* – 'do not attempt to conceal the workings of translation', but instead 'actively foreground translation as a cultural practice, suggesting the nomadic nature of the sonnet as a form'. Zooming in on the most turbulent time in the history of Europe – the Second World War – Thomas Vuong offers in the next chapter a wide-ranging survey of what it meant for wartime poets to be translating from German, French, Italian, Spanish or Portuguese, asking whether poetic translation, of the sonnet in particular, remained a tool for a better understanding between cultures. Examining cases such as the various French translations of Shakespeare, Hölderlin or Rilke produced by Résistant poets or the poignant story of Jean Cassou, imprisoned in a Vichy jail and composing and translating sonnets in his mind as he awaited execution, Vuong argues that sonnet translation maintained its 'civilizing' function, though he also highlights that certain poets – Roy Campbell or Eleonore Lorenz – could also use the exercise to further their ethnonationalistic politics.

Taking us to the far edge of Europe and to another strained period of history, Dmitri Manin, in the second practice-based piece of this volume, translates and presents the work of Russian avant-garde dissident Genrikh Sapgir. During the Soviet era, Sapgir could only publish translations and children's poems, but in 1975 he was given the opportunity to show his work – three sonnets he immediately decided to write on old shirts – as part of an exhibition of 'unofficial artists'. This work, expanded and republished after Perestroika, constitutes a striking response to the tenets of 'high' Socialist Realism and to ideas of what 'good' art should be about. The sonnets are presented here for the first time in English with a discussion of what it means to translate them into this language today. Moving from Europe to South-East Asia, Tse Hao Guang examines the early work of two contemporary Singaporean poets whose choice to write sonnets goes against the grain of the free verse generally used in Singaporean poetry. As the two poets – Joshua Ip and Jee Leong Koh – each reinvent the sonnet in their own way, both take liberties with the structure of the form and with its content (an open development on themes of gay love). This creative approach – on a par with Jakobson's concept of 'intralingual' translation – enables them to reappropriate the English language in a form of postcolonial 'glocalization' (notably through Ip's English–Singlish code switching) through which the poets widen their readership and go beyond the divide between tradition and innovation.

The fourth and final section of the book is largely devoted to intersemiotic translation – the transfer or transcoding of the sonnet to a different medium or code rather than a different vernacular tongue. This section also encompasses some critical debates that were set in motion by sonnet translation and adaptation. Jean-Luc Nardone opens the section with a diachronic study of dramatic adaptations of Petrarch's *Canzoniere*. Tracing the origins of the dramatic sonnet in Italian medieval lauds, the chapter focuses on French theatre and its reception from the early modern period to the early twentieth century, with occasional parallels to the English stage. The next essay examines a key text in considering the sonnet as a code, Oulipo founding member Raymond Queneau's *A Hundred Thousand Billion Poems*. This astronomical number of sonnets occurs as a result of combining the fourteen lines of ten base sonnets initially written by the poet and shuffled at will by means of strips of paper or using a computer interface. Natalie Berkman looks at this seemingly 'unreadable' text, examining its origins, influences and constraints, and elucidates Queneau's use of mathematics as a deep political and artistic commentary on both surrealism and mass production. Following this is the final practice-based piece in this book, by musician and poet Paul Munden, accompanied by translator Anouska Zummo. The authors investigate the role of the sonnets inserted in to the *Four Seasons* violin concertos and attributed to Vivaldi himself. In a hybrid creative-critical study, Paul Munden reinterprets and retranslates these sonnets through the lens of the musical performance of British violinist Nigel Kennedy. Last in the collection of essays, and circling back to Shakespeare via Russia, is Alexander Markov's study of the poetic controversy created by the conversation around Samuil Marshak's translation of Shakespeare's sonnets in 1969. Markov suggests that this critical controversy created powerful aesthetic changes in poetry, resulting in great avant-garde work in the Russian sonnet. Finally, the author focuses on Olga Sedakova, showing how her translation of Petrarch demonstrates a type of respect for the classics (Petrarch and Pushkin) that combines the aesthetics of postmodernism with the 'foreign' psychology of distant eras. Marshak wrote that 'Poetry is impossible to translate. Each time it is an exception to the rule' (quoted by Etkind 1999, 346); we hope our readers enjoy discovering and revisiting each one of the exceptions presented in this volume.

Notes

1. Although scholars now show that these difficulties could be circumvented and that several models exist (Cohen 210).
2. Wyatt was not the first English poet to translate part of Petrarch's *RVF* – Chaucer, who had visited Italy and been inspired by the three Italian humanists Petrarch, Dante and Boccacio, had also translated parts of Petrarch, most famously 'S'amor non è' as part of 'The Clerk's Tale' (Rossiter), but he did not attempt to reproduce or emulate the stanzaic shape of the sonnet.
3. See the literary translation journal by the same name: https://www.asymptotejournal.com/.

Works cited

Alduy, Cécile. *Politique des 'Amours': Poétique et genèse d'un genre français nouveau (1544–1560).* Droz, 2007.
Aroui, Jean-Louis and Andy Arleo, eds. 'Metrical structure of the European Sonnet'. *Towards a Typology of Poetic Forms: From Language to Metrics and Beyond.* Benjamins, 2009, pp. 385–401.
Atkins, Tim. *Petrarch Collected Atkins.* Crater Press, 2018.
Balsamo, Jean, ed. *Les poètes français de la Renaissance et Pétrarque.* Droz, 2004.
Berman, Antoine. 'La terre nourrice et le bord étranger'. *Communications,* vol. 43, 1986, Le croisement des cultures: pp. 205–224.
Bervin, Jen. *Nets.* Ugly. Duckling Presse, 2003.
Birkan-Berz, Carole and Zoe Skoulding. 'Translating Sound and Resonance in Experimental Poetry from the UK: A Cross-Channel Perspective'. *Palimpsestes,* vol. 28, 2015: pp. 97–116.
Bök, Christian. *The Xenotext, Book I.* Coach House, 2015.
Bonney, Sean. *Baudelaire in English.* Veer, 2011.
Brogan, T. V. F., Lawrence J. Zillman and Clive Scott. *Sonnet.* Edited by Alex Preminger et al. Princeton University Press, 1993.
Cohen, Sharmila and Paul Legault, eds. *The Sonnets: Translating and Rewriting Shakespeare.* Nightboat Books, 2012.
Cohen, Walter. *A History of European Literature: The West and the World from Antiquity to the Present.* Oxford University Press, 2017.
Coldiron, A. E. B. 'How Spenser Excavates Du Bellay's *Antiquitez*: Or, the Role of the Poet, Lyric Historiography, and the English Sonnet'. *Journal of English and Germanic Philology,* vol. 101, no. 1, 2002: pp. 41–67.
Dasenbrock, Reed Way. 'Wyatt's Transformation of Petrarch'. *Comparative Literature,* vol. 40, no. 2, 1988: pp. 122–133.
Duché, Véronique, ed. *Histoire des traductions en langue française, sous la direction de Jean-Yves Masson et Yves Chevrel, XV et XVIème siècles, 1470–1610.* Verdier, 2015.
Ellrodt, Robert. 'Comment traduire la poésie?'. *Palimpsestes,* numéro spécial, 'Traduire ou vouloir garder un peu de la poussière d'or'. Edited by C. Raguet-Bouvart. 2006: pp. 65–76.
Etkind, Efim. *Un art en crise: essai de poétique sur la traduction poétique.* L'Âge d'homme, 1982.
Etkind, Efim. 'What Is Untranslatable?' *Translation of Poetry and Poetic Prose: Proceedings of Nobel Symposium 110.* Edited by Sture Allén. World Scientific, 1999, pp. 337–346.
Finkin, Jordan. 'What Does It Mean to Write a Modern Jewish Sonnet?: Some Challenges of Yiddish and Hebrew'. *Journal of Jewish Identities,* vol. 7, no. 1, 2014: pp. 79–107.
Folkart, Barbara. *Second Finding: A Poetics of Translation.* University of Ottawa Press, 2007.

Forte, Frédéric. *33 Sonnets Plats*. Éditions de l'Attente, 2012.
France, Peter, ed. *The Oxford History of Literary Translation in English*. Oxford University Press, 2008.
Franco, Marcia Arruda. *Sá de Miranda, poeta do século de ouro*. Angelus Novus, 2005.
Girotto, Carlo Alberto, Jean-Charles, Monferran and Rémi Vuillemin. 'Early Modern Theories of the Sonnet: Accounts of the Quatorzain in Italy, France and England in the Second Half of the Sixteenth Century'. *The Early Modern English Sonnet: Ever in Motion*. Edited by Rémi Vuillemin, Laetitia Sansonetti and Enrica Zanin. Manchester University Press, 2020.
Greene, Roland. 'Thomas Wyatt'. *The Cambridge Companion to English Poets*. Edited by Claude Rawson. Cambridge University Press, 2011, pp. 37–52.
Hadfield, Andrew. 'Edmund Spenser's Translations of Du Bellay in Jan van der Noot's *A Theatre for Voluptuous Worldlings*'. *Tudor Translation*. Edited by Fred Schurink. Palgrave Macmillan, 2011, pp. 143–160.
Hamrick, Stephen. '"Tottel's Miscellany" and the English Reformation'. *Criticism*, vol. 44, no. 4, 2002: pp. 329–361.
Hersant, Patrick. 'Portraits du traducteur en préfacier'. *Palimpsestes*, vol. 31, 2018: pp. 17–36.
Helgerson, Richard. *A Sonnet from Carthage: Garcilaso de la Vega and the New Poetry of Sixteenth-Century Europe*. University of Pennsylvania Press, 2007.
Hill, Geoffrey. *The Triumph of Love*. Houghton Mifflin Harcourt, 2000.
Hilson, Jeff. *Dans les Essarts, onze sonnets sur soixante-neuf*. Théâtre typographique, 2021.
Hilson, Jeff. *Reality Street Book of Sonnets*. Reality Street, 2008.
Hosington, Brenda. 'Tudor Englishwomen's Translations of Continental Protestant Texts: The Interplay of Ideology and Historical'. *Tudor Translation*. Edited by Fred Schurink. Palgrave Macmillan, 2011, pp. 121–142.
Hudson, Robert J. 'The Petrarchian Lyrical Imperative: An Anthropology of the Sonnet in Renaissance France, 1536–1552'. Unpublished dissertation, University of California, 2008.
Iannaccone, Mariana. *John Florio's Italian and English Sonnets*. Lulu, 2021.
Ip, Joshua. 'Prends le temps'. Translated by Pierre Vinclair. *L'Atelier en ligne*. 19 July 2017. https://vinclairpierre.wordpress.com/2017/07/19/joshua-ip-prends-le-temps/. Accessed 3 January 2022.
Jack, R. D. S. 'Petrarch and the Scottish Renaissance Sonnet'. *Petrarch in Britain: Interpreters, Imitators, and Translators over 700 Years*. Edited by Martin McLaughlin, Letizia Panizza and Peter Hainsworth. Oxford University Press for the British Academy, 146, 2007, pp. 259–273.
Kay, Sarah. *Subjectivity in Troubadour Poetry*. Cambridge University Press, 1990.
Kennedy, William J. 'Iberian, French, and English Petrarchisms'. *The Cambridge Companion to Petrarch*. Edited by Albert R. Ascoli and Unn Falkeid. Cambridge University Press, 2015.

Kennedy, William J. *The Site of Petrarchism: Early Modern National Sentiment in Italy, France, and England*. Johns Hopkins University Press, 2003.

Lindner, Erik. *Un Autostoppeur et son accident: poèmes. Une traduction du néerlandais via d'autres langues*. Translated by Bénédicte Vilgrain. Théâtre typographique, 2018.

Malech, Dora and Laura T. Smith, eds. *Sonnets from the American: An Anthology of Poems and Essays*. University of Iowa Press, forthcoming.

Masseau, Paola. *Une traductologie de la poésie est-elle possible? La traduction du poème toujours renouvelée*. Publibook, 1999.

Melehy, Hassan. *The Poetics of Literary Transfer in Early Modern France and England*. Ashgate, 2010.

Mesa, Francisco José. 'The Translation of Lexical-Semantic Elements in Enrique Garcés's Los sonetos y canciones del Petrarca: The Case of Sestina RVF 30'. *Translating Petrarch's Poetry: L'Aura del Petrarca from the Quattrocento to the 21st Century*. Edited by C. Birkan-Berz, G. Coatalen and T. Vuong. Legenda, 2020, pp. 63–81.

Meschonnic, Henri. *Critique du rythme*. Verdier, 1982.

Meschonnic, Henri. *Poétique du traduire*. Verdier, 1999.

Müller, Timo. *The African American Sonnet: A Literary History*. University Press of Mississippi, 2018.

Nardone, Jean-Luc. *Pétrarque et la poésie européenne: Anthologie pétrarquiste bilingue*. Jérôme Millon, 2021.

Navarrete, Ignacio. *Orphans of Petrarch: Poetry and Theory in the Spanish Renaissance*. University of California Press, 1994.

Pastior, Oskar. *21 poèmes-anagrammes d'après Hebel*. Translated by Frédéric Forte and Bénédicte Vilgrain. Théâtre typographique, 2008.

Paterson, Don. *Orpheus: A Version of Rilke's Die Sonette an Orpheus*. Faber & Faber, 2006.

Pfister, Manfred. 'Inglese Italianato-Italiano Anglizzato: John Florio'. *Renaissance Go-Betweens: Cultural Exchange in Early Modern Europe*. Edited by Andreas Höfele and Werner Von Koppenfels. De Gruyter, 2005, pp. 32–54.

Prescott, Anne Lake. 'Two Annes, Two Davids'. *Tradition, Heterodoxy and Religious Culture*. Edited by Chanita Goodblatt and Howard Kreisel. Ben Guiron University of the Negev Press, 2007, pp. 311–330.

Raimondo, Riccardo. *Le Phenix Poëte et les Alouëtes: Traduire les Rerum vulgarium fragmenta de Pétrarque en langue française (XVIe-XXIe siècles): histoires, traditions et imaginaires*. Peter Lang, 2022.

Ramazani, Jahan. *A Transnational Poetics*. University of Chicago Press, 2009.

Regan, Stephen. *The Sonnet*. Oxford University Press, 2019.

Reynolds, Matthew. *The Poetry of Translation: From Chaucer & Petrarch to Homer & Logue*. Oxford University Press, 2011.

Robinson, Peter. *Poetry & Translation: The Art of the Impossible*. Liverpool University Press, 2010.

Ricoeur, Paul. *Sur la traduction*. Bayard, 2004.

Rossiter, William T. *Chaucer and Petrarch*. D.S. Brewer, 2010.

Rushworth, Jennifer. *Petrarch and the Literary Culture of Nineteenth-Century France: Translation, Appropriation, Transformation*. Suffolk, 2017.
Scott, Clive. *Literary Translation and the Rediscovery of Reading*. Cambridge University Press, 2012.
Scott, Clive. *Translating Baudelaire*. University of Exeter Press, 2000.
Scott, Clive. *The Work of Literary Translation*. Cambridge University Press, 2018.
Serjeantson, Deirdre. 'The Book of Psalms and the Early Modern Sonnet'. *Renaissance Studies*, vol. 29, no. 4, 2015: pp. 632–649.
Seymour, Mayne. *Ricochet: Word Sonnets/Sonnets d'un mot*. Translated by Sabine Huynh. University of Ottawa Press, 2011.
Skoulding, Zoe. *The Noise of Lyric*. Liverpool University Press, 2020.
'Le sonnet dans le monde'. *Inalco*. http://www.inalco.fr/evenement/sonnet-monde. Accessed 12 January 2020.
Spiller, Michael R. G. The Development of the Sonnet: An Introduction. Routledge, 1992.
Spiller, Michael R. G. 'The Scottish Court and the Scottish Sonnet at the Union of the Crowns'. *The Rose and the Thistle: Essays on the Culture of Late Medieval and Renaissance Scotland*. Edited by Sally Mapstone and Juliette Wood. Tuckwell, 1998, pp. 101–115.
Stamatakis, Chris. *Sir Thomas Wyatt and the Rhetoric of Rewriting: Turning the Word*. Oxford University Press, 2012.
Steenson, Allison L. *The Hawthornden Manuscripts of William Fowler and the Jacobean Court 1603–1612*. Routledge, 2020.
Taylor, Karla. 'Writers of the Italian Renaissance'. *The Oxford History of Literary Translation in English, Volume 1: To 1550*. Edited by Roger Ellis. Oxford University Press, 2008. 390–406.
Turbil, Alessandro. 'Petrarch and the French Reception of the Triumphi: An Age of Transition'. *Translating Petrarch's Poetry: L'Aura del Petrarca from the Quattrocento to the 21st Century*. Edited by C. Birkan-Berz, G. Coatalen and T. Vuong. Legenda, 2020, pp. 48–62.
Ughetto, André. *Le Sonnet: une forme européenne de poésie: étude, suivie d'un choix de sonnets italiens, espagnols, anglais, allemands, russes et français*. Ellipses, 2005.
Ullrich, Heiko. *Privatmann – Protestant – Patriot – Panegyriker – Petrarkist – Poet: Neue Studien zu Leben und Werk Georg Rudolf Weckherlins (1584–1653)*. Ralf Schuster Verlag, 2018.
Verweij, Sebastiaan. *The Literary Culture of Early Modern Scotland: Manuscript Production and Transmission, 1560–1625*. Oxford University Press, 2016.
Vinclair, Pierre. 'Extracts from Le Confinement du monde'. Translated by Joshua Ip. *Quarterly Literary Review Singapore*, vol. 19, no. 2, 2020: http://www.qlrs.com/issue.asp?ID=73. Accessed 3 January 2022.
Vinclair, Pierre. 'Une couronne/ A Crown'. Translated by Joshua Ip. *Eunoia Review*, 2020: https://eunoiareview.wordpress.com/2020/07/20/une-couronne-a-crown/. Accessed 3 January 2022.

Westling, Donald. *The Chances of Rhyme: Device and Modernity*. University of California Press, 2021 [1980].

Westover, Jeff. 'African American Sonnets: Voicing Justice and Personal Dignity'. *A Companion to Poetic Genre*. Edited by Erik Martiny. Wiley-Blackwell, 2011, pp. 234–240.

Wyatt, Michael. *The Italian Encounter with Tudor England*. Cambridge University Press, 2005.

Part One

Revisiting early modern circulations

1

Poetic furor in translation: Spenser's and Sylvester's sonnet collections

Pádraic Lamb

The French poet and theorist Joachim du Bellay (1549) is one of many who set their faces against poetic translation. Poetic translation cannot produce an 'œuvre digne de prix' because of the impossibility of translating 'ceste Divinité d'Invention [...] ceste grandeur de style [...]: bref ceste energie, et ne sçay quel Esprit, qui est en leurs escrits, que les Latins appelleroient *Genius*' (Du Bellay 2001, 90). The task of the translator is to come as close as possible to the 'Author'. What 'grandeur' to see a 'second language respond in every point to the elegance of the first', while preserving its own, muses Jacques Peletier (1555). Such use of language is impossible, he regrets: 'il ne se peut faire' (246; cf. 297).

In this chapter, I wish to discuss poetic furor used as a justification for translation in two translated sonnet-sequences. I will argue that two poetic translators, Edmund Spenser and Josuah Sylvester, appropriated a Platonic discourse of poetic inspiration to overcome this view of poetic translation as intrinsically inferior to the work of the 'Poëtes' or 'Auteur[s]' (Du Bellay, Bellay 2001, 90; Peletier 243).[1] Through representing their translations as themselves inspired, I will argue, these translators lay claim to the 'Divinité d'Invention' with which Du Bellay defines the poet to thus make possible poetic translation through supernatural guarantees. Edmund Spenser bypasses Du Bellay's own injunction in *Ruines of Rome: by Bellay* (part of *Complaints*, 1591), a translation of Du Bellay's *Le premier livre des antiquitez de Rome* (1558); Josuah Sylvester translates Jean du Nesme's *Le miracle de la paix en France* (1598) almost immediately as *The Miracle of the Peace in Fraunce* (1599). I wish to show that Spenser and Sylvester appropriate poetic furor to represent their work as acts of inspiration. I will argue that negative perceptions of poetic translation are resisted by claiming the 'psychagogic, revelatory and invigorating' efficacy of poetry expounded in Platonizing discourses on the furor (Borris 39) for both the figure of the translator and the translated text.

Poetic furor is the essential starting-point of Platonic poetics, which defines poetry as arising from the possession of the poet, by a god or one of the Muses: 'a certain *enthousiasmos* and celestial inspiration', as E. K. put it in commenting on Spenser's *The Shepheardes Calendar* (Spenser 1989, 170): the descent of the furors ultimately enables the ascent of the enraptured soul. Older critical perspectives on poetic inspiration as mere commonplace 'orthodoxy' (Heninger 221) have been revised by recent critical work on furor in representational strategies to legitimize vernacular poetry (Huntington; Galand-Hallyn et al.; Borris). Borris's review of sources points to the prevalence and availability of the theory of poetic furor. The more complete English treatments include critical works by Richard Wills, Thomas Lodge, E.K., William Webbe, George Puttenham and Philip Sidney (Borris 38–44).[2] Despite these new critical perspectives, furor and translation are rarely considered together in studies of non-scriptural English Renaissance poetry, with the notable exception of George Chapman's poetic Platonism in relation to Homer (Schoell; Clucas).

Constraints of space mean I can only evoke briefly the complex background evolution of furor in sixteenth-century French and English poetics.[3] In the *Ion* (533d–6d), in the famous image of connected magnetic rings, the possession of the poet through the Muse-sent furor allows the poet to enrapture the reader in turn and reproduce its divine effects through poetic speech. The furor can then enrapture later poets, performers or rhapsodes of that poem, such as the eponymous Ion. In a detail striking for discussion of imitation and translation, an inspired poet such as Homer becomes a Muse himself and inspires other poets: 'And from these first rings – the poets – are suspended various others, which are thus inspired' (536b). In Plato's text, no special credit is given to the human mouthpiece of the gods. In humanist Platonic poetics, however, such as those of the Pléiade of Du Bellay and Pierre de Ronsard, the central enabling experience of furor is emphasized in tandem with the necessary erudition of the poet, shown especially through the individual poet's affinity-based imitation of select Greek and Latin poets (Du Bellay 2001, 128–130). The fusion of imitation and inspiration in the early Pléiade defence and illustration of the vernacular poet draws on diverse (even contradictory) influences, such as Vida's Platonizing *De Arte Poetica* and Erasmus's anti-Ciceronian *Ciceronianus*, to credit the poet's personal erudition, as well as valorizing his or her persona as chosen by a divine source (the Muses or other divine figures). The defence of vernacular poetry takes an emphasis on personal self-expression from anti-Ciceronian discourse to exploit the claims of Platonic poetics that the highest form of poetry is to be achieved through sublime literary effects.[4] This results in a poetics of what Lecointe has called 'la fureur revendiquée par le moi' (316–371): that is, a poetics claiming for itself the most powerful verbal efficacy in a personal appropriation of furor. Despite the exalted figure of the inspired poet in the *Deffence*, Du Bellay's ethical postures also relate him to an evangelical version of furor (Noirot-Maguire).

In earlier applications of furor theory in Reformist translations of the Psalms, the absolute dependence on poetic furor, explicitly identified as emanating from God, figured the abasement of the human poet as a mere instrument of the divine word, as in Marot's liminary poem to his translations of Psalms (Jeanneret; cf. Raimondo). Marot gives an example of a Protestant Platonic poetics tending to produce an instrumental conception of the poet who piously refuses praise for this intermediary role.

The texts of Du Bellay and Du Nesme convey differing, interrelated versions of vernacular French Platonic poetics. Du Bellay was close to evangelical circles (Gadoffre); Du Nesme claims an exclusively Christian furor but his Platonic poetics owes a debt to the Pléiade. In fact, the four texts of the primary corpus are closely related. Du Bellay initiated the non-amorous sonnet collection in French and was an influence on Du Nesme, while Guillaume du Bartas's epic-writing was Du Nesme's chief model. Spenser stated his admiration for Du Bartas in the original sonnet appended to the *Ruines of Rome*, while Sylvester, of course, is known as the translator of Du Bartas's Christian epics, the *Semaines*, and was an admirer of Spenser ('our mysterious ELFINE oracle') despite disapproving of his use of non-Christian motifs of inspiration (Du Bartas 1965, 272). This network of texts suggests affinities with the epic, the genre explicitly identified as a product of the poet's furor in the *Ion*. Indeed, Spenser and Du Bartas do evoke 'goodly fury' (Spenser 1987, 6.Proem.2.6) and 'divine fureur' (*Uranie* line 13) as prompting and maintaining the enraptured and enrapturing poetic speech of their epic poems. This ennobling connection to the epic is echoed in the use to which the sonnet is put in these works. It is here used for religious and political meditation while knowingly playing with the debased amorous tradition. In Du Bellay's case, the beloved is arguably sublimated in the figure of Rome (Rebhorn; Brown 90). Similarly, Du Nesme's speaker addresses a female deity, Peace (wittily transfigured after the arrival of peace into the goddess of justice, Astraea). This intertextuality – in Genette's sense of citation, plagiarism and allusion (Genette 8) – indicates the self-conscious attempt made with these translations to dissociate the sonnet from 'the follies and faynings of love', yet without engaging in the biblical paraphrase of 'Spirituall Sonnets' (Southwell 1) that some proposed for religious reasons.

Larger structural patterns in both texts indicate that a conception of inspiration is central, not only to the source texts themselves, but also to the translators' enterprise. The thirty-two sonnets of the *Antiquitez* are preceded by a sonnet 'Au Roi': the number thirty-three, Christ's age when he died, evoking 'resurrection, immortality and heavenly perfection', is an important signifying structure in the *Antiquitez* (Smith 90), reinforcing the central purpose of the *Ruines* collection: the vernacular project to revive the spirits of Latin literature. Spenser reproduced this significant number in the *Ruines* in the *Complaints* volume. The invocation of the 'Divins esprits' ('Ye heavenly spirits') in the first two words of the collection signal it as an attempt at extended communication with them in order to win poetic immortality in the vernacular.

Not a numerological but a thematic structure underlies *Le Miracle/The Miracle*. It similarly foregrounds the question of inspiration through a metamorphosis of the presiding deity. Peace is invoked as the poet's Muse for the majority of the volume – the thirty-nine sonnets which follow an initial sonnet and quatrain addressed to the king. A verse-dialogue of eighty lines between Democritus and Heraclitus on the 'Troubles Past' forms a kind of interlude before Peace metamorphoses into her personification as Astraea in an ode and two sonnets. The nature of the Muse solicited for her poetic furor (Peace or Astraea) determines the type of poetry produced (political or amorous sonnets).

These structural patterns produce a formal beauty and significance in order to reinforce the presentation of the poetic text as contingent on the poet's furor. One reason for the extremely rare integral translation of these two lyric volumes is related, I believe, to recognition of that structural pattern whose effective translation must thus be integral. Both texts advertise themselves as translations: *Ruines of Rome: by Bellay* and *The Miracle of the Peace in Fraunce: Celebrated by the ghost of the diuine Du Bartas*. I hope to show that the translated texts also reveal, in liminary sonnets and through translative choices made, an attempt to represent the poetic furor of the source texts as a translative furor.

A performative use of language is essential to representation of poetic furor in both source texts. To take the case of the invocations of inspiration, 'the issuing of the utterance is the performing of an action' (Austin 6). Du Bellay invokes the ancient furor and represents, through the sacred quaking ('saincte horreur'), and, thus, possession of the poet-speaker's body, the concurrent ('En ce pendant que') poetic enunciation as indeed inspired:

A haulte voix trois fois je vous [Divins Esprits] appelle:

J'invoque icy vostre antique fureur,

En ce pendant que d'une saincte horreur

Je vays chantant vostre gloire plus belle. (Sonnet 1, lines 11–14)

Du Nesme describes in very similar terms the Christian enthusiasm which provokes his praise of Henry IV. The poet-speaker's powerlessness and the subjugation of his will are foregrounded in the alliterative (v) repetitions which precede the advent of the irresistible 'sacred furor' and the praise of the monarch in line 11. The forceful ravishment of the poet-speaker, *nolens volens*, represents the enunciation of praise as expression of the furor:

> Une saincte fureur d'un feu doux-violent
> M'invite et me ravit voulant ou ne voulant
> A bruire d'un HENRY la gloire et le trophée. (Sonnet 11, lines 9-10)

I have taken these two passages in order to give an idea of how furor, though a theme in itself, conditions the very representation of poetic speech in these works.

We may look now at Spenser's handling of this opening sonnet. Spenser maintains this schema of inspiration by enacting a translative furor, a transfer of the original inspiration to his new iteration of the text. I will elucidate Spenser's refiguring of Du Bellay's text as a Muse through his emphases and substitutions in translation, which insist on the operation of furor.

Du Bellay's French text contains notable allusive reminiscences of Virgil's description of the Sibyl's inspiration: 'horreur' is a Latinism which is a sign of a transcendental presence. Sounding these Latin voices in the vernacular, the poetic voice re-articulates the solicited 'antique fureur' in all its terrible power and thus demonstrates poetically furor's operation:

Divins Esprits, dont la poudreuse cendre	Ye heavenly spirites, whose ashie cinders lie
Gist sous le faix de tant de murs couvers,	Under deep ruines, with huge walls opprest,
Non, vostre los, qui vif par vos beaux vers	But not your praise, the which shall never die
Ne se verra sous la terre descendre.	Through your faire verses, ne in ashes rest;
Si des humains la voix se peult estendre	If so be shrilling voyce of wight alive
Depuis icy jusqu'au fond des enfers,	May reach from hence to depth of darkest hell,
Soient à mon cry les abysmes ouvers,	Then let those deep Abysses open rive,
Tant que d'abas vous me puissiez entendre.	That ye may understand my shreiking yell.
Trois fois cernant sous le voile des cieux	Thrice having seene, under the heavens veale,
De vos tumbeaus le tour devocieux,	Your toombs devoted compasse over all,
A haulte voix trois fois je vous appelle:	Thrice unto you with lowd voyce I appeale,

J'invoque icy vostre antique fureur,	And for your antique furie here doo call,
En ce pendant que d'une saincte horreur	The whiles that I with sacred horror sing
Je vays chantant vostre gloire plus belle.	Your glorie, fairest of all earthly thing.
(Sonnet 1)	(Sonnet 1)

The first sonnet thus accomplishes the resuscitation it calls for, in ways scrupulously preserved by Spenser. The present tense of the verbs chosen by Du Bellay and Spenser ('appelle', 'invoque', 'vays chantant', 'appeale', 'call', 'sing') and the use of the hortatory mood ('Soient', 'let') situate the act of poetic speech in the *hic et nunc* of performativity and of inspiration. Spontaneity was a quality of speech seen as signifying divine possession of the poet, achievable with rhetorical labour (Cave 125–156). The deictic immediacy of the oralized poetic voice seeks to signify the presence of the divine: 'J'invoque icy vostre antique fureur', 'And for your antique furie here doo call'. It carries out the invocation, which is at the same time an instance of its efficacy: the poet's voice invokes the furor of the 'heavenly spirites'; its enunciation claims to be the furor in action. Further rhetorical confirmation of the inspired nature of the utterance is provided by the vivid representation of the poet's physical presence; the oral performance as well as the bodily reaction of the poet are emphasized, explicit traditional signs of divine possession: 'A haulte voix trois fois je vous appelle', 'Thrice unto you with lowd voyce I appeale'. The poetic *Je*/I is animated with a 'saincte horreur', 'sacred horror', the bristling hair and trembling which form the *actio* of inspiration, recalling the Sibyl in the *Aeneid* ('*horrendae* [...] *Sibyllae*', Virgil 6.532, 6.538). Spenser's translation preserves these signs of external inspiration and, on occasion, reinforces them. The impersonal 'Si des humains la voix se peult estendre' is made particular to the 'I', who qualifies his own utterance with a supernatural epithet: 'That ye may understand *my shreiking yell*' (emphasis added). This is an auditory image of the translator's voice losing its control, ravished by the violent incursion of the furor. This type of reinforcement draws attention to the special status of the text as a reiteration of the furor of ancient Latin poets, actuated by a new transmission of the 'antique furie' through and beyond Du Bellay's 'antique fureur'. The violence being done (again, the immediacy of the present tense is important) to the poet is, then, quite different from the 'goodly fury' inducing rapture in *The Faerie Queene* (6.Proem.2.6). The representation of the translator quaking and roaring reflects a correlation of furor and style: the 'horror' of Virgil's representation of the Sibyl is replicated in the style of Du Bellay and Spenser's poetic texts. This ambiguity of the Roman 'heavenly spirites' is developed in Sonnet 5.

'Nature', 'Art' and 'Heaven' are listed in Sonnet 5 as the three factors in the original construction of Rome as well as in the project of its poetic resuscitation through its 'escripts' ('brave Writings'), which is imaged metaphorically as a necromantic act: to see Rome, 'C'est comme un corps par magique sçavoir / Tiré de nuict hors de sa sépulture' ('It's like a Corse drawn forth out of the Tomb / By Magick Skill out of eternal Night', lines 7–8). This supernatural metaphor foregrounds 'Heaven' without obliterating the natural disposition of the poet or learned poetical-rhetorical technique. The critique of pagan but also papal Rome in the evangelical Du Bellay's text is made stronger by the English anti-Papist context of Spenser's translation; Du Bellay's 'Ombre', 'esprit' and 'idole' used to evoke the corpse of Rome become 'Shade', 'spirite' and 'Idole' in Spenser. The moral danger posed by this potentially pagan and idolatrous Catholic 'Idole' in the volume signifies the fascination this necromantic furor exerts over the poet and translator, and implicitly over the reader. Rhetorical vivid description is presented as necromantically conjuring up the Roman spirit, and so poetic enunciation achieves necromancy in the re-actualisation of the Roman poetic furor ('brave Writings'), and visualization of the 'Idole' rearing up out of the 'Dust', which poetically confirms the supernatural transaction taking place in the verse:

Mais ses escripts, qui son loz le plus beau	But her brave Writings, which her famous Merit
Malgré le temps arrachent du tumbeau,	In spight of Time, out of the Dust doth rear,
Font son idole errer parmy le monde.	Do make her Idol through the World appear.
(Sonnet 10, lines 12–14)	(Sonnet 10, lines 12–14)

Latin intertexts are again at the heart of the poetic and translative procedure in Sonnet 25, where Spenser elevates his predecessors and in so doing, raises himself to their stature.[5] This poem is concerned with placing the poet in a line of illustrious predecessors; Virgil is named as a model in Du Bellay's version:

Peusse-je au moins, d'un pinceau plus agile	Or that at least I could with pencill fine,
Sur le patron de quelque grand Virgile	Fashion the pourtraicts of these Palacis,
De ces palais les protraicts façonner:	By paterne of great Virgils spirit divine;
J'entreprendrois, veu l'ardeur qui m'allume,	I would assay with that which in me is,
De rebastir au compas de la plume	To builde with leuell of my loftie style,
Ce que les mains ne peuvent maçonner.	That which no hands can evermore compile.
(Sonnet 25, lines 9–14)	(Sonnet 25, lines 9–14)

The modesty of the conditional mood ('Peusse-je au moins [...] J'entreprendrois') is a form of preterition, which allows Du Bellay to imply he has realized his objective (cf. Brown 78–80). The indirectness of preterition is exploited by Spenser to reinforce the inspired nature of his poetic discourse, itself rendered far more explicitly than in Du Bellay's text. For Borris, 'Platonizing mimetic idealism' is central to Spenser's poetics (17–18, 155–189). Here, to proceed 'By paterne of great Virgils spirit divine' means that the divinized Virgil is identified as the immediate source of the Platonic Idea to be expressed poetically.[6] This mimetic idealism is not lessened or lost through translation, as Du Bellay implies in the *Deffence*; rather translation is the means of reproducing through inspiration 'Virgils divine spirit' in a vernacular language.[7]

After figuring Virgil as Muse-figure, there is an allusive re-centring on the person of the poet-speaker, who occupies both subject and object positions in the next verse: 'J'entreprendrois, veu l'ardeur qui m'allume', 'I would assay with that which in me is'. Du Bellay's line balances the effort of the poet with vatic ardour. Spenser's formulation evokes allusively – with reference to the '*est deus in nobis*' from Ovid's *Fasti* (318–319) and the Psalmic 'all that is within me praise his holy Name'[8] – his speaker's possession by an internal god, and the will ('would') of the speaker gives an image of the translative process here as a combination of the three causes cited in Sonnet 5 ('Heaven', 'Art' and 'Nature') within the speaker. The biblical intertext suggests a Protestant inflection being given to Du Bellay's project, through the personal efforts of the presumably Protestant first-person speaker. Spenser notably departs from Du Bellay's text with the result that the model of Platonic inspiration in view of idealized mimesis of Virgil is made significantly clearer. The effect of this, I believe, is to engender a self-reflective focus on the text as a translation, itself participating in the mysterious inspired patterning through the medium of the translator.

The very last sonnet in the *Ruines* is original to Spenser, and adopts a distinctive rhyme scheme. Setting aside the common English rhyme scheme used for the body of his translation, in an act of poetic emancipation, Spenser innovates with an ABAB CDCD DEDE FF rhyme scheme for his original 'L'Envoy'. The form is Spenser's but the theme is Du Bellay himself: this mixture signals at one and the same time independence and homage.[9] This reading allows us to see how the sonnet 'Au Roi' which opens Du Bellay's sequence has thereby been effectively transformed into an envoy addressed chiefly to Du Bellay. By transforming this sonnet, Spenser preserves the numerological significance of thirty-three but re-orients it for his own poetic enterprise. The Muse-like capacity attributed to Henry II in Du Bellay's sonnet is thus structurally transferred to Du Bellay by Spenser. To represent Du Bellay as a Muse is to bolster Spenser's own claim to inspiration as a translator. *Les Regrets*, published as the preceding collection in the same volume as the *Antiquitez*, ends with an appeal to the French king to 'set at large' his power and bestow it on the poet.[10] The 'L'Envoy' modifies the necromantic motif of the opening 'Au Roi' sonnet, transferring the power of the poetic word to Du Bellay and Du Bartas:

> Bellay, first garland of free Poësie
> That France brought forth, though fruitfull of brave wits,
> Well worthie thou of immortalitie,
> That long hast traveld by thy learned writs,
> Olde Rome out of her ashes to revive,
> And give a second life to dead decayes:
> [...]
> Thy dayes therefore are endles, and thy prayse
> Excelling all, that euer went before;
> And after thee, gins Bartas hie to rayse
> His heavenly Muse, th'Almightie to adore.
> Live happie spirits, th'honour of your name,
> And fill the world with never dying fame. (L'Envoy 1–14)

Spenser not only appropriates the text, but reconstitutes the spirit of Du Bellay as a Spenserian inspiration, a poetic Muse, in the place of the French king. Du Bellay stands as Muse to Spenser as Homer was to Ion. His 'learned writs' function as do the 'brave Writings' of Virgil. The imperatives of lines 13–14 are performative, as Spenser's poem partakes of the transmission of Du Bellay's 'happy spirit' and necromantic poetic word.

Spenser's principal relation here is, of course, with Du Bellay, but he also numbers Du Bartas in his song: this is an unambiguous Protestant inflection of the text, acknowledging Du Bartas's kindred poetics based on the afflatus of furor. It falls to Sylvester, however, to 'fill the world' with the 'happy spirit' of Du Bartas, through his translation in this case of the Bartasian epigone Jean du Nesme (1570/1575–?).

Little is known of Du Nesme's career. *Le Miracle de la paix*, his first known work, was published in Paris in 1598 to celebrate the promulgation of the Edict of Nantes and the official toleration of Protestantism. His religious affiliation at this point is unknown but his commitment to the peace, as shown in *Le Miracle*, is certain (Barbier). The surprising announcement on Sylvester's title-page that the volume's author was the 'Ghost of the Divine Du Bartas' (Du Bartas himself had died in 1590) might in part be explained by the fact that the Parisian edition used did not feature Du Nesme's name on the title-page, but as we shall see, this ghostly authorship has a broader significance.

Du Nesme's most evident stylistic and lexical affiliation is with Du Bartas (exemplified by compound epithets and invocation of a Christian Muse), though Du Bellay, too, is present.[11] In fact, Du Bartas's praise of personified Peace (without mention of Astraea) in *Les Artifices* certainly prompted Du Nesme's whole enterprise, which amounts to a post-mortem continuation (Du Bartas 1965, 357). Sylvester, in turn, recognized this link and proclaims on the title-page that he is translating from the original of the 'Ghost of Du Bartas', as well as inserting praise of Elizabeth as Astraea in to his translation of *Les Artifices* (Du Bartas 1965, 359). This demonstrates Sylvester's analysis of the affinity between the two French poets as a phenomenon of inspiration; it expresses intertextuality through furor and recalls the resuscitation so important in the *Antiquitez*. The publication history of the text corroborates this reading, as *The Miracle* was published as an annexe to Du Bartas's poems from 1605 onwards (Du Bartas 1979, 66–108). Sylvester highlighted the spiritual connection between Du Bartas and Du Nesme in order to represent *The Miracle of the Peace* as a new expression of Du Bartas's Muse, Urania.[12] Du Nesme's explicit Muse, Peace, is directly assimilated in to Christian grace by Sylvester, who, in an affected polyptoton combining inspiration and the translator's art in the initial dedicatory sonnet to Anthony Bacon, uses the comparison to identify the Muse as grace and signify his modesty and piety in handling such a 'Theame': 'this sacred MIRACLE: / A *gratious* Theame (if I *disgrace* not it)' (lines 10–11). This establishes the volume as unambiguously Christian in outlook, though non-scriptural.

The sonnet to Anthony Bacon uses an ABBA ABBA CDCE EE rhyme scheme, which, with enclosed rhyme quatrains and five rhymes overall, is the closest equivalent to the traditional French schemes used by Du Nesme.[13] This formal imitation, though it strains Sylvester's capacities,[14] expresses the proximity of their respective Muses. For the main body of sonnets, Sylvester uses two variant rhyme schemes – Surrey's ABAB CDCD EFEF GG and the unusual ABBA CDDC EFEF/EFFE GG – to render Du Nesme's sonnets. The enclosed rhyme of the quatrains attempts to carry over the harmony of ideas of the French octave, but Sylvester always adheres to the couplet ending.

This translation conceives of itself in terms of a Protestant Platonic poetics. It reproduces the successively magnetized rings of the *Ion* with the roles of the rings or Muses taken up here by Peace, Du Bartas, Du Nesme and then Sylvester. Sylvester refers to the 'Celtike Muses' of his own Muse in the liminary sonnet. *Gallia Celtica* is one of the three regions of Gaul; rare in English, more common in French, this usage perhaps inadvertently shows the French influence on his diction:

> Lo, heer I tune vpon mine humble Lyre
> Our neighbour Kingdomes vn-expected weale,
> Through suddain ceasing of Warres enter-deale;
> As Celtike Muses to my Muse inspire. (Lines 5–6)

Sylvester then proceeds to construe his text, thanks to his 'Celtike Muses', as the *translatio* of Du Nesme's inspiration for his own text. Du Nesme's use of the image of the magnetized rings ('force aymantine') is emblematic of his Christian Platonic conception of inspired poetry. Followed by Sylvester, he goes so far as to incorporate the biblical 'zeale' ascribed to the prophets into the Platonic system of furors.[15] This synonymy between furor and zeal aims to appropriate biblical authority for the poetic text and, despite Sylvester's protestations of modesty, likens the poet and translator to the righteous prophets. A pious scruple, though, perhaps limits this syncretism, and for this non-scriptural poetry the Platonic model seems to be privileged. Henry IV, who has brought about the peace, is acclaimed for escorting the personified Peace to earth, and thus acquires a Muse-like power, as Henry II possessed in Du Bellay's 'Au Roi'. Sylvester, naturally, preserves this image of the 'stile' (line 13) guided by transcendent force towards the magnetic 'Adamant', despite the poet's natural weakness:

Ton crayon sur le vif un zele m'a surpris,	[…] Let zeale my crime excuse;
Et mon fer est tiré par ta force aymantine.	My steele's attracted by thine Adamant.
(Sonnet 17, lines 7–8)	(Sonnet 17, lines 7–8)

In French, God, through the intermediary of *Paix*, is the inspirational vector of poetic expression. In Sylvester's translation, Peace and the 'Celtike Muses' are the vectors of the same inspiration.

The opening sonnet adopts the posture of Du Bartas's *Urania* and rejects the pagan inspiration represented by Phoebus. Instead, the speaker declares his worship of the angelic beauty of sacred Peace; Sylvester inserts a paraphrase of 'grace' and avoids an impious declaration of angel-worship:

Mais quel autre Soleil nos campagnes decore,	But what new Sunne doth now adorne our Land,
Et repeinct nostre Ciel si riant et si beau?	And gives our skie so smooth and smiling cheere?
Car ce n'est pas Phoebus où l'or de son flambeau	For 'tis not Phoebus; else his golden brand
Luit plus clair aujourd'huy qu'il n'a point faict encore.	Shines brighter now then't hath done many a yeere.
Angelique Beauté, saincte Paix que j'adore.	Sweet Angel-beauty, sacred PEACE, heav'ns present.
(Sonnet 1, lines 1–5)	(Sonnet 1, lines 1–5)

Sonnet 2 is a hymn of praise which names *Paix*/Peace as the Muse of this work. It is an invocation which takes the form of extensive antonomasia of her divine attributes, building to a climax in line 14, where she is finally named:

Fille du Tout-puissant, alme, riche, feconde,	Faire fruitfull daughter of th'Omnipotent,
Arbitre qui maintiens l'un et l'autre Univers,	Great Umpire that doost either World sustain,
Sans qui, comme jadis, tout iroit à l'envers	Without whose help all would returne againe
Horriblement confus és abysmes du monde:	Like hideous Chaos to confusion bent.
O mere des vivans et nature feconde	O Mother of the living, second Nature
De la flamme de l'eau, et de la terre et des airs,	Of th'Elements, Fire, Water, Earth, and Aire:
Grace par qui les cieux à l'homme sont ouverts,	O Grace (whereby men climbe the heav'nly stair)
[...]	[...]
Nourrice des vertus, des Muses le soustien,	Thou Nourse of vertues, Muses chief supportall,
Tutelaire des arts, et source de tout bien,	Patron of Artes, of Good the speciall spring:
Je te saluë ô Paix, qui le salut nous donnes.	All hail (dere Peace) which vs all heale doost bring.
(Sonnet 2, lines 1–14)	(Sonnet 2, lines 1–14)

This long invocation aims at the kind of performativity seen in Du Bellay/Spenser. This is the poetry of pure praise, assimilated to prayer, which consists in repeating the divine name, and results in the answering of the prayer. The naming of peace results in the peace that the speaker, in the name of a collective, receives. The identification of the salutation with salvific grace is absolute, through the homophony 'saluë'/'salut' in French, only slightly lessened in Sylvester's 'hail'/'heale'. The Platonic emphasis appears in the notion of enraptured ascent through a personified divine intermediary: 'O Grace (whereby men climbe the heav'nly stair)'.

Sylvester's translation of these lines illustrates his view of *The Miracle*'s relation to Du Bartas's epic project. Some phrasing in particular deserves our attention: 'Great Umpire' hearkens back to the translation of *Eden* published a year previously in London, which defines 'spirits, by faith religiously refin'd' as '(umpires) [who] mortall to th'immortall joyne' (Du Bartas 1965, 284). Peace is in *The Miracle* the 'Great Umpire', a personified divine force connecting the human and the divine. The means of this mediation is the poetic enunciation of her attributes.

The Platonizing character of Sylvester's translation is played out in further synonymy. The abundance of terms employed for the experience of inspiration is intended to capture the confusion of the poet's possession; the sweetness of Christian prophetic inspiration, though present, does not dominate. Rage, furor, Pentecostal flames and rapture are the qualities invoked as the poet is buffeted irresistibly ('Will-nill') by the divinity: 'sacred rage of some sweet furious flame / Will-nill-I, raps me' (Sonnet 11, lines 9–10). This ecstatic abandon is moderated in the section explicitly inspired by Astraea: the change in poetic inspiration produces a change in poetic style, towards adoration in ideal terms of female beauty.

The arrival of Astraea is a reference to Virgil's *Eclogue* (4.48–49) with political significance: this symbol of a return to the Golden Age was much used to praise Elizabeth as a divinely ordained monarch (Yates 29–59; Spenser 1987, 3.3.49). To figure Elizabeth as fulfilling the prophecy of Astraea is also to align the poet-prophet of *Eclogue* IV with the speaker in the present who solicits Astraea. Sylvester's exalted treatment of Astraea can be interpreted as participating in a consciously Platonizing strain of Elizabeth-worship (Jayne 100, 115). There is a return, not without irony, to the humble posture of Marot's Psalms in the representation of the speaker addressing a mythological symbol of the political ruler of England. Idolatry in the national cause is apparently permitted:

| Mon Tout par qui dans moy je ne possede rien | [...] I nothing doe possesse |
| Que ton rare pourtrait [...]. (Sonnet 40, lines 10–11) | Save thine Idea, glorious and divine. (Sonnet 40, lines 10–11) |

Sylvester Platonizes Du Nesme when the divinity's 'pourtrait' becomes 'Idea'; the breach between the speaker and Astraea widens as she is dematerialized. Sylvester's speaker proclaims his mimetic idealism on Spenserian lines, as his praise of Astraea depends wholly on mimesis of the transcendental paradigm of excellence: the 'Idea' of Astraea, 'glorious and divine'. This translative choice overreaches Du Nesme and draws attention to the text as an English appropriation and enunciation by Sylvester's speaker of the 'quelque divinité' that Du Nesme (Sonnet 39, line 13) perceives in Astrée. The brief detour via the Astraean section is important in that it shows the poet's inspiration is carried over from Peace to Astraea. The integral translation of the collection has poetically enacted the return of the Golden Age, in France but also specifically in Elizabeth's England.

The translators' representation of their inspired reception of the 'Divinité d'Invention' of their 'Auteurs', especially in paratextual and liminary material, allows translators to play with the range of emphases in Platonic poetics, alternately foregrounding the mediator and effacing the self to praise the divine source of poetry. The 'fidelity' required of the Renaissance translator (Norton 58–90), as well as the impossibility through natural means of poetic translation, is hyperbolically respected through authorial inspiration. The furor of translation seeks to show that the translator can stake a claim to 'the force of a divine breath' and the capacity to '[bring] things forth surpassing her [Nature's] doings' (Sidney 24–25), in ways quite contrary to Sidney's counsels in the *Defence of Poetry*.

Erato is the Muse of love poetry but she does not feature in these sonnets. Spenser, in the closing sonnet, figures his preceding *translatio* of the 'Romaine Daemon' (*Ruines of Time*, line 376) and 'Bellay' ('L'Envoy', line 1) as an impetus for further work. The initial publication of the *Ruines* in the *Complaints* realizes that wish and associates the work with diverse translations and compositions, and with a number of imaginatively related visionary poet-speakers (Ferguson). Similarly, Sylvester includes *The Miracle* in his epic translations, where it stands as a kind of a corroborating supplement to the Bartasian mediation of inspiration. Beyond themes of love, these collections mark attempts to inflect the sonnet form towards serious spiritual, moral and political themes. Their inspirations also testify to the generic 'undecidability' (Warley 10) of the early modern English sonnet, and indicate an affinity with longer forms. Fowler's claim that 'we should regard every Elizabethan sonnet sequence as a long poem in fourteen-line stanzas' (174) relies on contested numerological data. Inspiration, and the inspired poet-translator, mediates between the individual sonnet and the 'sequence', as well as between the sonnet and other genres, and may be the occasion to re-examine inspiration as a formal practice in English sonnet collections.

Notes

1 Cf. Quintilian's influential comments (10.2.10–11) on the inherent inferiority of imitations (pp. 326–327). Following Jayne (xiii), I refer to 'Renaissance Platonism' rather than the Neoplatonism of late Antiquity.
2 Borris says Wills's treatment of furor is without argument (p. 41); I consider that the *De Re Poetica* endorses furor strongly (Wills pp. 72–76). In any case, it explains the theory at some length.
3 I am currently preparing a thesis on this topic, under the direction of Richard Hillman, at the CESR, Université de Tours.

4   See Fumaroli (pp. 77–115) on the anti-Ciceronian controversy and especially Cave on Erasmus and Du Bellay (pp. 35–77). Lecointe's study remains indispensable.
5   Cf. the use of the hyponym in Sonnet 32 to extend the achievement of this poetry to England.
6   'Paterne' has a Platonic sense in October of the *SC* (Spenser 1989, p. 176) and denotes specifically Platonic ideas in Puttenham (p. 93).
7   See Lecointe (pp. 482–528) on Vida's evidently important use of Virgil as an inspiring model of imitation.
8   Cf. the use of the line in 'October'. It is the incipit of Psalm 103 (Brown p. 87).
9   See Melehy (pp. 90–93) and Brown (pp. 79–83) on (generic) 'independence' without structural inspiration.
10 'Élargissez encor sur moy vostre pouvoir' (Sonnet 191, line 12).
11 Cf., for instance, the excipit of his Sonnet 26 with that of Du Nesme's sonnet 16.
12 A liminary sonnet by P. Catelle, otherwise unknown, identifies Du Nesme as the author (line 11).
13 Du Nesme practises the usual French variety in the sestet: CC DEDE or CC DEED.
14 See the strain in lines 2–3 and the hyperbaton of line 11.
15 Huntingdon (pp. 306) mentions the pairing is repeated in *Love's Labour's Lost* to mock madness.

Works cited

Barbier, Jean Paul. *Dictionnaire des poètes français de la seconde moitié du XVIe siècle (1549–1615). C–D*. Droz, 2015.

Borris, Kenneth. *Visionary Spenser and the Poetics of Early Modern Platonism*. Oxford University Press, 2017.

Brown, Richard Danson. *The New Poet: Novelty and Tradition in Spenser's Complaints*. Liverpool University Press, 1999.

Cave, Terence. *The Cornucopian Text: Problems of Writing in the French Renaissance*. Clarendon Press, 1979.

Clucas, Stephen. 'To Rauish and Refine an Earthly Soule': Ficino and the Poetry of George Chapman'. *Marsilio Ficino: His Theology, His Philosophy, His Legacy*. Edited by M. J. B. Allen, Valery Rees and Martin Davies. Brill, 2002, pp. 419–442.

Du Bartas, Guillaume. *Bartas: His Devine Weekes and Works*. Edited by Francis Colin Haber. Translated by Josuah Sylvester. Scholars' Facsimiles & Reprints, 1965.

Du Bartas, Guillaume. *The Divine Weeks and Works of Guillaume de Saluste Sieur de Bartas*. Edited by Susan Snyder. Translated by Josuah Sylvester. Clarendon Press, 1979.

Du Bartas, Guillaume. *The Works of Guillaume de Salluste, Sieur Du Bartas*. Edited by Urban Tigner Holmes et al. The University of North Carolina Press, 1935.

Du Bellay, Joachim. *OEuvres poétiques*. Edited by Daniel Aris and Françoise Joukovsky. Classiques Garnier, 2009.

Du Bellay, Joachim. *La Deffence, et illustration de la langue françoyse*. Edited by Jean-Charles Monferran. Droz, 2001.

Du Nesme, Jean. *Le Miracle de la paix en France, au roy très chrestien de France et de Navarre Henri IIII*. T. Ancelin, 1598.

Ferguson, Margaret W. '"The Afflatus of Ruin": Meditations on Rome by Du Bellay, Spenser, and Stevens'. *Roman Images: Selected Papers from the English Institute*, vol. 31, 1982: pp. 23–50.

Fowler, Alastair. *Triumphal Forms: Structural Patterns in Elizabethan Poetry*. Cambridge University Press, 1970.

Fumaroli, Marc. *L'âge de l'éloquence: rhétorique et 'res literaria', de la Renaissance au seuil de l'époque classique*. Droz, 1980.

Gadoffre, Gilbert. *Du Bellay et le sacré*. Gallimard, 1978.

Galand-Hallyn, Perrine, et al. 'L'Inspiration Poétique Au Quattrocento et Au XVIe Siècle'. *Poétiques de la Renaissance: le modèle italien, le monde franco-bouguignon et leur héritage en France au XVIe siècle*. Edited by Perrine Galand-Hallyn and Fernand Hallyn. Droz, 2001, pp. 109–147.

Genette, Gérard. *Palimpsestes: la littérature au second degré*. Éditions du Seuil, 1982.

Heninger, S. K. *Sidney and Spenser: The Poet as Maker*. Pennsylvania State University Press, 1989.

Huntington, John. 'Furious Insolence: The Social Meaning of Poetic Inspiration in the 1590s'. *Modern Philology*, vol. 94, 1997: pp. 305–326.

Jayne, Sears Reynolds. *Plato in Renaissance England*. Kluwer Academic Publications, 1995.

Jeanneret, Michel. 'Marot traducteur des psaumes: entre le néo-platonisme et la Réforme'. *Bibliothèque d'Humanisme et Renaissance*, vol. 27, no. 3, 1965: pp. 629–643.

Lecointe, Jean. *L'idéal et la différence: la perception de la personnalité littéraire a la renaissance*. Droz, 1993.

Melehy, Hassan. *The Poetics of Literary Transfer in Early Modern France and England*. Ashgate, 2010.

Noirot-Maguire, Corinne. 'Plaisir et puissance "éthiques": style simple et renaissance poétique'. *Publije*, vol. 3, no. 1, 2013: pp. 2–12.

Norton, Glyn P. *The Ideology and Language of Translation in Renaissance France and Their Humanist Antecedents*. Droz, 1984.

Ovid. *Fasti*. Translated by James George Frazer. Harvard University Press, 1996.

Peletier, Jacques. 'Art Poétique'. *Traités de Poétique et de Rhétorique de La Renaissance*. Edited by Francis Goyet. Livre de Poche, 1990, pp. 217–314.

Plato. *The Statesman, Philebus, Ion*. Edited and translated by Harold North Fowler and Walter Rangeley Maitland Lamb. Harvard University Press; William Heinemann, 1975.

Puttenham, George. *The Art of English Poesy: A Critical Edition*. Edited by Frank Whigham and Wayne A. Rebhorn. Cornell University Press, 2007.

Quintilian. *The Orator's Education, Volume IV: Books 9–10*. Translated by Donald Russell. Harvard University Press, 2002.

Raimondo, Riccardo. 'Clément Marot, traducteur évangélique des Rerum vulgarium fragmenta de Pétrarque'. *Renaissance and Reformation*, vol. 43, no. 2, 2020: pp. 119–145.

Rebhorn, Wayne A. 'Du Bellay's Imperial Mistress: Les Antiquitez de Rome as Petrarchist Sonnet Sequence'. *Renaissance Quarterly*, vol. 33, no. 4, 1980: pp. 609–622.

Schoell, Franck Louis. *Études sur l'humanisme continental en Angleterre à la fin de la Renaissance*. Champion, 1926.

Sidney, Philip. *A Defence of Poetry*. Edited by Jan Adrianus van Dorsten. Oxford University Press, 1966.

Smith, Paul J. *Dispositio: Problematic Ordering in French Renaissance Literature*. Brill, 2007.

Southwell, Robert. *The Poems of Robert Southwell, S.J.* Edited by James H. McDonald and Nancy Pollard Brown. Clarendon Press, 1967.

Spenser, Edmund. *The Faerie Queene*. Edited by Thomas P. Roche and Patrick O'Donnell. Penguin Books, 1987.

Spenser, Edmund. *The Yale Edition of the Shorter Poems of Edmund Spenser*. Edited by William Oram. Yale University Press, 1989.

Virgil. *Eclogues, Georgics, Aeneid I-VI*. Translated by H. Rushton Fairclough and G. P. Goold. Harvard University Press, 1999.

Warley, Christopher. *Sonnet Sequences and Social Distinction in Renaissance England*. Cambridge University Press, 2005.

Wills, Richard. *De Re Poetica*. Edited and translated by Alastair Fowler. Blackwell for the Luttrell Society, 1958.

Yates, Frances Amelia. *Astraea: The Imperial Theme in the Sixteenth Century*. Routledge and Kegan Paul, 1975.

2

The fashioning of English anti-Petrarchism: Spenser and Shakespeare remembering Du Bellay

Line Cottegnies

Thanks to Anne Lake Prescott's work on the influence of Pléiade poets in England, we know more about the English reception of French poetry in the period, along with Italian poetry (Prescott 1978; Prescott 2013b).[1] We have also begun to better perceive the mediation of France in the reception of Petrarchism itself, and the importance of translation and imitation (for definitions of the protean movement of Petrarchism, see Dubrow 4; for imitation, see Greene; and Melehy 2005, 159–160). It has become increasingly clear that the fashioning of England's literary idiom took place in a European, transnational context (Boutcher). Joachim du Bellay, whom Spenser celebrated as 'first garland of free poësie / That France brought forth [...] well worthie [...] of immortalitie' (Spenser 1591, sig. S4) was well known in England, mostly thanks to Spenser's mediation. Spenser did much to popularize Du Bellay in English: first, he translated some of Du Bellay's *Songe* in Jan van der Noot's anti-Catholic *Theatre for Worldlings* (1569); then he adapted his *Antiquitez de Rome* as *The Ruines of Rome*, which were published in his 1591 *Complaints*. Spenser's interest in the Catholic Du Bellay has led to intense speculation but can be explained by the French poet's satirical treatment of Rome, which made him acceptable in a Protestant context (Coldiron; Belle and Cottegnies 45). Some of Du Bellay's sonnets were even discreetly absorbed into the English repertoire, as shown by Prescott (1978, 52–60). A minor Elizabethan poet, Sir Arthur Gorges, translated twenty-three of Du Bellay's poems, taken from works as diverse as *L'Olive*, *Les Antiquitez*, *Les Regrets*, *Poésies diverses* and *Divers jeux rustiques*, which shows the extent of Gorges's reading, alongside twenty sonnets by Desportes. It is impossible, of course, to say whether his manuscript poems circulated at all, but Samuel Daniel also included imitations of four Du Bellay sonnets from *L'Olive* in *Delia* (Prescott 1978, 58).

It is likely that Shakespeare had read some Du Bellay, and at least Spenser's version of *The Ruines of Rome*. A. Kent Hieatt has identified verbal and thematic echoes between the *Ruines* and Shakespeare's *Sonnets*. Shakespeare might have been drawn to the French poet, one of the most individualistic of the Pléiade sonneteers, for the irreverent anti-Petrarchan stance of his late poetry, most particularly in *Les Antiquitez de Rome* and *Les Regrets* (Prescott 2013a, 144–145). Whether Shakespeare had read Du Bellay's works (or those of any other French poet) in French directly is a moot point, although he had some French, as we know from his plays (see Kennedy 2006; Kennedy 2016, 219–221). Few critics have looked into Shakespeare's debt to French sonneteers, perhaps for lack of direct evidence, with the valuable exception of Hassan Melehy and Anne Lake Prescott (Melehy 2010, 205–220; Prescott 2013a). Shakespeare the lyric poet still baffles critics, as if his debt to the tradition was either undetectable or limited to the fact that he wrote sonnets.[2] Yet, as for Spenser, Shakespeare's engagement with various modalities of adaptation and imitation of European poetry was instrumental in shaping his response to the genre of the sonnet, as this essay argues.

Following Anne Coldiron, Melehy has reminded us of the importance of Du Bellay's plan for a defence and illustration of the vernacular for a whole generation of European poets, including Spenser (Coldiron; Melehy 2010, 17–30; Brown). But even he, and Prescott, can only argue for a *probable* influence of Du Bellay on Shakespeare, which they mainly detect in Shakespeare's notions about time, and in the immortalizing and embalming function he grants poetry (Melehy 2010, 205; Prescott 2013a). This essay cannot, unfortunately, produce groundbreaking evidence proving that Shakespeare had definitely read Du Bellay, but it argues for a change of tack. I suggest that instead of looking for sources, we should compare Shakespeare's free imitation of Petrarchism to Du Bellay's, for both poets challenge the Petrarchan fashion in a similar, impertinent manner. While Spenser's mode of imitation keeps close to the original (Melehy 2005, 159; Melehy 2010, 76), I argue that Shakespeare and Du Bellay share a form of productive imitation that differs in degree from Spenser's and moves away from the humanistic conception of imitation.

It seems established that Shakespeare's *Sonnets* include verbal and thematic echoes that recall Spenser's *Ruines of Rome*. Hieatt lists, for instance, the association between 'injurious' and 'time' (Spenser 1591, Sonnet 27; Shakespeare, Sonnet 63), the presentation of 'time' as 'devouring' (Spenser 1591, Sonnet 3; Shakespeare, Sonnet 19), the 'war' waged against time (Spenser 1591, Sonnet 27; Shakespeare, Sonnets 15 and 16) and the use of words like 'antique' and 'antiquities' ('extremely rare among other sonnets of the time', Hieatt 801), and, even rarer, the verb 'to ruinate'. One of the most obvious thematic 'resemblances' is the emphasis on time and mutability. Shakespeare's Sonnet 55 is thus often cited as the closest to

Spenser's *Ruines of Rome*. But, as Prescott reminds us, these echoes have their significance within the larger context of the European vogue for 'Ruinish', or the language of ruins (Prescott 2013a, 135). It has also been pointed out that Du Bellay's *Antiquitez de Rome* makes explicit the analogy between the decayed city and a ruined female body, through the personification of Rome (Rebhorn). Du Bellay's sequence has thus been read as a radical revisiting of a Petrarchan sonnet sequence, with the lost Roman glory in lieu of the lost Laura (Prescott 2013a, 144), a transposition which is made even more explicit by Spenser through the use of the third-person pronoun 'she' to designate the city of Rome: 'She, whose high top above the starres did sore' (Spenser 1595, Sonnets 4, 65). In his *Sonnets*, Shakespeare similarly makes an implicit analogy between his addressee, the youth, and ruins when he submits the young man's body to the 'bloody tyrant, Time' in Sonnet 16, just as he compared Lucrece's body to a ruined building in *The Rape of Lucrece*: 'her soul's house is sacked [...] Her mansion battered by the enemy' (quoted in Prescott 2013a, 142). In Sonnets 55 and 65, the youth is compared to ruined 'statues' and a 'work of masonry', a joint allusion to the end of civilizations and to a funerary monument 'besmear'd with sluttish time' (Sonnet 55).[3] The young man celebrated by the poet is thus, paradoxically, also constantly associated with the prospect of his demise; and when Shakespeare emphasizes the power of poetry to immortalize its object in a rewriting of the Horatian trope of the *exegi monumentum aere perenius*, it is, again, by overtly associating his explicit subject, the youth, with physical decay. But while many of these thematic 'similarities' are intriguing, they do not seem overly specific, and some of them go even as far back as Horace or Ovid; as such, they are shared by a generation of poets.

Yet both Shakespeare and Du Bellay wittily revisit the Petrarchan genre with an irreverence that few poets of their generations display (for Shakespeare's poetics of irreverence, see Venet 2016, 397–398). Both show a critical awareness of generic expectations and systematically distort and dislocate them to create a new poetics. While Du Bellay replaces his mistress with Rome and everything it stands for, Shakespeare substitutes the beautiful lady of the tradition with a fair young man in the larger section of the sequence, and a dark lady for the remaining section – also thereby revising the subgenre of the sonnet to the 'ugly woman' identified by Patrizia Bettella. Like Du Bellay in *Les Regrets* (1558), Shakespeare turns the sonnet sequence into a dramatic exploration of the speaking persona's self, and several overlapping themes emerge. These include not just the multifaceted meditation on ruins that we find in both sequences, but also the melancholy treatment of exile, as in Sonnet 31 of *Les Regrets* ('Heureux qui comme Ulysse', Du Bellay 1993, II: 54), which seems to find an echo in Shakespeare's

Sonnet 56 (Kennedy 2006, 108). Both Du Bellay and Shakespeare substitute blame for the praise that is usually expected from a sonnet sequence. This is particularly obvious in *Les Regrets*, where Du Bellay uses the sonnet form more creatively than in his former sequence, *L'Olive* (1549). *Les Regrets* includes a catalogue of his male friends and patrons, and does away with the fiction of a beloved, while the speaker mourns for the lost grandeur of Rome. For if Du Bellay's poems retain from Petrarch an elegiac tone, they are mostly about melancholy and the loss of Rome as a symbol of the passing of time. The sequence constructs a community of readers, who, as patrons and friends, are blamed and praised in turn, united through the agency of the poet's self-centred persona. Replacing social distinction with a form of literary election, the speaker inverts the conventional relationship of patronage, asserting the symbolic power of the poet over his social superiors. Shakespeare also subverts the power balance that lies at the heart of the patronage system, predominantly by turning a patron into the beloved of his sequence and repeatedly blaming him for his own corruption. Moreover, he ostensibly fails to give him a pseudonym, that 'surnom louable' ('praise pseudonym'), as the poet Maurice Scève called it in Dizain LIX of *Delie* (1544, 47), or the imaginary name often imbued with symbolic significance that was usually given to the beloved in sonnet sequences. He even ostensibly refrains from revealing his patron's name – in spite of the sonnet genre's affinity with onomastics in the period. Moreover, by constantly emphasizing the power of his verse to immortalize the young man's fame, the poet subverts the implicit exchange on which the relationship of patronage is based, turning it into a form of symbolic blackmail.

Du Bellay was generally quite vocal in his criticism of Petrarchism; his famous verse diatribe against Petrarchan poets, 'Contre les Pétrarquistes' ('Against Petrarchan Poets'), which was published in *Divers jeux rustiques* (1557), was well known in England. It was imitated, for instance, by Gorges:

J'ay oublié l'art de Petrarquizer,	Of love fayne woolde I frame my style
Je veulx d'Amour franchement deviser,	Yet nott to flatter nor beguyle
Sans vous flatter, and sans me deguizer.	For they that so their words doo fyle
(Du Bellay 1993, II: 190)	And use a glosinge kinde of vayne. (Gorges 50)

This poem includes a stanza on blazons, which Du Bellay's speaker dismisses as vain rhetorical exercises. Contrary to lovers who pilfer the heavens for comparisons and hyperboles, Du Bellay's persona is a down-to-earth lover, looking for a much more concrete satisfaction:

> Mais quant à moy, qui plus terrestre suis,
> Et n'ayme rien, que ce qu'aymer je puis,
> Le plus subtil, qu'en amour je poursuis,
>   S'appelle jouissance. (Du Bellay 1993, II: 194)

In his imitation, Gorges skips the explicit reference to 'jouissance', which evokes sexual fulfilment:

> For me I cannott reache soe hye
> Butt still my truth and faith shall trye
> That I am yours untill I dye
> And doo by me, by me desarts. (Gorges 52)

It is tempting to see this passage as anticipating Shakespeare's Sonnet 130 and perhaps offering a precedent for its no-nonsense lover: 'I grant I never saw a goddess go – / My mistress when she walks treads on the ground' (Sonnet 130). Shakespeare might have found an inspiring precedent in the playful treatment here of the Neoplatonic base on which Petrarchism relies.[4] First, Du Bellay revisits the androgyne of Plato's *Symposium* critically, to turn it into a metaphor expressing the perfect friendship between lovers seen as equals (Du Bellay 1993, II: 194). However, in a final twist, he feigns playfully to endorse the conventional Petrarchan topos of the beloved as perfection incarnate, and therefore its Neoplatonic basis, offering to take up his Petrarchan stance to continue wooing his lady as 'the most beautiful idea' ('la plus belle Idée', II: 196) if she so wishes, provided that she agrees to step down from her pedestal and let him kiss her. As the speaker turns the Petrarchan trope into a playful metaphor without substance, he also frankly acknowledges the reality of his sexual desire, which runs counter to the fiction of idealized courtship. In his imitation of the poem, Gorges characteristically omits both the reference to the androgyne and the cruder allusion to the physicality of desire (Gorges 50–52). In his *Sonnets*, Shakespeare combines an original treatment of the androgyne, as when he extols the 'master-mistress' (the 'Fair Youth') of his 'passion' in Sonnet 20, with the celebration of sinful physical desire in the sonnets to the 'Dark Lady'. In the spirit of Du Bellay's poem above, Shakespeare's sonnet sequence thus subverts orthodox Petrarchism by making physical desire the explicit subject matter in a series of sonnets that are about desire and consummation. One sonnet in particular is entirely devoted to depicting the psychology and physiology of lust, described as obsessional and sinful – 'Th' expense of spirit in a waste of shame / Is lust in action' (Sonnet 129) – while Sonnets 135 and 136 are based on a series of very explicit sexual jokes involving puns on the polysemous word 'will' and the proper name 'Will'.

Throughout his oeuvre, Du Bellay developed a whole range of strategies critical of the blazon. With Sonnet 91 of *L'Olive*, a poem that was itself inspired by two minor Italian poems, he writes a paradoxical blazon, which starts by blaming the lady, but ends with praise. The speaker cantankerously feigns to relinquish his unworthy lady, 'unblazoning' her line after line, commanding her to give up all her qualities one by one, because they are all usurped from nature – and in doing so, he literally deconstructs the conventional Petrarchan catalogue of physical beauties:

Rendez à l'or cete [sic] couleur, qui dore Ces blonds cheveux, rendez mil' autres choses: […] Rendez ces mains au blanc yvoire encore, Ce seing au marbre, et ces levres aux roses…. (Du Bellay 1993, I: 62)	Return to gold this colour which gilds This fair hair; Return a thousand other things […] Return these hands to white ivory This breast to marble, and these lips to roses…. (my translation)

The poem is, however, based on a witty reversal, which reads as blackmail: it ends on a volta introduced by the conjunction 'or' which overturns the poem's ostensible aggression towards the woman, and suggests the possibility of her keeping her status – if she accepts the speaker's advances. The final twist wittily suggests that the poet can renege on his cursing and start loving his lady again:

Ou aux rochez rendez ce cœur de marbre, Et aux lions cet' humble felonnie.	Or return to the rocks this marble heart, And to lions this humbling treachery.

The sonnet thus, paradoxically, reaffirms the validity of the conventional blazon after all. As for the typical catalogue of beauties, its hackneyed metaphors imply a form of literalization, as each body part is turned into a material substance: the lady's hair, for instance, is not described as being like gold, but *is* gold itself. The lady is thus turned into a beautiful object, a hybrid compound of material parts, as in one of Arcimboldo's contemporary mannerist composite object portraits. The poem, which reads until the very last couplet like a counterblazon, or a poem satirizing or blaming an ostensibly ugly woman, must finally be read as its opposite: a paradoxical blazon. The paradox on which it is based is the apparent unworthiness of the lady, which is ultimately reversed back into worthiness – although the strategy deconstructing the praise in the first twelve lines necessarily questions the very validity of the blazon.

This poem was known in England and was adapted fairly literally twice, successively by Gorges and Samuel Daniel. Intriguingly, they both overlook the final twist, to end on a straightforward rejection of the lady, failing to translate the witty irony of the original poem. In Sonnet 20 of his *Vannetyes and Toyes*, Gorges adds a final couplet in which the speaker simply dismisses his mistress:

> Restore agayne that colloure of the golde
> that garnishte hath those haires like golden streames
> And lett those eyes so heavenly to beholde
> resign unto the Sonn their borrowed beames
> […]
> And let that harte off hardened flynty stone
> return unto the rocks from whenc [sic] it came
> And then (oh love) if thow wilte heare my mone
> teach me withall how to foregett her name. (Gorges 23)

In Sonnet 18 of *Delia*, Daniel also alters the ending, adding one last particularly blunt line which sends the woman packing:

> Restore thy tresses to the golden Ore,
> Yeelde Cithereas sonne those Arkes of loue;
> […]
> But yet restore thy fearce and cruell minde,
> To Hyrcan Tygers, and to ruthles Beares.
>> Yeelde to the Marble thy hard hart againe;
>> So shalt thou cease to plague, and I to paine. (Daniel)

It is quite possible that Daniel was imitating Gorges's version here rather than Du Bellay's,[5] but it might also be the case that both Gorges and Daniel resisted the subtle tweaking of generic conventions which Du Bellay achieved with his final reversal of counterblazon into paradoxical blazon. It is plausible that a misogynistic poem entirely dedicated to blame (and to the rejection of the lady) was more appealing to a contemporary English readership, or that Gorges and Daniel perhaps found it more satisfactory for aesthetic reasons, because it did not contradict the rest of the poem.

Du Bellay uses a similar twist in Sonnet 91 of *Les Regrets*, an anti-Petrarchan parody, which is a rewriting of a sonnet by Mellin de Saint-Gelais, itself inspired by an earlier poem by Francesco Berni (Saint-Gelais 1, 184–185; Berni 95). The poem, again, plays with generic expectations, as it oscillates between a parodic blazon (as signalled by the meliorative adjectives and the repeated interjections) and an ironic counterblazon, with the woman seemingly praised but also associated with negative terms – until, brushstroke after brushstroke, it is the portrait of an ugly woman that finally comes together:

> O beaux cheveux d'argent mignonnement retors!
> O front crespe, et serein! Et vous face doree!
> O beaux yeux de crystal! ô grand' bouche honoree
> Qui d'un large reply retrousses tes deux bordz!
> […]
> O beau corps transparent! ô beaux membres de glace!
> O divines beautez! pardonnez moi de grace,
> Si pour estre mortel, je ne vous ose aymer. (Du Bellay 1993, II: 84)

Du Bellay's ending differs from both sources, however. Where Berni ended with a sarcastic comment taking stock of his lady's parodic portrait, and Saint-Gelais with an ironic mention of his pangs of love, Du Bellay ends on a final, coy withdrawal ('Oh, divine graces! Forgive me, / If being a mortal, I dare not love you' – my translation). The poet rejects the ugly woman he has vilified under the guise of a perfidious parodic praise, by simply withdrawing from the scene. In order to reject her, he modestly feigns to don again, in a final twist, the mask of the humble Petrarchan lover: as a down-to-earth human being, he finds himself eventually unworthy of this 'goddess' – even though he has erected a profoundly repellant idol. In these two sonnets, Du Bellay thus reworks his sources in a creative way, making full use of the final volta to baffle his readers' expectations.

Shakespeare shares with Du Bellay this critique of the blazon, which is aligned with his overall critique of Petrarchism. In his works, the blazon is treated in an exclusively parodic and satirical mode. In Sonnet 106, it is clearly associated with a poetic practice of the past – which reminds us that Shakespeare is writing almost fifty years after Du Bellay:

> When in the chronicle of wasted time
> I see descriptions of the fairest wights,
> And beauty making beautiful old rhyme,
> In praise of ladies dead and lovely knights,

> Then in the blazon of sweet beauty's best,
> Of hand, of foot, of lip, of eye, of brow,
> I see their antique pen would have expressed
> Even such a beauty as you master now.

There is not one instance in his œuvre where Shakespeare treats the blazon as straightforward praise. In *Henry V* (1599), the blazon is associated with the French princes and ridiculed: on the eve of the Battle of Agincourt, the arrogant French courtiers quarrel about whose horse and suit of armour are the most beautiful. Orleans mocks the Dauphin's hyperbolic praise of his horse: 'I have heard a sonnet begin so to one's mistress' (3.7.41).[6] The praise of the horse becomes an absurd, parodic version of a Petrarchan blazon. Meanwhile, Henry V describes himself as a down-to-earth English soldier unable to speak the language of courtship and refuses to woo the French princess in the manner of courtiers who can 'rhyme themselves into ladies' favours' (5.2.163). His manly plainness stands in sharp contrast with the sophistication of the effeminate French courtier, as if to signify that the conventional blazon and its continental Petrarchan poetics are either not truly English, or no longer fashionable.

Shakespeare's plays are full of Petrarchan lovers who are mocked for loving too closely 'by th' book', like Romeo rebuked by Juliet in *Romeo and Juliet* (1597, 1.5.109). In *As You Like It* (1599), Orlando, the arch-Petrarchan lover, is mocked for carving poems extolling the beauties and virtues of his lady into the bark of trees in 3.2 (see Venet 2014). In *Twelfth Night* (1603), the conventional blazon is turned by Olivia, to whom it is sent as a compliment, into an itemized list of body parts similar to a post-mortem inventory. This time Shakespeare shows the rebellion of the love object: the lady of the blazon appropriates her own praise to turn it upside down. The itemized inventory becomes an apt metaphor for the deadly dismembering carried out by the conventional blazon.

> VIOLA 'Tis beauty truly blent, whose red and white
> Nature's own sweet and cunning hand laid on.
> Lady, you are the cruell'st she alive
> If you will lead these graces to the grave
> And leave the world no copy.
>
> OLIVIA O, sir, I will not be so hard-hearted. I will give out divers schedules of my beauty. It shall be inventoried, and every particle and utensil labelled to my will, as, *item*, two lips, indifferent red; *item*, two grey eyes, with lids to them; *item*, one neck, one chin, and so forth. (1.5.228–238)

But it is with Sonnet 130, which reads like a distant rewriting of Du Bellay's *Regrets* 91, that Shakespeare offers his most explicit criticism of the blazon (Roulon). The sonnet extols the beauties of the 'Dark Lady', who has been alternatively described by critics as a brunette, an ugly woman or a Black woman (De Grazia). It is not exactly a counterblazon, since, in a similar fashion to Du Bellay's Sonnet 91 of *L'Olive*, it finally recuperates the conclusion of a conventional blazon, ending by affirming the superiority of the speaker's lady over other ladies: it can more accurately be described, therefore, as a parodic blazon, because it ends on a note of paradoxical praise. Like the two Du Bellay blazons discussed above, the poem is based on a surprising twist, and manipulates the readers' expectations, keeping them guessing until the very end:

> My mistress' eyes are nothing like the sun;
> Coral is far more red than her lips' red;
> If snow be white, why then her breasts are dun;
> […]
>   And yet by heaven, I think my love as rare
>   As any she belied with false compare.

Shakespeare playfully reworks the topos of the 'ugly' lady's parodic praise in a paradoxical blazon. The ending, however, contrasts with that of *Regrets* 91, as the woman, even though she has been described as not conventionally desirable, is not rejected, but eventually embraced *with* all her faults – and this is in keeping with the wider group of 'Dark Lady' sonnets, in which the speaker embraces sin. As with Du Bellay, the rhetorical target of the poem lies elsewhere: turning away from the woman herself, Shakespeare uses the paradoxical blazon as a poetic manifesto to deconstruct the conventions of the genre – whose inadequate, hackneyed rhetoric, reduced to 'false compare', is the real subject matter of the poem – while affirming the 'plainness' of his new poetic voice.

Shakespeare's treatment of the blazon here can perhaps be contrasted with Spenser's, which is also creative, but distinctively less critical of Petrarchism. Jonathan Sawday has argued that the gender of England's ruler gave the English blazon a peculiar tonality, making it markedly more chaste, less erotically charged, than on the continent (197). He also remarks that English sonneteers were encouraged to associate the genre with 'emerging discourses of commerce and trade', as well as imperialism (198). According to him, two blazons by Spenser best illustrate this. In a blazon embedded in his 1594 *Epithalamion*, Spenser plays with the convention, eulogizing his bride in a passage where she is described as a surrogate of the queen in Ireland. To this effect, the speaker summons a chorus of young maids, all daughters of merchants, to acknowledge his lady's beauty:

> Her long, loose yellow locks, like golden wire,
> Sprinkled with pearl, and pearling flowers atween,
> Do like a golden mantle her attire;
> And being crownèd with a garland green,
> Seem like some maiden queen.
> […]
> Tell me, ye merchants daughters, did ye see
> So fair a creature in your town before?
> So sweet, so lovely, and so mild as she,
> Adorned with beauty's grace and vertue's store? (Spenser 1595, [G8]-[G8v])

The poem then literally turns the beloved into an 'object of consumption', to be displayed and admired by this mercantile audience (Sawday 199), through the hyperbolic list of the precious comparisons: 'Her goodly eyes like Saphires shining bright, / Her forehead ivory white …'. Spenser uses a similar conceit in Sonnet 15 of *Amoretti* (1595):

> Ye tradefull Merchants that with weary toyle,
> Do seeke most pretious things to make your gain:
> And both the Indias of their treasures spoile,
> What needeth you to seeke so farre in vaine?
> For loe my love doth in her selfe containe
> All this worlds riches that may farre be found,
> If Saphyres, loe hir eies be Saphyres plaine,
> If Rubies, loe hir lips be Rubies sound:
> […]
> But that which fairest is, but few behold,
> Her mind adornd with vertues manifold. (Spenser 1595, B)

While it is tempting to read the rise of English protocapitalism and imperialism in these poems, this hypothesis takes a beating when we realize that both this sonnet and the passage of *Epithalamion* quoted above are close imitations of a sonnet of Desportes's *Diana* (Sonnet 32, Book 1, 1573), which Sawday overlooks – so much for national peculiarity. If a materialistic reading of such sonnets remains possible, they must be set in a transnational context, as reflecting a European trend. The 'English' blazon is not particularly English after all: if seen in a transnational perspective, it belongs to a European web of texts.⁷ Desportes's conclusion, however, differs from Spenser's:

> Marchands, qui recherchez tout le rivage more
> Du froid Septentrion et qui, sans reposer,
> À cent mille dangers vous allez exposer
> Pour un gain incertain, qui vos esprits dévore,
>
> Venez seulement voir la beauté que j'adore,
> Et par quelle richesse elle a su m'attiser:
> Et je suis sûr qu'après, vous ne pourrez priser
> Le plus rare trésor dont l'Afrique se dore.
> Voyez les filets d'or de ce chef blondissant,
> […]
> Cet argent, cet ivoire; et ne vous contentez
> Qu'on ne vous montre encor mille autres raretés,
> Mille beaux diamants et mille perles fines. (Desportes I, 92–93)

In this version, merchants are summoned to admire the lady, who has been turned into an icon, and to claim that she is more beautiful than all worldly treasures. This admission in turn renders their quest and their pilfering of all the world's riches vain. But in *Amoretti* 15, Spenser alters the original sonnet by adding a reference to the lady's hidden beauty, her mind, in the final couplet. The poem can therefore be read on two levels. First, as a variant on a conventional blazon, it ostensibly celebrates the lady's perfections, both physical and moral, as is obvious from the last line. Unsurprisingly, Spenser's lady is described as far superior to all the most precious material things, making the quest for material possessions futile, in a variant on the trope of the *sans pareille*. But a second, moral reading is also suggested, as the merchants also represent the vanity of mercantile pursuits, as evidenced by the negative connotations of terms such as 'weary toil', 'gain' and 'spoil', while the lady stands as the embodiment of steadfast moral perfection pitted against such toys. This interpretation chimes with the Neoplatonic tenor of Spenser's *Amoretti* as a whole (Bulger). But in one further turn of the screw, we can also read the poem through a reflective perspective as a metapoetic sonnet critical of the genre of the blazon, for the lady's portrait constructed through the poem is that of a materialistic idol, a grotesque embodiment of the mercantile dream. This reading helps us to read the penultimate line as a riddle, addressed perhaps to Spenser's conniving male readers: 'But that which fairest is, but few behold …'. This part of her which few can behold is, naturally, her virtuous mind, as we are told in the last line. Yet, for a short moment of suspense, the poem seems to suggest a playful sexual innuendo – it is as if two different, incompatible images were superimposed.

However subtle, Spenser's version of the Desportes blazon is still an imitation: the original poem remains identifiable and Spenser's wit lies in the way he interprets, imitates and alters his source. The same is true of Du Bellay's *Regrets* 91, in which the originals by Saint-Gelais and Berni are still present, according to Du Bellay's conception of imitation as defined in *Deffence and Illustration*. Melehy argues that Spenser, in turn, borrows his 'notion of poetic imitation from the Pléiade [...] in order to effect an imitative reworking of Du Bellay and the other poets', and to create 'an English literature that would rival that of Antiquity, and then ultimately surpass it' (Melehy 2010, 76). While we can call Du Bellay's and Spenser's conceptions of imitation humanistic, Shakespeare's attitude to imitation is different, not in nature – imitation for Shakespeare also implies 'reordering [pieces of a text], transforming them, and writing a text that addresses and contributes to the present context' (Melehy 2005, 159–160) – but, rather, in degree. Thus, even though Shakespeare's blazon in Sonnet 130 does not call to mind a direct source and is not opposed to a specific precedent, it can still be seen as a product of the culture of imitation, but of a different kind, less indebted to specifics. When literary reminiscences surface in the *Sonnets*, they are so well digested as to become unrecognizable and untraceable.

Keeping the precedent of Du Bellay's treatment of Petrarchism in mind, we can tentatively offer, to conclude, a reading of Shakespeare's sequence as creating a new poetics through a sustained revising of the metaphysical and aesthetic principles of Petrarchan poetics (for a different reading, see Kennedy 2016 and Edmondson and Wells in Shakespeare 2020). As argued above, the most visible twist to the genre is the substitution of a man for the more conventional mistress in the main of the sequence, but also important is the fact that the youth is presented as the embodiment of a Neoplatonic ideal, the perfect alloy of 'fair, kind, and true' (Sonnet 105), before his corruption shatters this essential Platonic trinity. Meanwhile, in the poems commonly associated with the 'Dark Lady', the woman is presented as neither beautiful nor virtuous, but an object of discourse; she becomes the wedge that splinters the world order and causes in the speaker a far-ranging epistemological crisis. When the Petrarchan tradition is still traceable, it has become so distorted that it seems like a grotesque reminiscence. Sonnet 20, for instance, still contains the echo of a conventional blazon, down to its erotic titillation, as the poet praises the different body parts of the youth, including that part that cannot be named. But the perfect youth does not simply take up the position of the lady of the sonnets: he supersedes women, as he is described as having a 'woman's gentle heart, but not acquainted / With shifting change as is false women's fashion'. Yet the poem retains, but distorts, the conventional topos of impossibility of the Petrarchan convention: the inadequacy of the 'supplement' of the youth's sexual anatomy renders him improper for the persona's love. Nature 'by addition me of thee defeated, / By adding one thing to my purpose nothing'. The sonnet thus suggests a new dichotomy between a more noble love ('thy love') and physical love ('thy love's use'), in a complete revision of the Platonic opposition between the celestial Venus and then terrestrial Venus presented in Plato's *Symposium*. This, in turn, subverts the topos of loss and failure that conventionally lies at the heart of the Petrarchan sequences by taking it into hitherto uncharted, queer, territory: the topos of impossibility no longer has anything to do with cruelty or absence, but with a supplement that is defined as privation.

The Platonic fable created in the first section of the *Sonnets* is soon denied, however, as the youth proves fallible: the final section is about a love experienced as explicitly sinful and dishonourable. Here the buoyancy of Sonnet 130 is undercut by a darker notion of love, where the persona's decision to call fair and true what is typically deemed ugly and false takes on subversive undertones, and leads to an explicit and systematic reversal, then confusion, of values; the paradoxical blazon of dark beauty becomes a metaphysical drama that takes on a more pessimistic dimension as the poet's perception of truth splits, with radical consequences:

> Thou blind fool, Love, what dost thou to mine eyes,
> That they behold, and see not what they see?
> They know what beauty is, see where it lies,
> Yet what the best is take the worst to be. (Sonnet 137, l. 1–4)

The speaker decides to call fair that which is foul, good that which is evil, true that which is false. By willingly embracing sin, he turns the world's order upside down, with potentially radical consequences, as 'fair' and 'foul', good and evil become interchangeable and indistinguishable. In this distorted episteme, the crisis to which the poet submits Petrarchan poetics symbolically informs a new creation, almost Satanic, and produces a metaphysical, moral and aesthetic crisis: 'For I have sworn thee fair, and thought thee bright, / Who art as black as hell, as dark as night' (Sonnet 147). In Sonnet 121, the speaker boldly declares 'I am that I am', a blasphemous echo of *Exodus* 3.14. The consequence, as Joel Fineman has shown, can only be a splitting of the speaking, perjurous subject: 'For I have sworn thee fair: more perjured I, / To swear against the truth so foul a lie' (Sonnet 152).

Never had the conventional paronomasia on 'eye' and 'I' acquired such an intense meaning, as the aesthetic and metaphysical crisis becomes a crisis of the subject. With the experience of sin opening up a space of interiority, the wilful 'I' discovers himself as impure and abject. These sexually explicit sonnets, which stage a subversive desire, seem to be the logical outcome of the metaphysical and moral demise that is staged elsewhere. Here Shakespeare leaves behind the dead remains of the Petrarchan tradition to venture into pastures new.

This essay argues that Du Bellay and Spenser adopted a form of imitation that could be called humanistic – in which the source remains identifiable – while Shakespeare did not. Commenting on Spenserian imitation, Melehy argues that *Complaints* constitutes 'a kind of "defense and illustration" of English poetry' (Melehy 76–77); then Shakespeare's *Sonnets* might best be considered as creating a new kind of poetry from the ruins and detached pieces of a poetry which, around 1600, appeared old-fashioned. It could be argued that Shakespeare was following the lead of Du Bellay after all, whose anti-Petrarchan stance he might have remembered, by authoring a poetry that is intensely self-reflexive, but also concerned with forging a radically new poetic idiom. The subversion of the conventional, often degraded, Neoplatonism inherent in the Petrarchan tradition is what, if this reading of Shakespeare's *Sonnets* has any traction, gives this most dramatic of sequences its peculiar shape. With his blazons of ugliness and celebration of impure desire, Shakespeare transforms the Petrarchan heritage beyond recognition.

Notes

1. For an earlier, much shorter version of this argument, see Cottegnies (2020).
2. Although Shakespeare's sonnets were collected and published in 1609 by Thomas Thorpe, Edmondson and Wells have suggested in a recent edition that Shakespeare did not compose them as an organized sequence (Shakespeare 2020). The present essay is based on a sequential reading of the sonnets, however.
3. All quotations from the *Sonnets* are from Shakespeare (2006).
4. For definitions of Neoplatonism in the period's literature, see Bulger, Medcalf and Roe.
5. For a similar suggestion about another poem, see note in Gorges p. 189.
6. All quotations from the dramatic works are from Shakespeare (2005).
7. For an earlier version of this argument, see Cottegnies (2018).

Works cited

Bellay, Joachim du. *L'Olive*. Paris, 1550.
Bellay, Joachim du. *Les Antiquitez de Rome*. Paris, 1558a.
Bellay, Joachim du. *Les Regrets*. Paris, 1558b.
Bellay, Joachim du. *Œuvres poétiques*. 2 vols. Edited by Daniel Aris and Françoise Joukovsky. Classiques Garnier, 1993.
Belle, Marie-Alice and Line Cottegnies, eds. *Robert Garnier in Elizabethan England*. MHRA Publications, 2017.
Berni, Francesco. *Rime*. Edited by Danilo Romei. Murcia, 1985.
Bettella, Patrizia. *The Ugly Woman: Transgressive Aesthetic Models in Italian Poetry from the Middle Ages to the Baroque*. University of Toronto Press, 2005.
Boutcher, Warren. 'Intertraffic: Transnational Literatures and Languages in Late Renaissance England and Europe'. *International Exchange in the Early Modern Book World*. Edited by Matthew McLean and Sara K. Barker. Brill, 2016, pp. 343–373.
Brown, Richard Danson. 'Forming the "First Garland of Free Poësie": Spenser's Dialogue with Du Bellay in *Ruines of Rome*'. *Translation and Literature*, vol. 7, no. 1, 1998: pp. 3–22.
Bulger, Thomas. 'Platonism in Spenser's Mutability Cantos'. *Platonism and the English Imagination*. Edited by Anna Baldwin and Sarah Hutton. Cambridge University Press, 1994, pp. 126–138.
Coldiron, Anne E. B. 'How Spenser Excavates Du Bellay's *Antiquitez*'. *Journal of English and Germanic Philology*, vol. 102, 2005: pp. 159–183.
Cottegnies, Line. 'Of the Importance of Imitation: Du Bellay, Shakespeare, and the English Sonneteers'. *Shakespeare Studies*, vol. 48, 2020: pp. 41–47.
Cottegnies, Line. 'Shakespeare et le blason anglais'. *Le Blason: anatomie d'une anatomie*. Edited by Julien Goeury and Thomas Hunkeler. Droz, 2018, pp. 477–499.
Daniel, Samuel. *Delia*. London, 1592.
Desportes, Philippe. *Les Premières oeuvres*. Edited by François Rouget and Bruno Petey-Giard. Classiques Garnier, 2014.
Dubrow, Heather. *Echoes of Desire: English Petrarchism and Its Counterdiscourses*. Cornell University Press, 1995.
Fineman, Joel. *Shakespeare's Perjured Eye: The Invention of Poetic Subjectivity in Shakespeare's Sonnets*. University of California Press, 1986.
Gorges, Arthur. *Poems*. Edited by Helen Estabrook Sandison. Oxford University Press, 1953.
Grazia, Margreta de. 'The Scandal of Shakespeare's Sonnets'. *Shakespeare: The Critical Complex: Shakespeare's Poems*. Edited by Stephen Orgel and Sean Keilen. Garland, 1999, pp. 89–112.
Greene, Roland. *Post-Petrarchism: Origins and Innovations of the Western Lyric Sequence*. Princeton University Press, 1991.

Hieatt, A. Kent. 'The Genesis of Shakespeare's Sonnets: Spenser's *Ruines of Rome: By Bellay*'. *PMLA*, vol. 98, no. 3, 1983: pp. 341–352.

Kennedy, William J. '*Les langues des hommes sont pleines de tromperies*: Shakespeare, French Poetry, and Alien Tongues'. *Textual Conversations in the Renaissance*. Edited by Zachary Lesser and Benedict S. Robinson. Ashgate, 2006, pp. 91–111.

Kennedy, William J. 'Shakespeare's Sonnets and the Economy of Petrarchan Aesthetics'. *Petrarchism at Work: Contextual Economies in the Age of Shakespeare*. Cornell University Press, 2016, pp. 219–312.

Medcalf, Stephen. 'Shakespeare on Beauty, Truth and Transcendence'. *Platonism and the English Imagination*. Edited by Anna Baldwin and Sarah Hutton. Cambridge University Press, 1994, pp. 117–125.

Melehy, Hassan. 'Antiquities of Britain: Spenser's *Ruins of Time*'. *Studies in Philology*, vol. 102, no. 2, 2005: pp. 159–183.

Melehy, Hassan. *The Poetics of Literary Transfer in Early Modern France and England*. Ashgate, 2010.

Prescott, Anne Lake. 'Du Bellay and Shakespeare's *Sonnets*'. *The Oxford Handbook of Shakespeare's Poetry*. Edited by Jonathan F. S. Post. Oxford University Press, 2013a, pp. 134–150.

Prescott, Anne Lake. *French Poets and the English Renaissance: Studies in Fame and Transformation*. Yale University Press, 1978.

Prescott, Anne Lake. 'Ronsard in England 1635–1699'. *French Connections in the English Renaissance*. Edited by Catherine Gimelli Martin and Hassan Melehy. Ashgate, 2013, pp. 179–191.

Rebhorn, Wayne A. 'Du Bellay's Imperial Mistress: *Les Antiquitez de Rome* as Petrarquist Sonnet Sequence'. *Renaissance Quarterly*, vol. 33, no. 4, 1980: pp. 609–622.

Roe, John. 'Italian Neoplatonism and the Poetry of Sidney, Shakespeare, Chapman and Donne'. *Platonism and the English Imagination*. Edited by Anna Baldwin and Sarah Hutton. Cambridge University Press, 1994. 100–116.

Roulon, Nathalie. 'Le sonnet 130 de Shakespeare ou le blason mis à nu'. *Renaissance and Reformation / Renaissance et Réforme*, vol. 37, no. 2, 2014: pp. 19–47.

Saint-Gelais, Mellin de. *Œuvres poétiques françaises*. 2 vol. Edited by Donald Stone Jr. STFM, 1993–1995.

Sawday, Jonathan. *The Body Emblazoned: Dissection and the Human Body in Renaissance Culture*. Routledge, 1995.

Scève, Maurice. *Œuvres complètes*. Edited by Pascal Quignard. Mercure de France, 1974.

Shakespeare, William. *All the Sonnets of Shakespeare*. Edited by Paul Edmondson and Stanley Wells. Cambridge University Press, 2020.

Shakespeare, William. *The Oxford Shakespeare: The Complete Works*. Edited by Gary Taylor, Stanley Wells et al. Oxford University Press, 2005, 2nd edition.

Shakespeare, William. *The Sonnets*. Edited by G. Blakemore Evans. Updated edition, with a new introduction by Stephen Orgel. Cambridge University Press, 2006.

Spenser, Edmund. *Amoretti and Epithalamion*. London, 1595.

Spenser, Edmund. *Complaints*. London, 1591.

Van der Noot, Jan. *A Theatre… [for] Worldlings*. London, 1569.

Venet, Gisèle. '"Ce n'est plus thym ny marjolaine": *As You Like It*, ou l'atelier de la réécriture.' *Études anglaises*, vol. 69, no. 4, 2016: pp. 387–409.

Venet, Gisèle. 'Préface'. William Shakespeare. *Comme il vous plaira*. Translated by Jean-Michel Déprats. Gallimard, 2014, pp. 7–62.

3

'Translated out of Ronsard'?: A misattributed translation of Petrarch's *RVF* 48 by Sir John Borough

Guillaume Coatalen

In 1638, Dudley North, third Baron North (bap. 1582, d. 1666), wrote a series of love poems which finally appeared in print in *A Forest of Varieties* in 1645. Among them, a twenty-four-line sonnet occurs, 'Made in imitation of a Sonnet in Ronsard', for which no source has been identified (Prescott 2013, 179–192).[1]

To at least one Caroline nobleman dabbling in poetry, Ronsard represented 'unrequited love', 'heat' and 'fire', the very tropes which the French poet had quarried from Petrarch's verse (Bellenger). Anne Lake Prescott notes, however, that Ronsard was rather neglected – although he had quite a few imitators, English readers preferred Du Bartas (1978, 76). Drummond, who did admire him, mentions him in a letter along with 'Homer, Virgil, Ovid and Petrarch' as well as the more recent 'Bartas, Boscan and Garcilasso' in order to criticize the obscurity of the new Metaphysical poetry (Lake Prescott 99; Lytle Harris 10–11). A few years earlier, Sir John Borough (d. 1643), also known as Burrus or 'Borroughs', the antiquary, herald, royal archivist and former secretary to Francis Bacon, copied out one of his own imitations, a sonnet headed 'Translated out of Ronsard', in British Library Harleian MS 1823. Little research has been carried out on Borough, and none on his verse, though it is typical of Jacobean lawyers and a valuable measure of poetic taste and practice at the time (Woolf). Since he was a student at Gray's Inn in 1611–12 and the manuscript's *terminus post quem* is 8 August 1635, a date indicated on fol. 43v, he must have been around forty years old, a fairly mature age, when he copied out the verse in the manuscript. He was already Garter King of Arms, a post befitting a serious scholar responsible for heraldry, which was a system regulating social order, wealth and power. Yet he seemed attached to what could be perceived as frivolous verse, whose composition may date back to the far-off days when he was a student at Gray's Inn (Coatalen 2005). After all, composing poetic toys could be for the

Garter King of Arms a way to impress refined courtly circles and improve his social status. The eye-skip ('~~quiet~~ /constant/ compasse quiet') or letter-inversion ('~~febals~~ befals') corrections are typical of someone copying a text from another manuscript. The trope on contraries, characteristic of Petrarch's love sonnets, which is developed in the first quatrain of the sonnet attributed to Ronsard suggested that the piece might in fact be by Petrarch. It eventually proved to be a translation of Petrarch's *Canzoniere* or *Rerum vulgarium fragmenta* (hereafter *RVF*) 48, beginning 'Se mai foco per foco non si spense'. This contribution examines the possible reasons for this misattribution and its implications for how translation practice and theory in early modern England should be envisaged. It also offers an edition of the vernacular verse contained in the manuscript, which includes, in addition to the translation of *RVF* 48, a loose imitation of one of Petrarch's most popular sonnets, *RVF* 189 'Passa la nave mia colma d'oblio', famously translated by Sir Thomas Wyatt as 'My galley, chargèd with forgetfulness' and included in Tottel's popular miscellany, *Songs and Sonnets* (1557). A better grasp of Borough's Petrarchan compositions partly depends on considering the neighbouring poems of a comparable nature with which they interact.

The contents of Harleian MS 1823 indicate that Borough had a number of friends in common with Ben Jonson, including Hugh Holland (the first item in the manuscript is a set of selective quotations from his *Pancharis* [1603]) and Thomas Farnaby. A neo-Latin 'sons of Ben' answer to Ben Jonson's 'Inviting a Friend to Supper', with the date 10 July 1631, occurs on fol. 24. There was quite a vogue for Latin responses to Ben Jonson's poems in the 1630s, in particular for responses to his 'Ode on Himself', which was written on the failure of his comedy *The New Inn* (first performed in 1629). In this context, the term 'Palmari', used in the 1808 catalogue of Harleian manuscripts to describe one of Burrus's Latin pieces on fol. 24, means 'the one who takes the palm', or 'the top poet' (Nares II 259). The bulk of the manuscript is made up of letters in Latin addressed to Philip Bacon, a friend from Gray's Inn (Foster 116) – Edward Bacon's second son and Francis Bacon's nephew. These were posthumously published in 1643 in *Impetus Juveniles*, which also contains Latin verse addressed to Philip and Francis Bacon (Borough). *The Oxford Dictionary of National Biography* states that *The Soveraignty of the British Sea*, written in 1633 and printed in 1651, was Borough's only work published during his lifetime (Baron). The vernacular verse, perhaps composed by Borough, was carefully excluded from *Impetus Juveniles*, which consisted entirely of writings in Latin, a language taken more seriously. However, a psalmic sonnet would not have affected his reputation and, like many poets, he may have wanted to keep verse in manuscript. Otherwise, the manuscript comprises the sonnet attributed to Ronsard, the imitation of Petrarch's *RVF* 189 and a religious sonnet (written on a smaller sheet bound with the other material), reminiscent of the psalms and comparable with some of George Herbert's verse in *The Temple* (1633). Borough also copied lines from an Italian song, adapted from *La Camilla* (first published in Venice in 1532), a collection of sonnets, madrigals and other popular tunes. These were often adapted from Petrarch, and were gathered together by Caio Baldassarre Olimpo degli Alessandri (c. 1486–c. 1540), who was one of François I's favourite Italian poets (Tomasi). *La Camilla* was reprinted up to 1700. Poetry is further represented in the manuscript by extracts from Virgil and Seneca in the original Latin.

The vernacular verse in Harleian MS 1823

The poems are transcribed diplomatically, with expanded abbreviations in italics, additions set in between slashes ('/'), illegible material between square brackets ('[]') and deletions with a single strikethrough line. Borough's legible secretary hand looks somewhat old-fashioned for a manuscript compiled shortly after 1635. The Petrarchan sources are given in full while other translations in English and French are indicated in parentheses beneath the transcriptions.

fol. 7r

Da'i tuoi bei occhi nasce il mio dolce amore
Dal dolce amore dolce desire
Dal dolce desire dolce ardore
Dal dolce languire dolce dolore
Dal dolce dolore dolce morire
Dal dolce morire morir contento
Che per voi dolce è tutto quel ch'io sento.

(*Camilla: opera molto dilettevole da intendere / composta da Baldessar Olimpio da Sassofer à requisition de' giovani innamorati, nella quale si contiene sonetti, ottave, canzoni, strambotti & madrigali*. In Verona: per Bortolamio Merlo, 1611, Sig. A7.)

Da bei vostr'occhi vsci il mio dolce amore;
E dal mio dolce amor, dolce desire,
E dal dolce desire, il dolce ardore,

E dal mio dolce ardor, dolce languire,
E dal dolce languir, dolce dolore,
E dal dolce dolor, dolce morire,
E dal dolce morir, dolce contento,
Che per voi tutto è dolce que ch'io sento.

fol. 14r

As in a ship which with the swelling floud
    And loud impetuous windes is mastered

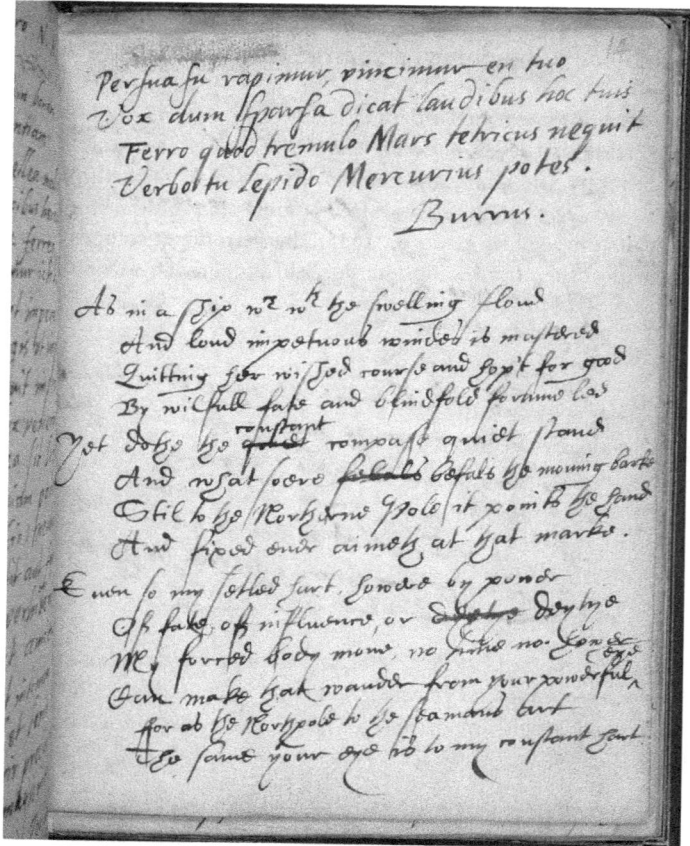

Figure 3.1 Harley_ms_1823_f014r. Reproduced by permission of the British Library.

> Quitting her wished course and hop't for good
> By wilfull fate and blindfold fortune led
> Yet dothe the ~~quiet~~ /constant/ compasse quiet stand
> And what soere ~~febals~~ befals the mouing barke
> Stil to the Northerne Pole it points the hand
> And fixed euer aimeth at that marke.
> Euen so my setled hart, howere by power
> Of fate, of influence, or ~~dyytye~~ deytye
> My forced body moue, no time no. hower
> Can make that wander from your powerful /eye/
> ffor as the Northpole to the seamans art
> The same your eye is to my constant hart.

(Shakespeare, Sonnet 116, Spenser, *Amoretti*, Sonnet 34.)

Petrarch *RVF* 189

> Passa la nave mia colma d'oblio
> per aspro mare a mezza notte il verno
> enfra Scilla et Caribdi, et al governo
> siede 'l signore anzi 'l nimico mio;
>
> à ciascun remo un penser pronto et rio
> che la tempesta e 'l fin par ch' abbi a scherno;
> la vela rompe un vento umido eterno
> di sospir, di speranze et di desio;
>
> pioggia di lagrimar, nebbia di sdegni
> bagna et rallenta le già stanche sarte
> che son d'error con ignoranzia attorto.
>
> Celansi i duo mei dolci usati segni,
> morta fra l'onde è la ragion et l'arte
> tal ch' incomincio a desperar del porto.

fol. 14v

Translated out of Ronsard

> As fier by fier is n'ere extinguished
> Nor Riuers by distilling showers made drye
> But as by like, like stil is nourished
> And contrarye oft help't by contrarye

Say (Loue) thou which our meeting thoughts dost fit
    And in ~~true~~ two bodys mak'st ~~o~~ one soule to dwell
    Why by strange meanes dost thou disable it
    Through much desiring our desire to tell.
Perhaps as Nilus dulls the neighbour coastes
    With hideous noyse falling from lofty shelfe
    Or as the sun dazels the gazers eyes
Euen so desire that striues within it selfe
    In his vnbrideled obiect soone is lost
    As to much ~~sup~~ spurring hinders him that flyes   'to': too
[   ]
                Burrus.

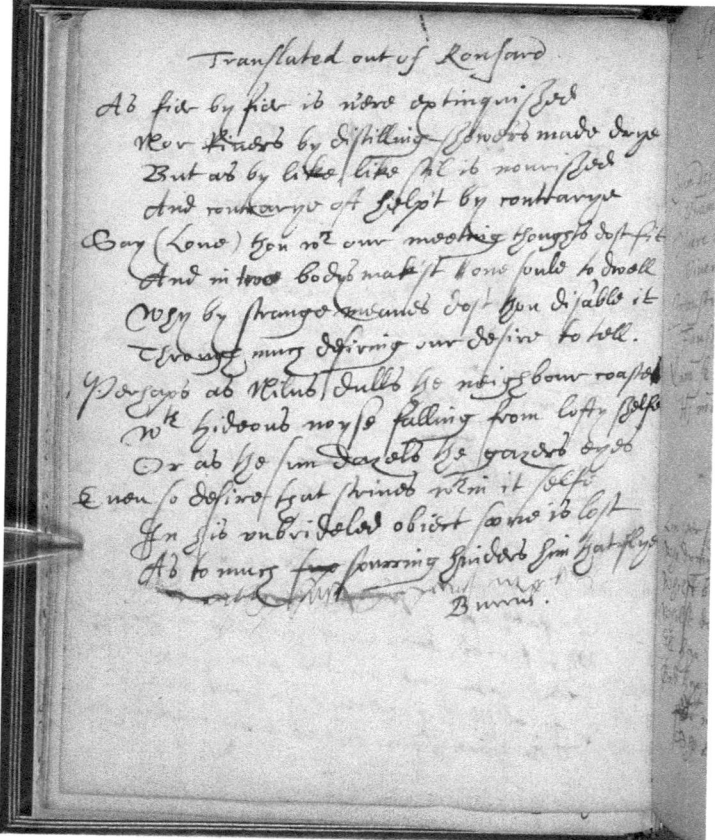

Figure 3.2 Harley_ms_1823_f014v. Reproduced by permission of the British Library.

(Philieul, 1555, CI; Maldeghem, 1606, XL.)

Petrarch *RVF* 48

> Se mai foco per foco non si spense,
> né fiume fu già mai secco per pioggia,
> ma sempre l'un per l'altro simil poggia,
> et spesso l'un contrario l'altro accense,
>
> Amor, tu che' pensier' nostri dispense,
> al qual un'alma in duo corpi s'appoggia,
> perché fai in lei con disusata foggia
> men per molto voler le voglie intense?
>
> Forse sí come 'l Nil d'alto caggendo
> col gran suono i vicin' d'intorno assorda,
> e 'l sole abbaglia chi ben fiso 'l guarda,
>
> cosí 'l desio che seco non s'accorda,
> ne lo sfrenato obiecto vien perdendo,
> et per troppo spronar la fuga è tarda.

(Surrey, 'The louer describes his restlesse state' (lines 5–8), *Tottel's Miscellany*, sig. Ciiiir.)

fol. 94r

> O whether shall I go? or whether flye?
> To heauen? there sits a iudge to punish sinne:
> To hell? there an accuser for revenge doth crye.
> To earth? there faulty accessoryes bin:
>
> Within me? there a guilty conscience lyes:
> Without me? there I finde a world of woes.
> Thus when his fauour God to man denyes,
> himselfe, earth, hel, and heauen, al turne his foes.
>
> Alas how can I flye whom sin doth binde
> Or if I could, how can I shun thy hand
> Or if I can, where shall I comfort finde
> Since without thee no blisse no ioy can stande

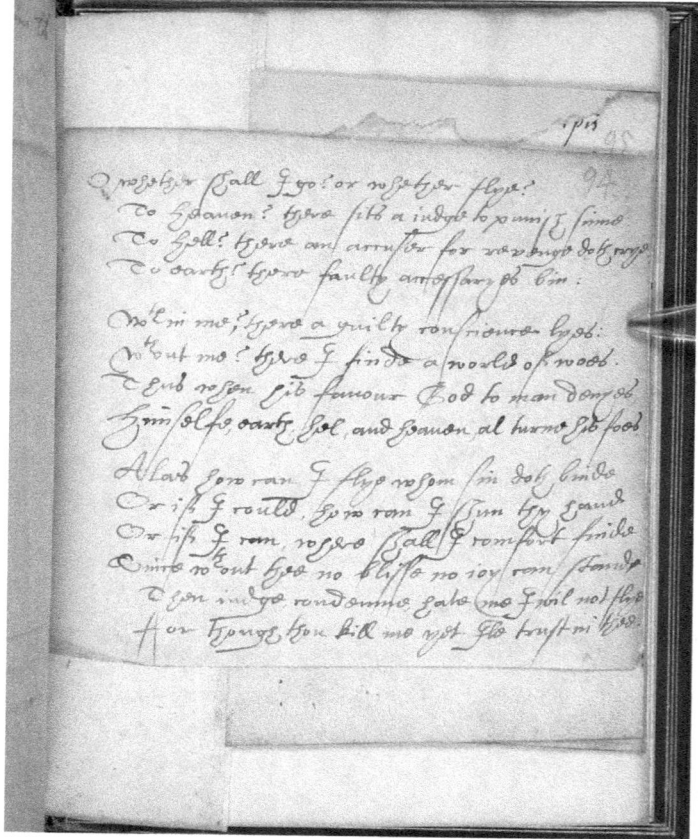

Figure 3.3 Harley_ms_1823_f094r. Reproduced by permission of the British Library.

> Then iudge, condemne, hate me I wil not flye
> ffor though thou kill me yet Ile trust in thee.

(See Psalm 139:7–10 (*KJV*)):

> Whither shall I go from thy spirit? or whither shall I flee from thy presence? / If I ascend up into heaven, thou art there: if I make my bed in hell, behold, thou art there. / If I take the wings of the morning, and dwell in the uttermost parts of the sea; / Even there shall thy hand lead me, and thy right hand shall hold me.

(The piece is also reminiscent of George Herbert's verse 'The Search': 'Whither, O, whither art thou fled, / My Lord, my Love?' (lines 1–2).)

Ronsard and Petrarch

Petrarch is present in three ways in the manuscript, even though he is not explicitly mentioned: a translation of *RVF* 48 is misattributed to Ronsard, another sonnet is silently imitated from *RVF* 189, and, finally, a popular song adapted from *La Camilla* is based on Petrarchan commonplaces, notably 'il dolce dolore' – the lover's sweet suffering. Caroline translations or imitations of Petrarch, from the original and from the French, were not infrequent: one need only mention Drummond's Sonnets I.6, 9, 15, 50 and 51 and II.7, from Parts I and II of *Poems* (1640), and Thomas Carew's 'The Spring' and 'Prayer to the Wind', published in *Poems* (1640) (Roche). The sonnet, as a form, is further present in the divine sonnet strongly reminiscent of the psalms. For the extract adapted from *La Camilla*, Borough may have had access to a 1622 Venetian edition while serving as secretary to the ambassador Thomas Howard, Earl of Arundel (Baron), or simply copied it from another manuscript.

The choice of *RVF* 48 is interesting in itself, since no extant translation of the sonnet dated from before the 1630s has survived (Watson, Boswell). Perhaps the focus on contraries appealed to Borough in an age when poets like John Donne were exploring paradoxes, even though parts of his translation echo Thomas Middleton's earlier (1597) *The Wisdome of Salomon Paraphrased*: 'Your hot affection cooled your hot desire, / Two heats once met make cool distilling showers' (lines 171–172). The neo-Platonic single soul in two bodies, 'And in two /true/ bodys mak'st one soule to dwell' – an allusion to the popular myth of lovers as separated twins developed by Aristophanes in Plato's *Symposium* (192c–193a) – is reminiscent of the 'Our two soules therefore, which are one' in John Donne's 'A Valediction: Forbidding Mourning' (line 21), a poem Borough may very well have been familiar with. The lines about the Nile may allude to a passage in Philip Sidney's *Apology for Poetrie*, 'you bee borne so neare the dull-making Cataract of Nilus, that you cannot heare the Planet-like Musicke of Poetrie', while the paradox of hindering spurs may have brought to Borough's mind lines six and seven from Shakespeare's Sonnet 51, 'When swift extremity can seem but slow? / Then should I spur, though mounted on the wind' (ed. Burrow, lines 6–7, 483). The mistress who dazzles the gazer's eyes is a Petrarchan commonplace which occurs in Sidney's Sonnet 76 in *Astrophel and Stella*. So, all in all, although Petrarch's *RVF* 48 was not the best-known of his sonnets, numerous details from it occur in Elizabethan and Jacobean Petrarchan songs and sonnets, and part of its appeal was surely that it contained a significant number of core Petrarchan commonplaces. In imagery and diction, the manuscript poem is perfectly typical of English post-Petrarchan poetry.

The sonnet loosely adapted from Petrarch's *RVF* 189, 'Passa la nave mia colma d'oblio', belongs to a rich tradition of texts in verse and prose which go back to a simile in Ovid's *Metamorphoses* (8.470–2) – 'utque carina, / quam ventus ventoque rapit contrarius aestus, / vim geminam sentit paretque incerta duobus' ['And as a Boate which tide contrarie beares / Against the winde, feeles double force, and is compeld to yeelde / To both' (in Arthur Golding's 1567 translation)] – and scriptural sources like Matthew 8:24 – 'there arose a great tempest in the sea, insomuch that the ship was covered with the waves'. It is based on the metaphorical image of the soul carried by a ship (the body) caught in the tempest of life. Closer in time to Borough, the Petrarchan tempest trope occurs in Shakespeare's definition of constant love in Sonnet 116: 'That looks on tempests and is never shaken; / It is the star to every wandering barque' (ed. Burrow, lines 6–7, 613). Edmund Spenser uses the simile in Sonnet 34 of his *Amoretti* – 'Lyke as a ship, that through the Ocean wyde' – and in *The Faerie Queene* (2.2.208) – 'As a tall ship tossed in troublous seas'. Nicholas Breton, too, offers a variation on the theme in part of his 'A Most Excellent Passion' in *The Phoenix Nest* (1593), beginning with 'These lines I send by waues of woe, / And bale becomes my boate' (Breton 65). While Borough must have known Petrarch's original sonnet and Wyatt's translation, from the second quatrain onwards his sonnet diverges from Petrarch's by laying the stress on love's constancy, like Shakespeare in Sonnet 116, as opposed to the vagaries of fortune. What does link it to Petrarch's sonnet is the trope of the mistress's eyes guiding stars to the seaman lover.

As for the divine sonnet, with its rhetorical questions and answers, it is rooted in the tradition of the psalms, illustrated by the likes of Francis Quarles and George Herbert in Borough's time (Höltgen). Taking the examples of Anne Lock, Henry Lok and Barnabe Barnes, Deirdre Serjeantson has convincingly shown how intertwined psalms and sonnets were in the second half of the sixteenth century. Borough's Caroline manuscript testifies to the same close connection between these major secular and religious lyric genres. The sonnet thus becomes a form devised to sing both secular and divine love. The strong formal link between the psalms and the sonnet is made apparent in the ABAB rhyming quatrains and the concluding sestet rhymed ABABCC, patterns extensively used, for instance, in the Hopkins and Sternhold 1562 psalter. In effect, Borough's imitation of *RVF* 189 and his divine sonnet chime in comparable ways, the slightly different rhyme scheme notwithstanding.

For *RVF* 48, Borough followed the rhyme scheme ABAB CDCD EFG FEG, which is Petrarch's for the tercets (EFG FEG) but not Petrarch's Flemish translator Philippe de Maldeghem's, who adopts the so-called Marotic rhyme scheme for the tercets (CCD EED) after the common ABBA ABBA for the quatrains. The two most frequent rhyme schemes Ronsard uses in his tercets are CCD EED and CCD EDE. For the other two sonnets, however, Borough chose the Shakespearean rhyme scheme with its defining concluding couplet, which had become the dominant form. The only metrically difficult line in the misattributed sonnet is line seven, 'Why by strange meanes dost thou disable it', where two scansions seem to be available: either 'WHY by strange MEANES dost THOU disAble IT' or, stressing 'strange', 'WHY by STRANGE MEANES dost THOU disAble IT', a more expressive scansion. The translation of 'gran suono' (*RVF* 48, line 10), literally 'big sound', by the relatively common expression 'hideous noyse' may echo Arthur Golding's translation of Ovid's *Metamorphoses* (1573), which uses it seven times. The phrase 'distilling showers' occurs in Shakespeare's *Venus and Adonis* (1593) and in Middleton's *The Wisdome of Salomon Paraphrased* (1597). '[S]welling flood' occurs in the Geneva Bible (1561), Michael Drayton's *Endimion and Phœbe* (Drayton, stanza 71, line 1, 310) and Edward Fairfax's translation of Tasso. All in all, Borough's style in his love sonnets is not too dissimilar to that of love sonnets written in the 1590s and 1600s, while the plain style in the religious sonnet is comparable with George Herbert's slightly later religious verse. So why did Borough ascribe Petrarch's *RVF* 48 to Ronsard? He may have forgotten the source or made a mistake. Another possibility is that the misattribution was deliberate. Ronsard's early love poetry was imitated in Scotland by Alexander Montgomerie and in England by Thomas Lodge (Grubb). William Drummond called him 'paragon of poets' (France 259). Undoubtedly, Ronsard's prestige was immense in England, which may partly explain the misattribution. Another more likely hypothesis is that Ronsard sounded like Petrarch, even though Ronsard did not translate a single entire sonnet by Petrarch. The *Canzoniere*'s presence in Ronsard's love poetry takes the form of countless rewritings of particular lines or borrowings of particular images made popular by Petrarch's translators and imitators (Gendre, Bellenger). Since Borough's translation of the original Italian sonnet is quite literal, it is possible that he had access to it, in particular given that he resided in Venice in 1622 (Baron), but it is of course highly unlikely that an Italian source would have been ascribed to Ronsard. It is therefore more probable that Borough used a French translation instead, which was erroneously attributed to Ronsard. Here again, the two most likely printed translations available to him, Vasquin Philieul's and Maldeghem's, are clearly presented as translations. Borough's translation gestures towards an intermediary version of the ultimate Petrarchan source, but if it was in English it has not survived. What seems to have happened is that Borough used a manuscript source in French with or without an attribution to Ronsard.

The confusion (which is not dispelled in the 1808 printed catalogue) between Petrarch and Ronsard is not surprising if one considers the extent to which Ronsard digested Petrarch's love poetry. Sixteenth-century translations co-existed with or were followed by a staggering number of sonnets written in the manner of Petrarch, first in France and then in England, to such an extent that the verb 'Pétrarquiser' was coined in France and recorded in Randle Cotgrave's 1611 dictionary: 'To Petrarkise it, to write like a passionate louer' (n.p.). It does not seem to appear in the *OED*, apart from Cotgrave's entry. The French sense, in Theodore Beza's *Abraham sacrifiant* and in Ronsard's 1552 *Amours*, seems to me to be wholly negative, unlike Cotgrave's. Borough attributed the sonnet to Ronsard and not to Philippe Desportes, the French Petrarchan poet who influenced Elizabethan sonneteers. Yet Desportes, too, stitched together multiple elements imitated from Petrarch's *Canzoniere* to write his own love sonnets (Rouget, Whitworth). Prescott has gathered ample evidence of the extent of Ronsard's reception in England from 1635 to 1699, a period when Ronsard was out of fashion in France. Our manuscript may be added to this testimony on Ronsard's pervasive presence some eighty years after the publication in French of his love poetry. As with Desportes, whose spiritual sonnets were translated in the 1630s (Coatalen 2013), imitations of Ronsard may have participated in a fervent nostalgia for Tudor literature. The misattribution seems to suggest that Ronsard had come to replace Petrarch as the ultimate source for Petrarchan tropes. It is difficult to ascertain when that happened, but by the last two decades of the sixteenth century, Desportes, Ronsard and Du Bellay, among other French sonneteers, had become significant sources for the booming production of Petrarchan love sonnets. The French Petrarchan poets of the *Pléiade* had not superseded the original Italian source but were probably consulted alongside the *Canzoniere*. Desportes and Ronsard may have been imitated as readily accessible exemplars of Petrarchanism, since more English readers would have known French than Italian (Gallagher 30).

A comparison between Borough's, Philieul's and Maldeghem's translations suggests Maldeghem's more literal version was Borough's source (Balsamo 2004). Borough's 'vnbrideled obiect' echoes Maldeghem's 'obiect débridé', while Philieul translates more literally Petrarch's 'sfrenato obietto' ('obiect frené'). Maldeghem's more recent 1606 translation may have been easier to get hold of than Philieul's 1555 collection. Philieul's work was not appreciated in France and fell into oblivion, making it still more unlikely that his translation served as the source text. When translating, Borough does try to develop his own style, and though he does not display the kind of *sprezzatura*, or effortless brilliance, which characterizes Sidney's or Shakespeare's love sonnets, he masters quite a few rhetorical tricks. He is particularly fond of figures of repetition, like diacope – starting with 'fier by fier' (line 1), the repetition of a word with words in between; epizeuxis – 'like, like' (line 3), the repetition of a word with no words in between; and polyptoton – 'desiring our desire' (line 8), words based on the same root.

As in the case of Spenser, who started his poetic career by translating Du Bellay's sonnets (Hatfield), Borough may have considered the loose imitation of Petrarch's *RVF* 189, the psalmic sonnet and the fairly close translation of Petrarch's *RVF* 48 as means to perfect his poetic style. It is impossible to establish whether he started by imitating Petrarch's verse before translating it, but imitation may have been a less exacting exercise. Thus, the manuscript offers an interesting case study in translation, imitation and the subtle transition from one to the other (Burrow, Pigman). Ironically enough, by imitating Petrarch, he was composing in the manner of Ronsard. While Tudor translation in general has been the object of growing critical attention (Morini, Schurink), a technical and systematic account of the various choices, from close to paraphrastic – Francis Davison notes one of his poems is 'paraphrast[i]cally translated out of Petrarkes 103' (Davison 24; Mortimer 25) – made by early modern English translators of Petrarch's verse remains to be written.

Ultimately, the exact source of a given sonnet may not have mattered that much to Borough, who misattributed one sonnet by Petrarch and freely imitated another without indicating a source. Imitation was embraced as the most natural way to write any type of text in the early modern period; while classical sources and scriptural ones were immediately identified by readers and duly recorded in print, the idea that vernacular authors should be treated likewise was not entirely accepted, even if authors like Edmund Spenser and Ben Jonson had succeeded in presenting themselves as classics. Borough did care who the author of the sonnet was; he thought, and the notion was far from being absurd, that the sonnet was by Ronsard. What characterizes his misattribution is the interchangeability of famous authors, and the desire for an authoritative source which took precedence over the desire for a particular author.

Note

1 I wish to thank Amy Bowles for taking pictures of Harleian MS 1823 and the readers for their excellent work.

Works cited

Balsamo, Jean. 'Philippe de Maldeghem ou le Pétrarque en Flandre (1600)'. *Les Poètes français de la Renaissance et Pétrarque*. Edited by Jean Balsamo. Travaux d'Humanisme et Renaissance 394. Textes et Travaux de la Fondation Barbier-Mueller pour l'étude de la poésie italienne de la Renaissance 1. Librairie Droz, 2004, pp. 491–505.

Baron, S. A. 'Borough, Sir John (d. 1643)'. *Oxford Dictionary of National Biography*. Edited by David Cannadine. Oxford University Press, 2004. https://doi-org.ezproxy.univ-paris3.fr/10.1093/ref:odnb/2913. Accessed 1 January 2023.

Bellenger, Yvonne. 'Quatre sonnets de Ronsard imités de Pétrarque *Amours* 1553, s. 12, 14, 60, 149'. *Échos des voix, échos des textes: Mélanges en l'honneur de Béatrice Périgot*. Edited by Odile Gannier and Véronique Montagne. Rencontres, no. 252, Colloques, congrès et conférences sur la Renaissance européenne, no. 79. Classiques Garnier, 2013, pp. 649–665.

Bellenger, Yvonne. 'Ronsard imitateur infidèle de Pétrarque'. *Petrarca e la cultura europea*. Edited by Luisa Rotondi Secchi Tarugi. Nuovi orizzonti, 1997, pp. 223–242.

Borough, Sir John. *Burrhi impetus juveniles et quædam sedatioris aliquantulum animi epistolæ*. Excudebat Leonardus Lichfield, 1643.

Boswell, Jackson Campbell and Gordon Braden. *Petrarch's English Laurels, 1475–1700: A Compendium of Printed References and Allusions*. Ashgate, 2012.

Breton, Nicholas. *The Phoenix Nest*. Set foorth by R.S. of the Inner temple gentleman. Iohn Iackson, 1593.

Burrow, Colin. *Imitating Authors: Plato to Futurity*. Oxford University Press, 2019.

Coatalen, Guillaume. 'An English Translation of Desportes' Christian Sonnets Presented to John Scudamour by Edward Ski[...]'. *The Review of English Studies (RES)*, vol. 65, no. 271, October 2013: pp. 619–646.

Coatalen, Guillaume. 'Unpublished Elizabethan Sonnets in a Legal Manuscript from the Cambridge University Library'. *The Review of English Studies (RES)*, vol. 54, no. 217, November 2003: pp. 553–565.

Cotgrave, Randle. *A Dictionarie of the French and English Tongues*. Adam Islip, 1611.

Da Sassoferrato, Baldassarre Olympo. *Camilla de Baldesar Olimpio da Sassoferrato nouamente corretta: & ristampata del MDXXXII doue si contiene mattinate, strambotti, madrigaletti, canzoni, epistole, sonetti, frottole, barcellete, & prose*. Nicolo d'Aristotile detto Zoppino, 1532.

Da Sassoferrato, Baldassarre Olympo. *La Camilla: opera molto dilettevole da intendere: nella quale si contiene sonetti, ottaue e strambotti Di nuouo ristampata, e di molti errori emendata.* Appresso Angelo Righettini, 1622.

Davison, Francis. *Dauisons poems, or, a Poeticall Rapsodie.* Printed by B[ernard] A[lsop] for Roger Iackson, 1621.

Drayton, Michael. *Endimion and Phœbe.* At London: Printed by Iames Roberts, for Iohn Busbie, [1595].

Edward Fairfax, *Godfrey of Bulloigne, or The recouerie of Ierusalem.* Ar. Hatfield, for I. Iaggard and M. Lownes, 1600.

Foster, Joseph. *Register of Admissions to Gray's Inn, 1521–1889.* Priv. print. by the Hansard publishing union, limited, 1889.

France, Peter. *The Oxford Guide to English Literature in Translation.* Oxford University Press, 2001.

Gallagher, John. *Learning Languages in Early Modern England.* Oxford University Press, 2019.

Gendre, André. 'Pierre de Ronsard'. *Les Poètes français de la Renaissance et Pétrarque.* Travaux d'Humanisme et Renaissance 394. Textes et Travaux de la Fondation Barbier-Mueller pour l'étude de la poésie italienne de la Renaissance 1. Edited by Jean Balsamo. Librairie Droz, 2004, pp. 229–251.

Grubb, Marion. 'Lodge's Borrowing from Ronsard'. *Modern Language Notes*, vol. 45, no. 6, 1930: pp. 357–360.

Hatfield, Andrew. 'Edmund Spenser's Translations of Du Bellay in Jan van der Noot's *A Theatre for Voluptuous Worldlings*'. *Tudor Translation.* Edited by Fred Schurink. Palgrave Macmillan, 2012, pp. 143–160.

Höltgen, Karl Josef. 'New Verse by Francis Quarles: The Portland Manuscripts, Metrical Psalms, and the "Bay Psalm Book" (with Text)'. *English Literary Renaissance*, vol. 28, no. 1, 1998: pp. 118–141.

Lytle Harris, Phyllis. 'Elizabethan Imagery in the Poetry of Drummond of Hawthornden' (1950). Graduate Student Theses, Dissertations & Professional Papers. 2209. https://scholarworks.umt.edu/etd/2209/.

Middleton, Thomas and Gary Taylor, eds. *Thomas Middleton: The Collected Works.* Clarendon Press, 2010.

Morini, Massimiliano. *Tudor Theory and Practice.* Routledge, 2006.

Mortimer, Anthony Robert. *Petrarch's Canzoniere in the English Renaissance.* Rodopi, 2005.

Nares, Robert, Stebbing Shaw, Joseph Planta and Francis Douce, eds. *A Catalogue of the Harleian Manuscripts in the British Museum.* 4 vols. Eyre and Strahan, 1808–12.

North, Dudley. *A Forest of Varieties.* Printed by Richard Cotes, 1645.

Ovid. *The. xv. Booke of P. Ouidius Naso, entytuled Metamorphosis, translated oute of Latin into English meeter.* Translated by Arthur Golding William Seres, 1567.

Petrarca. *Il Canzoniere.* Edited by Giancarlo Contini. Einaudi, 1964.

Petrarca, Francesco. *Tovtes Les Evvres Vulgaires De Francoys Petrarqve. Contenans Quatre Liures De M.d. Laure D'Auignon Sa Maistresse*. De L'imprimerie De Barthelemy Bonhomme. Auec Priuilege Du Roy, 1555.

Pétrarque and Philippe de Maldeghem. *Le Pétrarque en rime françoise avecq ses commentaires, traduict par Philippe de Maldeghem*. F. Fabry, 1606.

Pigman, G. W. 'Versions of Imitation in the Renaissance'. *Renaissance Quarterly*, vol. 33, no. 1, 1980: pp. 1–32.

Prescott, Anne Lake. 'Appendix: Ronsard in England 1635–1699'. *French Connections in the English Renaissance*. Edited by Catherine Gimelli Martin and Hassan Melehy. Ashgate Publishing, 2013, pp. 179–192.

Prescott, Anne Lake. *French Poets and the English Renaissance: Studies in Fame and Transformation*. Yale University Press, 1978.

Roche, Thomas. *Petrarch in Translation*. Penguin Classics, 2005.

Rouget, François. 'Philippe Desportes, médiateur du pétrarquisme français'. *Les Poètes français de la Renaissance et Pétrarque*. Travaux d'Humanisme et Renaissance 394. Textes et Travaux de la Fondation Barbier-Mueller pour l'étude de la poésie italienne de la Renaissance 1. Edited by Jean Balsamo. Librairie Droz, 2004, pp. 331–352.

Schurink, Fred, ed. *Tudor Translation*. Palgrave Macmillan, 2012.

Serjeantson, Deirdre. 'The Book of Psalms and the Early Modern Sonnet'. *Renaissance Studies*, vol. 29, no. 4, September 2015: pp. 632–649.

Shakespeare, William. *Complete Sonnets and Poems*. Edited by Colin Burrow. Oxford University Press, 2008.

Sidney, Philip. *Major Works*. Edited by Katherine Duncan-Jones. Oxford University Press, 1989.

Spenser, Edmund. *The Shorter Poems*. Edited by Richard McCabe. Penguin, 1999.

Tomasi, Franco. 'La Poésie italienne à la cour de François Ier: Alamanni, Martelli et autres cas exemplaires'. *La poésie à la cour de François Ier*. Cahiers V. L. Saulnier 29. Edited by Jean-Eudes Girot. PUPS, 2011. 68.

Watson, George. *The English Petrarchans: A Critical Bibliography of the Canzoniere*. Warburg Inst., 1967.

Whitworth, Charles. '"The Sweet Conceits of Philippe Du Portes": le poète français chez les élisabéthains. *Philippe Desportes, poète profane, poète sacré, Actes du colloque international de Chartres (14–16 septembre 2006)*. Edited by Bruno Petey-Girard and François Rouget. Champion, 2008, pp. 315–329.

Woolf, Daniel R. 'John Seldon, John Borough and Francis Bacon's *History of Henry VII*, 1621'. *Huntington Library Quarterly*, vol. 47, no. 1, 1984, pp. 47–53.

4

Paving the way for Opitz: The first German sonnets at the crossroads of European circulation networks, 1556–1604

Elisabeth Rothmund

With what is now commonly called a 'delayed Renaissance' (Valentin 1999, 827), the sonnet underwent a late development in the Germanic area during the so-called 'baroque' phase. The 1620s onwards saw Germany acquire a scholarly vernacular literature that helped it join the other nations of Western Europe. In literary history, this initial blooming of the German sonnet is mostly remembered for the works of the Silesian poet Martin Opitz (1597–1639), whose 1624 'Buch von der deutschen Poeterey' and 1625 *Poemata* offered the first rules and models written in German. Opitz thus paved the way for processes of mass production and appropriation, which critics often reduce to the reception of the French Pléiade model, either directly or via the Netherlands (to which Germany was both linguistically and religiously close).

But Opitz, who was indebted to Ronsard,[1] though a crucial figure in the development of the German sonnet, was not its inventor, nor was he the first poet to introduce it into the Germanic area. As early as the second half of the sixteenth century, the form was first transferred into German through texts which were few but very diverse, showing a profusion of possibilities thus far unknown, as well as a multiplicity of approaches, amongst which Opitz's influential translations of Ronsard were only one example. Consisting of what seem to be isolated and sporadic experiments that were often made spontaneously and largely independently from one another, this early phase in the discovery and acclimatization of the sonnet is all the more interesting as, unlike Opitz's approach, it was still detached from any real theory. To be more accurate, practice and theoretical thinking were consubstantial, and this practice, which often comprised translation, adaptation or imitation, resulted from the practitioners' perception of their own activity and of the cultural good they were transferring and acculturating.

Despite several pioneering works (Fechner/Forster 1972; Kimmich 1976; McNair 1982; Verweyen 1984; Aurnhammer 2000), the first German sonnets have remained undervalued. Paying great attention to versification, metre and prosody, scholars have mostly focused on the undoubtedly central issue of the German alexandrine rather than investigated the reception of the sonnet as a *form* – that is, a way of articulating poetic thought and discourse. The mainstream approach has remained very teleological, assessing early productions in comparison with the Opitzian model seen as an absolute norm, either to deplore apparent defects or, on the contrary, to rehabilitate other options that the Silesian poet's reforms nipped in the bud.[2] Incidentally, in overlooking the processes to focus on the results, experts neglect the experiences and expectations of the sonnet's practitioners and its readership. In addition, the first German sonnets have mostly been read as singular pieces, probably due to their isolated aspect and the fact that they were introduced as mere accidents or coincidences. Yet, as scattered as they may seem, these pieces show deep links to one another, and it is worth seeing them as a consistent whole which was itself part of a vast multilateral exchange and circulation network spreading throughout Europe. These apparently isolated phenomena were actually how Germany took part in a European circulation of the sonnet within a broader circulation of ideas, approaches, cultural goods and writing modalities – through correspondences between members of the European *respublica litteraria* and other sociable forms of writing such as *libri amicorum* combined with physical circulation, whether deliberately, as with travel for study or diplomatic missions, or under duress, as with temporary or definite migrations due to religious conflicts. At least partly linked to various forms of exile, the first German reception of the sonnet was an exclusively Protestant reality.

Each of these geographical movements accompanied a different form of circulation or migration of the sonnet, a form thus caught between various linguistic and cultural horizons, and various poetic systems or traditions, sometimes vernacular, sometimes in New Latin. The first sonnets written in German therefore show a wide array of interferences and hybridizations resulting from appropriation and acculturation processes as varied as literal translation (Wirsung, Van der Noot, Denaisius), adaptation, 'conversio' (Robert 226) of the sonnet into a locally established form or vice versa (Melissus), imitation through emulation (Fischart, Melissus) and others.

A comparative and contextualizing analysis of the first adaptations of the sonnet in the Germanic area will sketch the basis of an overall interpretation which, in taking into account the evolution from the initial discovery to the phrasing of a first normative definition, will be an opportunity to recontextualize the part played by Martin Opitz and better understand the ground on which he thrived. Indeed, a broad historical perspective reveals dynamics and continuities that cannot be unveiled by close readings, as essential as they may be. While the earliest translations also stemmed from Italian, Dutch and English sonnets, broadening the perspective to a European scale also highlights the dominance and multiple migrations of the French model.

*

It was thanks to the translation of a 1554 anti-papist treatise by the Italian Reformer Bernardino Ochino (1487-1564) that, in 1556, the sonnet first appeared in the Germanic area. This arrival was actually discreet and accidental: the translator, Christoph Wirsung (1500-1571), a doctor from Augsbourg, decided to keep Ochino's introductory sonnet,[3] even though the form was unknown to him. The first conscious and deliberate adaptations of the sonnet occurred twenty years later, first with the translation of two collections by the Antwerp poet Jan van der Noot (1536?-95/1601?) (van der Noot 1568a and b, 1572; 1576, 1579), who had taken refuge in Cologne, and then with a cycle of sonnets composed in imitation of the French which Johann Fischart (1546-91), then in Strasbourg, added to his translation of a Huguenot pamphlet (Fischart 1575 and 1593),[4] and with an original epithalamium composed in 1579 by the New Latin poet Paul Schede Melissus (1539-1602) and published as an appendix in Opitz's non-authorized *Pöemata* (Opitz 1624b, 171-172). Finally, in 1604, a first English sonnet was translated by Petrus Denaisius (1560-1610) in his German version of *Basilikon Doron*, a manual that James VI of Scotland (1566-1625) had written for his son.

It is not surprising that Ochino chose the sonnet as an introduction to his treatise, since it has been proven he was in contact with Cardinal Bembo (1470-1547) and the poet Vittoria Colonna (1490-1547) and was therefore undoubtedly familiar with this poetic form. However, it was probably unknown to Wirsung; although he kept the poem and did his best to respect most of its formal features (a problem the French translator dodged by replacing it with an epigram), he did not include the abbreviated form of the generic name ('SON'.), as if he had not identified it. Regarding the two major difficulties encountered in the process of transferring the sonnet into the German poetic system (creating a long line that would be an equivalent of the Italian *endecasillabo*, the common line or the French alexandrine, and following the rhyming scheme, which expresses the inner dynamics of the poem), it can be noted that Wirsung did not adapt the line in any way and chose to keep the one that was then commonly used in German poetry: the *Knittelvers*, simply defined by the amount of stressed syllables (four), but not by any metre or fixed number of syllables. However, under the probable influence of the isosyllabism commonly found in Lutheran hymns, Wirsung's *Knittelverse* are quite regular and are often close to octosyllables with an iambic tendency. The Italian rhyme scheme (ABBA ABBA CDE CDE) was preserved. Some interesting features (a daring enjambment and subtlety in the interweaving of alliterations and assonances) show a certain degree of experimentation:

O zeit fur andere torecht toll /	O secol piu ch'ogni altro sciocco e stolto,
O welt on witz / blind / viehisch / vnd	O bestiale, ignorante, e cieco mondo,
Die gantz vnd gar in finstern schlund	Poi che pur ti sei tutto in si profondo
Versenckt / verstrickt / vnd mangels voll.	E tenebroso abißo immerso e inuolto.
(Ochino 1556)	(Ochino 1554)

Wirsung identified most of the formal specificities of the sonnet and endeavoured to render them as scrupulously as possible, even though they did not correspond to anything known to him. His joining of the German tercets in a sestet proves he perfectly understood the bipartite structure: after two quatrains calling out to the world and the age, both corrupted, the tercets focus on the individual, the analogy being introduced by the comparative 'so'. If Wirsung's choice reinforces the semantic and syntactic unity of the sestet, it can also be explained by the linking function of the rhyme: it is only in their reunion that the tercets can find a poetic unity.

This first foray of the sonnet into Germanic lands nevertheless remains a curiosity: mostly functional, published in a work whose readers were unlikely to have any taste for poetic innovation, it was not immediately influential.

Translations of works by Jan van der Noot reveal the major part he played in the reception and broadcasting of the French sonnet, as well as the European dimension of the circulation network from which emerged the first sonnets deliberately translated into German.[5] A poet and a polyglot, an imitator of Ronsard exiled in London (1567–70?) and later near Cologne (1570?–78?), Van der Noot was a key actor in the first Dutch reception of the Pléiade poets.[6] Initially published in London in two original versions – one in Dutch and one in French – and then translated into English, his first collection to be translated into German was, like Ochino's, an anti-Catholic and anti-papist work that mostly consisted of theological commentaries on the Book of Revelation, but also included, in addition to four original sonnets, six translations of epigrams by Clément Marot translating Petrarch and, most importantly, an almost complete reproduction of Du Bellay's *Songe*, a sonnet sequence published after *Les Antiquitez de Rome* (Du Bellay 1558). The two original versions are equally good, the sonnet having conquered the Netherlands more quickly than Germany due to the bilingualism of the Netherlands' southern provinces (the first to be reached) and its compatibility with the *Referein* practised by the *Rederijkers* (the members of the Chambers of Rhetoric), an indigenous form close to the French Rhétoriqueurs' 'chant royal'. The evolution of the works of Lucas d'Heere (1534-84), who also remodelled the *Rederijkers'* long line to craft a Dutch alexandrine, constitutes a striking example (Vermeer; Eringa).[7]

It is very instructive to compare the German version with its almost contemporaneous English counterpart. The English translations of Du Bellay were entrusted to the young Edmund Spenser (1552-99), then a student at Merchant Taylors'. The school's headmaster was Richard Mulcaster (1530-1611), a man who was close to the London Dutch community (especially Charles Utenhove, 1536-1600, who had personally known Du Bellay in Paris), and attached great importance to the study of the literatures that were budding all around Europe. Spenser, who was translating from the French, curiously went for blank verse, thus turning Du Bellay's sonnets into unrhymed but scrupulously translated poems. However, his translation of Marot's epigrams into perfectly drafted English sonnets (ABAB CDCD EFEF GG) shows that he mastered the form. In fact, these texts were even included in his 1591 *Complaints*, in which he completely rewrote Du Bellay's sonnets (especially the tercets) to make them fit the Elizabethan mould.[8]

Unlike Spenser, who knew who Du Bellay was and what a sonnet was, the German translator and 'imperial lawyer' Balthasar Froe translated from Van der Noot's Dutch, relying on the closeness between what still seemed to be two dialectal variations of one Germanic idiom: Low and High German.[9]

Given the circumstances, this is a decent translation. Very literal and linear, it can be superimposed onto the original: cautiously following the original sonnets to the letter, Froe probably hoped to respect their spirit. His approach recalls Wirsung's, except that in choosing the *Knittelvers*, Wirsung shifted the sonnet towards a poetic system of which at least one element was familiar to him; freed from the metrical issue, he enjoyed a greater autonomy in adapting its other formal features. Although seemingly favourable, the similarity between Dutch and German turns out to be misleading, for it veils vast difficulties and narrows the translator's leeway. Froe bravely looked for

T'was inden tijd als Gods ghift' t'onsen loone	ZV zeitten wann Gott kompt zu vnserm lohne /
Ten soetsten compt in ons ooghen ghestreken,	Jn vnsere augen sussiglich geschlichen /
Doendé in ons soo een soet vergheten leken,	Vnd tut in vns ein suß vergessen streichen /
(Deur saechte[n] slaep) des daechs arbeyt gewoone:	Durch sanfften Schlaff des tags arbeit gewohne:
Als eenen gheest hem my vertoonde schoone	Als dann ein Geist er mir ercläret schone.
Ontrent den vloet die d'ou Roome[n] comt breken,	Zur zeit des Fals das alt Rom solt zerbechen /
Noemende my by mijnen naem, quam spreken	Bey meinem Namm mich nent / thet zu mir sprechen /
Segghende my, siet nae des hemels throone:	Seh her / vnd stell dein Gesicht zum Himmels throne:
Siet riep hy my, siet en wilt wel bemecken	Schaw ahn sprach er vnd thu es wol an mercken /
Al datter is onder des hemels ronde,	Alles was da ist vnder des Himmels runde /
Siet hoet al niet en sijn dan ydel wercken.	Jst anders nicht dann alles eittel Wercken.
En als ghyt merct, en verstaet deur d'anschouwen:	Wann du es verstehest vnd merckest durchs anschawen.
Ghemerct dat God alleené is ons ghesonde,	Befindst das Gott allein ist der gesunde /
En stelt niet el dan op hem v betrouwen.[10]	Darumb nur alleine auff jhn stell dein vertrawen.
(van der Noot 1568a)	(van der Noot 1572)

German equivalents of the Dutch common lines and alexandrines, mostly relying on the principle of exact reproduction, but he faced two difficulties: the rhyme, which could not always be preserved with the High German equivalents of the rhyming words, and, above all, the complex crafting of longer lines requiring a caesura and a rhythm of their own. While Spenser had captured the spirit of Du Bellay's sonnets without feeling (at least initially) bound to an outward form, the French version of which differed from the English model, and had adapted them to national specificities, Froe's extreme attention to this outward form made him less sensitive to the dynamics of the entire poem, which is particularly essential (and perhaps confusing) given that Du Bellay plays with the canonical structure of the sonnet. As their strict form was desired more by Van der Noot than by the translator, Froe's German sonnets were thus constructed on shaky ground. If they did constitute a major step in the German appropriation of the sonnet, they suffered from the unbridgeable gap that lay between Van der Noot's ambition and the limited means the translator had at his disposal, considering what German vernacular poetry then was. Later anonymously translated from the French by someone else, the sonnets from Van der Noot's *Extasis* are far better. The pieces – some of them perhaps originals, at least for which no hypotexts have been found – are so convincing that they remind one of Spenser's art in freely translating Marot's epigrams.

While Van der Noot willingly saw himself as the Brabantian (or even German) Ronsard, Fischart – an indefatigable conveyor of French texts he translated for his brother-in-law, the Strasbourg publisher Bernhard Jobin (before 1545–93) – had political and polemical ambitions rather than aesthetic or poetic ones. He discovered the sonnet in the Huguenot pamphleteering literature, and it was in an appendix to his translation of one such work, written in the midst of the polemics on the Saint Bartholomew's Day massacre, that he published his only foray into this poetic form: a cycle of seven 'original' sonnets, which were not translations but imitations from the French.[11] It has been suggested that these are satirical because of their licentious form, but the hypothesis cannot hold: if Fischart did have a satirical intention, his French models did not show any consciously playful deviation from poetic norms, and this approach would imply a knowledge of the orthodox form shared by him and his readership, which nothing confirms. As an 'urban' polemicist, he was not a practitioner of the erudite poetry written by contemporaries such as Melissus and Denaisius, who were also regular visitors to the Heidelberg Court and the Palatine Library, but his cultural background and experience as a poet were better than Wirsung's and Froe's: he could appreciate the dialogic and dialectic potential of the sonnet, relying as he systematically did on inductive reasoning based on a causal relationship (Aurnhammer). However, this passive but solid knowledge of the sonnet did not inform the details of the outward form: Fischart obviously had difficulty with the rhyme scheme of the octave, and, semantically as well as syntactically speaking, his sonnets only partially adopted the complex organization of the form's rhymes and its many components. When reading the complete cycle, one will notice the underlying persistence of the linear and juxtaposing practice that dominated pre-Renaissance German vernacular poetry (Forster 1983): probably influenced by the *Knittelvers* (which he preserved, like Wirsung), Fischart thought mostly in terms of rhyming couplets, these often forming syntactical units which, in the end, dismantle the subtle architecture of the sonnet:

> Solchs that er / weil er sich befahrt
> Sein Volck möcht jhn vmb tyranney
> Bekriegen / sich zumachen frey:

- -

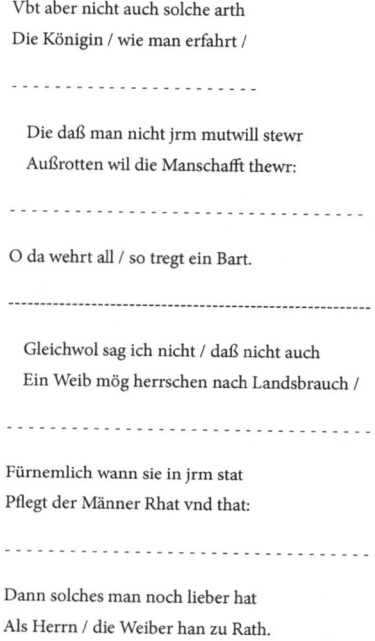

(Fischart 1593, Sonnet 6)

Fischart's sonnets, which still had an intermediary status, therefore resemble discreet palimpsests in which the ancient indigenous German tradition persists underneath the modernity of the Romance-inspired sonnet.

In 1579, an epithalamium composed by Paul Schede Melissus for Georges d'Averly and Adelheit von Grauwart shows, for the first time in German, a near-perfect mastery of the sonnet form (Fechner and Forster 1972). This is all the more impressive considering that this piece is this poet's only German sonnet to have survived: Melissus, a New Latin poet, did not publish anything in his mother tongue, apart from a partial translation of the Huguenot Psalter. It is, however, unlikely to have resulted from a sudden master stroke, since it is the first known sonnet to show the outcome of a painstaking process of appropriation. Like Van der Noot and so many other poets from this generation, Melissus was a polyglot engaged in an erudite social network whose members practised translation, rewriting, paraphrase, imitation and transpositions of all kinds in a multilingual form of poetic verbal jousting that was as much playful as it was serious, traces of which can be found in his collections (Melissus 1574, 1575).[12]

This appropriation process was specific insofar as it implied a third language: Latin, the utmost poetic idiom in Melissus's eyes, a kind of poetic 'mother tongue' that constituted both a translatory tool and a legitimation. The first step consisted in translating Italian and French sonnets into Latin epigrams:[13] a transfer from one canonical form to another, without any porosity or hybridization, entirely based on the spiritual kinship between two established forms whose respective poetic systems had similar functions. The Latin epigram remained intact. The second phase consisted in a 'sonnetisation' of the Latin epigram, now modelled on the formal features of the sonnet, as testified by the typographic disposition, which well reflects the structure of the sonnet.

The broadening of the New Latin practice through contact with the modern vernacular (Robert 221) remained within the limits of the singular translation: original epigrams that Melissus might have based on this model have been sought, to no avail. Therefore, the sonnetization of the epigram was not an end in itself: legitimizing the sonnet by proving its compatibility with an approved form (Robert 220), it authorized the move towards imitation in the language of discovery (French) and then, in a further emancipation, the transfer to German in the form of an original production that was more freely imitative, borne from emulation. In this regard, epistolary exchanges as well as physical circulation played a decisive part: Melissus sojourned in Paris, Geneva, London and Rome. In Heidelberg, he was benevolently helped by French-speaking counterparts from Lorraine or the Ardennes who were there as religious refugees or diplomats on a mission, such as the Averly brothers, who were in the Prince of Condé's service and accompanied Charlotte de Bourbon-Montpensier (1546–82) when she found refuge in the Palatinate after converting to Protestantism (1571/72). They imported to Germany their indigenous poetic practices, which spread all the more easily given that French was a popular communication language amongst the Reformed. Moreover, the friendly exchange that went on between Melissus and the Averly brothers, or the Lorraine poet Nicolas Clément de Trèles (1545–88?), often took on a pedagogic dimension. Receiving a sonnet from a French friend was like receiving versified instructions which Melissus brilliantly followed, the student often surpassing the master – as was the case in an exchange on the work of one of the painters of the royal court (Melissus 1575, 361–362). However, this emulation was not servile, since the two texts differed in their rhyme scheme (CDC DEE/CDD CEE).

Unfortunately, the absence of sources makes it hard to reconstitute with precision the genesis and motives of the transfer of Melissus's epithalamium into German, which was all the more improbable as nothing justified this linguistic choice: it was not the bride and groom's mother tongue, nor was it the language in which the poet wrote. The Averly brothers were no longer in Germany at that time, and nor was Melissus. It is probable that Melissus had been challenged by Nicolas Clément and merged in one text the form he had discovered with a learning process to which the Averly brothers had largely contributed, along with his German origins and the context of the place where they had met.[14]

> Was im Weltkreise rund allenthalb lebt vnd schwebet /
> Warhafft erhalten wirdt durch gleich eintrechtigkeit /
> Dann Gott vorkommen hat alle Zwyspaltigkeit
> Daß inn all seim Geschöpff keins widers ander strebet.

In this first example of a successful adaptation, everything contributes to turn the sonnet and the French Alexandrine (which now had a rhythm and a caesura, even though it was not yet metrically perfect) into the logical outcome of a totally consistent appropriation process, and a real poetic 'memorial' to friendship.

Relying on the French form to translate an English sonnet somewhere between the Spenserian and the Ronsardian models into German, Petrus Denaisius translated the opening sonnet that James VI of Scotland had written for the *Basilikon Doron* and dedicated to his son, in a way that testifies to the multiple migrations of the French sonnet and its spread all around Europe. The *Basilikon Doron*, a manual summing up James's vision of monarchy and the sovereign's duties, was initially destined for private use, but it was widely circulated around continental Europe when, in 1603, the King of Scotland succeeded Elizabeth I as King of England. Read as a political programme, the text was soon translated into Latin, French, Dutch, German and even Hungarian. Dedicated to the Elector Palatine, Frederick IV, this translation by Denaisius, a jurist and assessor at the Speyer Imperial Chamber Court, clearly partook of the Palatinate's anti-Catholic and anti-Habsburg diplomatic policy, which consisted in building up international alliances and led to the 1613 marriage between Frederick's son and the daughter of the King of England. This public aspect was enough to justify a (nearly) word-for-word translation of the opening piece.[15] The structure of the English sonnet was perfect to introduce a treatise in three parts: each part got a quatrain, while the final couplet phrased its ultimate recommendation. But James VI of Scotland and I of England relied on a very personal variation on the Spenserian sonnet. Used only twice in his works, it sounds like a propping up of royal speech, the only other example being an epitaph in memory of the poet Alexander Montgomerie (1550–98): as he had converted to Catholicism, his burial (which took place in a clandestine hush) at the Canongate Kirk of Edinburgh had been authorized by the intervention of the king, whose eulogy-like sonnet replaced the forbidden ceremony, as if royal poetic speech were making up for the silencing of the bells.[16] This singular form, in which the quatrains share the same external rhyme – ABBA ACCA ADDA EE – looks like a Frenchification of the Spenserian sonnet (see also Verweyen 1984).[17] Choosing the French model without hesitation (thus testifying to its dominance in Germany), Denaisius made good use of a rhyming scheme that was unusual in the tercets of the French sonnet (CDD CEE), probably very consciously chosen to stay close to the specificity of the hypotext, as it may have been intended to seal together the three parts of the treatise. Although it was translated from English, Denaisius's German sonnet thus stands out as the meeting point between two French influences, and the outcome of a nearly circular form of circulation.

*

The first sonnets to have been written in German are strikingly fortuitous. They often arose accidentally, at the periphery of projects whose main goals were not aesthetic: their stakes were theological controversy, confessional polemic or diplomacy and the search for international political alliances.

Beyond this aleatory and incidental aspect (the texts in which the sonnets feature could have never reached Germany; the sonnet form could have been discarded), interesting constants can be noticed. First of all, the sonnets (and the works that contain them) circulated in various traditional ways, such as correspondences between the citizens of the *respublica litteraria* or major axes for the trading of goods, with a significant part played by the peripheries of the empire, especially in the West and the Rhine area. Another key element was the physical circulation of people, who travelled with written works and writing practices (Van der Noot represented a European hub, as did Melissus, who discovered the French sonnet in Geneva and then Paris before enjoying the company of the French Huguenots in Germany). While the means of circulation were varied, the circles involved were homogeneous, gathering scholarly or at least lettered people who had reformed or sympathized with the Calvinist cause.

With the circulation of ideas, people, texts, mindsets and poetic forms of expression, the sonnet also moved between languages and the poetic systems practised by those involved in these communication and action networks, which often overlapped. In addition to literal translations which were sometimes blind attempts (what Wirsung and Froe wanted was to reproduce the outward shape of the sonnet), and less constrained translations that were closer to adaptation (Wirsung, Fischart and Melissus kept a familiar German or Latin versification, thus offering their own reading of a hitherto unseen form), there were also contrary moves *towards* the poetic object that was to be appropriated, by polyglots (Van der Noot, Melissus) who did not hesitate to practise it in French in order to get more familiar with it before transferring it to their mother tongue. As the sonnet's constraints were tight, this operation turned out to be particularly difficult: it was a real challenge for the translator to keep all the formal features of an unknown form (and understand its raison d'être in the first place!) then transfer them by adapting them to the linguistic, prosodic and (sometimes still blurry) metrical demands of the target language. When at least one familiar element could be preserved (versification, most of the time), the result was far more convincing.

Despite the contingency of these early manifestations and the multiplicity of the networks at stake, there is another striking factor: the persistence of the French model which was spreading throughout Western and Northern Europe and converged somewhat naturally in the German-speaking territories of the Holy Empire. Belatedly adopting the sonnet, Germany welcomed various influences and benefitted from the previous circulations of the French sonnet. This was not disconnected from the confessional issue, and the dominance of the French model owes as much to the power of the reformed networks as to the part France and its language played in Germany, and the argumentative, rhetorical potential of the sonnet of which the Huguenots had made much use. The last step in this introduction of the sonnet through translation (understood broadly) consisted in overcoming the contingency of singular cases in order to create a native tradition by phrasing a normative definition based on several model translations, thus allowing the emergence of a larger-scale production of originals. Opitz's 'Poeterey', a text largely inspired by Ronsard's *Abbregé de l'art poétique françois*, which the Silesian poet discovered in an unpublished 'opuscule' by the Prussian writer Ernst Schwabe von der Heyde (1598–1626) – who exemplified the first reception of the Italian and French vernacular Renaissance, mixing practice and theory – is an explicit return to the authority of the Pléiade poets. If Schwabe's and Opitz's exploration of the form was similar to their predecessors' (the first sonnets they brought out in 1618 were respectively translated from Petrarca and the Dutch *Bloemhof*),[18] they both opted without hesitation for the French sonnet form.

The fact that five out of the six sonnets in Opitz's 1624 'Poeterey' were translated from Ronsard and, above all, the fact that the first foreign text to be quoted is a sonnet by Ronsard (the only one for which Opitz included the original hypotext next to its German translation, which he clearly presents as partly autonomous)[19] show both his reliance on a tutelary authority he nearly pretended to equal, and the legitimizing value of a successful translation of the sonnet.

Translated from the French by Fanny Quément
with the editors of the volume

Notes

1. Out of the six sonnets quoted in Opitz's 'Poeterey', five were translations from Ronsard.
2. Especially as he introduced metrics respecting German prosody, based on a strict alternation between stressed and unstressed syllables.
3. 'Al Christanesmo Bastardo', 'Zu dem Bastardischen Christenthumb'. See also McNair.
4. Entitled 'An Ehr und Billigkeit liebende Leser. Etlich Sonnet', the German cycle was published under the pseudonym Uldrich Wysart.
5. Concerning Van der Noot, see: Forster (1977); Vermeylen; Westerweel (especially Bostoen pp. 49–61 and Waterschoot pp. 35–47); and Melehy.
6. Concerning the Dutch networks in England and the impact of London exile on the artistic and intellectual life of the Dutch-speaking community, see for instance, Forster (1967).
7. The *Rederijkervers* is longer than the Alexandrine, and its length varies according to province. Contrary to d'Heere, a member of a Chamber of Rhetoric in Ghent, Van der Noot did not cultivate any relations with the *Rederijkers*.
8. The 1568 literal translations, which had a rhythm but no rhyme, gave an imperfect idea of the elaborate architecture of the French sonnet, in which the 'catastrophe' lies in the turn between the two tercets rather than in the one between the octave and the sestet. In the 1591 version, Spenser reordered the elements of the tercets so that the catastrophe would fit into the final distich.
9. See the title page: 'in Oberlendisch teutsch', an obvious opposition to 'niederländisch deutsch' ('nederduytsch').
10. Du Bellay, *Le Songe*, Sonnet 1.
11. Probably based on the anonymous series *Sonnets (sur ce subject). Contre lesdits Italiens et Katherine de Medicis, Roine-Mère*. Published by Pierre de l'Estoile, it was already circulating in the summer of 1575, likely as a loose sheet. See Aurnhammer and Rothmund (2017).
12. Referring to improvised poems, the term 'schediasmata' in the title of these collections puns on the author's name (Paul *Schede* Melissus).
13. Petrarch, Sonetto CIIII (Petrarch p. 211); Ronsard, Sonnet XII (Ronsard 1555, pp. 9–10). Both translations are in Melissus (1575, pp. 102–103).
14. 'C'est trop vraiment, c'est trop, apris & entrepris; / Que feront cy-apres les hommes indigènes / Puis qu'un seul estranger égale leurs escris ? / Translate & n'escris plus en ces langues lointaines, / Ou ne te vante plus Melisse Franconois, / Mais polyglosse Grec, Latin, Teuton, François' (Melissus 1575, p. 214).
15. From a more bourgeois (and anti-monarchic) perspective, the English merchant Emanuel Thomson, the rival author of another translation, did not keep the sonnet form.

16 'Though to his buriall was refused the bell | The bell of fame, shall aye his praises knell' (final distich, Westcott pp. 31–32).
17 An amateur student of French poetry, James VI had, for instance, received Guillaume de Salluste du Bartas at the court of Edinburgh. Made Queen of France by her marriage with François II, his mother Mary Stuart had been a disciple of Ronsard.
18 *Bloem-Hof* (p. 53): 'Wat wil ic over bosch, wat wil ic over sant'; Opitz 1618, p. 9: 'Was wil ich über Pusch / was will ich über Sandt'.
19 'Ah belle liberté, qui me seruoit d'escorte' (*Sonnets pour Hélène*, 1578, livre II, Sonnet 67), chapter 3 (*Von etlichen sachen die den Poeten vorgeworffen werden; vnd derselben entschuldigung*).

Works cited

Primary sources

Basilikon Doron. Or His Majesties Instructions to His Dearest Sonne, Henry the Prince. Robert Walde-graue, 1603.
Basilikon Doron Oder Instruction vnd Underrichtung Iacobi deß Ersten dieses namens in Engelandt/Schottlandt/Franckreich/vnd Irrlandt Königs/an Seiner Kön. Mayt. Geliebten Sohn Printz Henrichen. Auß dem Englischen verteutscht. Melchior Harmann, 1604.
Den Bloem-Hof van de Nederlantsche Ieught [...]. Dirk Pieterß., 1608.
D'Heere, Lucas. *Den Hof en Boomgaerd der Poësie* [...]. 1565. Reprint by Werner Waterschoot: *Lucas de Heere, Den hof en boomgaerd der poësien*. 1969.
Discours merveilleux de la vie, actions & déportemens de Catherine de Médicis Royne mère. [...]. [s. l.] 1575. Critical edition by Nicole Cazauran: *Discours merveilleux de la vie, actions et déportemens de Catherine de Médicis, Royne-mère* [1575, ²1576]. 1995.
Du Bellay, Joachim. *Le Premier Livre des Antiquitez de Rome contenant une generale description de sa grandeur, et comme une déploration de sa ruine* [...]. *Plus un Songe ou vision sur le mesme subiect, du mesme autheur*. Paris: Fédéric Morel, 1558. (Du Bellay 1558).
Fischart, Johann. *Offenlichs vnd inn warhait wolgegründts Ausschreiben/der vbelbefridigten Ständ inn Frankreich* [...] *Inhaltend Die Wunderlich Beschreibung des lebens/verhaltens/thun vn[d] wesens der Catherine von Medicis* [...] *Aus dem Französischen inn Teutsch gepracht/Durch Emericum Lebusius*. 1575.
Fischart, Johann. *Wacht früe auff/Das ist. Summarischer/vnnd Warhaffter Bericht von den verschienenen/auch gegenwärtigen beschwerlichen Händeln in Franckreich* [...]. *Durch Eusebium Philadelphum Cosmopolitam. Mit angehenckter wunderlicher beschreibung deß Lebens/Verhaltens/Thun vnnd Wesens der Catharinen vonn Medicis/der Königinn Franckreich Mutter. Alles aus dem Frantzösischen ins Teutsche gebracht Durch Emericum Lebusinum*. [B. Jobin], 1593.

Melissus, Paul. *Melissi Schediasmata poetica*. Georg Corvinus, 1574.
Melissus, Paul. *Melissi Schediasmatvm Reliqviae*. Georg Rab, 1575.
Noot, Jan van der. *Cort begryp der XII. boeken Olympiados, Beschreven devr I. Ian Vander Noot, Patritius van Antwerpen. Abrégé des douze livres Olympiades, Composez par le S. Iehan Vander Noot, Patrice d'Anvers*. Gillis van den Rade, 1579. Critical edition by Zaalberg, C.A.: *The Olympia Epics of Jan Van der Noot* [...]. Van Gorcum, 1956.
Noot, Jan van der. *Das Buch Extasis* [...]. Felix Röschlin, ca. 1576.
Noot, Jan van der. *Het theatre oft toon-neel* [...]. John Day, 1568a.
Noot, Jan van der. *Le Theatre Avquel sont exposés & montrés les inconueniens & miseres qui suiuent les mondains & vicieux, ensemble les plaisirs & contentements dont les fideles ioüissent* [...]. John Day, 1568b.
Noot, Jan van der. *Theatrvm das ist Schawplatz darein die eitelheit der jrrdischen vnnd vergencklichen dingen vnd die vbertreffenlichste Gottliche vnd Himmlische sach getzeigt* [...] *wird* [...] *jetz aber in Oberlendisch teutsch vbergesatzt durch Balthasarn Froe Rechenmeistern zu Cöln*. Cervicornus, 1572.
Ochino, Bernardino. *Apologi nelli quali siscvoprano li abvsi, sciocheze, svpersitioni, errori, idolàtrie & impieta della sinagoga del Papa* [...], 1554.
Ochino, Bernardino. *Des Hochgelehrten vnd Gottseligen Bernhardini Ochini Apologi.* [...] *Durch Christoff Wirsung verdeütscht*, 1556.
Opitz, Martin. *Acht Bücher, Deutscher Poematum durch Ihn selber heraus gegeben, auch also vermehret unnd ubersehen, das die vorigen darmitte nicht zu vergleichen sindt*. David Müller, 1625.
Opitz, Martin. *Aristarchus sive De Contemptu Linguæ Teutonicæ*. Johann Dörffer, 1617.
Opitz, Martin. *Hipponax ad Asterien* [...]. Johann Rhambau, 1618.
Opitz, Martin. *Martini Opitii Buch von der Deutschen Poeterey* [...]. D. Müller; Gründer, 1624a.
Opitz, Martin. *Martini Opicii. Teutsche Pöemata* [...]. Zetzner, 1624b.
Petrarca, Francesco. *Il Petrarca. Con nvove, e brevi dichiarationi* [...]. G. Rouillé, 1551.
Ronsard, Pierre de. *Continvation des Amovrs de P. de Ronsard Vandomois*. V. Certenas [Sertenas], 1555.
Ronsard, Pierre de. *Les œuvres de P. de Ronsard Gentil-homme Vandomois* (Tome 1). G. Buon, 1578.
Spenser, Edmund. *Complaints*. W. Ponsonbie, 1591.

Secondary sources

Aurnhammer, Achim. 'Johann Fischarts Spottsonette'. *Simpliciana. Schriften der Grimmelshausen-Gesellschaft*, vol. 22, 2000: pp. 145–165.
Bostoen, Karel. 'Van der Noot's Apocalyptic Visions: Do You "See" What You Read?' *Anglo-Dutch Relations in the Field of the Emblem*. Edited by Bart Westerweel. Brill, 1997, pp. 49–61.

Eringa, Sjoerd. *La Renaissance et les Rhétoriqueurs néerlandais*. Matthieu de Casteleyn. Anna Bijns. Luc de Heere. Société d'imprimerie 'Holland', 1920.

Fechner, Jörg-Ulrich and Leonard W. Forster. 'Das deutsche Sonett des Melissus'. *Rezeption und Produktion zwischen 1670 und 1730. Festschrift für Günther Weydt*. Edited by Rasch, Wolfdietrich et al. A. Francke, 1972, pp. 33–51.

Forster, Leonard W. *Janus Gruter's English Years: Studies in the Continuity of Dutch Literature in Exile in Elizabethan England*. Leiden University Press/ London University Press, 1967.

Forster, Leonard W. 'Jan van der Noot und die Deutsche Renaissancelyrik. Stand und Aufgabe der Forschung'. *Kleine Schriften zur deutschen Literatur im 17.Jahrhundert*. Rodopi, 1977, pp. 101–118.

Forster, Leonard W. 'Über Reihen und Gliedern – Vornehmlich in mittlerer deutscher Literatur'. *Virtus et Fortuna: zur deutschen Literatur zwischen 1400 und 1720. Festschrift für Hans-Gert Roloff*. Edited by Joseph P. Strelka and Jörg Jungmayr. P. Lang, 1983, pp. 15–36.

Kimmich, Flora. 'Sonnets before Opitz: The Evolution of a Form'. *German Quarterly*, vol. 49, 1976: pp. 15–37.

McNair, Philipp. 'Zu dem *Bastardischen Christenthumb*. The Italian Background to the First Known Sonnet in Germany'. *From Wolfram and Petrarch to Goethe and Grass: Studies in Literature in Honour of Leonard Forster*. Edited by D. H. Green et al. Koerner, 1982, pp. 257–263.

Melehy, Hassan. *The Poetics of Literary Transfer in Early Modern France and England*. Ashgate, 2010.

Robert, Jörg. 'Deutsch-französische Dornen – Paul Melissus und die Rezeption der Pléiade in Deutschland'. *Abgrenzung und Synthese. Lateinische Dichtung und volkssprachliche Tradition in Renaissance und Barock*. Edited by Marc Föcking and Gernot Michael Müller. Winter, 2007, pp. 207–229.

Rothmund, Elisabeth. *Translatio – Imitatio – Eigenschöpfung? Frühe deutsche Rezeption des Sonetts im europäischen Kontext (1556–1604): Vorbilder, Interferenzen und Aneignungsprozesse*. Université Paris-Sorbonne, 2017.

Valentin, Jean-Marie. 'De Leibniz à Vico. Contestation et restauration de la rhétorique (1690–1730)'. *Histoire de la rhétorique dans l'Europe moderne. 1450–1950*. Edited by Marc Fumaroli. Presses Universitaires de France, 1999, pp. 823–878.

Vermeer, Wim. 'De sonnetten van Lucas d'Heere'. *Spiegel der Letteren*. Jaargang 21, 1979, pp. 81–100.

Vermeylen, August. *Leven en werken van Jonker Jan van der Noot*. De Nederlandsche boekhandel, 1899.

Verweyen, Theodor. 'Über die poetische Praxis vor Opitz – Am Beispiel eines Sonetts aus dem Englischen von Petrus Denaisius'. *Daphnis*, vol. 13, no. 1–2, 1984: pp. 137–165.

Waterschoot, Werner. 'An Author's Strategy: Jan van der Noot's *Het Theatre*'. *Anglo-Dutch Relations in the Field of the Emblem*. Edited by Bart Westerweel. Brill, 1997, pp. 35–47.

Westcott, Allan F., ed. *New Poems by James I of England*. Columbia University Press, 1911.

Westerweel, Bart, ed. *Anglo-Dutch Relations in the Field of the Emblem*. Brill, 1997.

Part Two

Sonnet translation as a space for poetic imagination

5

Keats's sonnets and the translation process: Mediation, conversion and response

Oriane Monthéard

John Keats, who wrote over sixty sonnets between 1814 and 1819, contributed to the Romantic-era sonnet revival first by experimenting on the sonnet as a form, and then by exploring its limits and attempting to solve the defects he perceived in its rhyme scheme. When Keats's poems are classified according to their patterns, it can easily be noticed that the young poet, who inherited both the Petrarchan and the Shakespearean traditions, favoured the first form at the beginning of his career, and then progressively turned to the second, sometimes altering both patterns with the aim of adjusting his poetic language to the various sonnet codes. Keats's most extreme experiment in this field may be found in 'O thou whose face hath felt the winter's wind', a hybrid form in blank verse, approaching the English pattern but inspired by epistolary prose – the poem being written as part of a letter and developing the epistolary discourse on indolence. Another sonnet, 'If by dull rhymes our English must be chain'd', written in May 1819 – that is, a few days before 'Ode to a Nightingale' – marked a turning point in this exploration, which eventually resulted in the creation of Keats's unique ode stanza. The poem, in which the poet claimed that the suitable sonnet stanza and the appropriate poetic language remained to be invented, was included in a letter to George and Georgiana Keats and was introduced by the following comment on sonnet patterns: the 'legitimate [the Italian] does not suit the language over-well from the pouncing rhymes – the other kind [the English] appears too elegaic [sic] – and the couplet at the end of it has seldom a pleasing effect – I do not pretend to have succeeded – it will explain itself' (Rollins vol. II, 108). Keats's ongoing formal quest thus points to the poet's wish to free his poetic language from the sonnet conventions and to untie the sonnet from its history, while at the same time acknowledging the necessity of submitting to this form, of consenting to its restrictions, as the speaker of 'If by dull rhymes' states: 'Let us find out, if we must be constrain'd, / Sandals more interwoven and complete / To fit the naked foot of Poesy' (lines 4–6). And though Keats's career was guided by the wish to experiment with different genres, he never turned away from the sonnet form.

Along with this formal search, which recognized both the sonnet's legacy and its potential, Keats's personal mode of sonnet writing was founded on his talent for using inspiration from his forerunners and his contemporaries, as well as his constant focus on the writing process, which he saw as deeply anchored in the past and at the same time forged by his own poetic project. In many poems, Keats firmly connects the writing of poetry not only to reading in general, but also to reading translated canonical texts. Thus, for Keats, writing partly entailed converting whatever was grasped through reading into poetic language.

Translated texts certainly played a major role in Keats's poetic apprenticeship and the making of his poetic identity, as is testified by his letters and poems, including his sonnets. For the young poet, who constantly framed and reframed his relationship to other writers, reading translated texts, responding to them and reflecting on translation was an indirect but essential means of strengthening that relationship. Keats's reliance on translated texts goes further than an intellectual stimulation; it acts as a powerful undercurrent, bridging reading and writing, receiving and producing. This chapter will thus try to examine how reading translated texts and translating, as a process, affected Keats's sonnet writing. Relying on several of Keats's sonnets, we will first explore his relation to translated texts and its effect on his poetics, and then analyse the poet's attempt to write a sonnet out of (mis)translation. Finally, we will discuss the question of how this concept of free translation may be linked to Keats's more general tendency to address other poets through poetic response.

Keats's relation to the translated text, or blindness overcome

Keats's letters and several of his sonnets bring to light the extent to which, to the young poet, translating and mediated reading were ascribed a social dimension. This social dimension played a significant part in writing, as 'On first looking into Chapman's Homer' illustrates:[1] written in 1816, this sonnet originates in second-hand contact with a canonical text and is presented as the result of a collective experience linking poets, translators and readers. The circumstances attached to the writing of the poem, related by Keats's friend and mentor Charles Cowden Clarke and inscribed in the sonnet, point to the value of mediation and shared reading. The facts are well known: one

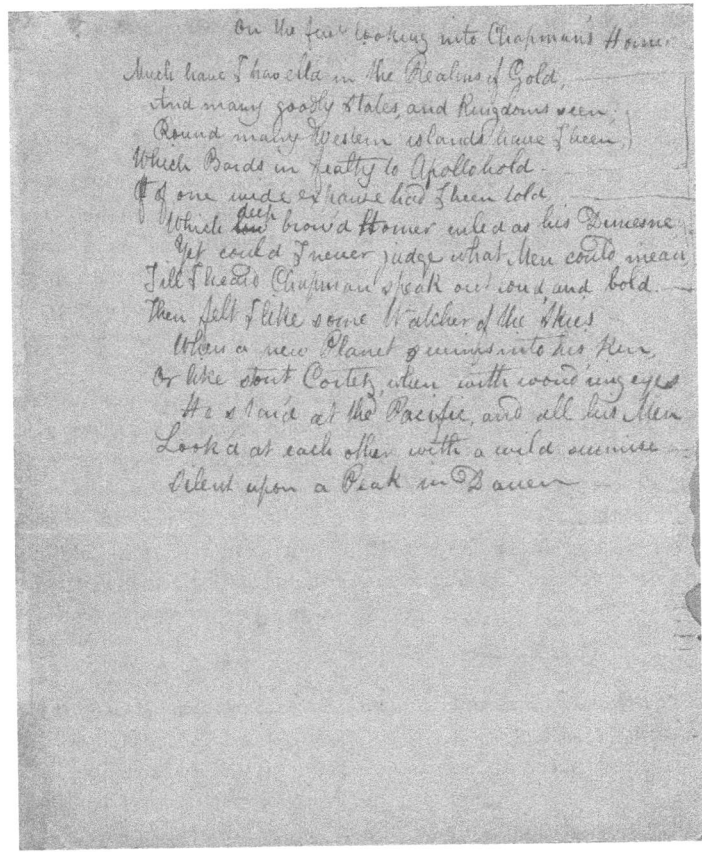

Figure 5.1 Keats, John, 1795–1821. Much have I travell'd in the realms of gold. A.MS., early draft. MS Keats 2.4. Houghton Library, Harvard University, Cambridge, MA. 49184486.

October night in 1816, Keats was introduced by Clarke to George Chapman's translation of Homer; he wrote the sonnet in the morning and had it sent to his friend, who found it on his breakfast table.[2]

Reading poetry as a collective experience, as well as writing contests, was certainly commonplace in Keats's circle and in his time in general. Yet he particularly valued those moments when, to use his words, this 'brotherhood in song' ('To George Felton Mathew', line 2) was sealed by reading and writing performances. That a poem on a translated version of Homer should emerge from such circumstances of togetherness and companionship is meaningful – all the more so since Clarke, to whom Keats later dedicated an epistle, had contributed to Keats's literary education. Thus, in more than one way, the poem is derived from second-hand knowledge and a process of exchange and transmission. After all, as Charles J. Rzepka has noticed, the original title of the poem, 'On *the* first looking into Chapman's Homer', 'seems to suggest Keats initially meant to celebrate, not just his own experience (he could have written "*my* first looking"), but the "occasion" of a common "first-looking" experienced by the two friends' (55). Line 8, which reads 'Till I heard Chapman speak out loud and bold', refers to Chapman's voice but may also evoke Clarke relaying the original voice by reading aloud to his friend. As these circumstances and the title's unfolding imply, Keats's poem is generated by a lineage of mediators to whom he pays tribute, and his gratitude is first directed to Clarke, the primary recipient of the text who received the poem as a gift in return for his assistance, then to Chapman, as the conveyor of Homer's text, and eventually to Homer, a revered but after all distant interpreter of the Troy myth.

These circumstances also remind us that Keats had come late to high culture and that he could read neither Greek nor Italian, which kept the close reading of major texts out of his reach. Marjorie Levinson perfectly describes this 'educational deficit':

> He knew some French and Latin, little Italian, no Greek. His Homer was Chapman, his Dante was Cary, his Provençal ballads translations in an edition of Chaucer, his Boccacio Englished. […] His absorption of the accessible English writers was greatly constrained by his ignorance of the originals upon which they drew and his nonsystematic self-education. (7)

This inability to read foreign languages had deep literary and social implications. Reading Chapman's Homer allowed Keats to 'breathe Homer's pure serene' (line 7): the metaphor, by involving vital functions, expresses the necessity and the importance of the discovery, and indeed, as Timothy Webb puts it, 'with Chapman's help, the poet [was] given lungs to breathe a rarefied atmosphere' (305). Yet the impossibility for Keats of reading Homer and others in their original languages was certainly seen, at first, as an obstacle to his poetic development and to his integration into more educated literary spheres. This cultural and social weakness provided grounds for the famous attack by John Gibson Lockhart in the *Edinburgh Magazine*, in which Keats's so-called immature language and vulgarity were partially ascribed to the poet's poor understanding of classical Greek culture.[3] From this perspective, the reading experience accounted for in the Chapman's Homer sonnet is about social and literary exclusion turning into a hope of inclusion.[4] Yet if we consider Keats's social status in general not as disabling in itself but rather as the necessary condition for integration into an unconventional 'culture of dissent',[5] Keats's inability to read and translate most foreign texts may be regarded as that which allowed him to relate indirectly to canonical texts, namely by turning a 'linguistic dispossession' into 'empowerment' (Webb 305).

Indeed, for Keats, this ignorance may lead to an intense aesthetic experience, resulting in a celebration of non-comprehension. 'To Homer', a sonnet written two years after the Chapman's Homer sonnet, offers another viewpoint on Keats's relation to Homer and on his experience of exclusion from the literary spheres of his time. Though the speaker remains marginalized from a cultural and intellectual point of view, the poem ironically draws parallels between what are barely comparable: the speaker's 'giant ignorance' (line 1) and Homer's supposed blindness. 'Of thee I hear, and of the Cyclades' (line 2): as though the image has been literalised, the culturally blind speaker has replaced reading with the oral reception of the text. As 'the veil was rent' (line 5) for Homer, whose extraordinary visionary power offset his disability, the veil was also partially rent for Keats, his ignorance mitigated thanks to Chapman's translation and other texts that promised further discoveries. For Homer and for the speaker, or for anyone, as the proverb-like tonality of the lines allows us to think, 'on the shores of darkness there is light' (line 9), 'there is triple sight in blindness' and blindness may be 'keen' (line 12): ignorance may allow acute vision, as the loss of visual perception might yield better imaginative abilities.[6]

But Keats's purported blindness – through the speaker's – may also allude to his inability to understand Homer's original language, a blindness that was never cured. Keats mentions the quality of this productive half-ignorance in an 1818 letter addressed to his friend John Hamilton Reynolds: 'I long to feast upon old Homer as we have upon Shakespeare. and [*sic*] as I have lately upon Milton. – if you understood Greek, and would read me passages, now and then, explaining their meaning, 't would be, from its mistiness, perhaps a greater luxury than reading the thing one's self' (Rollins vol. I, 274). First, like the speaker in 'To Homer', Keats hopes to *listen* to the original text and longs to experience linguistic incomprehension so as to, as one could imagine, relish the solely musical quality of a language that remains foreign to him. Moreover, the social aspect of translation that enacts the transmission process is once again essential. Here, Keats values the translated, or rather reconstituted, text more than 'the thing' itself, and values even more the process of mediation through reading and commenting, the performance of an improvised translation as it is addressed and received.

What also recalls 'To Homer' in this epistolary statement is the fertile notion of 'mistiness', induced here both by the Greek text and by its potentially approximate and subjective reconstitution. This wish to remain in the dark, or in half-light, is consistent with the negative capability principle, according to which Keats, in some circumstances, favours half-knowledge over full awareness, so that, in this context at least, his mind may remain open to imagination. Far from being an obstacle or causing a sense of failure, this effect of mistiness, created by the translator and received by his listener, allows for a freer translation and amplified imagination; it is 'not only an inhibitor, but also a facilitator, for thought and imagination' (Paterson 260).[7] As a matter of fact, Chapman's 1609–11 version led Keats to a rediscovery of Homer, since he knew Pope's translation or at least part of it. Very popular in Keats's time, and praised by Coleridge, Chapman's Homer was considered to be less literal than Pope's, and was viewed as a regeneration of the original text which sounded closer to its essence than Pope's version, while being a new poem in itself. In his preface to the reader, in the form of an epistle, Chapman presents his text as a 'conversion', a mode of translation that suited Keats's preference for a free and imaginative interpretation of the text (Reynolds 74–76). As the typically Keatsian ingestion metaphor ('I long to feast upon old Homer') also suggests, what matters most in the listening process is the possibility of an intimate reception of and connection to the text, however inaccurate or partial. Thus half-ignorance may provide a momentous opportunity to fuel inspiration, an intense aesthetic reading event and a source of imaginative power that is eventually converted into the sonnet. To Keats, understanding the text and its literal meaning is less important than the grasping or 'breathing' of its essence. In this context, misunderstanding and inaccuracy are not necessarily a loss, for whatever may disappear in the process of translation or reading is regained through invention, which Keats confirmed two years later in his translation from Ronsard.

Writing through mistranslation

While some of his contemporaries were accomplished translators (Coleridge translated Schiller, Shelley translated Homer, Plato, Calderón and Goethe, and Byron translated Dante), Keats's ability to translate was limited to French, Latin and Italian, and his relatively limited command of these languages never led him to translate regularly or to produce translations that might have been published. Yet he did translate most of Virgil's *Aeneid* as a schoolboy, and even though his friend Charles Brown described it as a 'literal prose translation' (41), Keats was awarded a major prize for his prose version.

Keats's inaccurate and truncated version of Ronsard's second sonnet in *Les Amours*, written in September 1818, is, then, his only translated text that was published and eventually acknowledged. The sonnet has long been dismissed as insignificant compared to other works,[8] and was first published in Richard Monckton Milnes's posthumous edition of Keats's writings, *Life, Letters and Literary Remains, of John Keats*. Yet it is included in more recent complete and selective editions, and even in Eavan Boland and Edward Hirsch's 2008 anthology of sonnets, *The Making of a Sonnet*, in the chapter titled 'The Sonnet Goes to Different Lengths', where it is presented more as a sonnet in itself than as a translation. To Andrew Motion, who includes the text in his short selected edition of Keats's poems, *Fugitive Poems*, this sonnet should not be 'ousted from our view' (8).[9] Indeed, however imperfect Keats's translation may be, it certainly deserves critical attention: it has a specific significance in Keats's work insofar as it illustrates how he explores the interaction between translation and poetic writing; the experiment in itself and the resulting sonnet also embody an attempt to relate to another poet and to another text.

The sonnet, which was almost literally written through a mist, pays tribute to Ronsard while being unfaithful to the original.[10] In a letter to Reynolds, Keats explains how he performed this 'free' translation without the original before him, relying on a somewhat blurred memory of the text, which he had read in a copy of Ronsard's volume borrowed from his friend Woodhouse.[11] Choosing the memory of the French text as a source instead of the original is the first stage in the transformation process, and proves that Keats accepted the risk of distortion and omission. By trusting his memory, however potentially fallible, Keats 'breathed in' the sonnet's 'pure serene', and thus recollected what his mind unquestionably perceived as the essence of the text, a highly subjective and already reshaped poetic material eventually leading to a creative mistranslation. This intuitive translation method, using the subjective appropriation of a text, raises the issue of the translator's responsibility: while this unfaithfulness is a refusal to commit to a proper translation, it also claims the translator's right to remain at a distance from the text, as though the memory of Ronsard's sonnet were more important than the text itself. Nevertheless, rather than a proof of disrespect for the source text, Keats's gesture should be regarded as an opportunity for him to translate from a very personal reading that takes the poem beyond language transposition.

Keats's sonnet undoubtedly imitates the general movement of Ronsard's text. In both sonnets, nature is endowed with a divine power and creates a perfect woman whose beauty is celebrated; Keats and Ronsard evoke a journey from the skies to the earth and from the world of ideas and allegory (Nature and Love) to the aching body of the speaking subject. Both poems stage a gradual shift from 'she', embodying nature and its beautiful creature, to the subject, 'I'. Yet, as might be expected, the translated sonnet is driven towards Keatsian poetics: Keats slightly rearranged the French poem, gave up a few elements and added and displaced others, so that the English sonnet sounds an echo of the French original:

Nature ornant Cassandre, qui devoit	Nature withheld Cassandra in the skies
De sa douceur forcer les plus rebelles,	For more adornment a full thousand years;
La composa de cent beautez nouvelles	She took their cream of Beauty's fairest dyes,
Que dés mille ans en espargne elle avoit.	And shap'd and tinted her above all Peers:
De tous les biens qu'Amour au ciel couvoit	Meanwhile Love kept her dearly with his wings,
Comme un tresor cherement sous ses ailes,	And underneath their shadow fill'd her eyes
Elle enrichit les graces immortelles	With such a richness that the cloudy Kings
De son bel œil, qui les Dieux esmouvoit.	Of high Olympus utter'd slavish sighs.
Du Ciel à peine elle estoit descendue	When from the Heavens I saw her first descend
Quand je la vey, quand mon ame esperdue	My heart took fire, and only burning pains
En devint folle, et d'un si poignant trait	They were my pleasures – they my Life's sad end –
Amour coula ses beautez dans mes veines,	Love pour'd her beauty into my warm veins – [13]
Qu'autres plaisirs je ne sens que mes peines	
Ny autre bien qu'adorer son pourtrait.[12]	

Not only does the English poem alter Ronsard's sonnet, especially through rewritten elements in the first and second quatrain (for instance, the 'slavish sighs' of the 'cloudy Kings' expand on 'qui les Dieux esmouvoit'), but Keatsian imagery and vocabulary can be recognized here and there: 'full' in 'full thousand years' echoes the numerous uses of the word and the idea of abundance and completeness that may be found in 'I stood tip-toe upon a little hill', in 'When I have fears that I may cease to be' and, repeatedly, in 'Ode to a Nightingale' and 'La belle dame sans merci'. In lines 10–11, the French speaker's emotional state, expressed in intellectual terms ('[M]on ame esperdue / En devint folle'), is transposed by Keats into images involving physical pain and sensations, with 'my burning pains' or 'My heart took fire' (recalling 'When I am consumed in the fire' in the sonnet 'When I sat down to read *King Lear* once again'). Beauty, abstractly referred to in French with 'cent beautez nouvelles', is invested with bodily features, colour and shape, more suitable to Keatsian ideals ('She took their cream of Beauty's fairest dyes / And shap'd and tinted her above all Peers'). The last line of the poem, 'Love pour'd her beauty into my warm veins', is reminiscent of the mingling metaphors which abound in Keats's poems, and may even prefigure the near-sonnet 'This living hand now warm and capable'.[14] Though the line perfectly translates 'Amour coula ses beautez dans mes veines' – and this is probably the only line in Keats's translation that faithfully copies one of Ronsard's – it is undeniably Keatsian in tone and inspiration.[15] The sonnet form itself is affected in the process of translation and takes the poem towards Englishness: Ronsard's sonnet, written in a French mode adapted from the Petrarchan pattern, is transformed by Keats into an irregular Shakespearean sonnet composed of three alternate-rhyme quatrains which re-uses in the second quatrain a rhyme from the first, an anomalous formal choice. Most strikingly, the sonnet stops after twelve lines. Indeed, as he wrote to Reynolds, Keats could not remember the closing lines of the French sonnet, and therefore produced only a partial translation.

Yet, even with the missing lines, the English poem as it is does not necessarily sound fragmentary, in part because some of line 13 in Ronsard's text is integrated into line 11 in Keats's ('They were my pleasures – they my Life's sad end –' mirrors 'Qu'autres plaisirs je ne sens que mes peines'). Moreover, while the French speaker ends on the lady's image as a final tribute and proof of his love, the lady in Keats's text disappears at the end, remaining only as a poisonous presence, and is replaced by the image of a passive, victimized subject embodied by possessive pronouns instead of 'I'. Though this alteration is partly due to Keats's selective memory, it may also reveal a choice by the poet, all the more so as this shift from 'she' to 'I' can be noticed in other love sonnets.[16] Finally, the last lines in the English version recall in many respects several of Keats's sonnet endings. As often in Keats's sonnets, the poem stages the process of conclusion by matching the image of death with the end of the sonnet: 'Life's sad end', which closes line 11, is reworded in the last line, which calls forth deathly poisoning. Moreover, this emphasis on conclusion is often counterbalanced by an attempt to delay the unavoidable ending, with the speaker's voice seeming to lower to silence reluctantly.[17] The tempo of the closing lines in 'Translated from Ronsard', which slackens their pace, also works poetically against the natural process of closure, along with repetitions ('they' and 'my'), the dash in the middle of the verse which creates a longer break in line 11, the [d] alliteration acting as an echo, and even the phonic composition in the very last line ('Love pour'd her beauty into my warm veins'), which abounds in bilabial consonants that seem to impede the fluidity of articulation. Thanks to the last lines, which reproduce the ambivalent ending pattern that can be found in other sonnets by Keats, this unfinished translation may be regarded as a finished text.[18]

Keats's translation seems, then, to effect a linguistic, poetic and formal conversion by turning the sonnet into a shortened yet complete sonnet-like and partly Keatsian poem. Keats's attempt is an active piece of reconstitution, a form of experimental appropriation consistent with his tendency to absorb and remodel any object he perceives and seeks to grasp. This appropriation is also a means for the young and self-doubting poet to reinforce his poetic authority and an opportunity to redefine his relation to another poet, mixing tribute and self-assertion, linguistic transposition and integration of the poem into his own poetic language. This attitude reflects a positive perception of influence, proving that, though pressured by an unavoidable anxiety posed by literary antecedents, Keats was not hampered by this but used it as a poetic subject so as to master it and reach out, in his own way, to the original.

From translation to response

Such a free conception of translation as Keats accomplished with Ronsard's sonnet, combining language transfer and rewriting, or his indulgence in what he called 'mistiness' when reading or hearing foreign texts, may be related to his tendency in some of his sonnets (and elsewhere) to convert writing from other texts and/or from other writers' languages. In this respect, Keats's complex relationship to non-English literature, together with his views on the translation process, is but one aspect of a wider picture, where his poems are often staged as products of transformation and take the form of replies. Indeed, several of Keats's poems are presented as directly and immediately resulting from the poet's reading of other works, which seems then to trigger poetic creation. While 'Translated from Ronsard' may be a poetic and linguistic adaptation that produces a less dramatic transformation, other sonnets by Keats written as responses to other texts remain more distant from the source text while at the same time openly pointing to the connection between the two works.

In these poems, the poet undertakes to bridge the gap between circumstance and writing, so that his text may appear as a natural extension of what inspired it. For instance, the circumstances preceding the writing of the Chapman's Homer sonnet make it a form of occasional poetry, but an exceptional one, directly written out of a powerful and almost epiphanic experience that acted as a catalyst. 'On sitting down to read *King Lear* once again' reproduces this pattern, since, as Keats explained in a letter to his brothers, 'the thing demanded the prologue of a Sonnet' (Rollins vol. I, 214), underlining how reading directly initiated writing in this case. By creating a sense of a continuity between his poem and another work – a writing practice also employed by other sonnet-writers, such as Wordsworth or Milton – Keats defines a link between reading and writing that recalls his conception of the translation process.

For Keats, representing the process through which texts are read, interpreted and then responded to implies an empathy with the other poet and the other text, which is often fulfilled thanks to the involvement of the speaker's body. Through the 'breathing' process evoked in the Chapman's Homer sonnet the poet expresses his desire for an intimate, physical relationship with the text: the body of the reader inhales the effluence of the text, in a very Keatsian transfer from one sense or ability to another which here deprives the act of reading of its intellectual dimension. In the title 'On sitting down to read *King Lear* once again', the act of reading is preceded by the physical movement with which it is associated; it is the poet's body that allows entry into the poem, relating an incarnated voice to the inspiring text. In this sonnet, Shakespeare's play seems to be literally assimilated by the speaker, who savours this 'bitter-sweet' 'Shakespearian fruit' (line 8). The poet's intimacy with the numerous texts he admires and praises may also appear in a more metaphorical form each time the poet-reader finds himself taken into the text he celebrates. 'Gone' 'in the old oak forest' (line 11) and 'consumed in the fire' (line 13), the speaker of the *King Lear* sonnet in turn experiences assimilation, as does the 'I' in 'This pleasant tale is like a little copse', who is kept within Chaucer's *The Flower and the Leaf*, 'in so sweet a place' (line 3). Self-portrayed as imprisoned in the body of the poems, these poetic voices fulfil the Keatsian fantasy of absorption into poetic objects and may also claim the poet's wish to fully grasp other poets' works.

This closeness and sense of continuity established with the source text are linked to Keats's interest in the process of transformation: in his letters, he often describes poetry writing in general in terms of conversion or chemical distillation,[19] as well as, as we have seen, breathing or ingestion. The nature and origin of the source text may vary – epistolary prose, longer poems and sonnets, whatever their language – but the transformation process itself, often mentioned in paratexts, titles and epistolary comments, is often an important component of the poetic scenes in the poems. Written in April 1819, the sonnet 'As Hermes once took to his feathers light' is a striking example that takes us back to the problematics of Keats's readings of translated texts: reading the Paolo and Francesca episode from Canto V of Dante's *Inferno* in H. F. Cary's translation inspired Keats with a powerful dream in which, as he explains in a letter to his brother and sister-in-law, he was taken to 'that region of hell' and felt, once again, as though he had been engulfed in the text and turned into one of its characters.[20] The dream, with all the distortions an unconscious mind may produce,[21] was then converted into a sonnet, which is thus the result of two transformations. Finally, the epistolary comments preceding the sonnet as copied out in a letter to George and Georgiana Keats provide a final prose version, presenting the subject of the sonnet, but also giving an account of the mental process that resulted in its composition. The title given to the poem for publication, 'A Dream, After Reading Dante's Episode of Paolo and Francesca', confirms Keats's tendency to connect reading, processing another author's work, and poetry writing. Was the sonnet meant to be on the scene from Dante's work, on the dream that it inspired, or on reading the translated text? The fact that this title avoids the usual 'Sonnet on [...]' pattern indicates that what prevailed, for Keats, was the origin of the poem and the transposition itself.

The sonnet on the Paolo and Francesca episode offers yet another facet of this closeness between source and target, since it was originally written in Keats's edition of Cary's Dante, as a contiguous piece of writing or a sort of gloss supplementing the original and meant to be part of a conversation between the translated original and its outgrowth. As Keats copied out other poems into his own books or those of his friends,[22] literally inscribing his works next to and within other poets' works, he explicitly sought to eliminate the distance between reading and writing and to enact the principle of breathing in the essence of texts, which to him required a reply, a very personal translation of his own emotion as a reader. Translating from his selective remembrance of Ronsard's sonnet, or writing a sonnet after reading another poet's work, may be seen, in Keats's poetics, as two forms of a creative extension of reading.

Though he was almost trapped in his own language, Keats remarkably turned this linguistic failing into major poetic material and a principle of writing. Sticking to the original text and focusing on language displacement, rarely possible and seldom performed in his work, was replaced by a constant search for the right balance between foreignness or, more generally, otherness and assimilation. When looking into the various translations of Keats's work into French, Yves Bonnefoy's selective edition stands out insofar as it particularly recalls this conception of translation as a creative response to the original version. Bonnefoy's translations in this collection, which sometimes seem distant from the original texts and imbued with his own poetic language, may be seen as openly and willingly unfaithful. However, these translations may also be regarded as an appropriate tribute and a suitable response to Keats's work for this very reason. For the French poet, who justifies his approach in a short preface, translating means above all taking poems towards his own poetic language and universe.[23] Bonnefoy goes even further by disrupting the sonnet form: in his edition, the 'Bright star' sonnet is extended to twenty lines arranged in two stanzas; 'The day is gone and all its sweets are gone' has twenty-one lines with one eighteen-line stanza and three closing lines; both are unrhymed. In doing this, Bonnefoy claims that Keats's sonnets may easily accept the distortion and at the same time proves how the mutability of the sonnet form can be revealed in the translation process.

Notes

1 Sonnets written shortly after the Chapman's Homer sonnet also celebrate social interaction in reading or writing. See 'Keen, fitful gusts are whisp'ring here and there' and 'On leaving some friends at an early hour'.
2 In his *Recollections of Writers*, Clarke wrote: 'A beautiful copy of the folio edition of Chapman's Homer had been lent me [...] and to work we went, turning to some of the "famousest" passages, as we had scrappily known them in Pope's version [...] Chapman supplied us with many an after-treat; but it was in the teeming wonderment of this his [Keats's] first introduction, that, when I came down to breakfast the next morning, I found upon my table a letter with no other enclosure than his famous sonnet' (pp. 129–130).
3 See Lockhart's article on *Endymion* in the *Blackwood's Edinburgh Magazine* August 1818 review: 'As for Mr Keats's "Endymion", it has just as much to do with Greece as it has with "old Tartary the fierce"; no man, whose mind has ever been imbued with the smallest knowledge or feeling of classical poetry or classical history, could have stooped to profane and vulgarise every association in the manner which has been adopted by this "son of promise".'
4 In his biography of Keats, Andrew Motion also sees the sonnet as 'a poem written by an outsider who wants to be an insider' (p. 112).
5 This is Nicholas Roe's approach in *John Keats and the Culture of Dissent*.
6 From this perspective, the experimental sonnet 'O thou whose face hath felt the winter's wind', in which the speaker is a thrush addressing the poet, may be read as an allegory of such an experience. In this sonnet, the question of linguistic ignorance is opened out to the wider scope of knowledge in general, and Keats seems to rewrite 'To Homer' and its several stages. The poem dialectically opposes winter and its mist to spring and its promise of harvest and abundance, yet 'supreme darkness' is already a light, and 'Triple morn' (line 8), sounds like an extension of the 'triple sight' evoked in 'To Homer'. The bird's prophecy, which celebrates the intensity of the light when darkness is overcome, and the paradox of learning through unconsciousness ('And he's awake who thinks himself asleep', line 14), sounds close to the experience related in the Chapman's Homer sonnet.

7 Keats also admits to being kept in the condition of seeing the world through the veil of mist as a letter writer, especially when overwhelmed by the pain of unrequited love. The lover's discourse equates mist with the intensity of emotional confusion, recalling the poet's state when creative imagination is most stimulated. See Rollins (vol. I, pp. 140–141).

8 George Steiner dismisses the sonnet for being 'jejune' and unworthy of any critical attention. See Steiner p. 189.

9 The value of this sonnet has also been acknowledged by composer William Hawley, who has adapted about a dozen of Keats's poems, among them 'Translated from Ronsard' (see http://www.williamhawley.net/scorepages/fourkeats/1ronsard.htm).

10 This lack of deference for the original text may be noticed elsewhere in Keats's writings: in his letters, he often misquotes other poets or writers to adjust the quotation to his own personal situation; the epigraph to 'Welcome joy and welcome sorrow', from Milton's *Paradise Lost*, is also inaccurate.

11 See Keats's letter to John Hamilton Reynolds, 22 September 1817: 'Here is a free translation of a Sonnet of Ronsard, which I think will please you – I have the Loan of his work – they have great Beauties […]. I had not the original by me when I wrote it, and did not recollect the purport of the last lines –' (Rollins vol. I, p. 371).

12 Ronsard wrote several versions of this sonnet, which is the second poem in *Le premier livre des amours*. Keats read the version which is included in Richard Woodhouse's copy and copied out in his commonplace book on page 139. See https://nrs.harvard.edu/urn-3:FHCL.HOUGH:3410865?n=262.

13 This version of the poem is Woodhouse's transcript, as copied in his commonplace book on page 140, and differs slightly from the version included in Jack Stillinger's edition. See https://nrs.harvard.edu/urn-3:FHCL.HOUGH:3410865?n=263.

14 See especially lines 5–7, which stage a similar scene of deathly blood transfusion: 'That thou would wish thine own heart dry of blood, / So in my veins red life might stream again'.

15 Before sending the whole translation to Reynolds, Keats mentions his sonnet in a letter to his friend Charles W. Dilke and sends him this very line, which confirms he was aware of the affinity between Ronsard's line and his own poetics. See Rollins (vol. I, p. 369).

16 This pattern may be found in the sonnets 'The day is gone, and all its sweets are gone' and 'Bright star, would I were as steadfast as thou art', and also in 'La belle dame sans merci'.

17 See, for instance, the closing lines of 'To Byron': 'Still warble, dying swan, – still tell the tale, / The enchanting tale – the tale of pleasing woe.' See also the ending of 'Why did I laugh tonight? No voice will tell': 'Verse, fame, and beauty are intense indeed, / But death intenser – death is life's high meed.'

18 Yet Milnes rewrote the ending of Keats's sonnet by adding these lines: 'So that her image in my soul upgrew, / The only thing adorable and true' (Milnes p. 241).
19 For instance, Keats evokes '[the] innumerable compositions and decompositions which take place between the intellect and its thousand materials before it arrives at that trembling delicate and snail-horn perception of beauty' (Rollins vol. I, p. 265). Keats's vocabulary to describe poetic creation in general is often related to chemistry, such as 'ethereal', 'distillation', 'essential'. See Gaillet.
20 See Rollins, vol. II, p. 91: 'I floated about the whirling atmosphere as it is described with a beautiful figure to whose lips mine were joined at it seem'd for an age.'
21 Peter Levine analyses Keats's distortions of the scene represented by Dante. 'Keats's introduction is extraordinary, for he says that he found "delightful enjoyment" in an imaginary experience of Hell. In *The Divine Comedy*, the kiss takes place on earth and leads to death, damnation and an involuntary conjunction of two tormented souls. In Keats's sonnet, the kiss occurs in the inferno, where it nevertheless generates eternal pleasure and warmth. Like Dante's tempest, Keats's wind stops and starts, but when it stops it deposits the lovers lightly on a vernal landscape' (p. 82).
22 Keats composed 'This pleasant tale is like a little copse' in Clarke's edition of Chaucer.
23 To him, translating means 'désirer rencontrer [les textes] au plus immédiat de soi-même, c'est-à-dire dans la langue où l'on a vécu ses propres découvertes du chant de l'oiseau dans l'arbre' (p. 7).

Works cited

Bonnefoy, Yves. *Keats et Leopardi*. Mercure de France, 2000.
Boland, Eavan and Edward Hirsch, eds. *The Making of a Sonnet: A Norton Anthology*. Norton, 2008.
Brown, Charles Armitage. *The Life of John Keats*. Oxford University Press, 1937.
Clarke Cowden, Charles. *The Life of John Keats*. Oxford University Press, 1937.
Clarke Cowden, Charles. *Recollections of Writers*. 1878. Centaur, 1969.
Gaillet, Florence. 'Poésie, alchimie et éthique'. *Keats ou le sortilège des mots*. Edited by Christian La Cassagnère. Presses Universitaires de Lyon, 2003, pp. 155–175.
Gentili, Vanna. '"Let Us Inspect the Lyre": Keats's Work on the Sonnet Form'. *The Challenge of Keats: Bicentenary Essays 1795–1995*. Edited by Allan C. Christensen, Giuseppe Galigani, Anthony L. Johnson and Lilla Maria Crisafulli Jones. Rodopi, 2000, pp. 79–94.

Hirsch, Edward. *John Keats: The 64 Sonnets*. Paul Dry Books, 2004.
Jackson, Heather Joanna. *Romantic Readers: The Evidence of Marginalia*. Yale University Press, 2005.
Levine, Peter. 'Keats against Dante: The Sonnet on Paolo and Francesca'. *Keats-Shelley Journal*, vol. 51, 2002: pp. 73–96.
Levinson, Marjorie. *Keats's Life of Allegory: The Origins of a Style*. Blackwell, 1988.
Monckton Milnes, Richard. *Life, Letters and Literary Remains, of John Keats*. E. Moxon, 1848.
Motion, Andrew, ed. *John Keats: Fugitive Poems*. Hesperus Press, 2004.
Motion, Andrew. *Keats: A Biography*. Faber and Faber, 1997.
Paterson, Alexandra. 'A Greater Luxury: Keats's Depictions of Mistiness and Reading'. *Romanticism*, vol. 18, no. 3, 2012: pp. 260–269.
Reynolds, Matthew. *The Poetry of Translation: From Chaucer & Petrarch to Homer & Logue*. Oxford University Press, 2011.
Rezpka, Charles J. '"Cortez: Or Balboa, or Somebody like That": Form, Fact, and Forgetting in Keats's "Chapman's Homer" Sonnet'. *Keats-Shelley Journal*, vol. 51, 2002: pp. 35–75.
Roe, Nicholas. 'A Cockney Schoolroom: John Keats at Enfield'. *Keats: Bicentenary Readings*. Edited by Michael O'Neill. Edinburgh University Press, 1997a, pp. 11–26.
Roe, Nicholas. *John Keats and the Culture of Dissent*. Clarendon Press, 1997b.
Rollins, Hyder Edward, ed. *The Letters of John Keats*. 2 vols. Cambridge University Press, 1958.
Steiner, George. 'The Dog Did Not Bark: A Note on Keats in Translation'. *The Persistence of Poetry: Bicentennial Essays on Keats*. Edited by Robert M. Ryan and Ronald A. Sharp. University of Massachusetts Press, 1998. 10–35.
Stillinger, Jack, ed. *Keats: Complete Poems*. The Belknap Press, 1982.
Webb, Timothy. 'Homer and the Romantics'. *The Cambridge Companion to Homer*. Edited by Robert Fowler. Cambridge University Press, 2004, pp. 287–310.
Woodhouse, Richard. John Keats Collection, 1814–1891; Common place book of Richard Woodhouse: transcripts of unpublished poems. MS Keats 3.2. Houghton Library, Harvard University, Cambridge, MA. https://nrs.harvard.edu/urn-3:FHCL.HOUGH: 3410865.

6

On translating *Les Chimères* by Gérard de Nerval

Peter Valente

The twelve sonnets of Gérard de Nerval's *Les Chimères* (including the five-sonnet sequence 'Le Christ aux Oliviers') were first published as a group in 1854, a year before Nerval's apparent suicide at the age of forty-six. They are thought to contain the quintessence of his metaphysical and aesthetic ideas; he 'endows each word with hermetic value, injecting each with multiple possibilities of meanings, rhythms, tonalities, colors. In doing so, he sets up a series of reverberations, associations within the body of the sonnet itself' (Knapp 237). It is these variable meanings and rhythms that make translating Nerval's sonnets a challenge and require the translator to hold the music and the meaning in his mind at all times. Often in the sonnets these associations and reverberations are brought to a moment of tension, where thoughts and emotions are in conflict until they are harmoniously reabsorbed into a provisional unity in the final tercet. This threat of destabilization of the real is built into the form of the Nervalian sonnet. When translating Nerval's *Les Chimères*, I aimed to maintain the flow and rhythm of Nerval's sonnet rather than attempt to reproduce the rhyme scheme, or strictly adhere to the formal structure. Instead, I tried to approximate the sound of the original French by finding a sonic equivalent in English because of 'the exquisite joy experienced in the musicality and engaging rhythms of [the sonnets'] lines' (Knapp 237). In this chapter, I present the intricate poetics of these sonnets in their historical and biographical context and touch upon some of my approaches to creative translation, in view of the issues that arose in the course of my translation.

Nerval's sonnets modernize the traditional Petrarchan pattern of the sonnet and revive the Ronsardian sestet, using the structure with new intent (Hudson 220). While in a Petrarchan sonnet the rhyme scheme in the octave is ABBA ABBA, the Nervalian sonnet usually has a different rhyme scheme in the quatrains: ABAB ABAB. As Robert J. Hudson writes, 'Typically, embraced rhymes within a stanza [ABBA] suggest an enclosed premise or a self-sustained idea, even protection (as in the physical embrace). On the contrary, the cross rhymes [ABAB] suggest conflict or disagreement; their point-counterpoint exchange presents such stanzas with an unresolved dialectic rather than a holistic harmony' (229). In 'Delphica', Nerval begins with a stanza that expresses desire, as the poet asks Daphne if she has heard the 'old song'; the quatrains obey the Petrarchan pattern for end rhymes, ABBA:

La connais-tu, DAFNE, cette ancienne romance,
Au pied du sycomore, ou sous les lauriers blancs,
Sous l'olivier, le myrte ou les saules tremblants,
Cette chanson d'amour... qui toujours recommence?

Reconnais-tu le Temple au péristyle immense,
Et les citrons amers où s'imprimaient tes dents,
Et la grotte, fatale aux hôtes imprudents,
Où du dragon vaincu dort l'antique semence?

Ils reviendront, ces Dieux que tu pleures toujours!
Le temps va ramener l'ordre des anciens jours;
La terre a tressailli d'un souffle prophétique...

Cependant la sibylle au visage latin
Est endormie encor sous l'arc de Constantin
– Et rien n'a dérangé le sévère portique.

Do you know, Daphne, the lyrics of that old song,
Heard at the foot of the sycamore tree or under the white laurels,
Beneath the olive tree, the myrtle, or the trembling willows,
That song of love that always begins anew?...

Do you recognize the Temple with the immense peristyle,
And the bitter lemons that bear the imprint of your teeth,
And that cave, fatal to imprudent visitors,
Where the ancient seed of the vanquished dragon sleeps?

They will return, these gods that you still mourn!
Time will bring back the religion of the old days;
The earth has trembled with a prophetic breath...

Meanwhile the sibyl with the Latin visage
Still sleeps under the arch of Constantine
– And nothing has disturbed the severe portico.

In the sestet, however, Nerval is suggesting that the old gods will return: the end rhymes follow a Ronsardian pattern [CCD EED], expressing a gap between desire and the actualization of that desire. Nerval would not ultimately see the fulfilment of his hope for the emergence of a belief in the old pagan gods. Writing about Emperor Julian in *Les Illuminés*, he says, 'Thus concludes the life of the last pagan. He renounced those gods who, doubtless, had not brought the expected consolations to his deathbed. The Nazarene still triumphed over his resuscitated enemies after thirteen centuries' (my translation; Nerval 2022, 271). To modern ears, the Nervalian sonnet evokes the uncertainty and anxiety of man faced with the realization that God is dead. Nerval writes, 'there is certainly something more frightening in history than the fall of empires: it is the death of religion' (Nerval 2022, 247).

Nerval's revived Renaissance sonnets emerged from the wreckage of the old world. He had become disenchanted with the political paralysis and hypocrisy of the Louis-Philippe monarchy (1830–48), as well as the Second Revolution and the rise of Napoleon. The sonnets also materialize his failure to actualize his vision of a lover (the divine feminine) in the actress Jenny Colon. Nerval's increasing mental instability, and his descent into the uncharted regions of himself – into darkness – would lead him to write in his short story 'Isis': 'O nature! O eternal mother! Have mortals come to the point of rejecting all hope and all prestige. O Goddess of Saïs! Has the most brazen of your followers, while raising your sacred veil, come face to face with death?' (Knapp 236). Colon had rejected him and he was alone; he had suffered many nervous breakdowns; and his final years were complicated with financial and emotional problems. Throughout his life, he had descended into the darker regions of his psyche, exploring the nature of dreams and occult mysteries, but he failed, in the end, to save his Eurydice. Nerval writes in 'My Uncle's Library' from *The Illuminated*: 'is there not something of reason to be extracted from madness [...]?' (my translation; Nerval 2022, 4). The twelve sonnets of *Les Chimères* are the luminous record of that journey into madness and back again. They were first published as a group in 1854, a year before Nerval's apparent suicide at the age of forty-six. It is as though the intensity of Nerval's mind, bordering on madness, collided with the very form of the Petrarchan sonnet to create intricate poems that could contain the contemporary historical and personal chaos experienced by the poet.

In translating Nerval's *Chimeras*, I remained close to a literal translation, departing from this only where necessary to create poems in English that were musical as well as faithful. I translated *Les Chimères* literally when I felt the poem demanded it or to preserve some essential quality, and I also used words that belonged to an earlier time, to suggest the Romantic quality in Nerval; on the other hand, I also focused on reproducing the music of the original French, as well as departing from the literal to creatively transform the language. Thus, I situate my translations of *Les Chiméres* between those of Robert Duncan and Robin Blaser, about whose work Andrew Mossin writes, 'Duncan's version of *Les Chimères* is as much imbued with his own project of recovering elements of High Romanticism as Blaser's is in moving Nerval's language to a similarly distant position from its original space in French-language culture' (109). I used approaches derived from both the Duncan and the Blaser translations to arrive at my own ideas of creative translation, which used all the methods at my disposal to 'liberate the language imprisoned in a work in [the translator's] re-creation of that work' (Benjamin 23). My translation of the famous first sonnet is as follows:

El Desdichado

Je suis le ténébreux, – le veuf – l'inconsolé,
Le prince d'Aquitaine à la tour abolie :
Ma seule étoile est morte, – et mon luth constellé
Porte le soleil noir de la Mélancolie.

Dans la nuit du tombeau, toi qui m'as consolé,
Rends-moi le Pausilippe et la mer d'Italie,
La fleur qui plaisait tant à mon cœur désolé,
Et la treille où le pampre à la rose s'allie.

Suis-je Amour ou Phébus ?... Lusignan ou Biron ?
Mon front est rouge encor du baiser de la reine ;
J'ai rêvé dans la grotte où nage la sirène...

Et j'ai deux fois vainqueur traversé l'Achéron :
Modulant tour à tour sur la lyre d'Orphée
Les soupirs de la sainte et les cris de la fée.

Ill Fated Destiny

I am the dark adept, – the widower, – the inconsolable,
The Prince of Aquitaine in his demolished tower:
My only *Star* is dead, – and this lute no longer resounds
to the music of the spheres, but to the *black sun* of despair.

In the darkness of the Tomb, you who comforted me,
O give me back Mount Posillipo and the Italian sea,
The *flower* that so pleased my desolate heart,
And the trellis where the grapevine intertwines with the rose.

Am I Amor or Phoebus?... Lusignan or Biron?
My forehead is still flushed with the kiss of the queen;
I have dreamed of sirens swimming in a grotto...

And twice victorious I have crossed the Acheron:
Modulating in turn on the lyre of Orpheus
The sighs of the saint and the cries of the siren

I translated 'ténébreux' as 'dark adept', whereas some translators have chosen to translate the word as 'the dark one'. The unstressed and stressed aspect of 'adept' alongside the single hard syllable of 'dark' gives the line a certain intense and dramatic movement, and 'dark adept' also suggests the unusual and dramatic life path of Nerval. The poet Gerritt Lansing writes the following about Nerval: 'As Lord Peregrinus he rode slowly toward the reddest dawn. He had been to the bottom of the sea' (251).

I translated 'Ma seule étoile est morte – et mon luth constellé / Porte le soleil noir de la Mélancholie' as 'My only *Star* is dead, – and this lute no longer resounds / to the music of the spheres, but to the *black sun* of despair', reinventing these lines in an attempt to get closer to Nerval's meaning in the poem. In doing so, I sought to convey what I saw as the complexity of this image: the sense that Nerval's 'sound' no longer resonates with the bright stars, but is darker, more complex, Orphic, as a result of his disenchantment, which I have suggested in the caesura breaks in the lines. I added 'resounds', in keeping with the idea of a lute. I translated 'Dans la nuit du tombeau' as 'in the darkness of the Tomb'. My addition of the exclamation 'O' was an attempt to suggest yearning for a lost memory and melancholic remembrance. In line 10, I translated 'rouge' as 'flushed' instead of 'reddened', giving the line a greater sense of ambiguity, suggesting both sexual discomfort and the red of the queen's lips; more importantly, however, it suggests the memory of an actual physical reaction. A literal translation of 'syrène' might be 'mermaid', but in keeping with the mythological references in the text, I decided to lay the emphasis on the famous tale in Homer's *Odyssey* in which Ulysses is lured by the song of the siren. 'Siren' is also closer to the sound of 'syrène'. In the last line, I chose to continue with the theme of the siren's song.

The second sonnet in the sequence titled 'The Christ in the Olive Groves' reads:

II

Il reprit : « Tout est mort ! J'ai parcouru les mondes ;
Et j'ai perdu mon vol dans leurs chemins lactés,
Aussi loin que la vie en ses veines fécondes,
Répand des sables d'or et des flots argentés :

« Partout le sol désert côtoyé par les ondes,
Des tourbillons confus d'océans agités …

Un souffle vague émeut les sphères vagabondes,
Mais nul esprit n'existe en ces immensités.

« En cherchant l'œil de Dieu, je n'ai vu qu'un orbite
Vaste, noir et sans fond, d'où la nuit qui l'habite
Rayonne sur le monde et s'épaissit toujours ;

« Un arc-en-ciel étrange entoure ce puits sombre,
Seuil de l'ancien chaos dont le néant est l'ombre,
Spirale engloutissant les Mondes et les Jours !

II

He began again: 'All is dead! I have travelled between the Worlds;
I lost my sense of orientation in their milky ways,
To such an extent that life, from its fertile veins,
No longer pours out the golden sands and silver waves:

'Everywhere I looked, I saw a wasteland surrounded by waves,
Disturbed hurricanes from restless oceans…

A vague breath influences the motion of the wandering spheres,
But no spirit exists in these immense regions of space.

'Looking for the eye of God, I saw only a single EYE
Vast, black and bottomless, and the darkness from within
Radiates out into the world growing ever darker;

'A strange rainbow surrounds this somber pit,
Threshold of the old chaos whose shadow is nothingness,
Spiral that engulfs the Worlds and the Days!

In my translation of the first stanza, I translated 'J'ai parcouru les mondes' as 'I have travelled between the Worlds', attempting to render Nerval's sense in the poem of a search. Throughout his life, Nerval was fascinated by the line that divided dreams from reality (two different worlds), and this led him on a search for the underlying nature of reality which he would eventually discover in the complex myths contained in the world's religions. I interpreted 'perdu mon vol' (literally 'lost my flight') first as 'I lost my sense of direction', and finally as 'I lost my orientation'. 'Orientation' has more to do with space: one loses one's orientation in empty space (suggested by the last line of the poem), where there is no specified sense of direction. I see a gnostic tension between light and darkness in the poem. Rather than translating 'orbite' as 'socket', I opted for a typographic effect and capitalized the word 'eye' to create the visual sense of a large EYE, vast, dark and bottomless, a void: not a source of light but of darkness. This is the blindness of God.

I translated the fifth sonnet of 'The Christ in the Olive Groves' as follows:

V

C'était bien lui, ce fou, cet insensé sublime…
Cet Icare oublié qui remontait les cieux,

Ce Phaéton perdu sous la foudre des dieux,
Ce bel Atys meurtri que Cybèle ranime !

L'augure interrogeait le flanc de la victime,
La terre s'enivrait de ce sang précieux…
L'univers étourdi penchait sur ses essieux,
Et l'Olympe un instant chancela vers l'abîme.

« Réponds ! criait César à Jupiter Ammon,
Quel est ce nouveau dieu qu'on impose à la terre ?
Et si ce n'est un dieu, c'est au moins un démon… »

Mais l'oracle invoqué pour jamais dut se taire ;
Un seul pouvait au monde expliquer ce mystère :
– Celui qui donna l'âme aux enfants du limon.

V

It was him, this madman, this sublime fool…
This forgotten Icarus who flew too close to the sun,

This Phaeton destroyed by the lightning of the gods,
This beautiful, emasculated Attis whom Cybele revives!

The augur examined the wound on the victim's side,
The earth was getting drunk on this precious blood of Christ…
The dizzy universe was unsteady on its axes,
And Olympus for an instant staggered toward the abyss.

'Answer,' cried Caesar to Jupiter Ammon,
'What is this new god being imposed upon the earth?
And if it is not a god, it must be a demon…'

But the oracle invoked had to be silent forever;
There was only one who could explain this mystery to the world:
– The hidden god who gave his soul to the children of clay.

In the first stanza, my translation of 'Ce bel Atys meurtri que Cybele ranime!' is 'This beautiful, emasculated Attis whom Cybele revives!'. Attis was the ancient Phrygian god of vegetation and consort of the great Mother of the gods, Cybele. The goddess, in order to punish him for his infidelity, drove him into a mad frenzy which caused him to castrate himself. 'Meurtri' has the sense of 'wound' and here suggests the effect of castration. I opted for 'emasculate', with its sexual connotation. Perhaps Nerval was thinking of the disastrous relationship, real or imagined, with the actress Jenny Colon.

Continuing with the fifth sonnet, I translated 'L'augure interrogeait le flanc de la victime' as 'The augur examined the wound on the victim's side', and the following line as 'The earth was getting drunk on this precious blood of Christ...'. My concern here was approximating the music of the original French and conveying the image of the earth absorbing the blood of Christ like a vampire. The last stanza, in my translation, is:

> But the oracle invoked had to be silent forever;
> There was only one who could explain this mystery to the world:
> – The hidden god who gave his soul to the children of clay.

I translated 'Celui qui donna l'âme aux enfants du limon' as 'The hidden god who gave his soul to the children of clay'. In adding the word 'hidden', I increased the mystery of the line, suggesting resonances with the idea of an alien god, a demon: 'What is this new god being imposed upon the earth? / And if it is not a god, it must be a demon...'. I also emphasized the sense that this 'hidden god' (perhaps a demon, Lucifer) is transferring his own soul to man: man is thus made in this god's image, underscoring the blasphemous nature of the poem. Thus the sonnet suggests Nerval's 'sympathy for the so-called demons: Lucifer, Prometheus, Judas, Cain [...] the fire beings' (Knapp 278).

Conclusion

Nerval's point of departure was the Petrarchan sonnet form, evoking a world where his Laura was deceased. This paradoxically led Nerval to create a poem based not on a desire to unify with the beloved, but on a descent into the underworld and resulting disillusionment. The Nervalian sonnet is not a closed, regular form, but rather open, suggestive, hermetic and with multiple variations in its rhyme patterns. In this, Nerval expresses a desire for the resurgence of the old, pagan gods. But transcendence is not possible in the modern world, and God is dead. Throughout his life, he had descended into the darker regions of his psyche, exploring the nature of dreams and occult mysteries, but he failed, in the end, as Orpheus, to save his Eurydice, Colon. The twelve sonnets of *Les Chimères* are the luminous record of that journey into madness and back again. Attempting to reproduce this record in translation requires a certain balancing act between literalness and inventiveness, between preserving, in Nerval's case, the hermetic, mysterious beauty of these poems, and creating an effective poem, in terms of sound, in English. As Dryden wrote, in his 'Preface to Ovid's *Epistles*', 'Tis much like dancing on ropes with fettered legs' (146).

Works cited

Benjamin, Walter. *Illuminations: Essays and Reflections*. Edited by Hannah Arendt. Houghton Mifflin Harcourt, 2019.

Dryden, John. *Selections from Dryden*. Edited by G. E. Hadow. Clarendon Press, 1908.

Hudson, Robert J. 'Nerval, Ronsard and the Orphic Lyre: Modulating Romantic Irony in *Les Chimères*'. *Nineteenth-Century French Studie*s, vol. 41, nos. 3 & 4, 2013: pp. 220–236.

Knapp, Bettina. *Gérard de Nerval: The Mystic's Dilemma*. University of Alabama Press, 1980.

Lansing, Gerrit. 'Test of Translation IX: Nerval's "Horus"'. *A Caterpillar Anthology: A Selection of Poetry and Prose from Caterpillar Magazine*. Edited by Clayton Eshleman. Doubleday & Company, Inc., 1971, pp. 77–88.

Mossin, Andrew. *Male Subjectivity and Poetic Form in New American Poetry*. St Martin's Press, 2010.

Nerval, Gérard de. *Œuvres complètes Tome IX: Les Illuminés*. Edited by Jacques-Remi Dahan. Classiques Garnier, 2015.

Nerval, Gérard de. *The Illuminated*. Introduced and translated by Peter Valente. Adelaide: Wakefield Press, 2022.

Reshaping Rilke: A comparative approach to the latest translations of *Die Sonette an Orpheus* into English

Frédéric Weinmann

Rainer Maria Rilke's treatment of the sonnet form in *Die Sonette an Orpheus* may be compared to the way Rodin quarried Orpheus's figure from the marble in 'Orpheus and the Menades', sculpted in the years Rilke was working as his secretary. This set of fifty-five poems, composed out of an unexpected moment of inspiration, was soon to be received all over Europe as a milestone in post-Romantic poetry and thought. Rilke had written a few sonnets in his early years, but his interest in this canonical form really appears in the *Neue Gedichte*, especially those written in July 1906, and in his transposition of Elizabeth Barrett Browning's *Sonnets from the Portuguese* begun in the same month (Kellenter 41–44). The particular poetics of *Die Sonette an Orpheus* results partly from a long-lasting experimentation with this form, either through original composition or translations into German of sonnets of Petrarch, Louise Labé, Michelangelo, Stéphane Mallarmé, Xavier de Magollon and Paul Valéry (Kellenter 19). This chapter aims to compare the many recent English translations of this sequence by focusing on a few essential aspects of Rilke's poetics. After surveying a spectrum of traditional and recent translations in the English language, taking into account their sometimes experimental nature, I examine how translators approach Rilke's use of the sonnet form (particularly rhythm and rhyme), as well as Rilke's neologisms and the musicality of his verse, especially the many echoes and repetitions.

A short history of *Die Sonette an Orpheus* in translation

Despite Rilke's renown in the world of letters, it was not until 1936 that *Die Sonette an Orpheus* – written in 1922 and published in 1923 – was first translated into English by James Blair Leishman. This initiative by the

London publisher Hogarth was soon followed by a similar undertaking in America and Mary Dows Herter, who in 1924 together with her husband William Warder Norton founded the eponymous publishing company, was able to produce her own version of the sonnet sequence in 1942.

Apart from these two somewhat official and often reprinted translations of *Die Sonette an Orpheus*, some concurrent publications saw the light before the copyright period ended in 1976. Some of these seem to have been almost private productions, first of all the translation by the British poet of Latvian origin Ruth Speirs, printed during her exile in Cairo by the Anglo-Egyptian Bookshop in 1942. A few years later, Eudo Colecestra Mason, a professor of German at Edinburgh University, published five sonnets 'freely rendered into English' 'by kind permission of Herr Anton Kippenberge [sic]' (Rilke 1948, 286). The openly anti-Semitic manager of Insel, Anton Kippenberg (Wilson 22), was obviously very open-minded towards foreign rights. In a letter to Hogarth dated 21 December 1934, two years before the publication of Leishman's translation of *Die Sonette an Orpheus*, he wrote:

> As you may know, we have no material interest whatsoever in the assignment of foreign rights to works by the poet Rainer Maria Rilke; we represent Rilke's heirs in this issue on a purely voluntary basis. The only thing that matters to us is that Rilke's work, as far as it becomes known abroad by virtue of translations, should keep being perceived always better and in a more perfect manner. Thus, the meaning of our letter and our reservation was only that we want to keep the way clear for some later master translation of Rilke's works, which is always within the realm of possibility, and must therefore abstain from granting foreign rights for a longer term. Of course, we have never thought of granting such rights for one and the same work to several publishers simultaneously. (my translation)[1]

Kippenberg was not quite honest on that point, or at least he was to change his mind, as is shown by the example of the French market, where the German Occupation during the Second World War opened up unexpected propaganda opportunities (Tautou 56–59) and no fewer than four translations of *Die Sonette an Orpheus* (by Angelloz, Bellivier, Betz and Ducellier) were published between 1942 and 1945. Three decades later, the expiration of W. W. Norton's copyright around 1975 resulted in a spate of American translations beginning with Alfred A. Poulin's version by Houghton Mifflin (Bauschinger and Cocalis 113). Though Rilke's work entered the public domain around the same time, there seem to have been no retranslations of *Die Sonette an Orpheus* in the UK until the first decade of this century.

Leaving aside the German Kippenberg's darker motives for wanting to see Rilke translated into other European languages, it is clear from the recent output that his desire for 'better and [...] more perfect' translation of Rilke is now being shared by many publishers in the English-speaking world. No fewer than eighteen translations of *Die Sonette an Orpheus* or of large parts of the sequence have been published since 2000, not to mention the translation of some selected sonnets by Estill Pollock or Mark Burrows, for instance. Natalia Voronevskaya identifies three different periods in her 'brief history of English translations of Rilke's *Sonnets to Orpheus*', explaining that the 'new wave of interest [in] Rilke between 1975 and 1977' owes much to the poet's 100th anniversary 'encourag[ing] many translators to produce new versions of one of his most prominent late works', but she does not explain the reason for the third wave 'at the end of the 20th and the beginning of the 21st centuries' (325–326). One can assume these projects to be as different as the translators themselves, especially since a kind of competition may prevail: the overwhelming majority (ten) are American and five are British, but there is also one Canadian translator and even one Frenchman – two of the translators (Stephen Cohn and Christiane Marks), being born in Germany, are properly bilingual. Yet almost all of them are academics or poets, sometimes both. From a cursory look at their prefaces, we can see that most of these translators wish to reproduce 'as many as possible of the formal features of the original' (Rilke 2005b, 21) or 'to replicate as much as possible the raw and original tone of Rilke's sonnets' (Rilke 2015b, 4).

Dissenting voices are few, apart from the sculptor and painter Stephen Cohn, who was born in Frankfurt-am-Main in 1931 and actually belongs to an older generation. Anita Barrows, Joanna Macy and David Cook all translate in the tradition of 'versioning': Cook writes in his preface that he hopes to have 'communicated some of [his] feeling of wonder and delight' and aims to 'provide an accessible and idiomatic English version' (Rilke 2012a, 6), whilst Barrows and Macy explain the necessity of omissions by the fact that some post-Romantic sentimental and overblown 'passages in Rilke risk diluting the effect of the whole and distracting today's readers, accustomed as they may be to a more concise poetic diction' (Rilke 2005a, 25). In his account of his predecessors' achievements ('On the Translation of *Sonnets to Orpheus*'), a representative of the third generation, Willis Barnstone, describes his own endeavour as an attempt 'to stay close in form, meaning, and voice, and hopefully to some of the austerely musical spirit that marks Alter's prose rendition of Genesis' (Rilke 2004, 95). In other words, he is eager to overcome the dilemma between meaning and spirit he claims to recognize in former translations in order to 'make the literal literary', as Jorges Luis Borges says in his own essay on translation (Rilke 2004, 95).

In an even more adaptive approach, Don Paterson pleads for a personal treatment of the original, even if for completely different reasons (see B. Goursaud's chapter in this volume). Like Robert Lowell in the early 1960s, Paterson rejects the mere translation in favour of imitations that he chooses, against T. S. Eliot's advice to Lowell (see Hahn Matthusen 281), to call 'versions': 'they must have' – he states in the first of his 'Fourteen Notes on the Version' – 'their own course, their own process, and have to make a virtue of their own mistakes; they will have, in other words, their *own* pattern of error and lyric felicity' (Rilke 2006, i). Further along on the spectrum of creative translation, the British conceptual poet and artist Ira Lightman, whose performances are blurbed by George Szirtes as 'Harpo Marx meets Rilke', has created 'a special collage/remix/rewrite' of the Sonette entitled *Rilke's Wellies*. In an interview with Will Barrett, Lightman defines his ambition concerning Rilke as follows:

> I've found the sonnets a revelation. I started reading them last summer, and immediately wanted to try to reproduce some of what they were doing. The mad mystical openness, the outrageous rhymes. I thought, from many English translations, that he was pious, a philosopher. He's much more naughty than that. (Barrett n.p.)

Looking at this great number of publications only confirms Karen Leeder's statement that 'today translation of Rilke has become something of an industry in itself' (190) – one that allows each translator to fulfil his or her own creative project. Using two of the organizing metaphors of *Die Sonette an Orpheus* – mirrors and metamorphosis – this chapter next focuses on places of symmetry and asymmetry in form, before considering areas where the translator's creativity is expected to *transform* the source text – Rilke's sound effects as well as neologisms and idiosyncratic turns of phrase.

Mirror effects: Layout, punctuation, prosody, rhyme

Composed over the course of a few days, *Die Sonette an Orpheus* forms a two-part sequence from a chronological as well as an architectural point of view. The first half was written between 2 and 5 February 1922 (with very few modifications in the following days); the second, written between 15 and 23 February, underwent a more extensive readjustment: II.5 and II.6 were composed first, whereas II.1 was the last (Rilke 1996, 706). This choice reveals Rilke's search for a coherence of the whole: after Orpheus is murdered by the Thracian women in the last poem of the first section, his resurrection in part II begins with the word *Atmen* ('Breathing'), defined in the same line as an 'invisible poem'. In other words, Orpheus, coming back from the dead, enjoys eternal life through lyric. Each translation of the whole sequence respects this overall structure, containing two parts of twenty-six and twenty-nine poems, respectively. Paterson's *Orpheus* even highlights this architecture by means of additional titles (e.g. 'Breath' for II.1), while Barnstone for his part takes the first words of the poems as headlines. Most of these editions being bilingual, the latest translations of the sonnets read as mirror translations, inviting a comparison between the text or at least the form of the original and its reflection in English. In fact, all without exception are written in verse and comprise fourteen lines distributed in two quatrains and two tercets: they look like sonnets at a single glance (except maybe those by Billias, who centres her poems instead of left-aligning them and offers a translation of II.22 condensed into thirteen lines). As Holding notes in the introduction to his 'New Approach to Translating', there is seemingly no other choice:

> when I began to revise the translation systematically with the help of Professor Dennis Mahoney, he suggested that the number of lines per stanza, as well as the number of stanzas, mirror that in the original. The more I thought about this, the more I agreed – if I am to transmit the information and content as closely to Rilke's original poems as possible, surely line and stanza length are integral in this process. (Rilke 2015b, 5)

The symmetry between original and translation is further reinforced by the punctuation, especially in conspicuous examples like a whole line in italics (II.11, 12), use of brackets (II.26, 6–7) or visual caesuras (I.20, 14 and II.11, 8)[2] – only Paterson, true to his definition of what a 'version' should be, systematically distances himself from Rilke's layout. The same applies to the use of ellipses (only Cohn and Barrows / Macy mostly ignore them) and italics (Cohn, Barrows / Macy and Paterson being joined in that case by Cook and – to a lesser extent – Polikoff). The other translators of the *Sonnets* seem to share Marks's opinion about punctuation: 'Preserving this fresh, spoken, quality became another important goal for me, particularly since it helps to reflect the poems' completely unanticipated, surprise arrival' (Rilke 2019b, xiv). Respect for the original form also shows in their treatment of enjambment. As Kellenter found out, the quatrains are sharply cut off from the tercets in forty-one of the original sonnets (75 per cent) and, compared to the *Neue Gedichte*, Rilke makes less frequent use of enjambment: in only sixteen of these sonnets (29 per cent) does a sentence continue into the next stanza, whilst ten of them (18 per cent) contain stanzas which end not with a period, but a comma (Kellenter 80). Nevertheless, the examined translations almost always follow the original pattern in cases of enjambment between two stanzas, whereas they pay less attention to apparently unobtrusive divisions of a noun phrase such as '*aus dem klaren / gelösten Wald*' (I.1, 5–6), '*aus beiden / Reichen*' (I.6, 1–2) or '*das polyphone / Licht*' (II.5, 3–4).

The mirror effect of these transpositions results from the conviction that seems to be shared by most contemporary translators that the content of the original should be mirrored line by line in the translation. Whereas half of them translate in this manner, the others tend to avoid reorganizing the semantic material exceedingly. Even Paterson in his versions follows this current tendency in poetic translation. A progressive slip over four lines and even into the next stanza, as in Billias's transposition of the first quatrain of II.9, is extremely rare. Nevertheless, all of them, from the highly rigorous Marks to the resolutely non-conformist Paterson, have defined translation units of one or two lines.

Mirrors: There's never been true description of what, in your innermostnature, you are.	Mirrors: no one's had the skill to speak about your secret lives.
(Rilke 2019b, II.3, lines 1–2)	(Rilke 2006, II.3, lines 1–2)

However, even strict mirror effects prove difficult to maintain to the end: for instance, to the best of our knowledge, in Sonnet II.3, in fact dedicated to mirrors, no English-language translator has reproduced the diametrical reflection of the very last word (*Narziss*) in the first one (*Spiegel*) or the echo of the '*klaren / gelösten Wald*' of the first sonnet (I.1, 5–6) in the '*klare, gelöste Narziss*' at the end of II.3.

Conversely, what contemporary translators into English either seem to neglect or outwardly reject is the attempt to mirror Rilke's prosody, despite its important part in the modernity of *Die Sonette an Orpheus*, for if 'iambic pentameter definitely dominates' the global history of the sonnet (Kellenter 14), it governs only eight poems of the sequence, whilst eight more consist of trochaic pentameters. The further thirty-nine freely alternate trochees and dactyls (Kellenter 88). The significance of this musical aspect of Rilke's poetry fully reveals itself when we pay attention to the difference between the first and the second parts of the sequence: in the first section, the lines are more compact and regular than in the second one. Only the three last sonnets of the first part comprise lines of five dactyls or even six stresses: 'Here, the influence of the [*Duino*] *Elegies* which has been emerging between both parts of the sequence already makes itself felt; it suggests what is coming' (Kellenter 90, my translation). Because the poet largely reorganized the second part, Kellenter says further, the movement from classical metre towards elegiac verses in the dactyls is finally less obvious than initially, but the change in the rhythmic structure corresponds nonetheless to a change in content:

> In general, all iambic and trochaic sonnets, compared to the dactylic ones, have a calm and explanatory tone which deals with tensions in a more contemplative way. [...] Because the rhythm of many sonnets is interspersed with elegiac elements, not running smoothly but often torn off, it is apt to express stronger emotions and above all antitheses. (Kellenter 91, my translation)

This metrical freedom leads to significant differences in the length of the lines, as the confrontation of I.23 and I.24 in the original best illustrates, but also has an influence on the melody and the meaning of the poems. If Rilke's mastery in this regard still had to be proven, evidence would be found in Sonnet I.5, which consists entirely of iambs except for the third foot of the third line, a trochee, to emphasize the possessive reference to Orpheus: 'Seine Metamorphose'. Cohn – a native German speaker – mentions this point in his introduction:

> Rilke's rhythms support the content as well as carrying the sheer sound and movement of his poetry; nowhere more so than in the *Sonnets to Orpheus*. Part of the *Auftrag* of translation here might be to make lines that move in a manner that respects Rilke's own pace and ear. (Rilke 2000, 9)

Note however the slight rhythmical variation in the otherwise regular Sonnet I.8, composed in trochaic pentameters: 'Triumph *knows*. Yearning soon surrenders. Only [...]' (I.8, 9), equivalent to 'Jubel *weiß* und Sehnsucht ist geständig'.

Claude Neuman, who set out to publish a trilingual edition of the sequence, insists even more on the importance of metrics and gives a detailed account of his conception: 'The rhythm of each Sonnet (as heard by the translator) is noted at the bottom of the page presenting the German text, stanza by stanza' (Rilke 2017, 22). In his version, 'Longing avows, if jubilation *knows*' (Rilke 2017, I.8, 9). The bilingual translator Marks also tackles this issue explicitly and is probably the one who comes closest to this objective:

> at a time when some readers have become less conscious of the possibilities of the meter, consider it dated, I have chosen to duplicate

> the original meter. The meter is integral to these thoroughly modern poems – a part of their 'message' – and Rilke's natural way of composing. (Rilke 2019b, xvii)

Apart from the technical difficulty, the distance to which the original metre is taken in the newest translations arises from the widespread suspicion expressed by Crucefix referring to Charles Tomlinson's example: 'The aim of these translations has been to preserve not the metre, but the movement of each poem' (Rilke 2012b, 11). Today's English-speaking translators patently refuse the metrical constraint. Barnstone, for instance, considers this to be characteristic of earlier translations:

> Both the Leishman and the MacIntyre are formalist versions, keeping the sonnet prosody in English. […] When they fail, they have most often resorted to archaic speech, alien to Rilke's modernity, and sometimes they fall into a forced metronymic evenness, also alien to Rilke. (Rilke 2004, 92)

Yet Holding writes a decade later about Barnstone himself:

> He attempts to replicate the general meter and rhyme scheme of the poems, which helps explain why the translations lacked Rilke's tone, and in certain places even seemed horribly contrived. (Rilke 2015b, 4)

Whether it is right or wrong, this opinion might point to an overall trend in the translation of (German) poetry into English in the early twenty-first century. There is a real fear of seeming formalistic by coercing the lines into a regular pattern – even when the poet himself did so – and the reader may therefore miss the contrast between extremely regular (or classical) lines and wilfully anarchistic ones, which is after all one of the main features of *Die Sonette an Orpheus*.

Lastly, this statement has to a certain extent also applied to rhyme. In Rilke, rhyme matters indeed, because according to Kellenter his choice of 'the densest, the most closed' lyrical form is largely due to an 'inner need to tame' his feelings and thoughts (45). But instead of demonstrating his talent by always complying with the same rhyme scheme as poets in ancient times, he exhibits the technical range of his instrument by varying the combinations at will, especially in the tercets: eighteen follow the pattern EFE/GFG, thirteen EFG/EFG, ten EEF/GGF, three EFE/FGG and eleven more unusual ones such as EEF/GFG, EFF/EGG, EFF/GEG, EFF/GGE or even CDC/EED and EFF/EFE (Kellenter 85). Besides, a similar creativity distinguishes the treatment of feminine and masculine rhymes. In ten of the sixteen transpositions examined, the interpreters have nevertheless disregarded rhyme, or considered themselves not in a position to meet the challenge of writing a rhymed translation. Only a few of them try, and sometimes prove that it is possible, even though they often use unsophisticated rhymes and never, strictly speaking, attempt to emulate Rilke's subtle combinations.

Orphic metamorphosis?

The shift of attention away from form results from other priorities set by translators. Nancy Billias for one, in her long and rich introduction to her translation *Orphic Listening: Rilke's Sonnets to Orpheus*, explains that translation – especially of poetry – is not a matter of mechanical transposition of a form or even music, but an attempt at hearing the breath of the poem. She writes:

> Now the poem is not a face, but a breath which sustains me, a current on which I am carried deeper into the poem's essence. In this breath I begin to understand the concept of *Weltinnenraum*, the notion of infinite interior space which was so important to Rilke as he moved towards writing the *Sonnets*. [...] I cannot name the breath which blows in and through the poem: is it 'a divine afflatus' or merely the sighing of wind through emptiness? In either case, as I continue to breathe the poem's rhythm, the poignancy of the link almost overwhelms me. (Rilke 2013, xxiii)

Polikoff, for his part, summarizes his strategy at the end of his introduction as follows:

> In these respects, too, I have sought not mechanically to reproduce the poetic effects of Rilke's German, but to write poetry that – insofar as such is possible – reincarnates the quality of his art in the English language. I have striven, that is, to accomplish what I hold to be the true (and truly Orphic) end of the art of translation: namely, to effect a *metamorphosis* that preserves the spirit of the original even if it transforms its linguistic body; a version that achieves – not mimetic representation of Rilke's words – but rather something akin to a transubstantiation of the soul of the *Sonnets*. (2015c, 19)

In this quasi-mystical definition of translation, one recognizes the author of *In the Image of Orpheus: Rilke, A Soul History*, linking Orpheus to the notion of metamorphosis in Rilke, whose conception of the mythical singer with the lyre echoes Books 10 and 11 of Ovid's *Metamorphoses*. For Rilke, Orpheus is a god who lives on after his death in the movement and breath of nature. In that sense, death does not mean an end, but a new beginning: 'all that's perfected returns / home to Beginnings' (Rilke 2019b, I.19), he writes in one of his sonnets. The cycle of the seasons, the water in the fountain, the dancer's spinning, the ring of the bell from the belfry and the reflection in the mirror are all manifestations of the eternal return to which the sequence is devoted. Rilke only once uses the word *Metamorphose*, already mentioned above, but repeatedly uses the Germanic root *wandeln*, which means both 'to change' and 'to stroll' and derives from *wenden* (to turn) or *winden* (to wriggle or writhe) – both of course related to the English verbs 'to wind' and 'to wander'. There is *der Wandel* (I.19, 5), *wandeln* (I.19, 1; II.4, 3; II.12, 14 in the sense of changing, I.10, 4 in the sense of erring), *die Wandlung* (I.1, 4; I.12, 1), *verwandeln* (I.12, 13; II.12, 13), *die Verwandlung* (II.12, 2; II.29, 6), *wenden* (II.12, 4) and *die Wendung* (I.11, 7). Rilke's knowledge of the German language is so thorough that he manages to reactivate the etymology of the word *Wand* (the wall) – which results from *winden* because walls were once made out of plaited branches – by combining the rarer form *Wandung* with the substantive *Wendung* so as to describe the spinning of the dead young dancer to whom the sonnets are dedicated. In the expression '*Wandung der eigenen Wendung*' (II.18, 14) culminates the near-homophonic phenomenon already visible in Sonnet II.12, which opens with the order '*Wolle die Wandlung*', and in which the conspicuous repetition of the sound [v], especially at the beginnings of words, conveys the idea of mutation.

Reproducing such echoes or even trying to re-embody this poetic effect of Rilke's German poses great difficulty. *Wandlung* is quite often translated as 'transformation', but can also be rendered – in one and the same translation – as 'change', 'exchange', 'transfiguration', 'transmutation' or even 'metamorphosis' (although the term *Metamorphose* is also used elsewhere in the *Sonette*, as discussed above). When reading Sonnet II.12, one would even say that most translators have avoided using the same word despite the repetition of *Wandlung* in these fourteen lines, not to mention the alliteration '*Wolle die Wandlung*' that mostly becomes 'Will transformation' (Barnstone, Good, Kline, Polikoff, Snow) or 'Seek (the) transformation' (Crucefix, Paterson), alongside 'Desire the transformation' (Holding), 'Seek renewal' (Cook), 'Want the change' (Barrow/Macy), 'Will metamorphosis' (Polikoff), 'Will to be transformed' (Temple), 'Wish to be transformed' (Neuman) and even 'Long ardently to be transformed' (Billias). Marks is the only one who systematically strives to reproduce Rilke's alliterations. She writes here 'Trust transformation', just as she says four lines later 'its pivoting point' for '*den wendenden Punkt*' (I.12, 4) or elsewhere 'beginning, beckoning, and transformations' for '*neuer Anfang, Wink und Wandlung*' (I.1, 4), 'Trail and turning' for '*Weg und Wendung*' (I.11, 7) and the 'wall of your own winding turn' for '*Wandung der eigenen Wendung*' (II.18, 14). Certainly, the [v]-echoes on the scale of the sequence are lost, but there is at least an attention to phonetic effects that elsewhere can only be found in the French Neuman. The three-fold alliteration and the polysemic meaning of the noun phrase '*ein wandelndes Lied*' (I.10, 4) are not easily rendered in English, and the solutions proposed are the following: 'a wandering song' (Barnstone, Good, Polikoff) or 'meandering song' (Billias, Holding, Marks, Snow). Other isolated solutions include 'ambling song' (Jennings), 'journeying song' (Cohn), 'shifting song' (Crucefix), 'travelling as a song' (Temple) or even 'wand'ring choruses' (Neuman) and 'half-remembered songs' (Paterson). In translating this line, all translators have had trouble integrating the meaning of 'transformation' given to the verb *wandeln* in the sonnet sequence. The mutation of Rilke's song therefore remains quite a cautious one.

In that regard, another point needs to finally be addressed: Rilke's lexical creativity. One of the main features of Rilke's poetry is the way he invents new words in German. It is sometimes difficult to differentiate real neologisms from rare or older words, but at least ten words in the sequence prove to be absolutely Rilkean. They sometimes result in interesting translations but translators often choose established phrases: 'achievers' (Cohn) for *Vermöger* (I.25, 7), 'the biddable hours' (Cohn) for *rufbare Stunden* (II.6, 14), 'gatelike open' (Snow) for *thorig offen* (II.9, 7), 'marking with their marrows' (Jennings and Holding) for *durchmärken* (I.14, 8), 'resonator' (Holding) for *Ertöner* (I.26, 1) and 'soot-framed' (Marks) for *umrusst* (II.2, 9) are examples of imaginative translations. For the rest, the adjective *mädchenhändig* (I.8, 10) is usually rendered as a noun phrase ('her girlish hands') and *Ruhewink* (II.5, 8) by means of a glossing-over like 'the sunset's call' (Good, Snow) or simply 'the call' (Paterson), 'the falling sun about to come' (Barnstone) or 'the hushing gesture' (Billias) – to quote just a few equivalents – while the striking adjectives *unabgeschmackt* (II.25, 4) and *weitzurückgeschnellt* (II.5, 9) usually result in standard terms such as 'unspoiled' or 'untasted' for the former, and 'outstretched', 'rippling', 'unfurled' or 'widely open' for the latter. This list allows several observations: all translators of *Die Sonette an Orpheus* into English in the early twenty-first century encounter the same difficulties and offer more or less similar alternatives, but often overlook the resonances within the sonnet sequence and hesitate before going against common usage.

Moreover, there is also a series of words that are not properly speaking neologisms, but are rare words, not listed in the definitive German dictionary (*Duden*) but in the *Digitales Wörterbuch der Deutschen Sprache* (DWDS), either by integrating information from older dictionaries like the brothers Grimm's German dictionary or by generating articles out of electronic resources. Some of them are easy to translate into English and therefore vanish as poetic effects: *frühen* (I.8, 6) is almost always rendered as 'to dawn', while *sternisch* (I.11, 12) generally becomes 'starry' and thus loses its actual signification, explained in the Grimms' dictionary where it reads: 'only used in the fields of divination, mysticism and astrology' (vol. X, II, column 2499, line 19, quoted after DWDS, my translation). On the other hand, most translators avoid the substantive *Unbetretbarkeit* (II.3, 8), rather well translated as 'impenetrability' (Barnstone, Marks) but probably too prosaic to their minds, even if they thereby lose the coherence of the parallel between mirrors and deep, dark forests. A fair number of them are also apprehensive about using a word such as 'the darer' to translate *der Wager* (II.24, 2), and Billias is the only one to risk the substantive 'ballaster' for *Beschwerer* (II.14, 5), mostly rendered through a verb (to burden), an adjective ('heavy'), an apposition ('weighed down') or a comparison ('like weights'). Only Kline thinks of the verb *beschweren* and writes 'complaining' (II.14, 5), and obviously no one has realized that the word *Beschwerer* – which only exists in standard German as part of the compound *Briefbeschwerer*, i.e. paperweight – is an orthographic variant of *Beschwörer*, 'exorcist', as it reads in the Grimms' dictionary. Overall, it might seem that Rilke's translators are relatively more attentive to the logical and linguistic correctness of their translations than to the musical and metaphorical dimension of the poems.

To conclude in an Orphic way, I would like to turn back to origins and show in chronological order the way translators transmute the first line of the first sonnet: '*Da stieg ein Baum. O reine Übersteigung!*' (I.1, 1). *Übersteigung*, a rare substantive typical of Rilke's love for abstract words and realities, echoes the growth of the imaginary tree through Orpheus's singing and, because of the prefix *über*, makes up a kind of superlative of *stieg*. Rilke describes the way the music of the divine singer gives birth to a fictive, holy forest, and the animals stop making noise in order to listen to his song. The exclamation is part of an admiring direct speech that may be the last words of living creatures before they fall silent, since the second line is in the present tense ('*O Orpheus singt!*') whereas the description of the wonderful metamorphosis is in the past tense. As Holding explains:

> It conveys transcendence, but also alludes to the rising of the tree, as well as the sap within it. While *transcendence* serves to provide the

abstract meaning of the word in this context, it does not have the concrete semanticity of the original. *Surmounting*, however, has both a concrete and abstract semantic meaning, and is therefore a more accurate translation. This complexity is the crux of the collection and is warranted in every line. (Rilke 2015b, 3)

I hope that the above gloss, combined with the following array of English translations and transformations, appropriately recaptures the way Rilke's intellectual and sensual poetics is reshaped in translation.

> A tree climbed there. O pure arising! (Kline)
> A tree rose up – O apogee of rising! (Cohn)
> A tree sprang into life. O clear transcendence! (Barnstone)
> A tree rose up. O pure transcendence! (Good)
> A tree arose. O pure transcendence! (Snow)
> A tree rose there. A pure arising. (Barrows/Macy)
> A tree rose from the earth. A pure transcendence – (Paterson)
> There the tree rises. Oh pure surpassing! (Temple)
> A tree sprang up! O pure and lofty yearning! (Cook)
> There upped a tree. O absolute outstripping! (Crucefix)
> A tree arising. There. (What pure excess!) (Billias)
> There rose a tree. Oh pure excess! (Jennings)
> There grew a tree. A pure surmounting! (Holding)
> A tree rose up. O pure transcendence! (Polikoff)
> There a tree ascended. A pure transcendence! (Neuman)
> There, see – a tree ascended. Pure transcendence! (Marks)

Notes

1   'Wie Sie vielleicht wissen, haben wir an der Vergebung der fremdsprachigen Rechte an Werken des Dichters Rainer Maria Rilke keinerlei materielles Interesse, sondern wir vertreten in dieser Hinsicht nur rein ehrenamtlich die Rilkeschen Erben. Uns liegt nur daran, dass das Werk Rilkes, soweit es im Ausland durch Uebersetzungen bekannt wird, immer besser und vollkommener wahrgenommen wird. Der Sinn unseres Schreibens und unseres Vorbehaltes war also nur der, dass wir für eine, immer im Bereich der Möglichkeit liegende, etwaige spätere Meisterübersetzung der Rilkeschen Werke den Weg freihalten wollen und daher von der Vergebung der rechte auf längere Zeit absehen müssen. An eine gleichzeitige Vergebung von Rechten an ein und demselben Werk haben wir natürlich von vornherein nie gedacht.'

I kindly thank Dr. Caroline Jessen, scientific director of the research project 'Transatlantlantischer Bücherverkehr' at the Deutsches Literaturarchiv in Marbach, for the most valuable piece of information with the reference number SUA:Insel-Verlag/Autoren/Rilke.
2   The unusual distortion of the overall shape in Temple's translation of II.11 is for sure an involuntary mistake, the new line after the caesura in the middle of line 8 causing an incredible mess in the following tercets, in which he moreover reads '*Traum*' instead of '*Trauern*'.

Works cited

Barrett, Will. 'Meet the Digital Poet in Residence: Ira Lightmann'. *Poetry School*, 2015. https://poetryschool.com/interviews/meet-digital-poet-residence-ira-lightman. Accessed 15 February 2021.

Bauschinger, Sigrid and Susan L. Cocalis. *Rilke-Rezeption/Rilke Reconsidered*. Francke, 1995.

Hahn Matthusen, Heather. 'Rainer Maria Rilke und Robert Lowell. Die Differenz des Übersetzens'. *Rilke und die Weltliteratur*. Edited by Manfred Engel and Dieter Lamping. Artemis & Winkler, 1999, pp. 281–298.

Kellenter, Sigrid. *Das Sonett bei Rilke*. Peter Lang. 1982.

Leeder, Karen. 'Rilke's Legacy in the English-Speaking World'. *The Cambridge Companion to Rilke*. Edited by Karen Leeder and Robert Vilain. Cambridge University Press, 2010, pp. 189–205.

Mason, Eudo C. *Rilke, Europe, and the English-Speaking World*. Cambridge University Press, 1961.

Prince, D. A. 'The Missing Voice' (Review of *Rilke's Wellies* by Ira Lightman). *HappenStance*. Sphinx: Press, 2019. https://www.sphinxreview.co.uk/index.php/1028-ira-lightman-rilke-s-wellies. Accessed 15 February 2021.

Rilke, Rainer Maria. *Fifty Selected Poems, with English Translations by C. F. MacIntyre*. University of California Press, 1940.

Rilke, Rainer Maria. *Five of Rilke's Sonnets to Orpheus Freely Rendered into English*. Translated by Eudo C. Mason. *German Life and Letters*, July 1948: pp. 286–287.

Rilke, Rainer Maria. *Gedichte 1910 bis 1926, hrsg. von Manfred Engel und Ulrich Fülleborn*. Insel (Kommentierte Ausgabe Bd 2), 1996.

Rilke, Rainer Maria. *Sonnets to Orpheus with Letters to a Young Poet*. Translated by Stephen Cohn. Carcanet, 2000.

Rilke, Rainer Maria. *The Poetry of Rainer Maria Rilke*. Translated by Anthony S. Kline. CreateSpace (Poetry in Translation), 2001 [only 15 sonnets].

Rilke, Rainer Maria. *Sonnets to Orpheus*. Translated by Willis Barnstone. Shambhala, 2004.

Rilke, Rainer Maria. *In Praise of Mortality: Selections from Rainer Maria Rilke's Duino Elegies and Sonnets to Orpheus*. Translated by Anita Barrows and Joanna Macy. Riverhead Books, 2005a [only 35 sonnets].

Rilke, Rainer Maria. *Rilke's Late Poetry: Duino Elegies, the Sonnets to Orpheus and Selected Last Poems*. Translated by Graham Good. Ronsdale Press, 2005b.

Rilke, Rainer Maria. *The Sonnets to Orpheus*. Translated by Edward Snow. North Point Press, 2005c.

Rilke, Rainer Maria. *Orpheus: A Version of Rilke's Sonette an Orpheus*. Translated by Don Paterson. Faber & Faber, 2006.

Rilke, Rainer Maria. *Sonnets to Orpheus. A New English Version with a Philosophical Introduction*. Translated by Rick Anthony Furtak. USP, 2008.

Rilke, Rainer Maria. *The Sonnets to Orpheus*. Translated by Robert Temple. Robert Temple Website, 2010.

Rilke, Rainer Maria. *The Sonnets to Orpheus*. Translated by David Cook. Redcliff, 2012a.

Rilke, Rainer Maria. *Sonnets to Orpheus*. Translated by Martyn Crucefix. Enitharmon Press, 2012b.

Rilke, Rainer Maria. *Orphic Listening, Rilke's Sonnets to Orpheus*. Translated by Nancy Billias. Fisher, 2013.

Rilke, Rainer Maria. *The Rilke of Ruth Speirs. New Poems, Duino Elegies, Sonnets to Orpheus & Others*. Edited by John Pilling and Peter Robinson. Two Rivers Press, 2015d.

Rilke, Rainer Maria. *Sonnets to Orpheus*. Translated by Daniel Joseph Polikoff. Angelico Press, 2015c.

Rilke, Rainer Maria. *The Sonnets to Orpheus* I. Translated by Joshua Jennings. ShortWorks (Poetry Issue), 2015a [only the first part, i.e. 26 sonnets].

Rilke, Rainer Maria. *'That Which Cannot Be Said': A New Approach to Translating Rilke's Sonnets to Orpheus*. Translated by Aidan C. Holding. University of Vermont College of Arts and Sciences College Honors Theses 8, 2015b.

Rilke, Rainer Maria. *Les Sonnets à Orphée. The Sonnets to Orpheus. Deutsch – Français – English*. Translated by Claude Neuman. Ressouvenances (Polychrome 18), 2017.

Rilke, Rainer Maria. *The Sonnets to Orpheus*. Translated by Ira Lightman. Amazon (Kindle), 2019a.

Rilke, Rainer Maria. *Sonnets to Orpheus*, translated by Christiane Marks. Open Letter, 2019b.

Swallow, Allan. 'A Review of Some Current Poetry'. *New Mexico Quarterly*, vol. 16, no. 4, 1946: pp. 491–496.

Tautou, Alexis. 'Traduire et éditer Rainer Maria Rilke sous l'occupation'. *Atlantide* no. 5 (Traducteurs dans l'histoire, traducteurs en guerre), 2016: pp. 43–64.

Voronevskaya, Natalia Viktorovna. 'On the History of English Translations from R. M. Rilke's Poetry'. *Oxford Journal of Scientific Research*, vol. iv, no. 1 (9), January–June 2015: pp. 325–331.

Wilson, W. Daniel. '"Global Mission": The Goethe Society of Weimar in the Third Reich', *Goethe Yearbook*, vol. XXVI, 2019: pp. 19–40.

8

Fernando Pessoa's sonnets – dislocations in form, persona and language

Carlos A. Pittella

Dislocations in form

Fernando Pessoa is the poet-name for a galaxy of 140 different personae, all orbiting the same real-person creator – the modernist Portuguese trilingual poet born in Lisbon in 1888 as Fernando Antonio Nogueira Pessôa. The poet would gradually simplify his signature: first, by omitting its middle elements; then, in 1916, by dropping the circumflex in order to bear a more cosmopolitan last name when publishing certain English poems (Pessoa 1945, 79), surely aware of the etymology of his last name (from the Latin *persōna*, theatre mask). While the author shortened his birth name to 'Fernando Pessoa', which became his *orthonym*,[1] he also published as three other poets with distinct styles – Alberto Caeiro, Álvaro de Campos and Ricardo Reis, known as his *heteronyms*[2] – plus a *semi-heteronym* by the name of Bernardo Soares, the second fictional prose writer of *The Book of Disquiet*.[3] If, during his lifetime, Pessoa was known by five different names appearing in several journals and as the author of the awarded collection *Mensagem*, his posthumous fame yielded a much longer roll call.

After the poet's death in 1935, the *corpus* of orthonym, heteronyms and semi-heteronym grew as unpublished texts were discovered. What's more, over one hundred fictional authors were identified as created by Pessoa, who had recognized, 'Eu sou uma antologia' [*I am an anthology*]. This phrase is the fitting title of a book that carried out the most comprehensive study of Pessoa's *personae* to date (Pessoa 2013c), including biographical notes for 136 fictional authors, plus an extra chapter dedicated to the orthonym: 136+1=137. Since then, the inclusion of one more name has been suggested:[4] 137+1=138. If we consider Pessoa's own signature to represent not one but three voices (an English, a French and a Portuguese),[5] we arrive at 140 personae: 137+3=140.

For a poet who was so many, it seems appropriate that *about* fourteen of his selves would have authored sonnets – one for each line of the traditional form. This 'about' is important, for it is challenging to be precise in the fluid world of Pessoa's characters, who tend to inherit poems from one another. Besides, depending on how we stretch the definition of 'sonnet', more or fewer authors would be considered sonneteers in Pessoa's coterie.

The first attempted census of Pessoa's sonnets was made in 2012 (Pittella 2012, 24). It amassed 282 poems: 104 originally written in English, 177 (or 176.8) in Portuguese, and 1 (or 1.2) in French. The decimals are due to the sonnet 'Tu és o outomno', primarily written in Portuguese while also including segments in French, and even rhyming between those languages:

> Tu és o outomno da paysagem-eu
> E que nevoas em mim o teu perfil!
> O teu voo ao passar por meu anil
> É o rhythmo de um meu ser que se perdeu...
>
> Adejo cego o extase teu subtil
> Com o incorporeo rosto de ser teu.
> Condessa outr'ora, quem? Tardes de ceu
> Sobre Versailles... Abbé, y-a-t'il?
>
> Plus d'autrefois que d'ombre en ton silence?
> (Se tudo isto não for verdadeiro?)
> La Pompadour e o seu criado, France.
>
> Escureceu teu corpo meu em mim
> E que Versailles realmente o cheiro
> Das rosas que não ha no teu jardim!

How does one approach this bilingual sonnet? How does it reverberate across Pessoa's known *corpus*? As with most unsigned poems, it is implicitly attributed to the orthonym; however, the sonnet was drafted in 1914, at a time when Pessoa's heteronyms were just being born. That ongoing multiplication of selves provides a key to interpreting the *self-landscape* ('paysagem-eu') in line 1 of the sonnet, quickly unravelling a web of connections throughout Pessoa's work, as well as with a poem by Ângelo de Lima, another daring sonneteer.

Numbered '1' on the manuscript, 'Tu és o outomno' commences a series of four poems transporting the reader to different places and times. Sonnet 1 takes us to France (2 to the Renaissance, and 3 to Ancient Greece), but the lyrical landscape is interrupted by a voice (in line 10) challenging what is being described: 'Se tudo isto não for verdadeiro?' [*What if all of this is not true?*]. Such an interruption questioning the reality of fiction and/or the fiction of reality is a trope in Pessoa, who would later craft the famous line 'O poeta é um fingidor' [*The poet is a forger*], dated April Fool's Day, 1931 (Pittella and Pizarro 161–162). The crashing descriptive/metalingual landscapes constitute what Pessoa named *intersectionism*, further developed in 'Chuva Oblíqua' in *Orpheu 2*. The first issue of the modernist journal *Orpheu* (1915), featuring Pessoa, Campos and six flesh-and-blood poets, triggered passionate reactions in the press, which called the poets 'insane' and invited the opinion of Dr Egas Moniz, who would win the Nobel in 1949 for inventing the lobotomy! The psychiatrist wanted the orphic group committed to a proper asylum, such as the infamous Rilhafolles Hospital (Pittella and Pizarro 198–202). In response, Pessoa invited his friend Ângelo de Lima – who was at the time actually committed to Rilhafolles – to open *Orpheu 2*; amongst Lima's pieces, there was an anything-but-traditional sonnet that, like Pessoa's Portuguese-and-French poem, also rhymed between languages – in this case Portuguese and Italian.

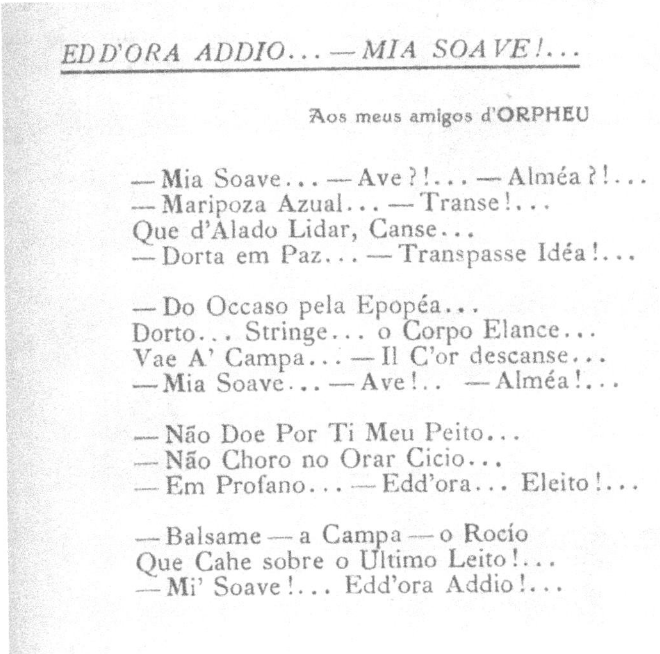

ED D'ORA ADDIO... — MIA SOAVE!...

Aos meus amigos d'ORPHEU

— Mia Soave... — Ave?!... — Alméa?!...
— Maripoza Azual... — Transe!...
Que d'Alado Lidar, Canse...
— Dorta em Paz... — Transpasse Idéa!...

— Do Occaso pela Epopéa...
Dorto... Stringe... o Corpo Elance...
Vae A' Campa... — Il C'or descanse...
— Mia Soave... — Ave!.. — Alméa!...

— Não Doe Por Ti Meu Peito...
— Não Choro no Orar Cicio...
— Em Profano... — Edd'ora... Eleito!...

— Balsame — a Campa — o Rocío
Que Cahe sobre o Ultimo Leito!...
— Mi' Soave!... Edd'ora Addio!...

Figure 8.1 Lima-Orpheu2-15-detail. Biblioteca Nacional de Portugal.

In merely formal terms, both Pessoa's and Lima's poems are Petrarchan sonnets with enclosed rhymes in the quatrains, a fairly common cut in Portuguese literature. Pessoa's piece has the expected decasyllables, while Lima's borrows the shorter lines of popular songs (*redondilha maior*) – already a departure from the sonnet tradition, but far from the most unusual thing about that poem. It is in their mixed languages that these sonnets appear most surprising; and the disparity between traditional form and groundbreaking content makes their transgression ever more striking.

The fourteen-line poem is versatile in Pessoa, in both content and form. The poet not only wrote English sonnets in the Shakespearean mould and Portuguese sonnets in Petrarchan fashion, but also crisscrossed traditions, writing more than thirty *English* Petrarchan sonnets and at least four *Portuguese* Shakespearean sonnets.

The sonnet form allows for a privileged view of Pessoa's poetry, a microcosm through which to study the complexity of the poet's debts to and ruptures with multiple traditions. It offers not only a stable frame to appreciate the diversity of tropes and personae but also an outline for the editor, as it becomes objectively simpler to transcribe Pessoa's handwriting following schematics of metre and rhyme (Ferrari 2012). The specificity of the enclosed rhyme pattern, for example, helps to identify incomplete sonnets. While scanning the hundreds of unpublished English texts in Pessoa's archive, the eye sometimes catches a strophic pattern; regardless of proliferating variants, the series of three quatrains followed by an indented couplet suddenly flags a Shakespearean sonnet:

> Tell me again that story of the Prince, –
> That fairy tale of when I was a child.
> It cannot now sustain me nor convince
> But it can make my sullen soul feel wild.
>
> The improbable is ours because we love.
> Awake in me once more the sleeping tale
> That my old heart its stubborn youth may prove.
> Who knows the Prince may find the Holy Grail.
>
> Tell me again the story. He was bold,
> He fought against bad giants and at last
> That princess cloistered since old age was old
> Was wakened by him and won. This is the past.
>
>   What the blind future holds let us forget,
>   Knowing it or not knowing, we regret.

Fernando Pessoa's Sonnets

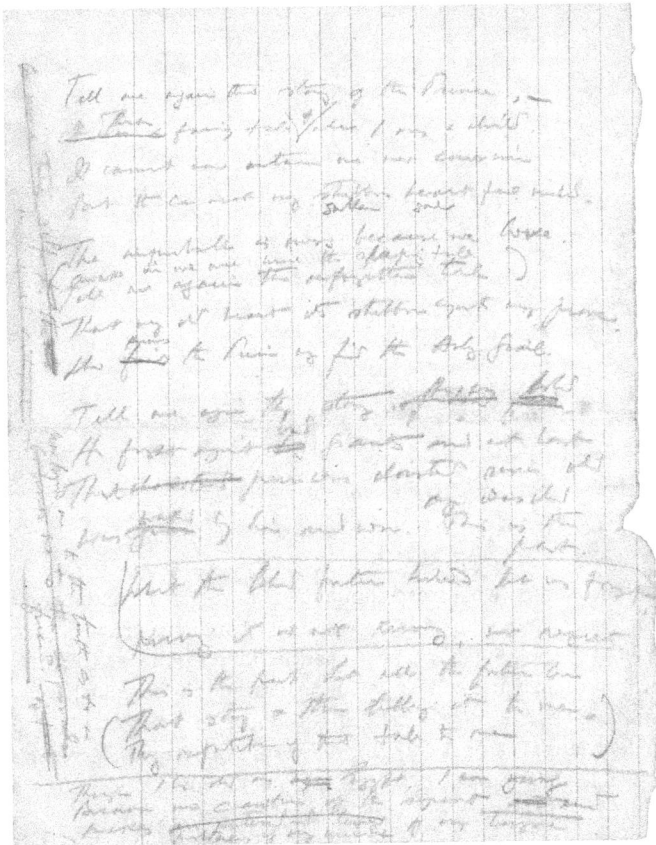

Figure 8.2 BNP-E3-49A7-9v.

Like the three unpublished sonnets at the end of this chapter, 'Tell me again that story of the Prince' was written in 1933. Thus, recent scholarship proves the poet was still creating in English long after the publication of his well-known *35 Sonnets* (one of the four English chapbooks Pessoa self-published between 1918 and 1921). Pessoa's sonnets from 1933 are strikingly simpler – with a much more direct syntax – than the archaizing language used in *35 Sonnets*. Before all of Pessoa's sonnets are edited, it remains dangerous to generalize about a body of work marked by plurality and fragmentation. And even in poems Pessoa saw printed, he did not consider the work complete, as evidenced by emendations made after publication.

Take poem VIII from *35 Sonnets*. One of the copies kept by the poet shows his hesitation around a word on line 8, generating a dilemma for Pessoa's

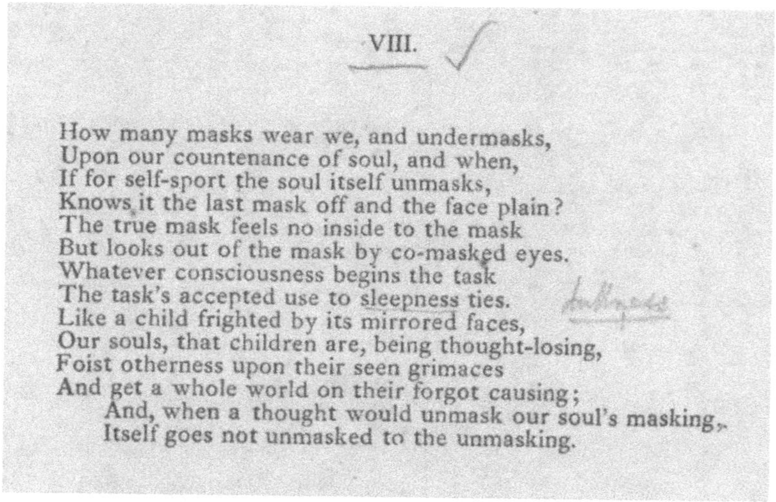

> VIII.
>
> How many masks wear we, and undermasks,
> Upon our countenance of soul, and when,
> If for self-sport the soul itself unmasks,
> Knows it the last mask off and the face plain?
> The true mask feels no inside to the mask
> But looks out of the mask by co-masked eyes.
> Whatever consciousness begins the task
> The task's accepted use to sleepness ties.
> Like a child frighted by its mirrored faces,
> Our souls, that children are, being thought-losing,
> Foist otherness upon their seen grimaces
> And get a whole world on their forgot causing;
>   And, when a thought would unmask our soul's masking,
>   Itself goes not unmasked to the unmasking.

Figure 8.3 BNP-E3-98(1)-2v-detail; cf. Pessoa 1918: [10].

posthumous editors: what word should be featured as the authoritative text and which relegated to the critical apparatus? Should one privilege 'sleepness' as printed in the poet's lifetime, or the handwritten 'dullness'? The marginalia effectively breached the sonnet form, generating editorial instability. João Dionísio, responsible for the critical edition of *35 Sonnets*, opted for the marginal variant (Pessoa 1993, 70), defending the tenet of privileging the last deducible version of a poem (32–33). Yet, by doing so, Dionísio altered a published text, disagreeing with Jorge de Sena, the previous editor of Pessoa's collected English poems. Eventually, Dionísio reconsidered his position (358).

Even if one sees this as editorial bickering, the version finally edited matters, as it becomes a citation, a textbook, a memory – and the multiple editions of a poem end up substantively different. As Pessoa's work is intrinsically incomplete, the ethics of those decisions generate endless controversies and what Pizarro calls *the anxiety of unity* (288), with scholars oftentimes chasing completeness where there is none. And the sonnet in question matters, with its first quatrain constituting a labyrinthine question in which form, content and biography are intricately woven in an *ars poetica*:

> How many masks wear we, and undermasks,
> Upon our countenance of soul, and when,
> If for self-sport the soul itself unmasks,
> Knows it the last mask off and the face plain?

Here we have a Portuguese poet writing in English; a modernist borrowing a Shakespearean form to use its many turns to sing the manifolds of a fragmented ego; a metalingual sonnet about lyrical selves; a poet with dozens of personae meditating under his own name about how many masks one wears…

Dislocations in persona

The first count of Pessoa's 282 sonnets from a total of fourteen personae was not exhaustive: it cautioned that there were unpublished English pieces that could not be transcribed in time to be included (Pittella 2012, 21). Multiple sonnets have been edited since then, growing the *corpus* to 312 pieces.[6] Also, Frederick Wyatt was revealed as the last English persona created by Pessoa (Ferrari and Pittella 2018); and, even though Wyatt's poems were an inheritance from Alexander Search (so no new sonnets to tally), the total of Pessoan *sonneteers* had to be updated as well. Authorship is fluid among Pessoan sonneteers, and Charles Robert Anon loses poems to Alexander Search, who loses poems to Wyatt.

Sometimes, this tangle of authors is mindboggling. Take the *mise en abîme* of Carlos Otto's sonnet 'Sonho de Gorgias' [*Dream of Gorgias*], in which the famous Greek rhetorician recounts a dream – a dream of a persona of a persona!

      Sonhei uma cidade informe e colossal
      Fóra da sensação e idéa de existir
      Á qual nem o amôr saberia sorrir
      Tão extranha ao que nós alcunhamos real.

      □ □ □ □

      □

      Uma figura □ de pedra de cansaço
      Que do conhecido não □ traço.

      O sceptro do Pavôr cahira d'algum braço
      E jaziam ao pé ôcamente partidas
      As estatuas do Sêr, e do Tempo, e do Espaço.

Two unsigned 'sonnets' – with fourteen decasyllables but no end-rhymes – generate attribution questions. Pessoa, under his own name, frequently rhymes in lyrical poems, so a sonnet in blank verse would not fit squarely in to the poetics of the orthonym. The heteronym who regularly uses blank decasyllables, generally but not always alternating them with hexasyllables, is Ricardo Reis; but it is unlikely that Reis, an adherent of classical odes, would espouse a poetic form invented in the thirteenth century. These unrhymed pieces could be intended for verse dramas such as Pessoa's *Fausto*; but multiple dramas, in English and in Portuguese, remain unpublished (Freitas), impeding a thorough assessment of the problem. Hence the conjectural authorship and the unstable sum of Pessoan sonneteers.

One way to approach this fluidity of attribution is to inquire *when* and *why* it happens, leading us to three different circumstances: (1) when a poem is written before attribution or when attribution is external to its genesis; (2) reattribution; and (3) attribution *a priori*.

Regarding the first of these circumstances, between 1905 and 1907, Pessoa penned eight political sonnets in English, four of them completed and four fragmentary, evoking prominent names (Pittella 2018).

At this point one must note the importance of Pessoa's formative years in South Africa between 1896 and 1905 (with an interruption between 1901 and 1902 to visit family in Portugal and the Azores).[7] The writing of these political sonnets began shortly before Pessoa definitively left Durban for Lisbon. While the four incomplete poems were left unsigned, the finished ones were all attributed to Charles Robert Anon (and years later appropriated by Alexander Search).

If the final copy of the curse on Chamberlain is signed by Search, its first draft is unsigned (BNP/E3, 144N-7ʳ), just like 'Kitchener'. The reason some sonnets were attributed in the first place is that Pessoa needed a pseudonym to submit such militant pieces to the *Natal Mercury*, the same journal where Pessoa's 'C. R. Anon' had published a satirical poem in July 1904, scoffing at a translation made by one of his teachers (Jennings 46–47).

Pessoa was aware of the Miltonian tradition of employing the sonnet to address historical figures and events (Ferrari 2015, 7). He retrieved 'Anon' as a punny abbreviation of 'Anonymous' to sign, in July 1905, a letter to the 'Man in the Moon' columnist of the *Natal Mercury*. Identifying himself as an Englishman, Anon confesses to be 'somewhat astonished' by the British journalists who had mocked 'every reverse and disaster of the Russian army' in the Russo-Japanese war (1904–5); asking for 'such publicity as has been extended to writers on the other side', the poet submits a few political sonnets, which are rejected. The attribution to Anon is, thus, incidental, serving the specific purpose of concealing authorship; the

Joseph Chamberlain and Kitchener

Joseph Chamberlain	Kitchener
Their blood on thy head, whom the Afric waste	Oh hireling son of tyranny & hate
Saw struggling, puppets with unwilful hand,	Salaried salesman of distress and death,
Brother and brother: their bought souls shall brand	☐
Thine own with horrors. Be thy name erased	☐
From the full mouth of men; nor be there traced	☐
To thee one glory to thy parent land;	☐
But 'fore us, as 'fore God e'er do thou stand	☐
In that thy deed forevermore disgraced.	☐
Where lie the sons and husbands, where those dear	Hadst thou no mother? Never sawst thou love?
That thy curst craft hath lost? Their drops of blood,	☐
One by one fallen, and many a cadenced tear,	☐
With triple justice weighted trebly dread,	☐ the power ☐ fell
Shall each, rolled onward in a burning flood,	Thou layest faith in ☐
Crush thy dark soul. Their blood be on thy head!	God and revenge and punishment and hell.

poems submitted to the newspaper should thus be studied together with the unattributed political sonnets, with which they form a coherent set (Pittella 2018, 48).

Regarding reattribution, one interesting case is that of Frederick Wyatt, a poet who did not write any poems, having simply inherited, in 1913, a selection of twenty-one pieces (including five sonnets) previously attributed to Search, who had a corpus of over one hundred poems. The selection is judicious, exclusively made of songs and sonnets – just like the *oeuvre* of his namesake, Sir Thomas Wyatt; Pessoa's Wyatt incarnates an effort to create coherence among loose poems (Ferrari and Pittella 2018).

Though one cannot prove the intentions of a poet with rhizomatic projects, attribution seems to have also happened *a priori* – when Pessoa apparently knew in advance who was writing the sonnet, and why. Álvaro de Campos resorts to the sonnet sparingly but always to push its limits – while confessing to push its limits – in metalingual poems. The last poem by Campos (Pessoa 2014a, 326) has that quality in spades, opening with the claim 'Ha quanto tempo não escrevo um soneto' [*So long I haven't written a sonnet*]. But the most remarkable example of Campos stretching the limits of the sonnet is 'Meu coração, o almirante errado' [*My heart, the erroneous admiral*], with this second stanza:

E assim, prolixo, absurdo, postergado,	And thus, prolix, absurd, procrastinated,
Dado ao que nos resulta de se abster,	Given to what results from our abstaining,
Não foi dado, não foi dado, não foi dado	Wasn't given, wasn't given, wasn't given
E o verso errado deixa-o entender.	And, broken, that line leads to understanding.
(Pessoa 2014a, 319)	(my translation)

With heroic decasyllables being regularly stressed on the sixth and tenth syllables, the line repeating 'Não foi dado' (*Wasn't given*) is an outlier, stressing the seventh and eleventh – a transgression that is not only performed but also explained by the sonnet. Campos's heart, that erroneous admiral, creates the paradox of being wrong and right at the same time, and we hesitate: does Campos erupt already performing a caustic sonnet, or does irony beg Campos to undersign it? Either way, persona and poem seem interdependent. After 1914, Campos is the only one Pessoa invokes besides himself to regularly write sonnets, with the clear agenda to make fun of the form through the form.

Dislocations in language

The boundaries between inspiration and imitation are not always clear, and the current ethics of citation evolved over time. If, nowadays, an intertextual relationship may be pointed out by an 'après/after...' note or by quotation marks to flag borrowed lines, that was not the case when Luís de Camões (1524–80) wrote his sonnets in intertextuality with the work of Francesco Petrarca (1304–74).

One of the most famous sonnets in the Portuguese language, uncontentiously attributed to Camões, begins as a clear translation of a Petrarchan sonnet:

Alma minha gentil, que te partiste	Quest' anima gentil, che si diparte,
Tão cedo desta vida descontente,	Anzi tempo chiamata a l'altra vita,
Repousa lá no ceo eternamente,	Se lassuso è, quanto esser dê, gradita,
E viva eu cá na terra sempre triste;	Terrà del ciel la piú beata parte.
(Camões son. 19)[8]	(Petrarca 49)

By juxtaposing the first quatrain of each sonnet, one reads how Camões distances himself from his model after translating the first two Italian lines (likely through an intermediary Spanish translation).[9] As of the second stanza, Petrarca remains meditating on the ethereal locations of the departed soul, whereas Camões's gaze turns to himself on Earth and to his overwhelming loss. Reading the final tercets side by side, their divergence is vivid:

Roga a Deos que teus annos encurtou,	Nel quinto giro non abitrebbe ella;
Que tão cedo de cá me leve a verte,	Ma, se vola piú alto, assai mi fido
Quão cedo de meus olhos te levou.	Che con Giove sia vinta ogni altra stella.
(Camões son. 19)	(Petrarca 50)

Is this mere coincidence? Could Camões have once read Petrarca's lines and then forgotten their source, only to write a sonnet using them as a subconscious topic for a gloss? But this was not a one-off incident, as multiple Camonean sonnets either begin or conclude with lines borrowed from Petrarca.[10] Yet, the innovative craft of Camões is indisputable: even when appropriating lines, the result is more than a translation. Dislocating the inspiration into new cultural territory, the Platonism of Petrarca becomes earthbound in Camões (Lourenço).

One can imagine Camões's initial inspiration to translate Petrarca turning into a challenge, into a competitive urge to respond with 'a calculated re-writing' – to use George Monteiro's words in his comparative study of English renderings of 'Alma minha gentil' (Monteiro 1996, 133). Amid the translations, there is one by Pessoa, who established several such competitive intertextual relationships with authors both dead and alive, and in different languages.

If Camões had a complex intertextual relationship with Petrarca, Pessoa established layers upon layers of intertextuality with Camões – from announcing in 1912 the advent of a 'Supra-Camões' who would lead a renaissance in Portuguese poetry to the publication of *Mensagem* in 1934, a book that, among many things, is a retelling of Portuguese navigations that forms a dialogue with *The Lusiads* and a project that began as early as 1910 as a confessed imitation of Camões (Barbosa et al. 79).

In purple ink on a loose piece of paper, Pessoa typed his English rendering of 'Alma minha gentil' around 1912.[11] The translation works through metre and rhyme, following Pessoa's philosophy of translating rhythmically in accordance with the original (Saraiva 46–47; Bothe). Note how Pessoa takes pains to recreate the '-ente' end-rhymes as '-ent' in English, though all publications of this translation incorrectly published Pessoa's 'blent' as 'blest'.[12]

> Oh gentle spirit mine that didst depart,
> So early of this life in discontent,
> With heavenly bliss thy rest be ever blent
> While I on earth play wakeful my sad part.
>
> If in the ethereal seat where now thou art
> A memory of this life they do consent,
> Forget not that great love self-eloquent
> Whose purity mine eyes here showed thy heart.
>
> And, if thou see aught worthy of thy light
> In the great darkness that hath come on me
> From thine irreparable loss's spite,
>
> Pray God, that made thy years so short to be,
> As soon to haste me to thy deathless sight
> As from my mortal sight he hasted thee.

In evaluating this translation, Monteiro invokes a note by Pessoa's Campos (Monteiro 1996, 135), attacking Camões's sonnet as derivative, still a translation of Petrarca's – if not of his words, of his poetic form – and too conformist to venture outside the limits of the sonnet:

> Camões laments the loss of his gentle soul; but finally the one who laments is Petrarch. Had Camões felt this emotion sincerely, he would have found a new form, new words – least of all the sonnet with its ten-syllable line. But no; he employed the decasyllabic sonnet even as during his life he might have worn black to show mourning. (Álvaro de Campos, trans. Monteiro)

Fernando Pessoa's Sonnets   143

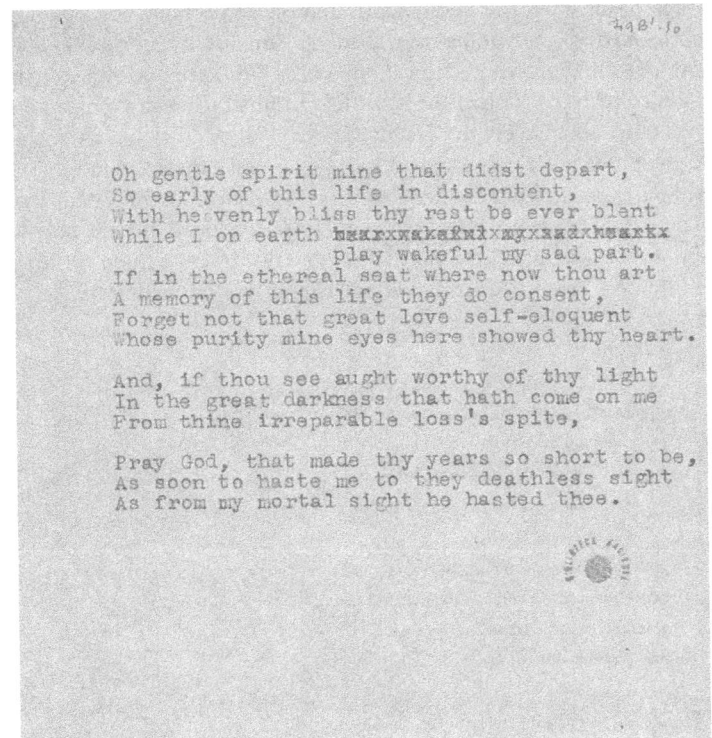

Figure 8.4 BNP-E3-49B1-10r.

What Campos accused Camões of doing was also done by Pessoa himself, long before Campos existed – and it is a phenomenon at the very root of Pessoa's sonnet as a process of dislocations in form, persona and language. In 1902, barely fourteen years old, Pessoa left a note on an otherwise blank page of his notebook titled 'Sonetos | Lendas | etc.' [*Sonnets | Legends | etc.*] (Fig. 8.5).

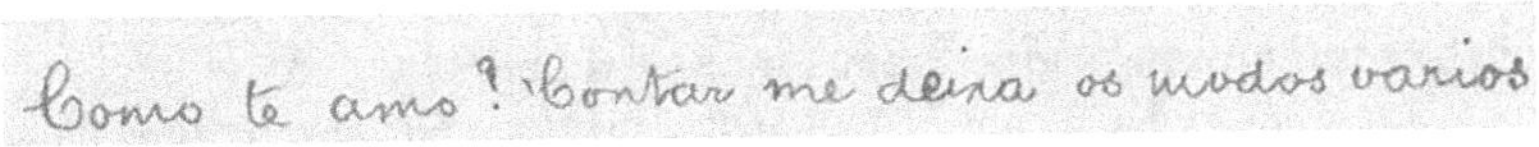

Figure 8.5 BNP-E3-153-18r-detail.

Three pages after, the line (slightly modified) becomes the opening of an unfinished sonnet under the heading 'Sonetos d'Amor (~~de Eduardo Lança~~)' – with the cryptic dedication 'A xxx' (*To* xxx) and the Roman 'I' signalling a planned series. This is the first original piece not crossed out in Pessoa's notebook. Except the first line is not at all original, but a translation of the incipit of a celebrated sonnet – 'How do I love thee? Let me count the ways', Sonnet XLIII from *Sonnets from the Portuguese*, by Elizabeth Barrett Browning (1850). With only two quatrains developed in the notebook, Pessoa's sonnet would be completed in a loose document written c. 1907 (but dated '1902') – now titled 'Antígona' and signed by Pessoa himself.

Antígona

> Como te amo? Não sei de quantos modos varios
> Eu te adoro, mulher de olhos azues e castos;
> Amo-te co' o fervor dos meus sentidos gastos;
> Amo-te co' o fervor dos meus preitos diarios.
>
> É puro o meu amor, como os puros sacrarios;
> É nobre o meu amor, como os mais nobres fastos;
> É grande como os mar's altisonos e vastos;
> É suave como o odor de lyrios solitarios.
>
> Amor que rompe enfim os laços crús do Ser;
> Um tão singelo amor, que augmenta na ventura;
> Um amor tão leal que augmenta no soffrer;
>
> Amor de tal feição que se na vida escura
> É tão grande e nas mais vis ansias do viver,
> Muito maior será na paz da sepultura!

When the poem was first published in its notebook version, there was no mention of the first line being a translation (Blanco 34–35); nor when the complete version appeared (Lourenço and Oliveira 86; Lopes 1990b, 166–168). The first one to notice the influence of Barrett Browning seems to have been George Monteiro (Monteiro 2000, 69–73), who recounts the birth of this unusual sonnet from a translated line.[13]

Pessoa's library has a copy of *The Poetical Works of Elizabeth B. Browning*, containing all 'Sonnets from the Portuguese' – as well as 'Catarina to Camoens', which Pessoa would translate in 1911–12, likely using this volume as the source text (Saraiva 112–123).[14] Though the book displays no printed date, we can ascertain it was *not* where Pessoa encountered the poem that inspired his 1902 sonnet, because the volume bears the stamp of 'The English Library', a bookstore Pessoa would frequent in Lisbon *after* he returned from Durban in 1905.

When the source for Pessoa's translation was found, it turned out to be a treasure trove of intertextual relationships. Kept in a private collection since 1973, the anthology *Sonnets of This Century* (i.e. the nineteenth century) bears reading marks and partial translations by Pessoa on 194 of its pages (Pittella 2017).

The source text – with a 'Sublime' handwritten comment – sheds light on the initial translation that became Pessoa's sonnet.[15] In fact, 'Antígona' is the second sonnet ever written by Pessoa (Pittella 2012, 102). By employing alexandrine verse while the traditional Portuguese sonnet prefers decasyllables, and by exemplifying one of the first cases of Pessoan reattribution, 'Antígona' embodies dislocations in form and personae. But it adds a layer of a linguistic dislocation that would characterize Pessoa's poetics as a whole:

> always forced to choose whether to express himself in English or Portuguese, Pessoa thus made a virtue of the self-alienation imposed on him by his having to hesitate between either of the two languages that remained, through this very choice, both equally familiar and foreign to him. (Roditi 40)

The dislocation in language follows the intercontinental corporeal dislocations of a life marked by early tragedies. In July 1893, when Pessoa had just turned five, his father died, and a few months later his baby brother Jorge passed away. In 1895, Pessoa's mother remarried and, in 1896, she went with Fernando to South Africa to join her new husband, who had been appointed Portuguese consul in Durban (Jennings 28–30). The couple would have five children, but only three would survive infancy, as the poet would lose two half-sisters: Madalena Henriqueta (1898–1901) and Maria Clara (1904–6). In August 1901, when Fernando and two siblings accompanied their parents on vacation from Durban to Portugal and the Azores, they also brought with them the remains of the recently deceased Madalena to be buried in the homeland (Cavalcanti Filho 78).

Once this recent death of a sister is known, it becomes hard not to factor it into the reading of 'Antígona' – a title that evokes the archetypical loyal sister who tried to secure a proper burial for her brother; in this case, Pessoa buries his sister, being himself Antigone (Pittella 2012, 249). The love sung in the sonnet suddenly becomes more fraternal than erotic, in a reading very different from the youthful romantic relationship interpreted by Blanco (34), or the reluctant farewell to a damsel read by Lopes (Lopes 1990a, 95).

Reading biographical events into a poetics of depersonalization is always risky. Still, the sonnet seems to mark a watershed; certainly a biographical goodbye to a loved one – whether to a sister who died, or a girlfriend who stayed in the Azores, or a mother returning to Durban with her new family and leaving the poet alone in Lisbon for the first time in his life (Pittella 2012, 248). But the transformation of a famous English line into an original Portuguese sonnet also hints at a linguistic departure: even though Pessoa would still return to Durban for a few more years of Anglophone education, this is the moment when he starts reentering his native Portuguese language while saying goodbye to a lost innocence, condemned to see language from the inside and the outside at the same time.

This self-distancing between languages is perhaps most felt in Pessoa's *35 Sonnets*, for a long time judged as second-rate (Sena) under an overwhelming influence of Shakespeare (Castro 32). But recent criticism has reclaimed those sonnets as complex modernistic creations. Performed by a 'self constituted in and through language' (Portela 173), they innovate both at the metrical level (Russom) and in their epistemological scepticism (Ramalho-Santos). Moreover, the influence of Barrett Browning has been noted in the *35 Sonnets* as well, challenging the assumption that Pessoa would be dialoguing with Shakespeare alone (Cearns 82).

Within an archive of tens of thousands of manuscripts, the *corpus* of Pessoa's sonnets is finite but complex enough to allow for a unique glimpse into the poet's *drama in people* ('Tábua'). But their finitude is still far from being exhausted, as the three unpublished sonnets that follow attest, inviting us to reconsider what we think we already know.

Appendix: Three unpublished English sonnets from 1933

This appendix includes three sonnets Pessoa wrote in 1933, here edited with their last complete variants (whenever legible). I thank Patricio Ferrari for collaborating on a preliminary transcription of these pieces.

1. [SOMETIMES A SOFTNESS]

> Sometimes a softness steals into my heart
> Like a scent in the night, and I know not
> If there is something that doth it impart
> Or some unthinking manner of my thought.

Am I remembering someone, something
From antenatal gardens come astray
The sorrow of whose loss doth falsely cling
Because it hath come and yet cannot stay?
Am I aspiring to some golden hour,
Placed now in some place future yet to be,
Whose shadowy forecast shows it as flower
That blossoms in the grace of mystery?
    I know not, nor why not; but this I know:
    It is mine, it is not, & it is so.

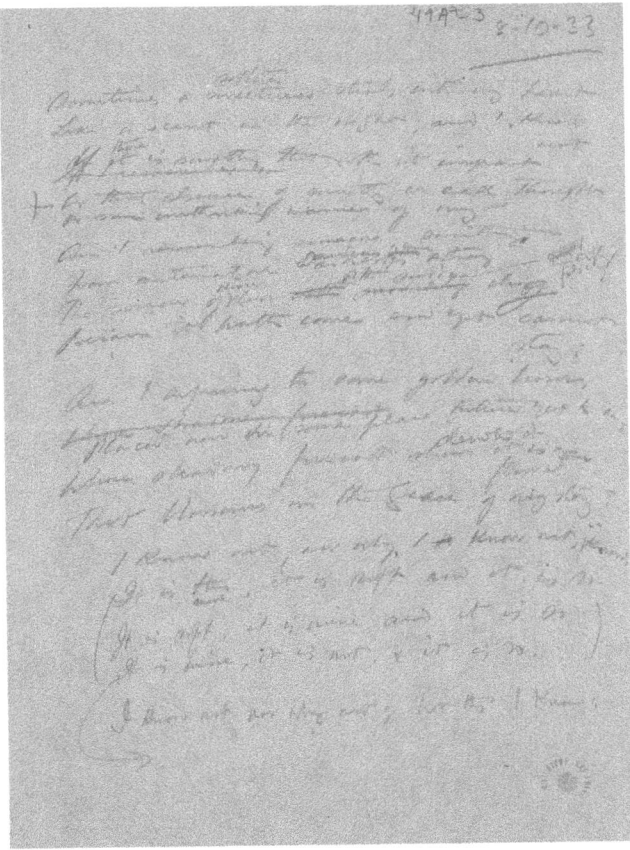

Figure 8.6 BNP-E3-49A7-3r – *(164 × 226 mm) Fragment of woven dun paper, unruled, with a medial horizontal fold, written in gray pencil on both sides and dated October 5, 1933; the verso displays the sonnet 'Oft in the great'.*

2. [Oft in the great]

Oft in the great void silence of the night,
Away from sleep & from the stars, I stare
Into the blackness of my room, with sight
That sees my outward thoughts such as they are.
How, though no pictures that dark sight doth find,
Nor pageants promised in the hope amaze,
In the projected space of my seen mind,
Visions I cannot see hold my lost gaze.
Then from a dream stranger than dreams I wake,
From something where no destiny was born,
Yet did some link within my senses break
Between me and the world, and left forlorn
    Some sacred void in me, some grieving night
    That neither dreams nor dawns can render bright.

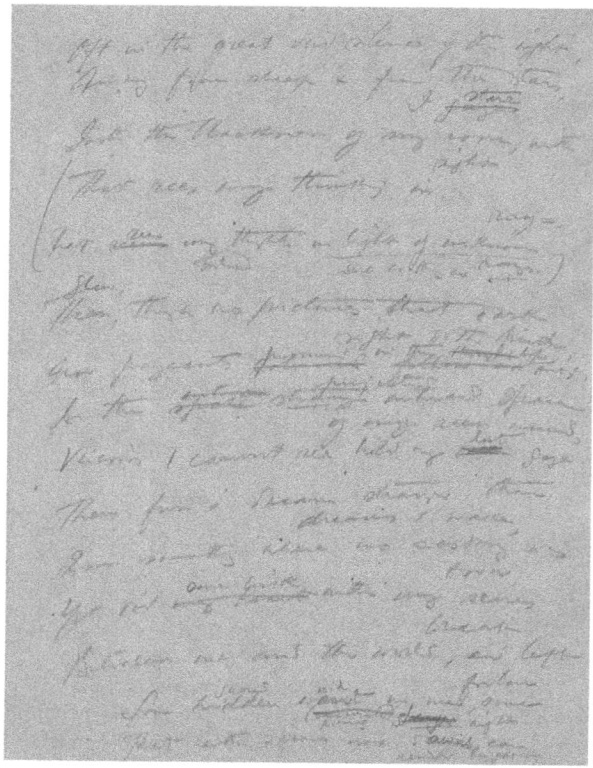

Figure 8.7 BNP-E3-49A7-3v – *Verso of paper with 'Sometimes a softness'.*

3. [The night holds things]

The night holds things more curious than the day
Although the day can mock the curious night.
Once in a mood of fancy as I lay
In my delight forgetting my delight,
There came to me a story of my past
That never had been, and I lived again
By a recomposition strange to taste
In a free joy of soul what had been pain.
Now, wherefore, and I ask my waking mind,
Make fancies to the past, as from dead flowers
A careful posy? Were it not more kind
To dreams we make from to dream future hours?
    But mine own question heard I not, that had
    Nor past nor future, because I was glad.

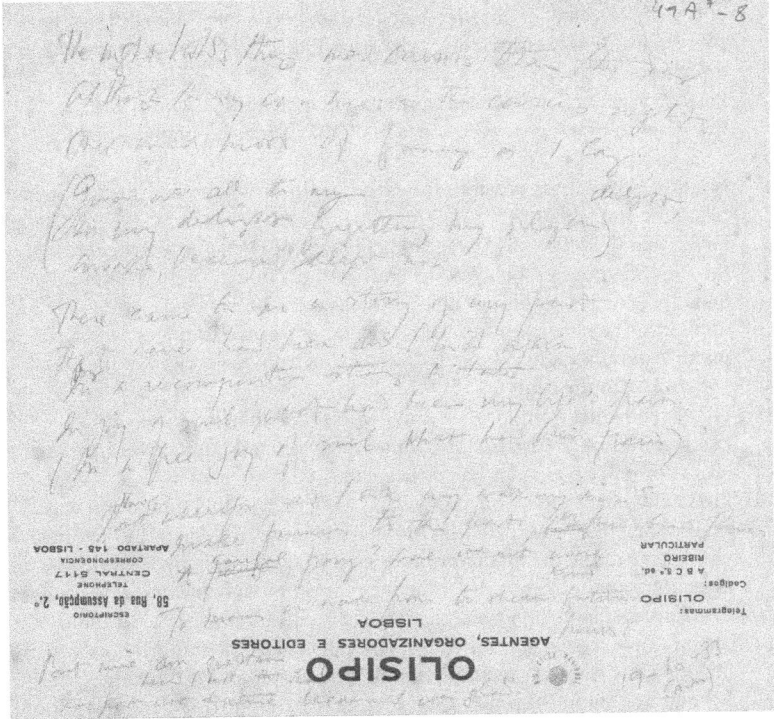

Figure 8.8 BNP-E3-49A7-8r – *(200 × 201 mm) Fragment of paper with the* olisipo *letterhead, unruled, with a vertical fold, written in grey pencil, dated October 19, 1933.*

Notes

1. Pessoa created this terminology; in 1928, he defended the appropriateness of the categories *orthonym/heteronym* (as opposed to *autonym/pseudonym*) to his works, but complicated the classification by also using pseudonyms and a semi-heteronym (Pittella and Pizarro pp. 175–180).
2. Though the *heteronyms* were created in the order Caeiro>Campos>Reis, the sequence in which they first appeared in print was Campos (1915), Reis (1924) and Caeiro (1925).
3. Pessoa uses 'semi-heteronymo' to describe Bernardo Soares, whose personality was not independent from his creator's (Pessoa 2013c, p. 560). The first published fragments of Soares's *Livro do Desassossego* appeared in 1929.
4. An article on 'D. Miguel Roupinho', the 137th persona (besides the orthonym), is still to be published, though Roupinho has been known since 1982, when Teresa Rita Lopes first mentioned him.
5. Sena highlighted how Pessoa was less vanguardist in English than in Portuguese (p. 36).
6. The 'new' sonnets comprise: two in Portuguese (Pessoa 2013b, p. 113; Pessoa 2013c, p. 323), eight in French (Pessoa 2014b) and twenty in English (various sources, including Ferrari and Pittella 2015; Pittella 2018; and the appendix to this chapter).
7. Pessoa's years in South Africa were studied by Jennings, who wrote the first English biography of Pessoa, a book that remained unpublished for decades.
8. I follow, as closely as possible, the orthography and punctuation of Camões (as in the 1607 edition).
9. Given that Castilian was the second language of Portuguese writers at the time, Camões probably didn't read Petrarca in the original Italian. Sena (pp. 56–57) points out that Petrarca's own sonnet (and Camões's, via Petrarca's) may have begun as a translation of Roman Emperor Hadrian's poem 'Animula vagula blandula' – departing from its farewell to life and apostrophe to the soul.
10. Other renowned Camonean sonnets with Petrarchan lines are: 'Eu cantarei d'amor tão docemente', 'Tanto de meu estado m'acho incerto' and 'Transforma-se o amador na cousa amada'.
11. First edited in 1947 by Braybrooke and King (p. 34), this translation was republished by many, including Monteiro (Monteiro 1996, p. 145). Some wrongly attribute the first publication to a 1939 opuscule by Ley, which does not contain the poem – though Ley was probably the one who brought the translated sonnet to the attention of the editors of the 1947 anthology.
12. The multiple reprints of this translation follow the 1947 publication, which included one silent correction (editing 'thy' instead of the typo 'they' on line 13) and two errors: misediting 'blest' instead of 'blent' on line 3, and 'thou do' instead of 'they do' on line 5.

13 Monteiro notes other traces of Barrett Browning's influence on Pessoa's work, such as 'Todas as cartas de amor são / Ridículas', a famous Campos poem that may be dialoguing with 'My letters! all dead paper, mute and white!' (Sonnet XXVIII in *Sonnets from the Portuguese*).

14 Pessoa translated several other English literary works, including Edgar Allan Poe's 'The Raven' (Saraiva pp. 152–159), and noted that the rhythmic structure of Poe's poem reveals the influence of Mrs. Browning (Pessoa 2013a, p. 215).

15 In his copy of *Sonnets from This Century*, Pessoa also deems Barrett Browning's Sonnet XIV 'Sublime' and 'The Soul's Expression' a 'very fine' poem; the only other sonneteer with more than one poem praised this highly is Dante Gabriel Rossetti (Pittella 2017, p. 288). This seems to be genuine admiration; yet, on the margins of a dreadfully misogynistic volume by P. J. Moebius (1906), the young Portuguese poet pencilled 'E. B. Browning' and 'Ch[ristina] Rossetti' as examples of poetesses who, according to Moebius, only walk paths already trodden by men (Barreto).

Works cited

Barbosa, Nicolás, et al. 'Portugal, o Primeiro Aviso de *Mensagem*: 106 Documentos Inéditos'. *Pessoa Plural*, no. 17, 2020: pp. 76–229.

Barreto, José. 'As Leituras'. *Misoginia e Anti-feminismo em Fernando Pessoa*. Ática, 2011, pp. 97–121.

Blanco, José. 'Fernando Pessoa: Jovem Poeta Português'. *Colóquio-Letras*, no. 88, 1985: pp. 27–36.

Bothe, Pauly Ellen. 'Algunos Apuntes hacia una Teoría de la Traducción y la Creación Literaria en Fernando Pessoa'. *Pessoa Plural*, no. 11, 2017: pp. 236–254.

Braybrooke, Neville and Elizabeth King, eds. *Translation, Second Series*. Phoenix Press, 1947.

Browning, Elizabeth Barrett. *The Poetical Works of Elizabeth Barrett Browning*, series I & II. Collins' Clear-Type Press, 1908.

Camões, Luís de. *Rimas*. Pedro Crasbeeck, 1607.

Castro, Mariana Gray de. *Fernando Pessoa's Shakespeare*. Diss. King's College London, 2010.

Cavalcanti Filho, José Paulo. *Fernando Pessoa: Uma Quase Autobiografia*. Record, 2011.

Cearns, Jennifer. 'The Ventriloquist Behind the Shattered Mirror: A Study of Pessoa's Bilingual Oeuvre'. *Pessoa Plural*, no. 6, 2014: pp. 78–103.

Dionísio, João. 'Integridade e Genuinidade na Obra de Fernando Pessoa'. *A Arca de Pessoa*. Edited by Steffen Dix and Jerónimo Pizarro. ICS, 2007, pp. 353–365.

Ferrari, Patricio. 'Genetic Criticism and the Relevance of Metrics in Editing Pessoa's Poetry'. *Pessoa Plural*, no. 2, 2012: pp. 1–57.

Ferrari, Patricio. 'Pessoa and Borges: In the Margins of Milton'. *Variaciones Borges*, no. 40, 2015: pp. 3–21.

Ferrari, Patricio and Carlos Pittella. 'Four Unpublished English Sonnets (and the Editorial Status of Pessoa's English Poetry)'. *PLCS*, no. 28, 2015: pp. 227–246. https://archive.org/details/fernandopessoaas00ferr

Ferrari, Patricio and Carlos Pittella. 'The Poems of Frederick Wyatt'. *Inside the Mask: The English Poetry of Fernando Pessoa*. Edited by Patricio Ferrari. Gávea-Brown, 2018, pp. 226–263. Originally published in *Pessoa Plural*, no. 10, 2016: pp. 226–301.

Freitas, Filipa de. '"O Amor": Uma Peça Inédita de Fernando Pessoa'. *Pessoa Plural*, no. 12, 2017: pp. 670–684.

Jennings, Hubert D. *Fernando Pessoa, the Poet with Many Faces: A Biography and Anthology*. Edited by Carlos Pittella. Tinta-da-China, 2019.

Ley, Charles David. *A Inglaterra e os Escritores Portugueses*. Seara Nova, 1939.

Lima, Ângelo de. 'Poemas Inéditos'. *Orpheu*, vol. I, no. 2, 1915: pp. 87–93.

Lopes, Teresa Rita. *Pessoa por Conhecer, vol. I – Roteiro para uma Expedição*. Estampa, 1990a.

Lopes, Teresa Rita. *Pessoa por Conhecer, vol. II – Textos para um Novo Mapa*. Estampa, 1990b.

Lourenço, Eduardo. *Poesia e Metafísica: Camões, Antero, Pessoa*. Sá da Costa, 1983.

Lourenço, Eduardo and António Braz de Oliveira, coords. *Fernando Pessoa no seu Tempo*. BNP, 1988.

Monteiro, George. *Fernando Pessoa and Nineteenth-Century Anglo-American Literature*. The University Press of Kentucky, 2000.

Monteiro, George. *The Presence of Camões: Influences on the Literature of England, America, and Southern Africa*. The University Press of Kentucky, 1996.

Pessoa, Fernando. *Álvaro de Campos – Obra Completa*. Edited by Jerónimo Pizarro and Antonio Cardiello. Tinta-da-China, 2014a.

Pessoa, Fernando. 'A Nova Poesia Portuguesa Sociologicamente Considerada'. *A Águia*, ser. II, no. 4, 1912: pp. 101–107.

Pessoa, Fernando. *Apreciações Literárias*. Edited by Pauly Ellen Bothe. Imprensa Nacional-Casa da Moeda, 2013a.

Pessoa, Fernando. *Cadernos I*. Edited by Jerónimo Pizarro. INCM, 2009.

Pessoa, Fernando. *Cartas a Armando Côrtes-Rodrigues*. Editorial Confluência, 1945.

Pessoa, Fernando. 'Como se eu fluísse …'. *GRANTA Portugal*, no. 1, 2013b: pp. 95–117.

Pessoa, Fernando. *Eu Sou uma Antologia: 136 autores fictícios*. Edited by Jerónimo Pizarro and Patricio Ferrari. Tinta-da-China, 2013c.

Pessoa, Fernando. *Fausto*. Edited by Carlos Pittella, collab. Filipa de Freitas. Tinta-da-China, 2018.

Pessoa, Fernando. *Poèmes Français*. Edited by Patricio Ferrari, collab. Patrick Quillier. Éditions de la Différence, 2014b.

Pessoa, Fernando. *Poemas Ingleses I: Antinous, Inscriptions, Epithalamium, 35 Sonnets*. Edited by João Dionísio. INCM, 1993.

Pessoa, Fernando. 'Tábua Bibliográfica, Fernando Pessoa'. *Presença*, no. 17, 1928: p. 10.

Pessoa, Fernando. *35 Sonnets*. Monteiro & Co., 1918.

Petrarca, Francesco. *Le Rime*. Edited by Giosuè Carducci and Severino Ferrari. Sansoni, 1899.

Pittella, Carlos. 'Chamberlain, Kitchener, Kropotkine – and the Political Pessoa'. *Inside the Mask: The English Poetry of Fernando Pessoa*. Edited by Patricio Ferrari. Gávea-Brown, 2018. pp, 42–69. Originally published in *Pessoa Plural*, no. 10, 2016: pp. 34–65.

Pittella, Carlos. *Pequenos Infinitos em Pessoa: Uma Aventura Filológico-literária pelos Sonetos de Fernando Pessoa*. Diss. PUC-Rio, 2012.

Pittella, Carlos. 'Sonnet 101 with Prof. Pessoa: Fernando Pessoa's Marginalia on an Anthology of 19th-Century English Sonnets'. *Pessoa Plural*, no. 11, 2017: pp. 277–375.

Pittella, Carlos and Jerónimo Pizarro. *Como Fernando Pessoa Pode Mudar a sua Vida*. Tinta-da-China, 2017.

Pizarro, Jerónimo. 'A Ansiedade da Unidade: Uma Teoria da Edição/L'Ansia di Unità: Una Teoria dell'Edizione'. *LEA*, no. 5, 2016: pp. 284–311.

Portela, Manuel. 'Putting Your Heart to Sleep with Pentameters: A Prosodic, Lexical, and Syntactic Analysis of Pessoa's "Sonnet X"'. *Pessoa Plural*, no. 10, 2016: pp. 173–192.

Ramalho-Santos, M. Irene. 'Blindfolded Eyes and the Eyable Being: Pessoa, the Senses, and the *35 Sonnets*'. *Pessoa Plural*, no. 10, 2016: pp. 135–150.

Roditi, Édouard. 'The Several Names of Fernando Pessoa'. *Poetry*, vol. 87, no. 1, 1955: pp. 40–44.

Russom, Geoffrey. 'Metrical Complexity in Pessoa's *35 Sonnets*'. *Pessoa Plural*, no. 10, 2016: pp. 151–172.

Saraiva, Arnaldo. *Fernando Pessoa. Poeta – Tradutor de Poetas*. Lello, 1996.

Sena, Jorge de. 'O Heterónimo Fernando Pessoa e os Poemas Ingleses que Publicou'. Preface. *Poemas Ingleses Publicados por Fernando Pessoa*. Fernando Pessoa. Ática, 1974, pp. 13–87.

Sharp, William, ed. *Sonnets of This Century*. Walter Scott, 1902.

Soares, Pedro Matos and Carlos Pittella. 'Pessoas com Relações com Pessoa'. *Pessoa Plural*, no. 16, 2019: pp. 414–445.

9

English sonnet spaces in Jacques Roubaud's *Churchill 40*

Thea Petrou

Jacques Roubaud's poetry volume *Churchill 40*, subtitled 'et autres sonnets de voyage' [and other travel sonnets], is a collection of the poet's travels from the spiralling streets of Paris to the heights of Mount Fuji, all expressed through innovative excursions in the sonnet form – there are, among others, prose sonnets, curtal sonnets, extended sonnets and upside-down sonnets.[1] These journeys are framed by Anglo-Saxon spaces, with the poet's experiences in the United States taking up the opening chapters of the book, and a series of sonnets that evoke London, the British countryside, and English art and literature comprising the volume's eponymous closing section. The title common to the volume and its final series of poems points to a single place, language and moment in history. Why does Roubaud choose to situate his book of 'travel sonnets' in these particular coordinates of space and time?

This chapter will be the record of a journey into the 'English sonnet spaces' of *Churchill 40*, explored in three stages. I begin with some close readings of the intersections between French and English in the sonnets, exploring the ways in which wordplay, rhythm and rhyme create a sense of multiplicity and multidimensionality in the poems. I will then consider the spaces that Roubaud shares in his book with other poets, particularly those writing in the English and American sonnet traditions. The form becomes a palimpsest that points beyond its own boundaries to that which has come before. Finally, I look at the representations of England in art, history and literature that make up the final chapter of poems in the book. This collective ode to England represents spaces that Roubaud yearns to inhabit in his poems, but does the poet appropriate these spaces, or is he simply passing through?

French–English intersections: Sonnet–multidimensional object

At the opening of his autobiographical prose volume *Poésie:*, Roubaud is trying to remember a sonnet (37–50). The poem is Góngora's and its themes speak to the narrator, who has reached his climacteric year: the age of sixty-three, considered in ancient Greek astrology to be the most dangerous turning point in one's life. The poem speaks of falling, precipices, earth that collapses beneath the poet's feet and buildings that fall into ruin, leaving only a memory traced in dust. The failure of these structures to hold the speaker in this world might be compared to the existential panic that seizes Roubaud at this symbolic turning point in his life; the poet describes waking in the early hours, paralysed by 'une angoisse compliquée' [a complicated anxiety], whose source was the knowledge – the certainty – that he was going to die (Roubaud 2000a, 56).

Roubaud reflects on his early encounters with Góngora's sonnet and his efforts to commit the poem to memory. He recalls a mnemonic process whereby some of the outer edges of the poem are seen in the mind's eye as an inverse set square, or 'équerre renversée':

En este occidental, en este, oh Licio,
        vida,
        caída,
        precipicio.

        jüicio.
        unida.
        prevenida
        edificio?

        venenosa,
        desnuda,
        humano!

        ponderosa
        muda,
        soberano! (Roubaud 2000a, 48)

He would memorize the poem's first line and 'la liste de quatorze mots-rimes' [the list of fourteen rhyme-words], with 'Licio' described as the cornerstone (41). The vertical column of the memory structure is more than a list, however. Roubaud specifies: 'une séquence écrite rythmée' [a rhythmic written sequence] (42).[2] The divisions in the structure of the poetic form are key to the process of memorization. The rhyme scheme shapes the pattern of words into groups of four and three: the ends of the quatrains and tercets that make up the sonnet. Once the first feat of memorizing these has been accomplished, the poet assures his reader that the rest of the rectangle is easy to fill in (49).

Roubaud has referred to 'un quatuor de forms' [a quartet of forms] in the poetry reading process:

> Il faut distinguer, par exemple, la page superficielle de la forme-poésie écrite de la page interne de la forme-poésie dans la mémoire. [...]
> De la même manière la forme-poèsie a une composante *orale*, externe et une composante *aurale*, interne. [...]
> Elle est faite de ces deux couples formels, l'un externe, l'autre interne.

> [We must distinguish between, for example, the superficial page of the written poetry-form and the internal page of the poetry-form in memory. [...]
> In the same way, the poetry-form has an external *oral* component and an internal *aural* component. [...]
> It is made up of these two formal pairings, the one external, the other internal.] (Roubaud 1995, 126–127)

As the poetry reader follows with her eyes the words printed on the page, an interiorized reading of the same poem unfolds aurally. When the poem is recited or heard, on the other hand, it is simultaneously visualized on 'la page interne' [the internal page] of our inner eye. The poem achieves its fullest existence possible, its quartet of dimensions, only when its words and rhythms are activated by the intermingling of its visual and aural aspects. Simultaneously, the interdependence of the aural and the visual is what facilitates the insinuation of the poem into memory. There it becomes a space to be invested with our thoughts and the recollections and associations that it stimulates: 'C'est la mémoire qui ira chercher ce qu'il y a dessous, derrière, au-delà de la notation, au-delà de l'exécution. [...] Ce n'est qu'en entrant dans la mémoire intérieure de qui le reçoit et fait sien qu'il accède à un nombre de dimensions respectable, qu'il devient vraiment un poème, et plus une partition' [It is memory that will seek out what is beneath, behind, beyond the notation, beyond the execution. [...] It is only upon entering the inner memory of the person who receives it and makes it his or her own that it reaches a respectable number of dimensions, that it really becomes a poem and is no longer a score] (Roubaud 1995, 128). The prepositions used by the poet – 'dessous, derrière, au-delà' [beneath, behind, beyond] – point beyond the poem on the page for the fulfilment of meaning. The spatial description of the poem itself expanding its dimensional properties during the reading process foregrounds Roubaud's view that a poem exists differently for each reader, growing with the various resonances created through the workings of its visual and phonic effects.

In *Churchill 40*, the tendency of some of the sonnets to slip between French and English adds to this already layered reading of a poem. 'Ma nouvelle casquette' [My New Cap] recounts the comical events that lead to the replacement of Roubaud's cap:

Cadeau d'un Secrétaire Définitivement Provisoire
Ou Provisoirement Définitif, P.F., de l'Oulipo
Ma neuve casquette s'harmonise, grise (agréable ton)
Avec ma veste grise aussi (c'est un gris de chez Hollington,

Un peu plus clair). Sur mon crâne (qui ne porte pas de chapeau)
Elle vient suturer l'absence de celle, perdue sans gloire,
Laissée dans la hâte et dans l'Amtrak (un changement à Trenton,
Anxieux, vers la New Jersey Line en direction de Prin-ce-ton).

[A gift from a Definitively Temporary
Or Temporarily Definitive Secretary, P.F., of Oulipo
My new grey cap (lovely shade) matches
My jacket, also grey (it's a Hollington grey,

A little bit lighter). On my head (which is hatless)
It sutures the absence of that other cap, lost without glory,
Left in haste on the Amtrak (a change at Trenton
(Anxious) for the New Jersey Line to Prin-ce-ton). (Roubaud 2004, 24)]

The poem is dedicated to Paul Fournel, Oulipo secretary and, in this instance, gift-giver. There are open-end rhymes in French, but in the second two lines of each quatrain, as Mònica Güell writes, 'il s'agit de rimes pour l'œil qui mêlent le français et l'anglais: "ton/Hollington, Trenton/Prin-ce-ton"' [it is a matter of visual rhymes which combine French and English: ton/Hollington, Trenton,/Prin-ce-ton] (273). The homographic endings match visually, but the French and English sounds differ when spoken aloud. English – or American – words and place names fit into the sixteen-syllable lines, pointedly so when it comes to the mute 'e' that would normally go unpronounced in 'Princeton', but which Roubaud here marks out with dieresis to be voiced: 'Prin-ce-ton'. Adjusting the American place name to fit the syllabic count of the French metric line creates a stumbling point when reading aloud, making the word stand out further and adding to the comedy of the poem.

The palindromic structures underlying the poem's rhyme patterns mirror a series of doublings that run through the sonnet's themes: the double definition of Paul Fournel's role in the Oulipo, the new cap that replaces the old, the harmonious shades of grey. Further parallels appear in the tercets that follow:

Et si le mot 'suturer' vient d'apparaître, là, dans un sonnet
(Compté sous mon crâne), en adéquation douteuse à son sujet
(Ma nouvelle casquette prenant le relais de son, hélas!

À jamais perdue prédécessoeure londonienne, hélas!)
C'est sans doute que de Paul Fournel le crâne (pas assez dur)
S'est récemment fendu sur quelques inches. Cause: la rupture

d'une selle de vélo
avec chute subséquente
pas dans la descente
d'un col
haut
mais dans une salle de sport
à Saint-Francis
co

[And if the word 'sutures' appears here, in a sonnet
(Counted out in my head), in a tenuous link to its subject
(My new cap taking over from its, alas!

Forever lost London predecessor, alas!)
It is without doubt because Paul Fournel's head (not very hard)
Was recently split open a few inches. Reason: a broken

bicycle saddle
and a subsequent fall
not downhill
on a steep
pass

> but in a sports hall
> in San Francis
> co]
> (24–25)

The cap 'on' Roubaud's head is linked with the sonnet's metre counted 'in' his head, and the unusual reference to a suturing that first appears in reference to the new helmet in the second quatrain of the poem gains its full resonance in an anecdote that tells of the stitches needed by Paul Fournel after he fell off his bicycle and sliced open his own head.[3] The interaction of English and French, and the play on visual and acoustic rhymes contribute to this sense of doubling in the piece, enriching the phonic texture of the poem and highlighting the relations (or moments of disconnection) between its aural and visual dimensions.

English place names come up elsewhere in a poem named 'Camden Lock':

Nue au bord de son tub la peau velours et soie
D'un rose retouché par crainte de scandale
Une beauté d'antan prise en miroir ovale
Offre sa bonbonnière et ses seins premier choix
Le brouhaha marchand du bric-à-brac étale
Nippe et frippe et papier, le métal et le bois
Visiteur de hasard le canal se tient coi
Avant de disparaître un temps jusqu'à Chapel

Street. Des clous de girofle de pluie assaisonnent
L'eau barbouillée de détritus. Le vent savonne
Ses nuées trimbalées depuis la Cornouaille
Elles ont survolé le Saut de Tristan où
Prospèrent les escargots, Stonehenge, Wimble-
Don, et sont entrées par le West-End. *Nimble*

Clouds. Ils s'éloignent. La Mer du Nord est au bout.

[Naked on the edge of her tub her skin of velvet and silk
A pink retouched to avoid a scandal
A beauty of old captured in an oval mirror
Shows off her bonbonniere and quality bosoms
The market hubbub flaunts odds and ends
Rags and scraps and paper, metal and wood
Chance visitor, the canal remains quiet
Before disappearing for a while until Chapel

Street. Cloves of rain season
The water daubed with rubbish. The wind whips into a lather
Its heavy clouds dragged up from Cornwall
They have flown over Tristan's Leap, where
The snails thrive, Stonehenge, Wimble-
Don, and come in through the West End. *Nimble*

Clouds. They move away. The North Sea is in the distance. (Roubaud 2004, 177)]

The reader is lured into this sonnet through her sense of sight, the first adjective, 'Nue' [Naked], proving irresistible in its prominent position at the head of the poem's first line. The sensuality intensifies towards the end of the opening line, where skin of velvet and silk evokes the sense of touch, but we must continue reading until line three to find out who or what is qualified by the poem's opening word. The image of the nude becomes one of the many objects laid out for sale at the bric-a-brac stall, her beauty captured within an oval-shaped mirror and described as 'retouché' [retouched] just in case the reader was in any doubt as to the nature of her existence. While looking at this image, the reader is drawn into the hustle and bustle of Camden Market. Alliteration, onomatopoeia and internal rhyme create echoes that compound the sense of the proliferation of materials visible at the stall in the lines 'Le brouhaha marchand du bric-à-brac étale / Nippe et frippe et papier, le métal et le bois' [The market hubbub flaunts odds and ends / Rags and scraps and paper, metal and wood]. The division of the classic alexandrine into hemistichs of six syllables throughout the opening verse produces a familiar rhythm that seems to run away with the enumeration of the objects that we see. But the reader is stalled mid-flow by the enjambment of 'Chapel Street' across the first two stanzas, its *rejet* of a single syllable and its English pronunciation, which introduce an exception into the rhyme scheme.

Beyond this phonic hurdle, the stimulation of the senses continues into the second strophe of the sonnet with smell and taste conjured up in the cloves of rain that season the canal, but this time our vision is directed away from our immediate surroundings and upwards towards the clouds. The poet traces the clouds' journey over the literary and mystical settings of Cornwall and Stonehenge to the West End, and away again towards the North Sea before a second enjambment takes place over the space of a stanza break with '*Nimble / Clouds*'. In a poem filled with various treasures – a beauty from another time, objects that have had a life before now, places with a mythical story to tell – the English interruption brings its own associations into the piece. The enjambed expression recalls the *nimbus* clouds, those classified as grey and heavy with rain. The reader might think also of the *nimble* girl, sat on the edge of her bath, particularly with the allusion to the clouds as soapy bubbles. The italic font, rushing ahead and finer than the rest of the print on the page, suggests the movement and the lightness of the clouds. Above all, the adjective 'nimble' chimes amusingly with the 'Wimble' of 'Wimbledon'; it is not a common or easy rhyme, and it stands out for sounding particularly 'English'.

The poet envelops us in the poem by stimulating our senses. He engages our concentration with the development of lists and trajectories; the regular rhythm and rhyme pattern, too, lull us into a sense of familiarity. However, both instances of English enjambment seem to represent limit points in the sonnet: the disappearance of the canal as it flows away from view towards Chapel Street and the floating ahead of the clouds; the end of first the quatrains and then the tercets of the sonnet. Each example of enjambment has a particular phonic effect too, interrupting or standing out somehow in the piece. Perhaps these instances of enjambment might be described as the cornerstones of the poem, like 'Licio' in the Góngora sonnet encountered in Roubaud's autobiographical narrative. They outline the shape of the sonnet on the page and they mark out the physical space in which the poet stands, observing the clouds above. The English interruptions are also points for the memory of the reader to hold onto when reading the poem, framing its spaces to be invested with her own associations.

In these poems the use of English stands apart: words are marked visually by hyphenated dieresis and italics, appearing in prominent positions at the ends of lines and stanzas; American-English pronunciation is contorted to fit the French metric count and uncommon rhymes are comical or particularly evocative. English terms do not blend harmoniously into the largely French text in these examples. Instead they stand out or complicate the reading process, offering the reader multiple points of interaction with the poem and opening out further dimensions.

Spaces shared: Sonnet–palimpsest

Rhyme and metre do not dominate all of the sonnets in *Churchill 40*. Roubaud approaches the prose form of the poem through Pierre Jean Jouve's translations of Shakespeare's sonnets. Roubaud explains that Jouve's translations acquired a certain autonomy from Shakespeare's poems and he saw in their prose a new sonnet form to be valued in itself: 'c'étaient des sonnets d'une espèce non encore reconnue, non identifiée comme telle. C'étaient des <u>sonnets en prose</u>' [they were a type of sonnet that was not yet known, not identified as such. They were prose sonnets] (Roubaud

2000a, 470). Roubaud's conception of the prose sonnet reflects the English sonnet form. Three paragraphs of prose are followed by a shorter tail, just as three quatrains would be followed by a couplet in the Shakespearean tradition. Roubaud saw in this discovery the potential for further distortion of the sonnet. The prose poem could be extended and curtailed in the same way as the lyric sonnet, leading Roubaud to invent, or discover, '[le] <u>sonnet court en prose</u>' [the short prose sonnet] (Roubaud 2000a, 472).[4] Roubaud arrives at his short prose sonnet through the reasoning of what is perhaps the most famous manifestation of this contortion in the lyric form: Gerard Manley Hopkins's curtal sonnet, whose parts are proportional reductions of the conventional sonnet. Hopkins takes the Petrarchan sonnet as his base, shrinking the octave (or two quatrains) into a sestet, and transforming the original sestet into a verse of four and a half lines. The curtal sonnet is a mathematically proportional reduction of the Petrarchan form, with the latter represented by the sum 8+6=14 and the former described by the equation: $\frac{12}{2}+\frac{9}{2}=\frac{21}{2}$.

The first prose sonnet of *Churchill 40*, 'Hotel Boulderado', is an extended one, made up of four prose sections followed by a tail of two lines. In the notes at the end of the volume, Roubaud designates this a 'sonnet de type shakespearien en prose' [Shakespearean prose sonnet] (184). What the reader sees is a palimpsest; for between Roubaud's formal innovations in 'Hotel Boulderado' and Shakespeare's tradition referenced in the note to the poem surely comes Jouve, who first transposed the English sonnets into French prose. The title of the sonnet, also the name of the hotel in which it is set, alludes to this notion of hybridity and absorption. In the opening lines of the poem, Roubaud discusses the wordplay of the title, whose blend of Boulder and Colorado is an example of a 'mot-valise': 'Le nom n'est pas "valise" exactement […], mais annexion onomastique (*hopefully*) par la ville de Boulder de tout l'état de Colorado' [the name is not exactly a 'suitcase' […], but an onomastic annexation (hopefully) by the town Boulder of the entire state of Colorado] (19). The term 'mot-valise' is a translation from the English 'suitcase word', which was originally a metaphor for the linguistic phenomenon of putting one word inside another, as into a case.

The third stanza of the poem is made up of the literature advertising 'Boulder's Pulse', the hotel's fitness centre:

« *As a guest of the Hotel Boulderado* », je *could be,* moi aussi « *a guest of* <u>Boulder's Pulse</u> *(Aerobics and Fitness Center) : Nautilus / Stationary Bicycles / Rowing Machines / Aerobics / Body Conditioning / / Heavy Hand Classes / Cross Country Ski Machines / Stairmaster* (Comment dégainer plus vite que son ombre dans les escaliers) */ Whirlpool / Free Weights / / / Please ask at the Front desk for more information.* (19)

The stanza points beyond itself. The English language and italic font, contrasted with short asides from the poet in French ['I *could be*, me too' and '*Stairmaster* (How to draw faster than your shadow in a duel on the stairs)'], signal a different source: the welcome brochure of the hotel. Meanwhile, the use of slashes to list the fitness equipment points beyond the prose form of the poem, since they are also used to mark the line breaks in citations of lyric poetry. When these words are laid out on the page in the manner suggested by the punctuation, the reader is faced with two stanzas of five lines, and an envoi. The result is a slight variation on Hopkins's curtal sonnet of ten and a half lines, which itself comprises a sestet, a quatrain and a half-line tail piece:

Nautilus
Stationary Bicycles
Rowing Machines
Aerobics
Body Conditioning

Heavy Hand Classes
Cross Country Ski Machines
Stairmaster (Comment dégainer plus vite que son ombre dans les escaliers)
Whirlpool
Free Weights

Please ask at the Front desk for more information.

Just as Boulder is a part of Colorado, and the gym an annex of the hotel, so too Hopkins's curtal sonnet appears within this larger prose sonnet form. It is not, as Roubaud writes, a 'suitcase' exactly, but one space that annexes another, an added dimension to a structure whose outlines already bear the traces of other sonnet traditions.

The curtailed lyric form is unfolded from within a verse of Roubaud's extended prose sonnet, which in turn grows from Shakespeare's lyric form and Hopkins's curtal sonnet. Roubaud's playful series of annexations obscures the sequence of the sonnet's evolution, and as one modified sonnet is hidden in another, there is the sense that the form exceeds the mathematical equation from which it is generated. Roubaud classifies the sonnet as 'une forme implicite' [an implicit form] in contrast, for example, to the sestina, which he describes as 'une forme explicite, dont la mutation n'est possible que par mathématisation (formalization explicite) réfléchie' [an explicit form whose mutation is only possible through considered mathematisation (explicit formalization)] (Roubaud 2014a, 109). While the rhyme scheme of the sestina is based on a set of mathematically calculated permutations, Roubaud explains that there is no common factor linking the various manifestations of the sonnet.[5] He gives the example of Lichtenberg's knife to clarify the ways in which the various parts of the sonnet are interchangeable:

> changez la lame, c'est encore lui, changez le manche, c'est lui toujours.
>   Autrement dit, chercher une *constante* de la forme, que ce soit dans le nombre ou la longueur des vers, dans la disposition rimique ou strophique [...], ne peut conduire qu'à constater son évanouissement. S'il y a une "théorie" du sonnet, ses "axioms" semblent changer avec le temps; et les lieux. En même temps, l'identité est évidente, comme celle du couteau: un sonnet appartient à l'espèce du sonnet.
>
> [change the blade, it's the same knife, change the handle, it's still the same.
>   In other words, seeking out a *permanent feature* of the form, whether in the number or length of the lines, in the arrangement of rhymes or stanzas [...], can only lead to the confirmation of its disappearance. If there is a "theory" of the sonnet, its "axioms" seem to change depending on time and place. At the same time, its identity is clear, like that of the knife: a sonnet belongs to the sonnet species.] (Roubaud 2014a, 33)

There is no single common denominator; any attempt to hone in on one or other of the sonnet's traits – length, verse structure, rhyme scheme – results in the impossibility of fixing a substantial and lasting definition, ruling out any sustainable theory of the form. Like all living things, the sonnet species evolves, adapting to the time and place in which it finds itself.

In order to approach a definition of the sonnet form, Roubaud proposes 'une exploration de ses moments [...] particulièrement attentive à ce qui bouge lors des franchissements des "frontières du dialecte" [...] *i.e.* de son adoption dans une langue nouvelle: français, anglais, espagnol, par exemple. L'intervention de la transformation-traduction est decisive' [an exploration of its moments [...] that pays particular attention to what shifts when 'dialectal boundaries' are crossed [...] i.e. when it is adopted into a new language: French, English, Spanish, for example. The intervention of translation-transformation is decisive] (Roubaud 2014a, 109). The poet suggests tracing the movement of the sonnet as it crosses the frontier of language: it is in translation that the shifting boundaries of the form are revealed. As a journey in form, 'Hotel Boulderado' therefore shows ways in which the sonnet annexes different traditions just as the town of Boulder annexes the state of Colorado.

The sonnet is also a space shared with American poets in *Churchill 40*. The setting of the volume's fifth poem is a poetry reading in New York:

> St Mark's on the Bowery. C'est tout près St Mark's
> Place. I remember (a sweet and sour remembrance). Louise.
> Ted sur son lit. Buvant des pepsis. Annabel me rappelle
> Une visite chez elle. *Her name now is Annabel Lee.*
> *(Married Mr Lee. divorced. but kept the name. Of course.*
> *Discussed we had, then, composition by numbers. She still does, she says.*
>
> 34s? 44s? *I mumble something about 31, 53, 37 & 73 Queneau numbers, etc.)*
> Ted wrote to me after Alix's death. Then died: (too many pepsis).
> Was buried to the sound of guns (he had been a marine
> Ron (Padgett) told me. Ron is here tonight).
> *I sit next to jackson mc low. He writes*
> Sans arrêt dans un cahier pendant les lectures:
> *Words he hears, or thinks of, listening, I think.*
> *I walk back* (13)
>
> [l. 1: It's very near *St Mark's*
> l. 3–4: Ted on his bed. Drinking pepsis. Annabel reminds me / Of a visit to hers.
> l.12: Non-stop in a notebook during the readings]

Poets Ted Berrigan, Ron Padgett and Jackson Mac Low are named in the poem and Edgar Allan Poe is alluded to through the tongue-in-cheek reference to Annabel Lee, the title of Poe's last complete poem, which explores the untimely death of a beautiful woman. St Mark's on the Bowery is the venue of the Poetry Project set up by Berrigan, a central site supporting the exploration of new poetry. The sense of a network is highlighted in the poem through the series of interactions and connections that unfold: 'Annabel me rappelle' [Annabelle reminds me], 'Ted wrote to me', 'Ron (Padgett) told me', 'I sit next to jackson mc low. He writes / [...] Words he hears, or thinks of, listening, I think'. Alison James points out the syntactical ambiguity towards the end of the sonnet, asking of the last link between the speaker and Mac Low, 'is the subject of the verb "listening" Roubaud, or Mac Low?' (254). The uncertain syntax establishes 'a link between the two poets' (James

254), and it also has the effect of multiplying the points in the network of interactions in the poem as a whole. A distinctly inherited form, the sonnet is a space that resonates with the voices of other poets, and it does so here against the backdrop of the physical setting in which writers come together to share their work. Listening, reading and writing are intertwined and the poem is generated by the connections formed between poets through these reciprocal acts.

Loss and memory are other prominent themes that run through the poem: the illness and death of the young Annabel Lee are echoed in the premature loss of Roubaud's late wife, Alix Cléo. Poe's own death followed shortly after his last poem was completed. Then Ted Berrigan dies. But the tone is swiftly lifted in the poem, the aside of '(too many pepsis)' a playfully ironic allusion to be picked up by those who know of Ted Berrigan and his writing.[6] This sometimes seemingly flippant air that alternates with moments heavy with loss and nostalgia, the brusque and fragmented phrasing, and the leaps from one name to another evoke Berrigan's sonnets. Friends and fellow poets of Berrigan often popped up in his poems through cursory references to their first names, 'in-jokes' that would resonate with his friends and fellow writers were frequent, and his sonnets were sometimes made up of fragments extracted from his other writings and rearranged in new formations. Stephanie Burt describes Berrigan's composition process in terms of 'collage': 'placing "found objects" (quotations or self-quotations, bits of other poems, overheard conversation) into the middle of what would otherwise sound like a lyric poem' (307). In her analysis of one of Berrigan's sonnets, Burt explains that the effect of his style 'feels less like dense crystals of argument, less like strenuously executed sculpture, than like lines taken out of order from diaries, or collages made out of transcriptions of telephone calls' (306). Roubaud's poem is thus also homage, memorializing Berrigan and his approach to poetry composition.

In his postface to the French translation of Berrigan's sonnets, Roubaud writes of a distinct 'Berrigan-sonnet' (101–102). However, despite compiling a set of axioms for its production, he casts doubt on the future survival of the form (98–99). The 'Berrigan-sonnet' is unlikely to become established as a 'forme poétique reconnue et identifiable' [a recognized and identifiable poetic form], in part because it has no fixed formal definition and precisely how far it leans on the traditional sonnet cannot be ascertained (106).

Roubaud suggests a glimmer of hope in the translated volume in the reader's hands: 'J'espère cependant que le livre de Berrigan en langue française viendra démentir cette conclusion' [I hope, however, that Berrigan's book in French will come to contradict this conclusion] (106). The translation will undoubtedly widen the readership of the sonnets, thus ensuring their continuity. But perhaps more importantly, the French translation of *The Sonnets* will bring the 'Berrigan-sonnet' into the consciousness of the French reader, where it will encounter various shapes and forms of sonnets she may have learnt in the French tradition and beyond. Translation brings one sonnet form up against another and Roubaud has shown that crossing the barrier of language is a way of expanding the parameters and possibilities of the form. Roubaud's 'Berrigan-sonnet' celebrates these networks of sharing and the interaction among poets nurtured by the ever-evolving sonnet tradition.

Memory: Sonnet–refuge

The final chapter of Roubaud's travel sonnets traces a journey through parts of London and the English countryside. The English spaces that form the setting of the sonnets in this section have a common theme: they are often fictional or derived from art. In the first poem of this concluding chapter, the England conjured up is one of childhood play. The poet remembers a game of make-believe in which he and his school friends took on the roles of world leaders against the backdrop of the Second World War:

'Winston Churchill à Carcassonne, octobre 1940'

Dans la cour de l'École Annexe jouons aux barres
Le préau s'est fait petit en septembre deux
Mille et tre, que je photographie à travers
La grille, et compare à mon souvenir d'octobre
Quarante, quand les marrons sortent de leurs bogues
Rousses, poudrés de neuf: on va jouer encore
À la guerre (verbale), reprenant nos rôles
Du printemps de l'« étrange défaite ». l'un fait
Mussolini (rires); un autre Hitler (Achtung
Biciclett' gro pneu!) – l'amiral Yama-
Moto qu'a été mis à pied. Moi je serai
Winston Churchill, par privilège familial
    D'une mère qui professe la langue. J'exalte
      La lutte, mâchouillant des sons pseudo-anglais.

English Sonnet Spaces in Jacques Roubaud's Churchill 40 169

'Winston Churchill at Carcassonne, October 1940'

[In the playground of the École Annexe we play prisoners' base
The yard looks small in September two
Thousand and three, I take a photograph through
The railings and compare it to my memory of October
1940, when the chestnuts escape from their burs
Red-brown, freshly powdered: we are going to play again
At war (verbal), taking up our roles
From the spring of the 'strange defeat'. one plays
Mussolini (laughter); another Hitler (Achtung
Biciclett' gro pneu!) – admiral Yama-
Moto who was stood down. I myself will be
Winston Churchill, through the family privilege
    Of a mother who teaches the language. I exalt
        The battle, chewing on pseudo-English sounds. (Roubaud 2004, 171)]

Roubaud makes no secret of his passion for England, writing frequently of his 'Anglomania' inspired by Churchill, who became a symbol of resistance for the poet during the Second World War (Roubaud 1993, 162). In a passage elucidating the scene of this poem in *La Boucle* Roubaud even refers to England as his 'Arcadie' [Arcadia] (426). A thread of childlike imaginings and otherness runs through the poem: the unexpected presence of Churchill in Carcassonne, simulated war battles, role-play and the attempts at speaking a foreign language so difficult and strange that it is reduced to object-like sounds that are chewed on. Yet these examples of otherness are countered with moments of repetition and familiarity: the chestnuts escaping their burs have a seasonal appearance; the friends play 'again' and they take up well-worn roles; even the language spoken by the young poet is only 'pseudo-anglais' and so not completely foreign.

The heading of the poem gives equal importance to the home setting of Carcassonne as to the historical figure Roubaud admired, and while the year '1940' resonates throughout history books, here 'octobre 1940' produces the singular memory unfolded by the poet over the lines of the sonnet. The childhood memory of play that Roubaud looks back on is distanced from the poet and the reader across time and space. He stands in a moment already past, in September 2003, looking back yet further into his past. As he memorializes the site through the capturing of a photograph, the railings demarcating the space of the playground establish a physical barrier that prevents the poet from entering. In this sonnet Roubaud's 'Arcadie' is not so much his ideal of England but the years he left behind in Carcassonne: the idyllic setting of his childhood and a time of nature and innocence always to be lost in a pre-war France.[7]

The ties between England and childhood in *Churchill 40*'s final series of poems continue in 'Constable Country, II: Stratford Mill ou Sept chapeaux noirs' [Stratford Mill or Seven Black Hats]. In this second of two poems dedicated to John Constable's landscape paintings, Roubaud describes 'Stratford Mill'. The memory narrated in the sonnet belongs to Mr Goodman, the main character of Roubaud's novella *Ciel et terre et ciel et terre, et ciel* (2009). In *Ciel et terre*, the character describes what he saw in one of four Constable paintings that adorned his bedroom wall as a child (33–37). He and his mother are in hiding in the south of France, waiting to escape the war by travelling to England – 'le pays de la liberté' [the country of freedom] – and he sees in these paintings representations of England, 'morceaux d'un lieu unique' [pieces of a unique place] (Roubaud 2009, 45–46).

In his description of Stratford Mill Mr Goodman takes the reader through a count of the seven men in the painting, each 'surmonté d'un chapeau' [topped with a hat]: 'Toute l'image, pour lui, était ainsi ponctuée de chapeaux, tous noirs' [The whole image, for him, was thus punctuated with hats, all black] (Roubaud 2009, 35). He recounts the way in which these hats structured his recollection of the painting, enabling him to piece together its details from memory:

> Une fois placées mentalement les sept têtes noires, fermant les yeux, ou les yeux ouverts dans la nuit quand il ne dormait pas, il pouvait reconstituer entièrement la scène: d'abord la rivière, la prairie, le moulin, la barque, le tronc d'arbre battu sur le devant, puis peu à peu tout le reste; laissant jusqu'à la fin vide le ciel tendre, sa tranquilité, de bleu et de blanc cousue.
>
> [Once he had mentally placed the seven black heads, closing his eyes, or with his eyes open in the dark when he couldn't sleep, he was able to reconstruct the entire scene: first the river, the meadow, the mill, the boat, the fallen tree trunk in the foreground, then bit by bit all the rest; leaving blank until the end the soft sky woven in blue and white, its tranquillity.] (35–37)

The sestet of the sonnet in *Churchill 40* closely reproduces this part of Roubaud's novella:

Un garçon chapeau	A boy black
Noir. Un homme à chapeau noir sur un petit mur.	Hat. A man in a black hat on a little wall.
Image ponctuée de sept chapeaux, tous noirs.	Image punctuated with seven hats, all black.

La rivière, la prairie, le moulin, la barque	The river, the meadow, the mill, the boat
Le tronc d'arbre abattu sur le devant, laissant	The fallen tree trunk in the fore, leaving
Le ciel tranquille, de bleu et de blanc cousu.	The tranquil sky, woven in blue and white.

(181)

Through memory, the character builds an escape from the darkness of insomnia. The mnemonic process whereby the young Mr Goodman reconstructs the image from memory may remind Roubaud's reader of the set square that helped the poet to learn Góngora's poem by heart. Roubaud aligns the sonnet form with what Constable's painting represents for his protagonist in *Ciel et terre*. As the alternative title to this poem suggests – 'ou Sept chapeaux noirs' [or Seven Black Hats] – it is not so much about a specific piece of England at all: the haven created in the reconstitution of the painting in memory is to be contrasted with the disappointment that the character of his novella encounters years later when he visits '*Constable Country*'. In the real setting of the paintings, Mr Goodman finds: 'rien qu'une reconstitution naïvement agressive, purement commerciale, de ce qui avait été le territoire mental du peintre, son pays d'enfance imaginaire, son invention' [nothing but a naively aggressive and purely commercial reconstruction of what had been the mental territory of the painter, the imaginary country of his childhood, his invention] (Roubaud 2009, 81–82). The 'pieces of a unique place' represented in these final sonnets of *Churchill 40* are therefore spaces to be inhabited in the workings of memory, imagined spaces that we make our own.

The sonnet as refuge or home is one of Roubaud's many spatial metaphors for the form. In his book of sonnets for children Roubaud likens the form to a house to evoke its endurance, describing it as 'ce qu'on peut faire de plus solide comme construction de poème' [the most solid poem construction] (Roubaud 1990, 84). Perhaps, then, Roubaud's set square-shaped outline is the doorway that leads inside, since it functions as an entry point for the reader's engagement with the form: it is a way of committing the poem to memory, where resonances grow and continue to enrich the reading experience beyond what is seen on the page. 'Constable Country, II' therefore paints an image of the possibilities that open out in the imagination of the sonnet reader: by first plotting the position of the seven black hats, the young Mr Goodman creates an entire landscape to wander through in memory.

The spaces that Roubaud creates in his poems engage and stimulate the memory of the reader; he draws us into a world of sonnets that are all the more interactive for their English and American dimensions. The poet creates spaces to be discovered through sequences in rhyme and rhythm, and the combinations of French and English multiply the possibilities of interaction between the 'aural' and the visual readings of the poems. The presences of English and American sonneteers, too, enrich Roubaud's sonnet forms and reveal layers of meaning to be discovered by the reader who is looking for them. The form becomes a palimpsest of ever-shifting lines that points beyond its own edges to those poets who have previously engaged with the sonnet. By crossing into the space of other languages, the poet and reader navigate the borders of the elusive sonnet form, prolonging its survival and contributing to its evolution. The representations of England in *Churchill 40*'s concluding chapter provide a space of fantasy and escape for the poet and his characters, and demonstrate that the reader too can journey through the sonnet form to spaces constructed in imagination.

Notes

1. All translations are my own.
2. Emphasis and typographical changes are reproduced from the original text in this and subsequent citations from Roubaud's works.
3. Roubaud evokes the cause of the accident in his careful arrangement of the extended sonnet's final verse in the shape of a bicycle saddle.
4. Roubaud describes his own experiments with the French curtal sonnet in *Poésie* (pp. 450–458).
5. The mathematical sequence that produces the permutation of the rhyme words in the sestina is explained by Roubaud in *Octogone* (pp. 147–153).
6. The words 'have a pepsi' appeared as a line in Berrigan's poem '10 Things I Do Every Day' (p. 164).
7. See in particular *La Boucle* for accounts of Roubaud's childhood memories in Carcassonne.

Works cited

Berrigan, Ted. *The Collected Poems of Ted Berrigan*. Edited by Alice Notley. University of California Press, 2005.
Burt, Stephanie and David Mikics. *The Art of the Sonnet*. Belknap HUP, 2010.
Güell, Mònica. '*Churchill 40*: voyages à travers le sonnet roubaldien'. *Jacques Roubaud, compositeur de mathématique et de poésie*. Edited by Agnès Disson and Véronique Montémont. Absalon, 2010, pp. 125–133.
James, Alison. 'Transatlantic Oulipo: Crossings and Crosscurrents'. *Formules*, vol. 16, 2012: pp. 249–262.
Roubaud, Jacques. *Les Animaux de tout le monde*. Seghers, 1990.

Roubaud, Jacques. *La bibliothèque de Warburg*. Seuil, 2002.
Roubaud, Jacques. *La Boucle*. Seuil, 1993.
Roubaud, Jacques. *Churchill 40*. Gallimard, 2004.
Roubaud, Jacques. *Ciel et terre et ciel et terre, et ciel*. Argol, 2009.
Roubaud, Jacques. *Description du projet*. Nous, 2014a.
Roubaud, Jacques. *La Fleur inverse. Essai sur l'art formel des troubadours*. Ramsay, 1986.
Roubaud, Jacques. *Octogone*. Gallimard, 2014b.
Roubaud, Jacques. *Poésie*. Seuil, 2000a.
Roubaud, Jacques. *Poésie, etcetera: ménage*. Stock, 1995.
Roubaud, Jacques. Postface. *Les Sonnets*. Ted Berrigan. Translated by Martin Richet. Joca Seria, 2013, pp. 91–106.
Roubaud, Jacques. *La Vieillesse d'Alexandre*. Éditions Ivrea, 2000b.

10

Lyrical gestures: The essence of the form and the spirit of the translated text in Don Paterson's 'versions' of sonnets

Bastien Goursaud

Traditional forms are central to Don Paterson's work, and the sonnet is by far the most recurrent. He has written more than a hundred original sonnets, edited an anthology of sonnets, published a commentary on Shakespeare's sonnets and published his own 'versions' of sonnets by various authors: two entire collections, one translated from Rilke's *Sonnets to Orpheus*, the other from Antonio Machado's work, as well as versions of Desnos, Rimbaud and Petrarch. Paterson has confessed to being obsessed with what he describes as the sonnet's ideal adequacy to a certain pattern of thought (see infra), which he relates to a rather surprising re-actualization of the Renaissance golden ratio, combined with a slightly provocative deterministic vision of poetic form in general, and of the sonnet in particular. One is in fact tempted to read Paterson's numerological description of the sonnet as a fixation on an abstract essence of the form.

Yet, Paterson's theoretical insistence on the intrinsic mnemonic and cognitive value of the form does not prevent him from breaking it up (see infra) or reshaping it to the point that it becomes hardly recognizable.[1] One can therefore observe how his work negotiates between a materialistic approach to the form inspired by cognitive science and the constant remodelling which he produces.

Paterson's conception of the poetic version is marked by an interest in what he calls the 'spirit' (Paterson 2006, 81; Paterson 1999b, 58) of the translated text: a surprisingly vague word for a poet capable of complex theoretical work,[2] and one that carries religious undertones at odds with the poet's materialistic pronouncements.[3] As a starting point to a reading of Paterson's versions, this chapter will attempt to shed some light on that apparent paradox. Its main contention will be that the notion of a 'spirit' of the translated text must be understood in reference to the etymology of the word, i.e. *spiritus* – breath, the underlying flow of expression and poetic diction. My interpretation will rely on Dominique Rabaté's reflections on lyrical gestures, which he defines as 'the congruence between what is said and an emotional state, the communication of an impetus crystallizing in the form of the poem' (Rabaté 2017, 90). In *Gestes Lyriques* (2013), Rabaté studies several types of gesture while affirming the open-ended nature of the list. His views are informed by Austin's theory of the performative – because of the plasticity of its form, the modern lyric utterance allows for the poem to convey a force, while the form itself is 'never completely fit' (Rabaté 2017, 89). This sense of a form conveying yet simultaneously betraying an impetus seems particularly appropriate to Paterson's attachment to, and freedom with, the sonnet form and its translation. Torn between formalism and materialism, between lyricism and an obsession with the central void of consciousness, the translation, or version, of a sonnet functions as a balancing act between a personal investment in literary history and the singular lyrical gesture.

Simultaneously, the entirety of this paper will underline that the interest in the 'spirit' of the sonnet goes hand in hand with the development of a poetics of lyrical effacement that has come to characterize some of Paterson's more recent work. The translation of a spirit understood as a lyrical gesture involves an impersonation, which, in Paterson's work, has so far tended to veer towards impersonality.

More broadly, it is interestingly in the context of the haunted work of translation that Paterson allows himself to resort to the language of spirituality. The absence of God, of a Spirit, leads to the exploration of what connects his voice to another – translation, or rather versioning, thus becomes a spiritual encounter rooted in the materiality of rhythm and, paradoxically, in the language of religion.

I will conclude by suggesting that the spirit of the translated text may also be read with reference to the poetics of the spectral that developed in Paterson's elegiac collection *Rain*. Ghosts and spectral presences are indeed omnipresent in Paterson's work, but in the elegiac context, the translation of a spirit is at once its bringing back to life within new letters, and an acknowledgement of the impossibility of retrieving it from the past.

The sonnet: A necessary form?

In his introduction to his anthology titled *101 Sonnets*, Paterson affirms that 'the reason we have the turn is that we just can't help it. The human brain craves disruption and variation just as much as it craves symmetry and repetition' (Paterson 1999b, xvii). In a 2010 essay published alongside his commentary on Shakespeare's sonnets, he explains that the natural length of a line is neurologically determined and roughly corresponds to the length of an iambic pentameter. He adds that in a 10–12-point type, a nice and unavoidably attractive square is produced by a 13–14-line poem, which leads him to conclude that '[a] sonnet is, first and foremost, just a square of text on a white ground. Wipe every sonnet from human literature and from the human memory, and it will reappear in pretty much the same form by tomorrow afternoon' (Paterson 2010, 486).

Similarly, the turn (or *volta*) is explained through a mathematical necessity: the presence within the sonnet of the famous golden ratio. In the same essay, he writes: 'The golden ratio is that natural division of roughly 8:13 that we find forming patterns everywhere – from the shell of the nautilus and the seedhead of the sunflower, to the spiral arms of the galaxies'; therefore, '[a]bout a week after the abolition and the reappearance of the sonnet, we'd see the emergence of the *volta*' (Paterson 2010, 490).

At times, it even seems like the sonnet's necessity functions as a metaphor for the possibility of an ordering within a materialistic, and therefore chaotic and potentially meaningless universe. Such is the narrative that underlies 'The Light' (Paterson 2003, 71), a meta-commentary on the sonnet's capacity for framing one's metaphysical interrogations.

Published in *Landing Light*, Paterson's next book of poems after *The Eyes* (his versions of Antonio Machado), this sonnet's characters (a cruel disillusioned mystic tells the speaker, a desperate monk, that '[t]here is no light') certainly owe much to the *via negativa* that is so central to the Spanish poet's work.[4] As Paterson's title suggests, his collection is full of plays on light and dark and chiaroscuro scenes – in this poem the light is quite obviously a metaphor for a godly presence, debunked by the mystic, and brought back to its physical nature: a mere 'square of late sun'. That square's framing of the monk's prayer mat in the final lines is reminiscent of the sonnet's – and poetic form's – minimal capacity to encompass a void, as well as Paterson's own depiction of the sonnet as merely 'a square of text on a white ground' (see supra).

'The Light' is indeed peppered with playful metapoetic allusions to the form: the speaker's 'thirteen years' as a prelude to the poem, his 'I was broken' echoed by the textual break of the sonnet's blank space at the turn, and the final self-referential line. These hints come as a materialization of the form within the grim parable told by the poem. Its response to the existential threat of nothingness found in Machado and Cioran's aphorisms[5] is a sort of Zen acceptance,[6] a reliance on the stability of the old forms 'frayed and framed', like the sonnet.

'The Light' does frame the creeping nothingness in this poem, as it appears to allow the speaker a distance, hence the final line ('I watched myself sit down for one last time.'), whose self-referentiality relates to his own disillusioned but serene attitude. It completes the form and the character's journey while remaining clear-eyed. The materialism of this poem functions as a sort of Derridean *pharmakon*, for the realization that light is just that, a physical phenomenon, comes with a reliance and a play on the material presence of a formal frame.

Dwelling at the boundaries

Yet, despite the apparent attachment to the necessity of the form, Paterson's use of it is extremely flexible. According to Hugh Haughton, '[i]t may be that despite – or because of – his fascination with the form, Paterson is obliged at some level to resist it, or at least to dwell at its boundaries' (44). Sonnets of rigorously traditional facture are indeed very rare in Paterson's work. Even when a sonnet presents itself as a sort of homage to the tradition, Paterson unsurprisingly fiddles with its form.

'Waking with Russell' (Paterson 2003, 5), a sonnet addressed to one of his sons, is an example of this. The poem clearly gestures at the unavoidable presence of the tradition: the perfectly iambic rhythm of the first and last lines and the final kiss and pledge would, for instance, not be out of place in a Shakespearean love sonnet. In addition to that, the direct quote from Dante ('I was *mezzo del cammin*'), although obviously not from a sonnet, adds a flavour of the Italian. This is partly Paterson's own variation on a definition of the sonnet as a vehicle and/or sign of the presence of literary history – something Stephanie Burt has described as one of the five characteristics of the contemporary sonnet.[7]

But history is also gently refashioned in this sonnet, for it simultaneously reflects on the undefinable difference brought about by the arrival of a newborn child in the life of the poet. The love experienced by the speaker is hard to define ('Whatever the difference is', the poem starts), and some familiar tropes of the love-sonnet tradition are recast – the river, the exchange, the path, the Neoplatonic sense of continuum, etc. – in an act of poetic recycling or rejuvenation. The form is also reshuffled, since the first sentence runs on for six lines and constitutes the argumentative sestet. Such reversal mirrors the poem's constant game of pitching back and forth ('I pitched back' recalls familiar scenes of father-and-son bonding), and so does the rhyme scheme, which is simplified into an alternation of masculine and feminine end-rhymes to echo the poem's merging of the familiar with the unfamiliar. Burt points out that the sonnet form recalls the 'white, privileged, European or male backgrounds that the most famous earlier writers of sonnets had' (246). Whilst he is in part heir to this tradition, Paterson also shows an awareness of its insufficiencies here. By letting his own account of the wonder of fatherhood be informed by the well-worn language of the courtly sonnet, he plays with a certain masculine inability to express oneself beyond the language of gendered roles. In fact, the penultimate line's self-satisfied exclusion of women ('How fine, I thought, this waking amongst men!') is also a moment of self-mockery – the address to the baby son makes it impossible to take its vaguely misogynistic implications too seriously. While Paterson acknowledges the continuity of his work with a clearly canonical history of the sonnet, he simultaneously attempts the balancing act of recognizing its artificiality, which in turn suggests that it might encompass a broader range of experiences.

Paterson's attachment to the sonnet form can at times seem entirely flexible, having more to do with an abstract sense of its patterns and inherent thought-mechanisms than with the details of the rhyme schemes and, perhaps more surprisingly, of the line counts. One central flaw in his representation of the sonnet as a structure supposedly informed by the golden ratio is that it would in this case have to be composed of thirteen lines. Paterson brushes aside the objection by simply explaining that 'a thirteen-line sonnet, with a turn after line 8, might be our Platonic form' except it 'would have produced a thirteen-line poem, and superstition (for one thing, Judas was the thirteenth disciple) would soon have legislated against that form ever achieving much popularity' (Paterson 1999b, xix). Only accidents of history have prevented the sonnet from reaching its essential form.

In his anthology *101 Sonnets*, Paterson also explains that the fourteen-line criterion is merely a practical one, that he could have included John Hollander's 'thirteen-line sonnets with thirteen-syllable lines', but also 'sonnetinos and double sonnets, cryptosonnets and curtal sonnets' as well as George Meredith's 'sixteen-line sonnets' (Paterson 1999b, xxiv). In that perspective, and given the previous allusion to Plato, one is tempted to understand Paterson's attachment to the sonnet as an attachment to an elusive essence of the form – a structure of symmetry and rupture, of harmony and disruption, which forces us to reread parts of his work as merely gesturing towards the sonnet. *Landing Light*, which was published between *The Eyes* and *Orpheus*, is pervaded with such fragments of sonnets and 'cryptosonnets'.

'Incunabula' (Paterson 2003, 7) may well be read as the early stage in the development of a sonnet: as an eight-line stanza placed after a sonnet, it unavoidably recalls an octave. Its ABBACDDC structure encourages such a reading, while other elements point at its incompletion: first, the poem only uses pararhyme, a type of incomplete rhyme, and secondly, the Latin word *incunabula* refers to 'the early stages or first traces in the development of anything'. It portrays 'tonsured scribes at facing desks', who are possibly from a pre-sonnet era, since an incunabulum is a book printed before 1501. The scribes are absorbed in the proofreading of manuscripts with their 'thumbs /

locked in their mouths', a bizarrely childlike attitude which echoes the original meaning of the title: swaddling clothes or cradle. This is an infant poem which, in effect, presents us with uncertain writers plodding through their work, for they know 'how little will make the difference'. Is this an image of the young sonneteer as a mere scribe, bound to scrupulously copy earlier models? Possibly, though Paterson's own practice of the poetic version shows a capacity for irreverence. But 'Incunabula' is made up of two questions: the first line and its amplification in the next seven lines. Its tone is therefore in keeping with the hesitant, uncertain attitude of the scribes.

'America', the next poem in the collection (Paterson 2003, 8), functions as a response to this attitude. Its six lines complete the octave of 'Incunabula', thus forming a sonnet, and the poem itself reflects on this completion by creating a sense of expectancy ('we stood watch') and its fulfilment. The latter comes through the syntax itself, via the use of a repetitive and expansive structure: with the polysyndeton that runs through the third and fourth lines, which mirrors the gathering movement of the wave, and with the repetition of 'second' ('for a second / and somewhere in that second'), which creates a moment of harmony and balance within the structure of the poem. The typographic shape of the text is also an echo of the precarious balance that is struck by the poem. It hangs 'perfected' – a word that immediately invokes Sylvia Plath's 'Edge'. Of course, in Plath's poem, written only a few days before her death, 'perfected' has to do with the rigidity of death. *Landing Light* is haunted by the rhythms of Sylvia Plath: her work seems to have acted as a catalyst for the collection. Another American voice, or 'global presence',[8] in Paterson's work is Robert Frost: the existential expectancy that opens the text on a very American wharf is probably indebted to Frost's own scepticism. It is therefore not entirely far-fetched to say that, in this sestet, Plath's detached voice and sculptural language (listen to the liquid consonants of the fourth line) combine with Frost's existential interrogation to form a response to the previous poem's hesitant, worried writers. Paterson composes a sort of history of the turn that took place in his career, a turn that might have had to do with middle age but which, in poetic terms, seems to have formalized through a conversation with other poets encapsulated here in this fragmented sonnet.

Translating the gesture, losing the ego

Simultaneously, the translation of sonnets by Machado and Rilke appears to have been a perfect space for Paterson to develop his own materialism in a framed and familiar context. Paterson's use of the sonnet form is more abstract and less conservative than it seems, and the sonnet's frame of thought has proved a fit vehicle for the progressive erasure of the lyric ego. This may seem surprising given the sonnet's link with the emergence of the modern, Renaissance self. Yet, as I want to suggest here, Paterson's versioning practice has allowed him to strive towards a paring down of his own lyric voice.

One of the central tenets of Paterson's thought, whose development coincides with his translation of Antonio Machado's poetry in *The Eyes*, is that the self is a fiction, a central void which emerged out of evolutionary necessity – much like the sonnet. Also, like the sonnet, it is described as a necessary illusion, one which the lyric poem cannot help but preserve while still toying with it and showing its inherent emptiness. Six years later, Paterson produced another collection of versions titled *Orpheus*, which was based on Rilke's *Sonnets to Orpheus*. The two books coincide with the shift in Paterson's work from a grim but playful, formalist game of masks, to a still playful but more fluent and impersonally lyrical, Zen-inspired posture.

Because it played such a pivotal role in the development of his own work, it might therefore seem unsurprising that Paterson chose to adopt a personal attitude to the work of translation. In the prefaces to both *The Eyes* and *Orpheus*, he describes his versioning of these poems as distinct from traditional translation. His ambition is not to translate what he calls the 'surface-sense' of the poem. In *The Eyes*, he declares his interest in 'A "Spirit" or "a vision"', which he deems 'a hopelessly subjective business' (Paterson 1999a, 56). It is surprising to find Paterson using such vague terminology, while elsewhere he enjoys being rather technical and precise in his theoretical discourse. It is of course possible to attribute such haziness to the difficulty of justifying entirely personal and indeed subjective choices in his versions. Yet, it is also significant that he should retain only the word 'spirit' when discussing his versions of Rilke in 2006: 'Versions fail when they misrepresent the *spirit* of the original, or fail in any one of the thousand other ways bad poems fail' (Paterson 2006, 81).

Paterson is probably aware that he is treading a dangerous path when using such a loaded word to describe the work of translation. I believe that it is a very significant choice – as was the case in 'The Light', the dubious biblical opposition it involves is in fact subverted into a material, linguistic one. For example, Paterson translated 'Profesion de fe', a sonnet from Antonio Machado's *Campos de Castilla* (Machado 164), a collection from his second period, when the *via negativa* and negative theology had not yet become entirely pervasive in the work of the Spanish poet: 'Thus the Creator / finds himself revived by his own creature: / he thrives on the same spirit he exhales,' say the last lines of the octave in Paterson's version (Paterson 1999b, 10), which it is tempting to read as an *ars poetica*.

Profesión de Fe	Profession of Faith

Dios no es el mar, está en el mar, riela	God is not the sea, is in the sea, shimmers
como luna en el agua, o aparece	like the moon on the water, or appears
como una blanca vela;	like a white sail;
en el mar se despierta o se adormece.	in the sea he awakes or sleeps.
Creó la mar, y nace	He created the sea and is born
de la mar cual la nube y la tormenta;	from the sea like the clouds and the storms;
es el Criador y la criatura lo hace;	he is the Creator and the creature creates him;
su aliento es alma, y por el alma alienta.	his breath is soul, and he breathes for the soul.
Yo he de hacerte, mi Dios, cual tú me hiciste,	I have to make you, my god, like you made me
y para darte el alma que me diste	and to give you the soul that you gave me
en mí te he de crear. Que el puro río	in myself I have to create you. May the pure river
de caridad que fluye eternamente	of charity that flows eternally
fluya en mi corazón. ¡Seca, Dios mío,	flow in my heart. Dry up, my Lord,
de una fe sin amor la turbia fuente!	the turbid fountain of a faith without love!

(my translation)

Paterson's dream of a singerless song and of a self-sustaining momentum in the poem is somehow reflected in his translation of Machado's pantheistic vision. Significantly, he chose not to translate the original chiasmus in the Spanish version ('su aliento es alma, y por el alma alienta'), a choice that lays less emphasis on the presence of the deity, and indeed allows for a more fluent and direct exhalation of the line.

On the whole, Paterson's poem is less repetitive and less focused on reversals and parallels than Machado's. Paterson's sestet does away with the repetitive and still chiasmic structures of 'he de hacerte'/'te he de crear' and 'mi Dios'/'Dios mío', which emphasized the interlacing of God with the speaker and the speaker with God. Instead, the version focuses on liquidity and a sense of flow. These qualities are already very present in the Spanish text with its pervasive liquid consonants, as well as the combination of two different kinds of lines: hendecasyllabic lines belonging to the traditional sonnet, and two shorter lines (heptasyllabic), belonging to *arte menor*, of popular origins.

However, they are amplified in Paterson's English with assonantal echoes of the sounds [u] and [ou], which indeed seem to flow through the lines, and with an entire stanza based on run-on lines, instead of just two in Machado's original sestet. The version is reminiscent of the musicality of 'Waking with Russell', which was published only four years later. It is clearly intent on emphasizing the free-flowing rhythmicality at the core of this pantheistic vision. It recreates a breath while neglecting its divine origin.

The spirit that Paterson translates is more rhythmical than spiritual, especially when one considers that the central image of Machado's sonnet, 'río de caridad', is translated as 'empty heart' in Paterson's poem. The change reads like a projection of Machado's later scepticism as well as Paterson's own atheism onto this text. It also reads at first as a bit of a contradiction with the rest, even in Paterson's own version, though not if one interprets it as a way for the Scottish poet to depart from a vision of the 'spirit' as religious in order to emphasize its lack of origin: it is a product of the celebration, i.e. a product of the poem itself. This in turn may function as a metapoetic comment in the context of a versioned text. It suggests that one might not want to consider the two sonnets solely as an original and its translation, but also as two separate poems sharing in the same spirit, the same lyric gesture. It shows an insistence on the flow rather than the source, on the texture of poetic diction rather than its origin, which will come to characterize most of Paterson's later work.

Rabaté describes gestures as 'more or less voluntary, more or less eloquent: they have to be practised, the way painters or martial arts masters practise in order to achieve the self-effacement necessary to execute their gestures in the most perfect way' (Rabaté 2013, 14, my translation). His reflections on lyrical gestures are a departure from a hypostatized view of the lyrical subject. In that respect, they seem particularly fit to describe the instability and fluidity that characterize the spirit of Paterson's versions.

But where does the sonnet form itself come into play? Where can we see its impact in Paterson's shift towards a poetics of self-effacement? About half the poems that he chose to translate in *The Eyes* are sonnets. The early development of his inquiry into the spirit of the translated text therefore coincides with the translation of mostly sonnets. My hypothesis is thus that Paterson's interest in the essence of the sonnet form provided both an ideal vehicle and a structuring counterpoint to his inquiry into the lyrical gesture of the text.

'Poetry' (Paterson 1999a, 28) is an interesting case in point. The Spanish poem it derives from was taken from a series of texts titled 'Otras canciones a Guiomar' (Machado 280), and was a fifteen-liner. Paterson chose to turn it into a sonnet, endowing it with a manifesto-like quality by renaming it 'Poetry'. Although the text riffs on a poetics of discretion and self-effacement, Paterson's hand in the reshuffling of the text is quite conspicuous, for he completely changes the order of the images and arguments. One of the most striking choices is the displacement of the central 'Bajo el azul olvido, nada canta, / ni tu nombre ni el mio, el agua santa' ('Under the oblivious blue of the sky, the sacred water sings nothing, neither your name nor mine', my translation) to the final couplet. The rest of the poem is therefore only one sentence – as was the case in the previous version, the sense of fluidity of the text is increased, through this image of water singing its own song. By affirming his presence as translator, Paterson paradoxically reinforces the sonnet's transparency.

Nonetheless, the sonnet form also provides a new structure to the argument of the poem, with a turn at line 9 clearly marked by a conjunction – 'but if it yields a steadier light'. Paterson's couplet is also separated from the rest by a line break; he emphasizes the sense of serenity of the last two lines by adding a respiration to the text, which (despite the absence of a clear rhyme scheme) is provided by the traditional framework of the Elizabethan sonnet. The blank space on the page is a reminder of the missing line, an insistence on the poem's movement towards silence, and a way to point at an underlying structure of poetic speech. The structure of the sonnet becomes a blueprint for the assertion of a poetics of disappearance of the self, as well as a discreet way to highlight the subverbal and potentially impersonal bodily function that breath constitutes.

In a sonnet from *Orpheus* titled 'The Spin', Paterson describes a dancer as a 'translator of all passing / into act' (Paterson 2006, 48), a rather distant version of Rilke's own 'Verlegung / alles Vergehens in Gang' (192). Significantly, the dancer's capacity to embody the ephemeral and the ungraspable is equated with the work of translation, as though Paterson's interest in the 'spirit' of the text also has to do with capturing a sense of the body at work – inextricably tied to speech, breath is possibly the most pervasive and yet the most fleeting lyrical gesture.

In his afterword to *Orpheus*, Paterson interprets the rose of Rilke's sonnets as a representation of the Austrian poet's own song: 'Below the layers of song upon song, there was nothing but the radiant nothingness to which he saw himself returned, and from which the song would emerge again, in the mouth of another Orpheus' (64). At times, Paterson's own versions sound like an amplification of Rilke's quasi-pantheistic interest in an elemental flow of poetic speech. In a review of *Orpheus*, American poet and critic Mark Doty writes that 'the marvel of these sonnets [is] that the nearly unsayable is given a spoken solidity, words that can point towards if not encompass the peculiar flowing fact of human presence' (n.p.). At first glance, Paterson's versions of Rilke are generally closer to the arguments and syntactic organizations of the original poems than were his versions of Machado; one could say that the translation process is more transparent. In that sense, it is consistent with Rilke's vision of an atemporal principle of singing operating through anonymous Orphic figures. Hence also the shortening of the title, for, as Adam Philips has pointed out, 'by calling the book Orpheus rather than Sonnets to Orpheus, Paterson keeps the address of the poems open; the book is at once by Orpheus to Orpheus and about Orpheus' (n.p.).

But such transparency can also be connected with an attachment to a certain lyrical gesture. Here's how Paterson translates Rilke's reflection on breath in the first poem of the second section in the *Sonnets to Orpheus*:

> Breath, you invisible poem –
> pure exchange, sister to silence, (Paterson 2006, 31)

If one follows Paterson's view that Rilke's sonnets 'constitute a kind of meta-essay on the possibilities of the sonnet form' (Paterson 2006, 62), Paterson's poem, which comes at the beginning of the second part of his collection (like Rilke's), is therefore placed at the turn of the meta-poem. Its evocation of respiration as a constant binary cosmic link may be read as a commentary on the sonnet form – possibly depicting the turn or *volta* as its natural locus of respiration.

The idea of the poet picking up a principle of singing is certainly central to this version about breath: one example of that is the way Paterson manages to preserve a relatively similar stress pattern in the first six lines of his poem, which might be said to form its argumentative sestet. The trochaic start to the first five lines is kept, possibly because of the inspiration/expiration movement it seems to mimic. Yet, in the sixth line, Paterson chooses to amplify the poem's rhythm of cosmic exchange with a series of three accented syllables that give the line a kind of slow tidal force ('by stealth, by the **same slow wave**'), as of a wave flowing in. Thus, Paterson's translation of the 'spirit' functions as an amplification of the sonnet's own breath. As the poem suggests, breathing is a deeply intimate and yet mostly unconscious bodily activity; as such, it combines the personal and the impersonal into an inextricable knot. Paterson's emphasis on the spirit of this sonnet works through the same paradoxical association, as its appropriation leads to an amplification of its sense of transparency and transpersonality.

Conclusion: Performing disappearance

In spite of Paterson's materialism and his emphasis on the spirit as a body-text gesture, related to breath, the spirit may also have to do with a more spectral approach to the translated text, with an attempt to make present an irremediably absent voice. *Rain*, Paterson's 2009 collection, can be read as a book-long elegy to his friend, the Irish-American poet Michael Donaghy, who died brutally in 2004. It contains several mourning sonnets, and two of them are versions. One is titled 'Miguel' (49),[9] after Cesar Vallejo's famous poem 'A mi hermano Miguel' (Vallejo 112).

In a translator's note to this poem, Paterson wrote:

> I couldn't bring myself to start work on a poem of my own, an elegy for the poet Michael Donaghy. […] I began fiddling with this poem for no good reason I could think of, oblivious even to the big fat clue of the title. Vallejo's original poem is no sonnet, but seems to me to have the soul of one. (Paterson and Vallejo 2008, 76)

'Miguel' is pervaded by silences and echoes, the most obvious one being located at the turn, where the tragic irony of the eighth line quietly resonates in the line break. The speaker is obviously haunted but refuses to admit the loss, and remains in the realm of play. Yet, 'hunting and hunting' is but one letter short of the admission that he is only looking for a ghost, something the repetition makes painfully obvious.

The 'soul' of Vallejo's poem is certainly akin to the organization of a sonnet: the late introduction of the brother's name is a sort of turn, for it echoes the initial 'Hermano' and marks the introduction of the story of his death. But the soul that Paterson alludes to is obviously twofold: the division that structures the text as well as the central lack that organizes it. In a book of aphorisms, Paterson writes that '[t]he self is a universal vanishing point' (Paterson 2007, 51). This poem's soul is certainly both an ungraspable presence and a central element of structure. In that sense also, it is a lyrical gesture.

'Miguel' riffs on the notion of play as a way to accept separation and domesticate loss. Despite Paterson's story about not realizing at first that his interest in Miguel was in reality a way of dealing with the loss of Michael, I believe that the poem does indeed have a soul or spirit that the sonnet form is used here to contain, in both senses of the word. In the same way that the hide and seek game of the two poems works as a metaphorical equivalent for mourning, a fort-da game of sorts, Paterson's versioning of Vallejo's text into a sonnet is a way of playing a mourning game with a spectral presence.

Two pages earlier in *Rain*, Paterson included a version of Robert Desnos's 'Le Paysage' translated as 'The Landscape' (47). Published at the end of Desnos's life, the sonnet is a sort of negative history of the love poem and its relationship to the landscape. Its very traditional form and acknowledgement of the impossibility of a definition ('Le mot qu'aucun lexique au monde n'a traduit') is reminiscent of Desnos's own departure from modernist and surrealist poetics. It insists on the elusive, the undefinable, while in the last stanza the lyric 'I' evokes a rigidity which is at once formal, physical and natural:

A vieillir tout devient rigide et lumineux,	As they age, all things grow rigid and bright.
Des boulevards sans noms et des cordes sans nœuds.	The streets fall nameless, and the knots untie.
Je me sens roidir avec le paysage.	Now, with this landscape, I fix, I shine.
(Desnos 57)	(Paterson 2009, 47)

Of course, such rigidity is also partly a rigor mortis, a sense of approaching death that finds its poetic echo in the return of formal constraint. American poet Dan Chiasson wrote that '"Rain" is a book of middle age, its Janus face looking back at youthful excess and wondering what on earth comes next' (n.p.). This tercet is partly a response to such puzzlement: if both sonnets perform a fatalistic acceptance of one's undoing, Paterson's version doesn't reach the discreet musical balance of Desnos's sonnet. In a note to his translation, he explains that 'Le Paysage' has long 'struck [him] as one of those poems so deeply folded in its own music, it almost defines "the problem of translation"' (Desnos and Paterson 63). Perhaps the music of Desnos's poem felt impossible to capture, but Paterson's translation certainly amplifies the sense of self-abandonment that is so central to the last stanza. While 'des cordes sans noeuds' cannot but evoke the Fates and the severance of all ties that comes with death, 'the knots untie' may also be read phonically as 'the nots unt-I', thus echoing a negation of the self performed through versioning and an attachment to the form. In Paterson's version, the repetition of the pronoun and the presence of the final assonantal [aɪ] rhyme literalizes the loss of oneself to the landscape/poem. This shines through the lines as a lyrical gesture that dislocates the 'I' through the rigidity of a form.

As a response to death, mourning and the unanswerable questions they conjure, Paterson turned to versioning as an art of absence and haunting. The stability of the form and the 'invisible poem' produced by the act of translation seem to have provided him with a space for the exploration of a series of lyrical gestures that perform disappearance.

Notes

1. The most striking example of this is 'The Version', a prose piece interestingly placed at the centre of Paterson's most recent sonnet sequence, *40 Sonnets*. Its resemblance to the sonnet lies mainly in its 8/6 proportions as well as in a dialectical structure. It is of course no coincidence that this experiment on the sonnet form should tell a playful story about translation and its perils which is itself presented, in a *mise en abyme*, as a version of Chilean poet Nicanor Parra.
2. For instance, in 2018, he published *Lyric, Sign, Metre*, a seven-hundred-page 'treatise'. With Paterson's characteristically informal approach to fundamental topics, its preface describes the book as an attempt to answer two questions: 'Firstly, does the existence of the poem point to a basic function of speech, and, if so, what is its purpose? Secondly, what *is* a poem?' He then goes on to describe the volume as practice-based poetic analysis, or 'an insider's perspective' (p. xiii).
3. For example, in *Lyric, Sign, Metre*: 'For millennia, religion allowed us to posit a distant parental overseer when we found ourselves unable to cope with the reality of our own cosmic orphanhood. [...] [We] still allow our thinking to be shaped by an idea just as perverse, one that I strongly suspect has its origins in our earlier theism: that "things mean something", and that there is some natural mechanism by which things are "lent meaning". The idea that that material objects, processes or events can somehow possess immaterial truths is, I suspect, a candidate for mankind's greatest errors' (p. 107).
4. The *via negativa* is a philosophical approach to theology which asserts that no finite concepts or attributes can be adequately used of God, but only negative terms. In the afterword to *The Eyes* Paterson wrote: 'The plan, in selecting from Machado's work, was to take a leisurely stroll down the *via negativa*; with Machado as guide, a less bleak route than the brochures describe' (p. 59).
5. At the end of his afterword to *The Eyes*, Paterson compares the influence of 'tutelary voices'. He explains that 'his own hand in the dark, Emil Cioran' had a similar role for him as Miguel de Unamuno for Machado (p. 60). Paterson has in fact emulated some aspects of Cioran's work in his own books of aphorisms: *The Book of Shadows* (2004) and *The Blind Eye* (2007).
6. Zen and quietist principles are present in Paterson's work, as his interest in traditional Japanese and Chinese poetry suggests. In *God's Gift to Women*, he included a blank page titled 'On Going to Meet a Zen Master in the Kyushu Mountains and Not Finding Him' (p. 39). He made a similar joke in *Rain* (p. 31), but he also included a Renku titled '*Renku*: My Last Thirty-Five Deaths' (p. 22) and a version of Tang dynasty poet Li Po (p. 43). Interestingly, Zen-inspired poetry becomes a less playful presence in Paterson's elegiac collection.

7   'Secondly, there is *a sense of history*: because we recognize the sonnet as a form from the past, a form with its own past, a poet who adopts it says that she cannot begin anew, that she acknowledges some sort of past in her poem' (Burt p. 246).
8   'I think he's been a sort of global presence [...] The complexity of his propositions and the depths of his thinking are really extraordinary' (Paterson 2012). He seems particularly interested in Frost's sonnets. For instance, he placed 'The Silken Tent' at the beginning of his anthology of sonnets, describing it as 'one of the most brilliantly sustained conceits in the English language, and as a fine a love poem as you'll ever read' (Paterson 1999a, p. 104). In 2010, he also gave a lecture titled 'Frost as a Thinker' at the Aldeburgh Poetry Festival, in which he discussed (among other poems) Frost's sonnet 'Design'.
9   This sonnet also echoes the opening poem of the collection, 'Two Trees', which is not a sonnet but a poem structured around union and division. Its first twelve lines tell the story of a 'Don Miguel' who one day decides 'to graft his orange to his lemon tree'. In the second stanza, the 'fused seam' has been split by the new owner and Don Miguel has disappeared. Despite a final line which states that 'trees are all this poem is about', the two trees and the disappearance of Don Miguel obviously recall the loss of Paterson's friend. Additionally, the poem's divided structure, as well as its final envoi, are certainly haunted by a sonnet-like necessity, but the twelve-line-long stanzas cannot but evoke sonnets devoid of their final couplets.

Works cited

Burt, Stephanie. 'The Contemporary Sonnet'. *The Cambridge Companion to the Sonnet*. Edited by A. D. Cousins and Peter Howarth. Cambridge University Press, 2011, pp. 245–266.

Chiasson, Dan. 'Forms of Attention'. *The New Yorker*. April 2010. https://www.newyorker.com/magazine/2010/04/19/forms-of-attention. Accessed 16 February 2018.

Desnos, Robert. *Contrée/Calixto*. Gallimard, 2013.

Desnos, Robert and Don Paterson. 'The Landscape'. *Poetry*, vol. 188, no. 1, 2006: pp. 62–64.

Doty, Mark. 'Review: Orpheus by Don Paterson'. *The Guardian*. 11 November 2006. http://www.theguardian.com/books/2006/nov/11/featuresreviews.guardianreview26. Accessed 16 February 2018.

Haughton, Hugh. 'Golden Means: Music, Translation and the Patersonnet'. *Don Paterson, Contemporary Critical Essays*. Edited by Natalie Pollard. Edinburgh University Press, 2014, pp. 34–48.

Machado, Antonio. *Poesías Completas*. Espasa Calpé, 1969.

Paterson, Don. *40 Sonnets*. Faber & Faber, 2015.

Paterson, Don. *101 Sonnets: From Shakespeare to Heaney*. Faber & Faber, 1999a.
Paterson, Don. *The Blind Eye: A Book of Late Advice*. Faber & Faber, 2007.
Paterson, Don. *The Eyes*. Faber & Faber, 1999b.
Paterson, Don. *God's Gift to Women*. Faber & Faber, 1997.
Paterson, Don. *Landing Light*. Faber & Faber, 2003.
Paterson, Don. *Lyric, Sign, Metre*. Faber & Faber, 2018.
Paterson, Don. *Orpheus: A Version of Rainer Maria Rilke*. Faber & Faber, 2006.
Paterson, Don. 'Poetry and Politics: Reading and Conversation with Don Paterson and Dan Chiasson'. Boston University. YouTube. April 2012. https://www.youtube.com/watch?v=rCDiMTS2eb8. Accessed 5 January 2021.
Paterson, Don. *Rain*. Faber & Faber, 2009.
Paterson, Don. *Reading Shakespeare's Sonnets, A New Commentary by Don Paterson*. Faber & Faber, 2010.
Paterson, Don and César Vallejo. 'Miguel'. *Poetry*, vol. 192, no. 1, 2008: pp. 75–77.
Philips, Adam. 'Review: Orpheus by Don Paterson'. *The Guardian*. 29 October 2006. http://www.theguardian.com/books/2006/oct/29/poetry.features2. Accessed 16 February 2018.
Rabaté, Dominique. *Gestes Lyriques*. Corti, 2013.
Rabaté, Dominique. 'A World of Gestures'. *Journal of Literary Theory*, vol. 11, no. 1, March 2017: pp. 89–96.
Rilke, Rainer Maria. *Les Elégies de Duino suivi de Les sonnets à Orphée*. Points, [1922] 2006.
Vallejo, César. *Obra poética completa*. Alianza Editorial, 1999.

Part Three

Sonnet migrations across and outside Europe: Translating as a political act

11

Translation and transnationalism: Reframing the contemporary Irish sonnet

Erin Cunningham

The prevalence of the sonnet in twentieth- and twenty-first-century Irish poetry has been the source of much recent commentary and criticism. Interventions by Alan Gillis, Stephen Regan and Tara Guissin-Stubbs have foregrounded the multiplicity and mutability of the sonnet by highlighting its various permutations across the modern history of Irish verse, drawing on a range of poets from the North and the Republic writing sonnets both conventional and experimental. Despite this variety in the Irish sonnet's contexts, contents and formal attributes, however, many critics read the form through a stubbornly Anglocentric lens, insisting on the English sonnet as the primary point of reference for its Irish counterpart. Helen Vendler, for example, proposes that W. B. Yeats understood the sonnet to be 'associated with the essential English lyric tradition' (147); Jason David Hall, writing on Seamus Heaney and the sonnet, describes it as 'an embodiment of standard English versification' (85); and Ronald Marken suggests that 'Irish poets have reconstituted the English sonnet's intricate machinery' (86). In many cases, these assessments are well justified; Irish poets often enter into dialogue with the English sonnet tradition, as demonstrated by engagements with Edmund Spenser such as Brendan Kennelly's *Cromwell*, Trevor Joyce's *Rome's Wreck* and Ciaran Carson's *The Twelfth of Never*, or recent rewritings of Shakespeare's sonnets by Paul Muldoon, Michael Longley, Bernard O'Donoghue and Nick Laird in Elizabeth Scott-Baumann and Hannah Crawforth's *On Shakespeare's Sonnets: A Poets' Celebration*. Some of these examples indicate the influence of their English intertexts, while others mount a postcolonial rebuke, using the sonnet as a site at which England's historical dispossession of the Irish can be rewritten and undermined. These complexities have lent themselves to many nuanced critical treatments of the relationship between the English and the Irish sonnet; Regan, for example, begins his study of the Irish sonnet by noting that 'the refinement of the English sonnet that begins with Sidney's *Astrophil and Stella* in 1591 coincides with one of the most decisive phases of English colonial settlement in Ireland', going on to consider use of the form by poets such as Thomas MacDonagh in order to assess 'how English lyric forms might be fused with Irish poetic forms like the *aisling* (or dream vision) in the creation of a new and distinctive Anglo–Irish poetry' (158). However, crucial as this negotiation between English and Irish poetics is to any critical consideration of the sonnet in Irish poetry, it is also imperative to consider the sonnet's origins in Italy and its prevalence in poetic traditions outside of England, and Irish sonnets' concomitant engagement with a range of national and international contexts. Indeed, as Gillis has noted, the English sonnet itself is various and ever evolving, 'giv[ing] the lie to simplistic ideas of a homogenized English sonnet tradition, against which the Irish sonnet must do battle' (570). Although it rightly draws attention to the postcolonial dynamics of Irish writers' use of form, a critical framework which takes the sonnet to be tied necessarily to Englishness risks replicating them through a failure to acknowledge Irish poets' independence from the English tradition. In this chapter, I examine the sonnet in Irish poetry with reference to various European poetic histories, considering Irish poets' use of translation and adaptation to posit alternative contexts for the form.[1]

The cross-national recurrence of the sonnet has been made apparent in recent years by the output of a group of Irish poets whose work has consciously and deliberately taken on international dimensions. In his 2015 monograph *Between Two Fires: Transnationalism and Cold War Poetry*, one of these poets, Justin Quinn, writes that 'the sonnet is one of the great transnational success stories of poetry, originating in Italy in the thirteenth century, and travelling into many other European languages over the subsequent centuries' (26). The sonnet therefore serves as a prime example of what Quinn terms 'the transnational dynamic', a defining principle in his critical writing, through which 'a poetry in another literary culture and language is recognized and interpreted, and then conveyed across the borders that intervene' (57). The form, which from its medieval Italian origins has assumed a central position in multiple national poetic traditions, is notable for its historical endurance and its geographical mobility; Regan writes: 'Its versatility and adaptability can be measured historically, through its extraordinary persistence among poetic forms, but also geographically, through the expansive terrain in which it has made itself at home' (392). The sonnet is historically a vector through which poetry has travelled across and between nations, and is a notable presence in Quinn's explorations of transnationalism.

In his *Cambridge Introduction to Modern Irish Poetry*, Quinn asserts a definitive contrast between the focused nationalist literary culture in full force at the beginning of the twentieth century and the purportedly more cosmopolitan, international poetic culture of its end. Examining the poets of his generation, including David Wheatley, Vona Groarke, Caitríona O'Reilly and Conor O'Callaghan, Quinn closes his study with the assertion that '[t]hese more recent poets do not move in concert with a larger nationalist objective, as the poets of a century before did. Rather, they bear witness to the multitudes the island contains, and have extended its borders to include a fair piece of the known world' (210). This is not to say that Irish poets working at the turn of the twentieth century entirely rejected transnational paradigms; Yeats, for example, turns to the European sonnet tradition in drawing upon the sonnets of Pierre de Ronsard. He uses Ronsard's 'Quand vous serez bien vieille' as a model for his poem 'When You Are Old', although he converts Ronsard's sonnet into a twelve-line douzaine, while a later homage to Ronsard, 'At the Abbey Theatre', retains Ronsard's original sonnet form. In replicating the appeal to the French poet Pontus de Tyard with which Ronsard begins his sonnet 'Tyard, on me blasmoit' with an address to 'Dear Craoibhin Aoibhin' (190), the pseudonym of Irish Revival scholar and president of the Gaelic League Douglas Hyde, Yeats draws upon French poetics to explore a parallel web of Irish artistic authority and influence. Vendler also notes that this is the first Shakespearean sonnet that Yeats published, meaning that his preliminary engagement with the sonnet's English form is, ironically, achieved by turning to France: 'At last, by an end-run through France, Yeats has been able to bestow the external form of the Shakespearean sonnet on an Irish poem' (168). 'At the Abbey Theatre' thus demonstrates the complexity of the various influences that came to bear upon the sonnet in Ireland, undermining any possibility of clearly delineating the sonnet's national allegiances and echoing the English sonnet's own permeability and its evolution from external influences. Nevertheless, as Quinn indicates, contemporary Irish poets have displayed a particularly potent interest in transnationalism and translation – one which is evident in their uses of the sonnet.

Quinn's definition of his generation's principles and priorities is clearly visible in the editorial workings of *Metre*, the poetry journal founded and edited by Quinn and Wheatley (along with Hugh Maxton, or W. J. McCormack, for its first issues), which ran from 1995 to 2005 and, although based in Ireland, advertised itself as a 'Magazine of International Poetry', with special issues dedicated to Australian, American and Central European verse, as well as one on Irish poetry and the diaspora. The journal had a clear emphasis on translation, featuring poems by and profiles of poets from around the globe. In addition to this, *Metre* is also notable for its emphasis on form, which is carried over into Quinn and Wheatley's poetry. Fran Brearton writes that their poetry, along with that of their contemporaries, demonstrates a 'fascination with form, a fascination worn on the sleeve' (631), while Conor O'Callaghan characterizes *Metre* by 'greater formal determinism, a more international perspective, empiricism, rationalism and wit' as compared to earlier Irish poetry (xv). O'Callaghan's bringing together of the 'formal' and the 'international' suggests an affiliation between the two, in the vein of a number of poetic movements which have signalled their cosmopolitanism through their recourse to established forms, many of them European.[2] In his introduction to *Metre*'s 'Irish Poetry and the Diaspora' issue, Quinn states of Irish poets living and working abroad: 'That one is far from the green, green grass of home might be just cause for many a maudlin moan but it can also provide a healthy dislocation for the imagination, as exhilarating as switching to free-verse after twenty years of sonnets' (7). However, despite Quinn's metaphorical association of free verse with the liberating qualities of travel and internationalism, both his poetry and that of Wheatley suggest that on a pragmatic level the opposite is true, with the poets frequently employing the sonnet to forge cultural connections beyond Ireland.

Wheatley's sonnets often acknowledge their debt to French poetry, responding to a range of poets including Corbière, Valéry and Baudelaire. 'The Owl', published in his 2006 collection *Mocker*, is subtitled 'after Baudelaire', and takes as its cue the French poet's sonnet 'Les Hiboux', from *Les Fleurs du mal*. Wheatley's poem translates the broad sense of Baudelaire's, but a series of changes both modernize it and critique its conclusions, revealing alternative convictions on Wheatley's behalf. 'The Owl' retains the loosely Petrarchan structure of Baudelaire's octave, with both versions employing a greater variety of rhyme words than the traditional Petrarchan sonnet; this enclosed structure is echoed by the first line – 'Owl at my window, window owl' – in which Petrarchan ABBA rhymes are reproduced rhetorically by Wheatley's use of chiasmus (25). This proscribed, contained structure is an apt vehicle for Baudelaire's owls – rendered singular in Wheatley's version – which sit '[s]ans remuer', or 'without stirring' (105). The sonnet uses the stationary figure of the owl to reflect symbolically upon the quality of wisdom, with Baudelaire writing that 'il faut en ce monde qu'il [le sage] craigne / Le tumulte et le mouvement', and that man '[p]orte toujours le châtiment / D'avoir voulu changer de place' (105).[3] Wheatley echoes this in his adaptation with the injunction 'don't just do / something, stand there!', a humorous inversion of the usual phrase which takes up Baudelaire's call to inaction and, in thus making a joke of it – mocking it, as per the title of his collection – also casts it into doubt (25).

The poem is full of alterations and details which subtly undermine Baudelaire's warning against 'changing places'. The black yew trees – 'ifs noirs' (104) – described at the beginning of Baudelaire's poem are replaced in Wheatley's by sycamores. Unlike the yew, which is native to Ireland and the United Kingdom and features in both Irish and English folklore, the sycamore, although now ubiquitous in both, is not indigenous to either country, and comes from mainland Europe. Wheatley, originally from Dublin and living and working in Hull at the time *Mocker* was published, therefore hints at the centrality of cultural import to his work, writing himself in a European form which has become similarly widespread across Britain and Ireland. The tree's 'midnight' colouring, an alteration of Baudelaire's 'black', also recalls Heaney's poem of that name, which describes the felling of Ireland's native trees by the English, its '[f]orests coopered to wine casks' – the idea of native or natural forms, inherent to a given nation, does not hold up against the changes wrought by history (Heaney 1972, 45). Wheatley draws out the connotations of international movement contained within Baudelaire's description of his owls as 'dieux étrangers' (104), or foreign gods, designating the owl as an 'alien' whose apparent stillness belies the precise mobility which Baudelaire condemns – '[his] red eye roves / while he sits tight' (25). Despite the 'unflappable' 'perfect calm' which appears to connote a preferred stillness, the poem is continually aware of movement, on both an intimate and a global scale, suggesting that the need to 'change places' is more inevitable than Baudelaire allows (25). This is enacted on a poetic level by Wheatley's translation of the sonnet, which transports the French poet across contexts, nations and languages.

The owl's quality of surveillance – his slightly mechanical 'red eye' – also adds a sinister quality to his stillness, connecting him to Wheatley's 'police copter or car alarm' (25) and Baudelaire's 'châtiment', or 'punishment' (105). This imbues the owl with an authoritarian character, questioning the extent and purpose of his wisdom. 'Bempton', a later sonnet in *Mocker*, invokes the Bempton cliffs, a Yorkshire nature reserve home to a range of seabirds. The poem's epigraph states that 'In past centuries it was believed that migrating birds would winter on the moon', and the poem itself, in defiance of the purported wisdom of the owl, accordingly celebrates travel and movement; the birds have 'always another sea to cross / Each sanctuary a new departure lounge' (39). The title of Wheatley's collection again comes into play; in contrast to the authoritarianism of the owl, the seabirds of 'Bempton' function as the rebellious 'mockers' to which it refers. They are described as 'jokers', 'mock-whiskered' with catches of fish, 'laughing', 'roaring', 'side-splitting', and 'guffaw[ing]' (39). Wheatley's collection, rather than the staid confines of prescriptive 'wisdom', celebrates freedom, irreverence, humour – all qualities which he connects emphatically to travel and movement, echoing the international vistas which he and Quinn seek to open up in *Metre*. However, this freedom of movement is not associated with a corresponding foray into free verse in 'Bempton'. Instead, Wheatley retains the sonnet and simply adapts it slightly to reflect his change in emphasis, rearranging the enclosed Petrarchan rhymes of 'The Owl' into a more open-ended cross-rhymed ABAB shape. Indeed, the sonnet represents the cultural movement and exploration that the owl's rigid injunctions attempt to quash, providing a means by which Wheatley can write across languages and cultures.

A similar variety of adaptive translation has appeared in the work of several contemporary Irish poets, frequently connected to the sonnet. Ciaran Carson's *The Alexandrine Plan* translates sonnets by Baudelaire, Mallarmé and Rimbaud, and, like Wheatley's 'The Owl', reflects some of the translator's background and preoccupations in its rendering of the poems. The first poem in the collection, 'The Green Bar', a translation of Rimbaud's 'Au Cabaret-Vert', uses both direct translation and metaphorical embellishment to alter the original national orientations of Rimbaud's sonnet. Charleroi, the Belgian city where 'Au Cabaret-Vert' is set, is translated as 'Kingstown', the former name of Dún Laoghaire (which would have been accurate in 1870, the year of Rimbaud's poem). The 'Cabaret-Vert' of Rimbaud's title becomes 'the old Green Bar', while 'la table / Verte' is translated as 'the shamrock / Table' (12–13). Using stereotypical markers of Irishness to relocate Rimbaud's sonnet, Carson suggests the instability of ideas of nation, conveying the falsity of such a version of Ireland by extracting it artificially from a completely separate national and linguistic context. In the same year as *The Alexandrine Plan* he published *The Twelfth of Never*, a collection of sonnets written in French alexandrine metre which subjects such depictions of Irishness to similar scrutiny, parodying an idea of Ireland as a mythologized, imaginary Neverland – a 'green hill far away', home to 'fairy cobblers' and 'schools of fishes' (*Poems* 351). Here, in his sonnet 'The Rising of the Moon', Carson combines French and Irish revolutionary imagery, as in the lines: 'She urged me to go out and revolutionize / Hibernia, and not to fear the guillotine' (357). This drawing together of French and Irish revolutions has its basis in history; the United Irishmen Rebellion of 1798 occurred while the French Revolution was ongoing, and also attracted French aid, with French troops sailing to Ireland to support the rebels there. Carson thus demonstrates an interest in cross-national European revolutionary histories which informs his use of the sonnet, and of the alexandrine specifically. As Tara Guissin-Stubbs notes in her study of the modern Irish sonnet, Carson's sonnets are deeply indebted to the form's French iterations above all others; he demonstrates an 'ultimate preference for French, rather than Elizabethan English, sonnet models' (119). *The Twelfth of Never* and *The Alexandrine Plan* are roughly coterminous with Wheatley and Quinn's publication of their first collections in the mid to late 1990s, and demonstrate the sonnet's place in a poetic landscape which was taking an increasing interest in translation and internationalism.

In a similar manner to *The Alexandrine Plan*, Derek Mahon's collection *Echo's Grove* consists of poems which 'aren't translations, in the strict sense, but *versions* of their originals [...] *adapted* from their originals' (15). Mahon's foreword defends approximation as a translative principle, writing that '"The poetry" hides in its language of origin and is not finally translatable; we can only approximate. This being so, the best plan may be to approximate with zest, to refuse pedantry and intimidation' (18). Nevertheless, many of the translations, or adaptations, in *Echo's Grove* do demonstrate a notable degree of fidelity to the poems on which they are based, with Mahon's interjections of novel vocabulary or rhyming patterns serving to draw out not only his own concerns but those of the poets he translates. Although the collection comprises a range of forms and poetic traditions, there are numerous translations of the sonnet from Italian, French, Spanish and German; the first two sonnets to appear in the collection are by one of its most notable Italian innovators, Petrarch. 'Bedroom' transposes into English Petrarch's 'O cameretta che già fosti un porto', sonnet 234 of his *Canzoniere*. The poem narrates the transformation of its speaker's bedroom from a 'haven / from daily tempests' to 'a fountain basin for tears shed', invaded by a 'harsh' love which 'asperges every night the little bed [...] with mournful hands from a prodigious urn' (69). The striking image of an urn of tears comes from Petrarch's poem, in which the 'lagrime nocturne' which soak the bed are poured from an urn: 'di che dogliose urne / ti bagna Amor, con quelle mani eburne / solo ver 'me crudeli a sí gran torto' (1073).[4] In Petrarch, the urn is characterized as 'mournful', while the 'cruel' hands of a personification of 'Love' 'bathe' the bed in its contents. However, in Mahon's retelling it is the hands themselves which become 'mournful', while the Italian *bagna* ('bathes') by contrast takes on a more positive aspect in its translation as 'asperges' – the action of blessing with holy water. In translation, the sonnet therefore takes on a complex of new ambivalences – love, while punitive, is also sorrowful, and the anguish it provokes is legible in some aspects as a form of blessing. Through these contrasts, Mahon echoes and develops the extreme paradoxes of Petrarch's sonnets, characterizing love as a divine ecstasy overlaid with agony; in the same fashion, the bed, here a site of solitary anguish, is haunted by the 'mournful' spectre of Love's hands, which evoke and yet deny an alternative sexual potentiality for the titular bedroom.

The rhyme scheme of 'Bedroom' transforms the characteristic ABBA ABBA CDE CDE patterning of Petrarch's sonnet into a very loosely rhymed ABBAABAA CDCEED. However, the 'haven' which closes the first line, although affiliated by this rhyme scheme with the four other end words throughout the octave that culminate in an *n* sound, also pre-empts the 'hated' that concludes the penultimate line of 'Bedroom'. This passage from 'haven' to 'hated' neatly encapsulates the trajectory of the sonnet, in which the speaker's bedroom is transformed from a place of 'consolation' to one of 'shame and scorn' (69). A similar structure undergirds 'Exequy', an adaptation of Petrarch's 'Gli occhi di ch'io parlai sì caldamente' which follows 'Bedroom' in *Echo's Grove* and describes the loss of a beloved figure, moving from a triumphant blazon outlining sensual details of 'face and figure', 'angelic' qualities which 'seemed to make a paradise below', to the reduction of these body parts to 'insentient dust' (70). The Petrarchan conceit by which the beauty of a sonnet's object renders her divine is thus stripped away in a harsh realization of her mortality, with the speaker professing to renounce poetry itself as a result: 'Now there will be no more love poetry / the vital flow has dried up in the vein' (70). For Regan, despite its themes of loss and renouncement, 'Exequy' 'shimmers with the possibility of renewal' by 'speak[ing] eloquently of the persistence and durability of the sonnet over centuries' (402), while for Guissin-Stubbs it emphasizes this poetic longevity at the same time as it reveals the submerged deathliness of the love poem: 'the ability of the sonnet to both enshrine the frailty of human experience and to outlive the individual means that wherever we find an amatory sonnet, death will never be far behind' (193). This connection between love and death recalls us to the 'urn' wielded by love's personification in 'Bedroom', while the 'whisper of insentient dust' that remains of the speaker's loved one looks forward to Mahon's 'Art and Dust', a translation of Michelangelo's 'Com'esser, donna, può quel c'alcun vede' which follows shortly after 'Exequy' in *Echo's Grove* and affirms the tendency of art to outlive its creator: 'nature is conquered once again by art' (72). The word 'whisper', notably, is an innovation of Mahon's, with Petrarch's original line reading 'poca polvere son, che nulla sente' – 'are a little dust, which feels nothing' (1297). While Mahon's 'dust' retains the insentience of Petrarch's, it also assumes the character of a 'whisper', reflecting the 'echo' of his collection's title, or his avowal in his foreword to allow his poems' sources 'to remain audible' (15). The word 'sonnet' is itself rooted, through the Italian *sonetto* ('little song'), in the Latin *sonus* ('sound'), and Mahon emphasizes these aural connections in his counterbalancing of bodily mortality with enduring echoed or whispered speech, conceptualizing adaptation down the centuries as a web of approximate or ambivalent voices.

Although his use of the sonnet often foregrounds its early modern English incarnations, Heaney is another practitioner of the form who engages with alternative national sonnet traditions. Appearing in 2001's

Electric Light, 'The Gaeltacht' is 'a sonnet // In imitation of Dante's' – specifically 'Dante a Guido Cavalcanti', a poem written within the tradition of the love sonnet but addressed to Cavalcanti, Dante's fellow poet and close friend. Dante pictures himself and Cavalcanti, along with Lapo Gianni, another Florentine poet, and three lovers, on an enchanted boat ride at sea (Dante 69–70). Heaney overlays this scene onto a memory of a trip with friends – 'you and Barlo and I' – on the Atlantic Drive in Donegal's Rosguill Peninsula, speculating on the transposition of Dante's scene into an Irish setting: 'I wish, *mon vieux* [...] that it was again nineteen-sixty / And Barlo was alive' (49). Although the sonnet suggests the possibility of connection and commonality across time and geographical space, it is notably unsure of the soundness of this connection, wondering 'if' the sonnet might prove an appropriate 'wildtrack' to the 'gabble' of Irish-language conversation between figures with such clearly nationally inflected names as Paddy Joe and Aoibheann Marren. These disjunctures are reflected in Rui Carvalho Homem's account of the poem's 'polyglot irony'; he notes that '[t]he opening line quaintly mixes English with a French tag to suggest the familiarity of a past convivial moment shared by a group of friends in a Gaelic-speaking environment', with Heaney bringing the sonnet 'into English as the target language, certainly and inevitably; but also into the territory of a third language, a territory whose very designation rests on a *resistance* to English' (51–52). These tensions mean that the poem's account of its own translation is fraught with uncertainty, with the posited relationship between Heaney and Dante based in aspiration rather than reality – 'it would be great' if Heaney's sonnet after Dante could be synchronized, in the manner of a wildtrack, to Heaney's memories, but this sentiment is weighted by its conditional phrasing. The same goes for a more ideal, less temporally bound version of the interpersonal relationships in the poem; Heaney imagines past selves conversant with present, living with dead, but this fantasy is again anchored in the phrase 'it would be great', combining aspiration and impossibility. The formal similarities between Heaney's poem and Dante's are imperfect – with differences in rhyme scheme and line length, for instance – but this imperfection echoes the more personal concerns of the poem, whose nostalgia, be it for departed friends or the Irish language itself, carries with it an attendant awareness of loss. Heaney extends these concerns to the question of literary inheritance, placing himself within a tradition of sonnet writing which ranges back to its origins in medieval Italy, while acknowledging the specific valences of his Irish context and his consequent inability to recover entirely the properties of Dante's writing, implying that the relationship of the European sonnet tradition to contemporary Irish poetry is in a state of continual adjustment.

Quinn's use of the sonnet to engage with a range of international poetries is particularly pronounced. His sonnets are frequently based on translation and adaptation of other European writers. 'They stand around…', from his 2002 collection *Fuselage*, takes the eighth of Rilke's *Duino Elegies* as its cue, converting the long-form, unrhymed shape of Rilke's poems into a Shakespearean sonnet (59). In Quinn's hands, the elegiac mode is therefore translatable into sonnet form, as are other varieties of writing; the fourteenth sonnet of his sequence 'Prague Elegies', for example, is a conversion into rhyme of an 1854 letter by Czech writer Jan Neruda, which Quinn, originally from Dublin and now living in Prague, saw quoted in newspaper *Lidové Noviny* in 2004 (Quinn 2006, 54; 78). The sonnet therefore serves as an act of formal translation, transposing the expansive forms of the letter and the newspaper into its own more condensed shape at the same time as it converts their language from Czech to English. Neruda, Quinn notes, was 'one of the foremost writers of the Czech national revival' (Quinn 2006, 78). Just as he claims that Irish poetry has moved from the concentrated nationalism of its own Revival to a more open cosmopolitanism, so Neruda, a nationalist writer, is recontextualized in a sequence which, while it has Prague at its centre, extrapolates outwards across Europe to the Byzantine and Roman Empires; cultural and historical figures from across Europe including Mozart, Chekhov, Cardinal Richelieu and, significantly, Petrarch; and such symbols of globalization as Coca-Cola and the World Bank. Several of Quinn's sonnets adopt and adapt the writing of Joseph Brodsky, while his sonnet sequence 'The Months' is 'loosely inspired' by Tuscan poet Folgore da San Gimignano's *Sonetti dei Mesi* (Quinn 2011, 77). However, the sequence does not return directly to the sonnet's medieval Italian roots, instead tracing a lineage of translation; Quinn writes in his note to its seventh poem that '[t]his version has been made from Jiří Pelán's Czech translation of the medieval Italian original', and also highlights that he has directly excerpted the phrase 'boiled capons, sovereign kids' from Dante Gabriel Rossetti's translation of the poem (77). The eleventh poem in 'The Months' is a sonnet in Czech – 'Lido di Dante v listopadu', by Petr Borkovec – which is placed alongside an English translation (Quinn 2011, 34–35). Quinn's sonnets do not attempt to conceal the workings of translation, or purport to pass effortlessly from one language to another, but instead actively foreground translation as a cultural practice, suggesting the nomadic nature of the sonnet.

Quinn's adoptive city of Prague features frequently in his poetry, particularly in 'The Months' and 'Prague Elegies'. The latter narrates a history of Prague, drawing on the work of predominantly Czech historians (Quinn 2006, 78). One of the sonnets notes a connection between Charles IV, the fourteenth-century Holy Roman Emperor and King of Bohemia, and

Petrarch; Petrarch petitioned Charles to bring peace and unity to Italy, urging him to travel to Rome (Quinn 2006, 47). Quinn's choice of form therefore has a direct connection to the history he relates, and in this case represents another instance of travel, tied to the conflicting national and civic allegiances generated by histories of empire. Elsewhere, he engages with his Czech contexts through translation. 'Jan Zábrana: City Life and Country Youth', published in his 2015 collection *Early House*, is a translation of a poem from Czech poet and translator Zábrana's 1968 collection of sonnets *Pages from a Diary* (45). *Pages from a Diary*, like Quinn's poetry, frequently made use of epigraphs and excerpts taken from the work of other poets representing alternative national traditions; in *Between Two Fires*, Quinn writes that 'some nations and poets call out for translation. Zábrana answered that call throughout his life, making himself a kind of Cold War conduit for some of the finest poetry of the twentieth century from both East and West [...]. By relinquishing personal expression, he achieves an astonishing originality' (91). Although Quinn, naturally, is writing outside of the Cold War context which lent the cultural interchanges of Zábrana and his contemporaries such political significance, similar concerns and methods are clearly visible in his own poetry; he locates 'originality' in an engaged relationship to transnational literary histories.

For Quinn the sonnet therefore becomes a vehicle for the exploration of themes of translation, transnationalism and travel, yoking his international outlook with an investment in what O'Callaghan terms the *Metre* poets' 'formal determinism'. *Close Quarters* contains another sonnet sequence, 'On the Translator's Art', which is dedicated to Martin Hilský, a Czech translator of Shakespeare. The first poem in the sequence uses *A Midsummer Night's Dream*, with its themes of transformation and transferral of affections, to consider the work of the translator. Indeed, Shakespeare explicitly figures the many transformations that take place within the play as a form of translation; upon the transfiguration of Bottom's head into that of a donkey, Peter Quince exclaims, 'bless thee! thou art translated' (186), while Puck later states of the same incident that he 'left sweet Pyramus translated there' (195). Quinn recalls the play through his descriptions of '[k]ings and asses, spirits at their games', and 'lovers straying in the forest', all of them 'constantly translated / by good fellows with wands, quills or machines' (18). The transformations, or translations, that occur within the play are therefore placed on a continuum with the text's subsequent history of translation; in this first poem's final lines, where '[t]he players come back out and take their bows / before the people underneath the flag / of the royal court of Athens, London or Prague' (18), we move from the play's setting through its first performances in London to contemporary performances, in translated form, in Prague.

The formal settings of Shakespeare's drama are also emphasized by the sonnets; the 'love and hate' of his characters 'plays through them like fated / rhymes and rhythms' (18). That these 'rhymes and rhythms' are 'fated' suggests that the players follow a pre-established pattern, contained by form as well as plot. Here, Quinn gestures to the Shakespearean play as an institution which has been continually reinvented, but also the sonnet itself, which has likewise pervaded various cultural contexts. Hilský translated Shakespeare's sonnets, along with his plays, into Czech, while Quinn's sonnets, although still in English, also in a sense 'translate' the Shakespearean sonnet. The sequence is relatively faithful to Shakespeare's conventional sonnet form, although there is a notable transgression of sonnet structure in this first sonnet, which runs an enjambed line over the volta, creating a sense of continuity where there would usually be a turn in the argument of the poem. Although Shakespeare's sonnets are more flexible in this respect than Petrarch's, enjambment over the eighth line, which signifies the end of a second quatrain if not always a volta, is uncharacteristic of the Shakespearean sonnet. However, in Quinn's sonnet this feature places the word 'translated' – emphasized further by its conspicuous irresolution within the line – at the sonnet's traditional centre, therefore retaining the archetypal transformation signified by the volta semantically if not syntactically.

This is echoed by the second sonnet in the sequence, which similarly ends its eighth line with the pivotal word 'translation', this time end-stopped (19). This sonnet figures the translator ironically as a treacherous figure akin to Shakespearean villains such as Edmund and Iago – much like the run-on line which denied the previous sonnet its volta, 'these quick snakes have slipped across the crease / between two nations' (19). In this, Quinn also addresses the relationship between nationalism and the transnational poetics that he advocates, hinting at his earlier critical assertions that his own poetic generation in Ireland entered into a knowing betrayal of the nationalist convictions of earlier poets. The final couplet of the poem, which asks, 'How could a theatre planned by Palacky / be moved by someone with an MBE?' (19), gestures at a similar shift in Czech culture. František Palacký was a prominent figure in the Czech National Revival, which, similarly to the Irish and other national revivals that flourished in Europe over the course of the nineteenth century, theorized nationalism as the reinstatement of an originary language and culture. He founded the National Theatre in Prague, which sought to promote Czech national theatre; Quinn implies that its staging of translations by Hilský represents a turn away from these nationalist origins. However, the distinction between national theatre and foreign influences is itself compromised; as Hilský himself and others have emphasized, Czech translations of Shakespeare's sonnets and plays proliferated during the Czech national revival (Hilský 142; Procházka, Gibińska and March 46).

In these examples of cultural exchange across languages, Quinn considers the diverse settings of Shakespeare's plays, indicating the playwright's own transnationalism:

> Why are they speaking English anyway –
> these Danes, these Picts, these most Italian Greeks?
> Why shouldn't they talk Czech as well […?] (20).

He returns to the image of chernozem from the second sonnet – a fertile black soil found in Eastern Europe – with an image of 'mud' in the third:

> What source is not a multilingual mud?
> How great and deep is England without recourse
> to Roman, Swedish, French and Irish blood?
> […]
> Go for a walk
> through Whitechapel: at stalls above the sewer
> the accents clash, making English pure (20).

Quinn invokes the popular use of 'soil' as a metaphor for home or nation (representing a fascistic nationalism in the case of the Nazi *Blut und Boden*) in order to reject it, suggesting that both language and physical territory are instead muddied, blended and indeterminate, with no clear allegiance to any discrete nation or identity.

It is vital to observe that this transnational turn is also palpable in Irish-language poetry, which is similarly embedded in networks of translation. While the sonnet is not as prominent a presence here as it is in contemporary poetry written in English by Irish poets, it features notably in the work of Máire Mhac an tSaoi, in a manner which emphasizes these transnational perspectives. Mhac an tSaoi is a translator; like Quinn, she has drawn on Rilke's *Duino Elegies*, translating these into Irish as *Marbhnaí Duino*, but she has also worked with the sonnet in translation, translating Yeats's 'Leda and the Swan' as 'Leda agus an tEala' in her 1999 collection *Shoa agus Dánta Eile*. Although the poems in this collection largely take other forms, it is framed by the sonnet, closing on the love sonnet 'Cian á Thógaint Díom' and employing the form for its title poem, 'Shoa'. This sonnet, which Mhac an tSaoi wrote in response to the Holocaust Memorial in Vienna, uses the image of an elderly Jewish man on all fours to dwell on the inhumanity of those in high places and the spiritual integrity of those they have downtrodden – like Quinn, she invokes 'mud' (Irish *láib*) in a valorizing context with the poem's final lines 'Beatha na n-éag insa láib, / An Bhrúid ar a bhonnaibh!' (23).[5] The brutishness of fascism depicted here echoes 'the brute blood of the air' of 'Leda and the Swan' (Yeats 322) – or 'mháistríocht bhorb san an aeir' ('brutal mastery in the air') in Mhac an tSaoi's translation (46) – another representation of the shaping of history by the violence of those in high places – in this case, the airborne Zeus in the form of a swan. 'Shoá' describes fascist authorities' elevation on 'gcuailli arda' (23), directly echoing the 'high stilts' of Yeats's late sonnet 'High Talk' (Yeats 467) at the same time as quoting, as Mhac an tSaoi highlights in a footnote to the poem, 'Caoineadh na Maighdine', an Irish song about the Passion of Jesus. Mhac an tSaoi thus represents the plight of Europe's Jews under fascism by drawing on imagery from her own Irish Catholic context, blending religions as well as languages and nations. Her sonnet, written in Irish and drawing upon the history of the sonnet in Irish poetry as represented by her Yeatsian intertexts, demonstrates the possibility of a transnational poetics which is both inward- and outward-facing; the poem's (and collection's) title, which uses the Hebrew word for 'Holocaust', emphasizes the continuity between a people's history and their language at the same time as it articulates the tendency of diverse languages to meet and interweave, and the capacity of texts to move between them.

In *Postnationalist Ireland*, which analyses a move away from nationalism in Irish politics, culture and philosophy, Richard Kearney interrogates various definitions of nationhood, including nation as territory – which 'lay[s] claim to a specific place or land which constitutes the so-called national territory' (3) – and 'nation as culture', under which he places questions of language (5). In the case of Ireland, both of these definitions of nationhood have proven fraught, and the handling of these concepts by the contemporary Irish poets explored in this chapter suggests that they are keen to underline their instability as foundational national categories. Indeed, these poets' ideas of nation frequently only possess integrity or unity when they are blended, as we see in the 'pure' nature of the clashing accents that close the third sonnet of Quinn's 'On the Translator's Art'. The sonnet, travelling between languages and nations in Irish poetry across the twentieth and twenty-first centuries, illustrates this, encompassing an expansive nexus of languages and national contexts within its compact form. Far from representing the confines of 'the green, green grass of home', the sonnet does not act as a static agent of tradition in modern and contemporary Irish poetry, but instead as a formal metaphor for transformation and cultural exchange, providing poets with a means of reaching across prescriptive national borders and, in doing so, effacing them.

Notes

1 The present chapter is limited to consideration of Europe due to spatial constraints, but it should be noted that the Irish sonnet also looks further afield; for example, Irene de Angelis has noted the influence of the Japanese haiku on Seamus Heaney's sonnet sequence 'Clearances' and Ciaran Carson's collection of sonnets *The Twelfth of Never* (pp. 28–29, 65–80).
2 The Parnassian movement in English poetry, for example, used French forms in order to signal a disdain for nationalism and an interest in cosmopolitanism. For more on the Parnassians and form, see Marion Thain (2019).
3 'In this world he [the wise man] must fear tumult and movement'; 'always bears the punishment of having wanted to change places.'
4 'nocturnal tears'; 'from that mournful urn / Love bathes you [the bed], with those ivory hands.'
5 'Eternal life in the mud, / The brute on his hind legs!'

Works cited

Alighieri, Dante. *Le opere di Dante: Testo critico della Società Dantesca Italiana*. Edited by Michele Barbi. Società Dantesca Italiana, 1960.
Baudelaire, Charles. *Les Fleurs du mal*. Gallimard, 2005.
Brearton, Fran. '"The Nothing-Could-Be-Simpler Line": Form in Contemporary Irish Poetry'. *The Oxford Handbook of Modern Irish Poetry*. Edited by Fran Brearton and Alan Gillis. Oxford University Press, 2012, pp. 629–647.
Carson, Ciaran. *The Alexandrine Plan*. Gallery Press, 1998.
Carson, Ciaran. *Collected Poems*. Gallery Press, 2008.
Carvalho Homem, Rui. *Poetry and Translation in Northern Ireland: Dislocations in Contemporary Writing*. Palgrave Macmillan, 2009.
De Angelis, Irene. *The Japanese Effect in Contemporary Irish Poetry*. Palgrave Macmillan, 2012.
Gillis, Alan. 'The Modern Irish Sonnet'. *The Oxford Handbook of Modern Irish Poetry*. Edited by Alan Gillis and Fran Brearton. Oxford University Press, 2010, pp. 567–587.
Guissin-Stubbs, Tara. *The Modern Irish Sonnet: Revision and Rebellion*. Palgrave Macmillan, 2020.
Hall, Jason David. *Seamus Heaney's Rhythmic Contract*. Palgrave Macmillan, 2009.
Heaney, Seamus. *Wintering Out*. Faber, 1972.
Heaney, Seamus. *Electric Light*. Faber, 2001.
Hilský, Martin. '"Telling What Is Old": Original, Translation and the Third Text – Shakespeare's Sonnets in Czech'. *Four Hundred Years of Shakespeare in Europe*. Edited by A. Luis Pujante and Ton Hoenselaars. Associated University Presses, 2003, pp. 134–144.
Joyce, Trevor. *Rome's Wreck*. Cusp Books, 2015.

Kearney, Richard. *Postnationalist Ireland: Politics, Culture, Philosophy*. Routledge, 1997.

Kennelly, Brendan. *Cromwell: A Poem*. Beaver Row Press, 1983.

Mahon, Derek. *Echo's Grove*. Gallery Press, 2013.

Marken, Ronald. 'Paul Muldoon's "Juggling a Red-Hot Half-Brick in an Old Sock": Poets in Ireland Renovate the English-Language Sonnet'. *Éire-Ireland*, vol. 24, no. 1, 1989: pp. 79–91.

Mhac An Tsaoi, Máire. *Shoa agus dánta eile*. Sáirséal Ó Marcaigh, 1999.

O'Callaghan, Conor, ed. *The Wake Forest Series of Irish Poetry, Volume III: Colette Bryce, Justin Quinn, John McAuliffe, Maurice Riordan, and Gerard Fanning*. Wake Forest University Press, 2013.

Petrarca, Francesco. *Canzoniere: Rerum Vulgarium Fragmenta*. Edited by Rosanna Bettarini. Einaudi, 2005.

Procházka, Martin, Marta Gibińska and Florence March. 'Shakespeare on Stage in Europe since the Late Seventeenth Century'. *The Shakespearean World*. Edited by Jill L. Levenson and Robert Ormsby. Routledge, 2017, pp. 40–59.

Quinn, Justin. *Between Two Fires: Transnationalism and Cold War Poetry*. Oxford University Press, 2015a.

Quinn, Justin. *The Cambridge Introduction to Modern Irish Poetry, 1800–2000*. Cambridge University Press, 2008.

Quinn, Justin. *Close Quarters*. Gallery Press, 2011.

Quinn, Justin. *Early House*. Gallery Press, 2015b.

Quinn, Justin. *Fuselage*. Gallery Press, 2002.

Quinn, Justin. 'Introduction: Irish Poetry and the Diaspora'. *Metre*, vol. 3, 1997: pp. 6–7.

Quinn, Justin. *Waves and Trees*. Gallery Press, 2006.

Regan, Stephen. *The Sonnet*. Oxford University Press, 2019.

Scott-Baumann, Elizabeth and Hannah Crawforth, eds. *On Shakespeare's Sonnets: A Poets' Celebration*. Bloomsbury Arden Shakespeare, 2016.

Shakespeare, William. *A Midsummer Night's Dream*. Edited by Sukanta Chaudhuri. Arden, 2017.

Thain, Marion. 'Parnassian Cosmopolitanism: Transnationalism and Poetic Form'. *Victorian Poetry*, vol. 57, no. 4, 2019: pp. 463–487.

Vendler, Helen. *Our Secret Discipline: Yeats and Lyric Form*. Oxford University Press, 2007.

Wheatley, David. *Mocker*. Gallery Press, 2006.

Yeats, W. B. *Yeats's Poems*. Edited by A. Norman Jeffares. Macmillan, 1996.

12

Sonnet translation and imitation during the Second World War: Maintaining the idea of Europe?

Thomas Vuong

The politics of translation during the Second World War

The part played by translation in the poetics of the Second World War has received very little recent attention: Linda M. Shires's foundational study briefly glosses Rilke's influence on English poets without dwelling on translations (62–63, 104); Rachel Galvin's brilliant comparative take on civilian poetry does not address translation either (117); Jonathan Hart's relevant chapter excludes the study of translation itself from its comparative frame, while Tim Kendall's remarkable *Oxford Handbook of British and Irish War Poetry* and *Modern English War Poetry* do not mention it – apart from a few lines about Geoffrey Hill. The subject has lately gained more attention in France, notably under the aegis of Christine Lombez.

This chapter aims to show how central translation has been in upholding a pan-European conception of poetry as dialogue between neighbouring cultures – that is to say, a certain idea of Europe itself. My focus will be specifically on the sonnet, as by 1939 the form had proven to be a common vehicle for dialogue between distinct European poetic traditions, especially through the prism of translation. Although mainly focused on France and to a lesser extent Britain, this short evocation of translative processes applied to the sonnet in wartime should help paint a bigger picture of the uses of elite culture, and specifically poetry, in times of harsh and nationalistic perceptions of European identities.

The specific subject of the sonnet during the Second World War has barely been considered in English. A. D. Cousins and Peter Howarth's remarkable *Cambridge Companion to the Sonnet* does not mention this period – only Auden's 1938 'In Time of War', which opens the era sonnet-wise.[1] Nor does Eavan Boland and Edward Hirsch's remarkable 2008 anthology contain more than one of Auden's and one of Barker's sonnets; and the other already mentioned works do not dwell on the significance of the form itself.

This chapter proposes a translator-based approach, in the footsteps of Andrew Chesterman and Christine Lombez (Lombez 2019, 15), with an emphasis on translation by poets. Beyond an idea of translation as the faithful rendering of works into one's language, this choice forces us to evoke it through the wider scope of imitation and direct influence, as a component of intertextuality (Bellos 320): the inclusion of poets in the following corpus irresistibly draws us towards the topic of poetics, which tends to enforce no strict border between reading and writing (Taravacci, Lombez 2019).

In those years when the dominant European project became a blood-soaked, totalitarian one, this chapter will investigate whether poetic translation, of the sonnet especially, did function as it had been progressively intended to – as a tool for better understanding and dialogue between languages, cultures and nations. However, one can only wonder whether the combined European dreams of refinement through the sonnet and understanding through translation – which Victor Hugo deems a 'civilising function' (348) – hold their own when these borders are the scene of dehumanizing, civilization-breaking wars, of which the Second World War might be the most striking occurrence.[2]

Translating Shakespeare into French: A militant act?

The case of Shakespeare's *Sonnets* is quite representative of the multiplicity of values translation bears in time of war, as four versions in French appear across four years of war, each one deserving consideration.

Giraud d'Uccle is the pseudonym of Léon Kochnitzky, an ambiguous and larger-than-life character (Vuong 2019a). Born in Belgium to a Russian father and a Polish Jewish mother, he stood alongside D'Annunzio in Fiume after the First World War when the Italian poet led nationalist irregulars to seize the Adriatic town for Italy, founding a short-lived, corporatist and somehow pre-fascist regime there. Hired to write Belgian propaganda at the outbreak of the Second World War, he probably translated Shakespeare's *Sonnets* during the Fall of France then sent the translation to Algiers publisher Edmond Charlot before escaping to the USA and the Belgian Desk of Roosevelt's Office for War Information.

Kochnitzky's translation includes only 126 of the 154 sonnets, eliminating the affair with the 'dark lady' – which may or may not suggest an emphasis on homoeroticism. His translation got eight reprints; trying to make sense of the German Occupation, his editor Albert Camus quotes a line from his rendering of Sonnet 27 in his notebooks (22). His translative choices are in tune with the era: blank alexandrines with a blend of archaism (Kochnitzky uses poetic inversions where Shakespeare does not) and a looseness regarding metrical tradition, aiming more at reaching twelve syllables than respecting the alexandrine's specific rules.

The urgency surrounding Kochnitzky's translation contrasts with the circumstances of André Prudhommeaux's more conservative take on the form. This anarchist refugee, who had settled in Switzerland thanks to his step-family, was forbidden by Geneva authorities to take part in intellectual activities and thus had time to write one of the most conservative translations of the twentieth century. Prudhommeaux sacrifices Shakespeare's images on the altar of the regular, rhymed alexandrine: thus in Sonnet 12 ('When I do count the clock that tells the time') the 'violet past prime' becomes 'Quand le temps sur la fleur a posé son cothurne' ('When Time on the flower has set its buskin') (Shakespeare 1945, 22). Other adjunctions such as 'sans appel' ('irrevocably') stand by erasures ('When I behold'), all in order to reach the right number of syllables and stresses at the end of each line. This target-oriented translation tries to render what an English readership could find in the sequence – only complicating it along the way. In his foreword, the French refugee poet avoids referring to the war, only evoking translation of the sonnet as 'a verbal, musical, logical, ornamental game' (Shakespeare 1945, 7). This overemphasis on complexity, search for equivalence and attraction to the classics appear surprisingly opposed to an anarchist *tabula rasa*; rather, translation here seems to be regarded as a form of challenge.

More interesting is the translation of twelve sonnets published in 1944 by French engineer and Résistant Maurice Blanchard. A surrealist and member of the semi-clandestine literary circle La Main à Plume, led by future Oulipo co-founder Noël Arnaud, and a man deeply engaged in the Résistance fight – he was hired by airplane firm Farman, from where he leaked key industrial information (Vuong 2019b, 85) – Blanchard adheres to Surrealism's ideal of total freedom. To resolve the conflicting energies of free-writing and sonnet-writing, he translated the sonnets into prose; the result is quite intriguing.

119	Sonnet CXIX
What potions have I drunk of Siren tears, Distill'd from limbecks foul as hell within, Applying fears to hopes, and hopes to fears, Still losing when I saw myself to win!	Quelles gorgées de pleurs de Sirène, distillées dans les alambics de l'enfer ai-je bues, m'appliquant frayeurs sur espoir, espoir sur frayeurs, toujours perdu quand je me voyais sauvé! (Shakespeare 1944, 30–31)

This paradoxical, intriguing rendering has echoes of Rimbaud's prose poems as much as of Nerval's sonnets, implying possible further influences. Blanchard transposes the *topos* of the inspired poet's spontaneity and effervescence onto the persona of the translator, claiming to have translated all of Shakespeare's sonnets, one per week between 1941 and 1944, then burnt the ones which weren't deemed good enough: all save twelve. Whether we believe him or not, he either kept or only chose to translate the ones most in accordance with his taste. More interestingly, translating the sonnets seems to have shaped the prose patterns Blanchard used in his own poetry: in *Les Pelouses fendues d'Aphrodite*, an underground surrealist collection published clandestinely, he wrote prose poems with the same four-paragraph rhythm, confirming the link between translation and prose sonnet in French (Chevrier 128).

The most directly engaged of these four translations comes from heavyweight academic Fernand Baldensperger, cofounder of the *Revue de Littérature Comparée* and US resident since 1935. From Berkeley, he published a full translation of the *Sonnets* in 1943, fully rearranging their order according to thematic divisions. This translation-cum-edition opens every section with a quote from an Italian, French or English poet: the omission of German is remarkable, especially in the case of this Vosges-born, German specialist academic. Baldensperger presents Shakespeare as one part of an entire poetic constellation, within which sonneteers shine bright: for this father of French comparative literature, both the sonnet form and its translation are acts of faith in a continent-wide culture.

Baldensperger explains in an essay published two years later that as the war broke, he had turned back to Shakespeare 'because he devoted himself, in a torn era, to find again what tore other times in a work of genius, which has become one of the intellectual charts of the West' (11). This academic translator also exemplifies the politics of translating Shakespeare: in 1943 he could foresee the Allies winning the war and leading the Western world, and thought it timely to translate the most significant common denominator – Bible excepted – in the English-speaking world. One can wonder whether the *Sonnets* are indeed such a ubiquitous text, more so than *Hamlet* or *Othello*, but their status as a classic – through both the name of Shakespeare and the sonnet form – seems to have weighed on the choice to translate them.

It is noteworthy that these translators of Shakespeare's *Sonnets* all operated either outside of mainland France (Prudhommeaux the anarchist in Switzerland, Baldensperger the academic in Berkeley, Kochnitzky the enigma in more loosely censored Algiers) or in semi-clandestine editions (in the case of the surrealist Blanchard): although no patriotic charge exists within Shakespeare's poems proper, the very act of translating a quintessentially English writer – or one deemed as such – could only be carried out from the margins.

German as a crucible for inspiration

At the other end of the linguistic–political spectrum are translations from German, which were particularly sensitive but nonetheless essential for several poets in the development of their *Weltanschauung* during the war. On either side of the Channel, two acquainted poets were influenced by Rainer Maria Rilke and Friedrich Hölderlin during the Second World War: Pierre Jean Jouve and David Gascoyne. Being neighbours and both heirs to the Surrealist quest for freedom of metaphors, Jouve and Gascoyne were fascinated by Alban Berg and psychoanalysis – Gascoyne even underwent therapy under Jouve's wife, Blanche Reverchon. After leaving France at the onset of the Second World War, Gascoyne went through a creative drought, but he nevertheless managed to pay homage to Jouve in 1941, translating five of his poems – the first an assonant, reversed sonnet, whose backwards form conveys Jouve's obsession with the time before the womb or after the grave; the limbo of the un-being.

Gascoyne resorts to simplification in his translation of Jouve's idiosyncratic style: the original's final juxtaposition, 'l'autre plus cendreux soleil', sounds more daring in French than 'the other more ashen sun' would in English, 'cendreux' being quite rare – much more so than 'ashen' – and the order of words less common in French. Nevertheless, Gascoyne settles for the simpler 'Towards the other more ashen sun', while the first lines of both Jouve's sestet and his octave are distorted. Gascoyne eliminates the remainders of rhyme that still subtly structure Jouve's reversed sonnet, compensating by an addition of syllables in order to reach the rhythm of the English pentameter; 'Weigh down on her who now is no more known', for example, is a rather expansive translation of 'Pesez sur elle qui n'est plus'.

La Femme et la Terre	Woman and Earth
Quand elle était, ce cœur était plus fort que la lumière	Was stronger than the light this heart which beat in her,
Son sang sous l'influence de la lune était plus ouvert	Her blood to the moon's influence more open lay
Que le sang répandu […]	Than lifeblood shed; […]
Et vous qui dormez ! autre granit et vieilles roses (Jouve 224)	Are sleeping now that other granite, roses overblown (Gascoyne 19)

Straying from Jouve's reversed Elizabethan sonnet, whose metrical lines gradually shorten in mimicry of the etiolation of the dying woman, Gascoyne does not manage to curtail the metrics of his translation. This departure from the original's metrical and rhyming dimensions, and from the two separate quatrains into which Jouve splits his octave – a mark of sonneticity in the French poet's often deconstructed take on the form – could suggest that Gascoyne's translation misses most of the original's formal characteristics. However, the mere fact of translating Jouve's at times nightmarish poetry does bring French formal experiments in depicting the death drive, relatively absent from British poetry of the late 1930s, into this latter context.

Gascoyne's 1938 *Hölderlin's Madness*, which includes several translations of the German poet, may have been one of the inspirations for the Hölderlin-inspired *Le Poète Fou* by Pierre Emmanuel, a French Résistant poet heavily influenced by Jouve. Hölderlin remained a crucible for inspiration, despite his use by German propaganda as proof of German genius (Tautou 2018) and emblematic pan-Germanism and the pivotal role of his legacy in the *Aktion Übersetzung* – the project for the translation of German classics in France, directed by the *Übersetzungsausschuss* (Enderle-Ristori).

A further case of influence is even more interesting, as it concerns a poet whose poetry appears to have been rather disconnected from its times. Indeed, Rilke's 1923 *Sonette an Orpheus* (*Sonnets to Orpheus*) were written at the remote Swiss Château de Muzot, where, away from the world, the poet finally emerged from an eight-year-long block on his *Duineser Elegien*. Influenced by Valéry's and Michelangelo's sonnets, which he translated during his sojourn in Muzot, with this meditative sequence the Austrian poet delivered a prominent instance of poetry as virtuosity, conceived at a distance from the world of politics.[3]

Nevertheless, the work of Rilke, who was both a Francophile and Francophone poet, is intimately connected to the politics of translation (Tautou 2016). For all his aestheticism and general un-Germanness according to the Nazi perspective on decadence, the Austrian poet could be used to prove a conjunction of interests between French and German literary scenes and was thus put forward by the *Deutsch-Französischer Übersetzungsausschuss*, the Paris-based committee for German–French translation. However, Tautou encourages us to apply nuance here, as no systemic overview sustained what would have needed to be a long-term policy, unfitted to the relatively short span of the Occupation and to the individualistic and detail-oriented process of translation. Thus, translations of the *Sonette an Orpheus* by Joseph François Angelloz or Geneviève Bianquis can either be read as collaborations with a compromised, however prestigious, collection of German classics financed by Germany, or as a way to claim the enemy's language and culture in order to defuse binary oppositions. Some translators went explicitly against the tide of collaboration, such as André Bellivier, whose foreword to his translation states that starting to translate the sequence planted a seed of hope when he was a war prisoner in an Oflag (Rilke 1943, n.p.). The list of different camps where he was imprisoned while working on his translations serves as a reminder of the actual hostility between countries, however much Franco-German institutions feigned accord.

Outside of France, Rilke also exerted influence on British Second World War poets such as Sidney Keyes (Hill 407) and Keith Douglas (Shires 62–63), through either imitation or opposition. Yet another English poet who somehow managed to unite both stances towards the Austrian poet is Auden, on whom Rilke's influence is well documented (Hoggart 27, 42, 136). I would like to suggest here that a possible turn within Auden's consideration of Rilkean ethics and aesthetics was instantiated by the experience of travelling with Christopher Isherwood through war-torn China in 1938, a journey that led him to compose his sequence 'In Time of War', included at the end of Isherwood's 1939 diary *Journey to a War*. Volker Klöpsch has even suggested that the very idea of a sonnet sequence stemmed from Rilke (87); it is true that Auden carried Rilke's *Sonette an Orpheus* in the original with him throughout his trip in China, and direct quotations thus appear in his sonnets – the thirteenth sonnet of 'In Time of War', for example. It is noteworthy that here, imitation allows the poet to interrogate and take a different stance from the original. Starting with Rilke's initial verse, 'Ruhmen, das ists' (Rilke 1997, 26) ('Praise, that's it' (Rilke 2012, 15), becoming in Auden's thirteenth sonnet 'Certainly praise' (271)), he interpolates the Austrian's sonnet into an evocation of the Chinese classical text the *Hundred Family Surnames*, or *Bǎijiāxìng*. He thus conflates and attacks several aristocratic perspectives on literature; the names of the Imperial dynasties developed in the classic Chinese text and Rilke's famed patronage by the Princess of Thurn und Taxis in Duino and the heir and merchant Werner Reinhart in Muzot are referred to as the mechanics of domination, 'the will of the unjust'. This sonnet's main point derives from this superficial opposition to Rilke: Auden not only juxtaposes two civilizations in order to focus on the failures of mankind, but actually denies the validity of a singular, Orphic poetry – 'History opposes our buoyant song' – that would somehow act upon the world, in order to emphasise the more global scale of suffering that he witnessed during his reporting of the 1930s wars. Back in Europe, Auden would similarly attack traditional conceptions of a somehow magical lyricism in the sonnet 'Rimbaud' and the short poem 'Orpheus'.

In the thirteenth sonnet of 'In Time of War', the sonnet's volta, occurring earlier than anticipated with line 5's 'But hear the injured weeping' (271), is used paradoxically to undermine early-twentieth-century ideas of lyricism as a way of bringing depth to a personal perspective on the world, as it is conceived in Apollinaire, Valéry, Lorca and Rilke himself. However, Auden can also sympathise with an individual plight, and writes thus of Rilke's personal writing drought:

XXIII (XIX)

[...]

Let us remember those who looked deserted:
To-night in China let me think of one

Who for ten years of drought and silence waited,
Until in Muzot all his being spoke,
And everything was given once for all.

Awed, grateful, tired, content to die, completed,
He went out in the winter night to *stroke*
That tower as one pets an animal. (281)

It should be noted that the first full French translation of the *Sonette an Orpheus*, by Angelloz, was printed only in 1943, when the publisher Aubier, subsidized by Germany, specialized in German literature. This is why, in the early years of the war, a young Swiss poet-to-be such as Philippe Jaccottet had to read Rilke's sonnets in German; unable to find them in bookshops, he would copy them and read one per day throughout 1942–43 (Jaccottet 2002, 46). These daily readings, along with weekly, if not daily, discussions of Rilke's sonnets with his mentor, the translator Gustave Roud, constituted Jaccottet's school of poetics during the war. This is a minor case of translation, restricted to the smallest private sphere: the foreign reader translating in his notebook, if not his own mind. If we accept Michel de Certeau's view of reading as a mental transformation of the read work into a new one (279), then reading in another language becomes an internal translation. Here, work on a small scale can turn out to be rather consequential: Jaccottet, arguably one of the major French-speaking poets of the second half of the twentieth century, carried out the first phase of his work under Rilke's influence (Jaccottet 2005, 60). However, Jaccottet would later consider this full-fledged lyricism to be a trap, and rather draw his inspiration more quietly from the poetics of Hölderlin (Lombez 2003, 66–81). Rilke and Hölderlin, both central to translation during the war, are thus seminal figures in the Francophone poetics of the mid-twentieth century.

Translating from German in the midst of death: Jean Cassou

More remarkable in its political intent than all of the prior examples in this chapter is Jean Cassou's only wartime translation from German, a take on Hofmannsthal's sonnet 'Die Beiden' ('Both', or 'The Couple'). Here, biographical circumstances need to be narrated in order to convey what translation can signify in times of war.

A first-time Résistant in newly German-occupied Paris, Cassou saw his Groupe du Musée de l'Homme dismantled by the German services in early 1941 and escaped to Toulouse, in the so-called 'free zone'. There, he joined Pierre Bertaux, a former translator of Hölderlin with whom he served as cabinet staff for left-wing rising star and Minister for Education and Culture Jean Zay (who would end up executed by far-right French militia during the war). Cassou and Bertaux set up a new Résistance network, whose leaders ended up denounced and arrested by the Vichy forces in December 1941. Cassou was among the last brought to the military jail Furgole Tower, a remnant of medieval fortifications; as a known left-wing figure, he was taken straight to an underground cell assigned to prisoners sentenced to death. Waiting for the executioners to come at dawn and unable to sleep, Cassou composed a few lines in his head, which he extended to a full sonnet the following night when it turned out he was not to be killed just yet. The French judges having no proof against him, he remained detained there for two months under conditions of military secrecy: no access to either his lawyer or paper and pen, no exercise outside of his cell, no communication whatsoever with the outside world. During these two months, Cassou composed about thirty sonnets in his mind, which he spent his days memorizing with his inmate.

The only sonnet composed with any direct external influence was a translation from Hofmannsthal, whose sonnet Cassou read in a German propaganda newspaper, *Die Pariser Zeitung*, left rotting in a corner of the jail:

| Die Beiden | IX Translated from Hugo von Hofmannsthal |

Sie trug den Becher in der Hand	At her lips she held a cup,
– Ihr Kinn und Mund glich seinem Rand –,	held it safely in her hand;
So leicht und sicher war ihr Gang,	sure and easy was her tread,
Kein Tropfen aus dem Becher sprang.	not a single drop was shed.

So leicht und fest war seine Hand:	Sure and steady was his hand,
Er ritt auf einem jungen Pferde,	and his horse high-spirited;
Und mit nachlässiger Gebärde	he with mastery pulled up,
Erzwang er, daß es zitternd stand.	made the startled creature stand.

Jedoch, wenn er aus ihrer Hand	Did the strong hand grasp the cup
Den leichten Becher nehmen sollte,	that the fair one offered up?
So war es beiden allzu schwer:	It was not done easily.
Denn beide bebten sie so sehr,	How they trembled, he and she!
Daß keine Hand die andre fand	Hand by hand was never found,
Und dunkler Wein am Boden rollte.	and the dark wine stained the ground.

(Hofmannsthal 50)   (Adès and Cassou 367, 55)

In this case, the external source is given further significance by the fact it is written in another language – a window on the wider world – with the overwhelming additional factor that this alterity belongs to the enemy. Freed and sent to a labour camp under a bargain finally struck by his lawyer, Cassou managed to set his mind-composed sonnets to paper and had them sent to Louis Aragon, the Communist figurehead of Résistance poetry. Aragon had this collection published by the clandestine Éditions de Minuit, with a long, political foreword where he devoted a few pages to the translation of Hofmannsthal:

> A sonnet by Hofmannsthal. A German sonnet to which the Patriot, from deep into the shadow, gives its French form. […] One will long dream about this adventure of the mind, set in the midst of this most terrible of wars; about this moment when Hofmannsthal and, let's call him Jean Noir, meet one another: then two poets bond as brothers and

their entente across irons heavily condemns jailors and that Germany to which they bow. (Cassou 1944, 35)

Aragon rightly notes that the jailed poet translated the Italian sestet (of an eccentric type) as a French one, starting with a distich, conveniently serving his own poetic and patriotic goal of promoting traditional forms in order to achieve cultural unity of the nation against the enemy – however, Cassou himself does not explicitly endorse these ideas, and the French scheme can also be read as a mere mnemonic help.

Cassou had prior interests in German poetry, having previously co-edited a study of German Romanticism. Nevertheless, his translation of a German sonnet – selected largely through coincidence – can be seen as the exact opposite of projects such as the carefully planned political 1943 anthology of German poetry in French translation edited by René Lasne and Georg Rabuse, which selected only authors compatible with the dictates of nationalism, omitting Jews such as Heinrich Heine and Max Brod and opponents of the regime such as Bertolt Brecht and Erich Kästner.

Another remarkable translation, this time from Cassou, taking his work from one medium to another, is the French composer Henri Dutilleux's song 'La Geôle', composed in 1943 or 1944 using a sonnet by Cassou, 'Je m'égare par les pics neigeux...'.[4] The original meaning of the Church Latin *translatio* (moving holy relics from one town to another) becomes operative in this case, as Dutilleux dedicated this composition to his brother, then imprisoned in Stalag VIII-C. Here, not only are Cassou's words translated into music, but his source-imprisonment is translated into Paul Dutilleux's target-imprisonment.

Translating from the Spanish: The ambiguities of a new Europe

While poets could translate sonnets from English or German as a political statement of their renewed faith in a common culture – a shared literary tradition embodied by the quintessentially European sonnet form – these translations largely remained in the domain of private poetics, which explains why translation proper co-exists alongside translation and imitation as inspiration for original works. The case of translations from the Spanish in Vichy France appears more institutional, as Iberian poetry came to occupy a prime position in publications that had to undergo censorship.

Pierre Darmangeat is both a key figure in this specific literary scene – one amongst few somehow allowed to thrive – and a touchstone for the politics of translation in Nazi-occupied France. A close friend and collaborator of left-wing publisher Pierre Seghers, arguably the most influential figure of the Résistance literary publishing landscape, Darmangeat wrote about poetry and translated from Spanish throughout the war. He edited the 1941 special issue of *Poésie 41* devoted to Spanish poetry, where, amongst dozens of poems mostly translated by him, sonnets can be found by Luis de Góngora and Antonio Machado.

In its foreword (4–5), Darmangeat defends the idea of Spanish poetry being both elitist and popular, the result of each poet's idiosyncratic research but also a very common art, easily read by a nation depicted as noble and poetic; he thus demonstrates a syntactic preciousness in common songs and poems and the influence of popular culture even in the most *cultos* (which means elaborate, if not convoluted, in Spanish Baroque poetics) of poets, Góngora.

On a continent suffering from the strain of war, and where poetry had temporarily reached a wider readership, this constant dialogue between elite and popular literature is at the core of the poetics of many Second World War poets, such as Aragon's. Nevertheless, the frequent focus on mystic and love poets actively eliminates polemics and politics from the stage: it is no coincidence that Darmangeat and his co-editor Bran did not choose Machado's emblematic 'Ya hay un español que quiere…', from the 'Proverbios y cantares' part of his main collection *Campos de Castilla*, for instance. Neither do they mention Machado's political engagement, nor even his place of death (Collioure in southern France), in fear of betraying the Republican refugee's true colours. Rather, the focus is on either picturesque poems, fitting with nationalism's domination of the European cultural landscape, or amorous or mystic sonnets, such as '¡Oh soledad, mi sola compañía…'.

Christine Lombez has examined Darmangeat's position within Résistance literary circles, retracing his anti-Fascist commitment and veiled criticism of Lasne and Rabuse's 1943 anthology (Lombez 2019, 123). It must be added that translating from Spanish under Vichy France was rather easier than from English, as Franquist Spain was a supposedly neutral country, although *de facto* an Axis ally, whose cultural policy highly valued the classics – one of the most prominent Franquist poetry periodicals was named *Garcilaso*, after Garcilaso de la Vega, the Renaissance soldier-poet who had popularized the sonnet in Spain. Thus, while a classic English writer such as Shakespeare held a certain subversive charge, translations of the Spanish classics remained firmly within the remit of conservative politics. While constrained by political factors restricting the choice of the translated poems, as seen in Machado's case, certain underlying statements about Spain remained: the prominence of Góngora over Quevedo in Darmangeat's anthology, for instance, served for connoisseurs as a reminder of the *Generación del 27*, which included major antifascists such as Federico García Lorca and Rafael Alberti who claimed the baroque poet as an inspiration.

It is noteworthy that Basque-country-born, Hispanophone Cassou was initially a prolific translator from Spanish. In 1939 he wrote the introduction to an anthology of contemporary Spanish war poems translated into French, where he defined 1930s poetry as a successor to the *romance*, both linked to popular culture and in dialogue with elite literary tradition, as exemplified by García Lorca and Machado (Cassou 1937, 7–10). Aragon would establish a French equivalent three years later, composing verse on the frontlines of the Battle of Belgium and the Fall of France, and subsequently during the military occupation of its Northern half.

Interestingly enough, one of the French Résistance's foremost poets, Robert Desnos, also claimed Góngora as a major influence on his wartime poetics. Desnos had been able to read the poet thanks to translations by Darmangeat, and as the former Surrealist composed a suite of hermetic poems named *Calixto* in German-occupied Paris, he wrote in his notes that the Spaniard, legendary for his hermeticism, constituted a model for him: 'L'hermétisme de Góngora. Ses recherches classiques périmées mais l'étonnante vie que gardent ses images' (1230). The hermeticism of *Calixto*, its Gongorist intricacies of allegory and metaphor, aims at undoing German censorship by dissimulating what is actually a commentary on the tortures inflicted by the Gestapo and the necessity of a fightback, through elevated, ultra-literary language. The Spanish baroque thus inflected Desnos's take on the sonnet form in *Calixto*, demonstrating the influence of translation within the French poetic landscape.

Camões, Stampa: The versatility of translation and imitation

Translating or imitating the sonnet can also facilitate political commentary: when former Surrealist, devout Communist and Résistance writer Louis Aragon went underground during the Vichy régime and subsequent Nazi occupation, he had to elaborate an entire set of poetic devices in order to conceal his politics under the guise of merely decorative writing – something he called 'poésie de contrebande' (smuggler poetry). He translated and subtly modified the Portuguese poet Luís de Camões thus (major changes by Aragon in italics):

	Imité de Camoens
Que me quereis, perpétuas saudades?	Que cherchez-vous de moi perpétuels *orages*
Com qu'esperanças inda me enganais?	De quels *combats* encore allez-vous me berner
O tempo, que se vai, não torna mais,	Lorsque le temps s'enfuit pour ne plus retourner
E se torna, não tornão as idades.	Et s'il s'en retournait n'en reviendrait plus l'âge
[…]	[…]
Aquillo a que ja quiz he tão mudado,	Ce que je chérissais jadis a tant changé
Que quasi he outra cousa; porque os dias	Qu'on dirait autre aimer et comme *autre douloir*
Tẽe o primeiro gôsto ja damnado.	Mon goût d'alors perdu maudit le goût que j'ai
Esperanças de novas alegrias,	Ah quel espoir trompé d'une inutile *gloire*
Não m'as deixa a Fortuna e o tempo irado,	Me laisserait le sort ni ce temps mensonger
Que do contentamento são espias.	Qui guette *mon regret comme un château* la Loire
(Camões 220)	(Aragon 82)

Aragon cleverly and provocatively smuggles in some more warlike terms: the famously untranslatable 'saudades' becomes 'orages' ('storms'), while 'esperanças' becomes 'combats' ('fights' rather than 'hopes'), and 'alegrias' turns into 'gloire' ('glory' rather than 'joy'). His use of the Old French 'douloir' is also significant in the context of his wartime poetics, which urge a return to the spring of French tradition. This choice is echoed in the final image of a Loire castle, which recalls not only the medieval origins of the sonnet, but also personal and national fate: the Loire was the boundary between occupied and 'free' France, and in 'Les Ponts-de-Cé' Aragon recalls that his battalion was defeated in 1940 on a bridge over the Loire.

However, at the opposite end of the political spectrum, a Commonwealth poet was also looking towards Camões, demonstrating the versatility of translation. The South African, London-settled Roy Campbell left the Bloomsbury group (after learning his wife had had an affair with Vita Sackville-West) and became a far-right Christian poet, travelled to Spain as a Franquist and later grew involved with the fascist intelligentsia in Rome. His 'Imitation (and Endorsement) of the Famous Sonnet of Bocage Which

He Wrote on Active Service Out East' draws on a sonnet by eighteenth-century Portuguese poet Manuel Maria Barbosa du Bocage dedicated to Camões. Campbell claimed Camões as a 'model' during his service in Eastern Africa ('Like yourself, from Chindwin to Zambezi / In wars and fearful penury I wander'), due to their respective fights for religion and country. One cannot help reading the original baroque fascination with death as an illustration of fascism's death impulse (Marcuse 1962) when Campbell translates Bocage's recommendation to Heaven – 'Meu fim demando ao Céu, pela certeza / De que só terei paz na sepultura' (Bocage 267) – by explicitly rendering it as a longing for death: 'I pray for sudden death to come tomorrow / And know that peace lies only in the tomb' (Campbell 386).

Thus a sixteenth-century Portuguese soldier and poet who served in the Indian Ocean was deployed as a reference for two very different manifestations of nationalism: Communist-inspired Résistance and proto-fascist jingoism set in a context of colonial expansionism.

Indeed, translation during the Second World War did not solely work against totalitarianism. As the Axis sought to build a new continental unity – with a focus on the Mediterranean for Italy and on the North Sea for Germany – so did far-right poets carry out translation according to a racist ideology partially inspired by poetry, as it arguably stemmed from German Romanticism's pan-German dream (Tautou 2018).

When it comes to the sonnet, a striking example of translative practices which reflected a racist frame of mind is found in Eleonore Lorenz. In her 1940 collection *Italianische Gesange* ('Italian songs'), this Dresden poet translated, alongside her own work, some sonnets by sixteenth-century poet Gaspara Stampa. Thematically introduced as 'Gleiches Blut' ('Same Blood'), a declaration of affinity between Germany and Italy, these translations of Stampa bear a strong political connotation, as both countries were core members of the Axis and are represented through the racial lens of blood ties:

der Süd dem Nord, der Nord dem Süd bereit.	South gives itself to North, North to South.
Kein Volk ist je dem andern so verbunden,	Never has a race with another mingled so much,
als das im fremden eignes Blut gefunden.	as if in the foreign one he found his own blood.

(Lorenz 46)

A clear example of the racist, pan-Germanist, Nazi-sponsored *Blut und Boden* (blood and soil) ideology, this sonnet forces us to read the Italian original under a new light: the form and the exchanges of the mind across Europe that it symbolizes are not impervious to the sinister manifestations of the continent's conceptualizations of race. One of Stampa's sonnets ('Chi vuol conoscer, donne, il mio signore...') chosen by Lorenz illustrates a convergence of the ideals of the Renaissance and of Aryanism when the speaker describes her beloved as a man 'der Wangen Blühn von blondem Haar umwallt, / sein Wuchs ist hoch, die Brust ist breit zu nennen' (Lorenz 72: whose blossom'd cheeks are by blonde hair circled, / his build is high, the chest is to be named wide).

Beyond the hijacking of an ancestral female sonneteer by the Nazi-aligned, if not Nazi-glorified, Lorenz (Leitgeb 208), a contemporary reader of poetry must recognize how problematic the traditional European stance on fairness of complexion is. Ironically, given her own intentions, Lorenz anticipates recent readings of Renaissance sonnets such as Shakespeare's 'dark lady' sequence by scholars such as Kim F. Hall, which force us to question the racist undertones of the thought of this foundational era.

In times of war, translation's role endures, although modified by dire circumstances: its goal is no longer to 'civilize', but to maintain civilization under considerable stress. It must nevertheless be stated that, as with the very concept of 'civilization', this mission is a double-edged sword; competing ideological projects – one neo-humanist, the other racist – can and do tap into this well of literary identities. Therein lies a foundational ambiguity of modern Europe, which is built upon dialogue between cultures which nevertheless consider themselves as foreign to one another. As one of European poetry's most emblematic forms, the sonnet remains reflective of these ambiguities; at a time when national identities flared up with total violence, translations of the sonnet could not escape the form's past and were revelatory of the ideologies of twentieth-century white Europe.

Notes

1   Dylan Thomas, Roy Fuller and Keith Douglas, and to a lesser extent David Gascoyne and Gavin Ewart, in Britain; Robert Desnos, Louis Aragon, Boris Vian, Raymond Queneau, Pierre Jean Jouve, Pierre Emmanuel and Paul Valéry in France; Eugenio Montale and Giorgio Caproni in Italy; and Bertolt Brecht, Reinhold Schneider and Marie-Luise Kaschnitz in Germany are but a few famous examples of this Second World War renewal of the sonnet on the war-torn continent.

2   Translations are mine where no translator is mentioned.
3   See other essays in this book by Frédéric Weinmann and Bastien Goursaud.
4   Played for the first time on 7 January 1945, it was published in 1946. Various claims about its composition circulate. Pierre Gervasoni quotes a score dated from late in the summer of 1944 (p. 133), while half a century later Dutilleux himself remembered it as having been composed in 1943 (p. 47).

Works cited

Adès, Timothy and Jean Cassou. 'Jean Cassou: Five Poems'. *Translation and Literature*, vol. 6, no. 2, 1997: pp. 219–233.
Aragon, Louis. *Les Yeux d'Elsa* (1942). Seghers, 2004.
Auden, Wystan Hugh and Christopher Isherwood. *Journey to a War*. Random, 1939.
Baldensperger, Fernand. *La Vie et l'oeuvre de William Shakespeare*. L'Arbre, 1945.
Bellos, David. *Is That a Fish in Your Ear? The Amazing Adventure of Translation*. Penguin, 2012.
Bocage, Manuel Maria Barbosa de. *Obras de Bocage*. Lello & Irmão, 1968.
Camões, Luis de. *Lirica Completa*, vol. 2. Impresa Nacional – Casa da Moeda, 1980.
Campbell, Roy. *Talking Bronco* (1946). *Collected Works, I, Poetry*. A. D. Donker, 1985.
Camus, Albert. *Carnets*. Tome 2, janvier 1942–mars 1945. Gallimard, 1964.
Cassou, Jean [Jean Noir]. 'Préface', *Le Romancero de la Guerre civile*. Dir. Georges Pillement. Éditions Sociales Internationales, 1937.
Cassou, Jean [Jean Noir]. *Trente-trois sonnets composés au secret*. Introduction by Louis Aragon [François La Colère]. Minuit, 1944.
Certeau, Michel de. *L'Invention du quotidien*. Tome 1, Arts de faire. Union Générale d'Éditions, 1980. Chapter XII: 'Lire: un braconnage'. pp. 279–296.
Chesterman, Andrew. 'The Name and Nature of Translator Studies'. *Reflections on Translation Theory: Selected Papers, 1993-2014*. John Benjamins, 2017 (2009), pp. 323–330.
Chevrier, Alain. 'Quelques versions du sonnet en prose. Forme & mesure. Cercle Polivanov: pour Jacques Roubaud / Mélanges'. *Mezura* no. 49. Inalco, 2001, pp. 127–139.
Cousins, A. D. and Peter Howarth, eds. *The Cambridge Companion to the Sonnet*. Cambridge University Press, 2011.
Darmangeat, Pierre. 'Foreword'. *Poésie* no. 41 (special issue: Poésie Espagnole), 1941.
Desnos, Robert. *Œuvres*. Paris, 1999.
Dutilleux, Henri. *Mystère et mémoire des sons*. Paris: Belfond, 1993.

Enderle-Ristori, Michaela. '1943, un tournant pour l'*Aktion Übersetzung*? Otto Abetz et l'organisation des traductions de l'allemand'. *1943 en traductions dans l'espace francophone européen*. Dir. Christine Lombez. Atlantide, no. 8, 2018: pp. 28–42.

Galvin, Rachel. *News of War: Civilian Poetry 1936–1945*. Oxford University Press, 2018.

Gascoyne, David. *Poems: 1937–1942*. Nicholson and Watson, 1943.

Gervasoni, Pierre. *Henri Dutilleux*. Actes Sud and Philharmonie de Paris, 2016.

Hall, Kim F. '"Those bastard signs of fair": Literary Whiteness in Shakespeare's Sonnets'. *Post-Colonial Shakespeares*. Edited by Ania Loomba and Martin Orkin. Routledge, 1998, pp. 64–83.

Hart, Jonathan. *The Poetics of Otherness: War, Trauma, and Literature*. Palgrave Macmillan, 2015.

Hill, Geoffrey. 'Sidney Keyes in Historical Perspective'. *The Oxford Handbook of British and Irish War Poetry*. Edited by Tim Kendall. Oxford University Press, 2007, pp. 398–418.

Hirsch, Edward and Eavan Boland, eds. *The Making of a Sonnet: A Norton Anthology*. Norton, 2008.

Hofmannsthal, Hugo von. *Sämtliche Werke*. Band I. Gedichte I. S. Fischer, 1984.

Hoggart, Richard. *Auden: An Introductory Essay*. Chatto and Windus, 1951.

Hugo, Victor. 'William Shakespeare (1864)'. *Œuvres complètes de Victor Hugo. Philosophie*, vol. 2. Albin Michel, 1934–1937.

Jaccottet, Philippe. *De la poésie*. Arlea, 2005.

Jaccottet, Philippe and Gustave Roud. *Correspondance 1942–1976*. Gallimard, 2002.

Jouve, Pierre Jean. *Matière Céleste*. Gallimard, 1937.

Klöpsch, Volker. 'Die Versuchung des Orpheus. Der Einfluss Rilkes auf das lyrische Werk von W. H. Auden'. *Fu Jen Studies*, vol. 16, 1983: pp. 77–109.

Leitgeb, Hanna. *Der ausgezeichnete Autor, Städtische Literaturpreise und Kulturpolitik in Deutschland, 1926–1971*. De Gruyter, 1994.

Lombez, Christine. 'D'une anthologie à l'autre: que transmettre de la poésie allemande en français pendant/après l'Occupation?' *Traduction et partages: que pensons-nous devoir transmettre?*. Edited by Ève de Dampierre, Anne-Laure Metzger, Vérane Partensky and Isabelle Poulin. Bibliothèque comparatiste, 2014, pp. 179–189.

Lombez, Christine. 'Pierre Darmangeat (1909-2004): L'Espagne poétique au coeur'. *Traduire, collaborer, résister: traducteurs et traductrices sous l'Occupation*. Dir. Christine Lombez. PU François Rabelais, 2019, pp. 123–136.

Lombez, Christine. *La seconde profondeur*. Les Belles Lettres, 2016.

Lombez, Christine, ed. *Traducteurs dans l'Histoire, traducteurs en guerre*. Atlantide, no. 5, 2016.

Lombez, Christine, ed. *Traduire, collaborer, résister: traducteurs et traductrices sous l'Occupation*. PU François Rabelais, 2019.

Lombez, Christine. *Transactions secrètes: Philippe Jaccottet traducteur de Rilke et de Hölderlin*. PU d'Artois, 2003.

Lorenz, Eleonore. *Italienische Gesänge*. F. A. Herbig, 1940.
Marcuse, Herbert. *Eros and Civilisation* (1955). Vintage Books, 1962.
Rilke, Rainer Maria. *Sonnets à Orphée* (*Die Sonette an Orpheus*, 1923). La Différence, 1997.
Rilke, Rainer Maria. *Sonnets à Orphée* (*Die Sonette an Orpheus*, 1923). Translated by André Bellivier. Kapp, 1943.
Rilke, Rainer Maria. *Sonnets to Orpheus* (*Die Sonette an Orpheus*, 1923). Translated by David Young. The Wesleyan University Press, 2012.
Shakespeare, William. *Douze Sonnets, traduits de l'anglais et présentés par Maurice Blanchard*. Translated by Maurice Blanchard. Quatre Vents, 1944.
Shakespeare, William. *Les Sonnets de Shakespeare, Essai d'interprétation poétique française par André Prudhommeaux*. Translated by André Prudhommeaux. Portes de France, 1945.
Shires, Linda M. *British Poetry of the Second World War*. Macmillan, 1985.
Taravacci, Pietro. 'Poesia da poesia. Alcune considerazioni sulla traduzione poetica dei poeti'. *Poeti traducono poeti*. Edited by Pietro Taravacci. Università degli Studi di Trento, 2015, pp. 7–23.
Tautou, Alexis. '1943, "l'année Hölderlin" vue de France'. *1943 en traductions dans l'espace francophone européen*. Edited by Christine Lombez. *Atlantide*, no. 8, 2018: pp. 65–87.
Tautou, Alexis. 'Traduire et éditer Rainer Maria Rilke sous l'Occupation'. *Traducteurs dans l'histoire, traducteurs en guerre*. Edited by Christine Lombez. *Atlantide*, no. 5, 2016: pp. 43–64.
Vuong, Thomas. 'Léon Kochnitzky, traducteur des *Sonnets de Shakespeare* et Européen en-dehors de l'Europe'. *Traduire, collaborer, résister: traducteurs et traductrices sous l'Occupation*. Edited by Christine Lombez. PU François Rabelais, 2019a, pp. 149–166.
Vuong, Thomas. 'Maurice Blanchard, traducteur de Shakespeare: une partie de l'histoire du sonnet en prose?'. *Traduire, collaborer, résister: traducteurs et traductrices sous l'Occupation*. Edited by Christine Lombez. PU François Rabelais, 2019b, pp. 83–100.

13

Translating Genrikh Sapgir's *Sonnets on Shirts*

Dmitri Manin

The sonnet is a beautiful gift to humankind.

Genrikh Sapgir

The story of *Sonnets on Shirts*

Genrikh Sapgir (1928–1999) was a leader of the Lianozovo group, an association of 'unofficial', avant-garde artists and poets. A prolific author, he was one of the many writers who worked outside the conventions of the officially sanctioned Socialist Realism aesthetics. Their works were never published during the Soviet era, and were spread through Samizdat channels (Von Zitzewitz).

Although Sapgir couldn't publish his own poetry, he published translations and wrote children's poetry and animation scripts, many of which became childhood staples for children born in the 1960s and 70s. In fact, many non-conformist but not outwardly dissident writers and poets in the Soviet environment had to derive income from translation and children's literature. Paradoxically, poetry translation flourished in the Soviet Union, at least to some degree, because it was the only publishing opportunity for such figures as Boris Pasternak or Nikolay Zabolotsky. Many early-twentieth-century Russian avant-garde writers wrote for children for the same reason (Shrayer & Shrayer 7–8; Ostashevsky xix; Khotimsky 345). Translation played a role here too, especially translation of English nonsense poetry. Both Chukovsky and the other defining figure of Soviet children's literature, Samuil Marshak, translated many traditional English Mother Goose rhymes.

In Sapgir's oeuvre for adults, the collection *Sonnets on Shirts* occupies a special place. It is the only book that was published three times before his death (in Paris in 1978, Moscow in 1989 and Omsk in 1991). Sapgir added poems to each new edition, which was also unusual: books were units of work for him (even if unpublished), and once they were completed he rarely revisited them (Orlitsky 331).

The genesis of *Sonnets on Shirts* was connected to a seminal event in Soviet cultural life: the 1975 exhibition of avant-garde art, the first of such shows to be officially sanctioned. The paintings of twenty artists, among them figures who would later achieve international renown such as Oscar Rabin, were displayed at the Exhibition of Achievements of the People's Economy (VDNKh). Needless to say, the official press published scathing reviews. The public, on the other hand, stood in long lines in freezing February weather to see the forbidden art. The show broke the monopoly of Socialist Realism and brought non-conformist art into a shadowy, but still visible, semi-legitimate existence.

Sapgir was friends with many of the avant-garde artists of the time and also participated in the VDNKh show. He recounted it in the foreword to the first, Paris edition of the sonnets:

> Here is how the title of the book, *Sonnets on Shirts*, came to be. In the fall of 1975, a show of 'left' artists was organized, by necessity at the VDNKh. My friends participated in it. To our public, at the time still inexperienced, I wanted to show examples of visual poetry. Two of my old shirts came in handy. With a red marker, I drew on their canvas backs two sonnets: 'Body' and 'Spirit'. They were hung this way in the exhibition pavilion on shirt hangers, one above the other. But just before opening night, the authorities ordered us to remove them, under the pretext that they hadn't gone through the censorship office. The third sonnet, 'She', was displayed in the same way the following spring at a Moscow apartment show.[1] [...] I think poems can be visually appealing and you can write them on clothes, wash-basins, tubs, bedsheets, luggage etc. This includes sonnets, a solemn form. Such a movement in poetry could be termed 'materialism'. (Sapgir 1978)[2]

This is what brought the first three sonnets to life, and in the next two or three years Sapgir wrote another sixty or so that were published in the Paris edition of 1978. They are not dated. In later editions, eighteen more poems were added as 'Sonnets-89', apparently written in 1989.

Sapgir and the modernist sonnet tradition

The sonnet is well established in the Russian poetic tradition. Even a brief survey would be beyond the scope of this chapter, but suffice it to say that Vladimir Sovalin's 1983 anthology *The Russian Sonnet* takes 500 pages to cover both original and translated poems created across two centuries from Trediakovsky to the Russian Silver Age. In the Soviet period, sonnets were also written and translated: notable examples include Pasternak and Marshak's translations of Shakespeare sonnets – discussed in Alexander Markov's chapter in this volume – and Joseph Brodsky's innovative *Twenty Sonnets to Mary Stuart*, written almost contemporaneously (1974) with the first *Sonnets on Shirts*.

Although the sonnet is an essentially traditionalist form, many avant-garde poets wrote sonnets. Since avant-garde art partly defines itself by the negation of convention, it needs the very thing that it negates to persist as a backdrop. Sapgir defined himself as a 'formalist' (Probstein 166). Indeed, poetic form is indispensable in his texts, which are often built on various kinds of sound patterning, not just end rhymes.

In his treatment of the sonnet form, Sapgir is relatively conservative. He largely preserves the broad logical structure of the sonnet, always keeping the two-part composition. About two thirds of the poems are in iambic pentameter, the canonical sonnet metre, and over three quarters are fully rhymed. Almost all of them consist of fourteen lines, except for two which are cut short and four which include a clearly marked extra line. In the rhymed sonnets, the rhyme scheme supports the division into octave and sestet, with the octave usually built on two rhyme chains and the sestet on three rhyme pairs.

At the same time, Sapgir's deviations from convention span a wide range of typologies in the collection. In the rhymed sonnets, unconventional rhyme schemes like ABAB BAAB CCD EED or ABAB BABA CDE CDE are prevalent. One sonnet, 'Winter in Maleyevka', is built on only two rhyme chains throughout the octave and sestet. There are sixteen blank verse sonnets (almost all of them among 'Sonnets-89') and two partially rhymed ones: in 'Muse', the octave is unrhymed and the sestet rhymed; in 'Crow', only the last two lines rhyme. Generally, rhymes range from exact to very loose, as is typical in contemporary Russian versification. In four sonnets, Sapgir rhymes words hyphenated across lines (as Hopkins did in English) or cut off entirely and left for the reader to complete.

Regarding metre, the third of the sonnets that are not in iambic pentameter are a motley collection. There is one in iambic tetrameter ('She') and three in amphibrachic tetrameter (both strict and loose). The sonnet titled 'Newspaper Editorial' is emphatically prosaic. The metre of 'Broken Sonnet' is best characterized as free verse. 'Something–Nothing' is written in lines of dolnik with variable lengths.[3] There is one polymetric sonnet with lines which are mainly accentual-syllabic, but in different metres ('A Walk to Ivanteyevka'). Of the sonnets that do not adhere to traditional accentual-syllabic metres, I would classify most as purely accentual verse with a more or less regular number of stresses per line, usually fluctuating around four.

Thematically, the sonnets cover a lot of ground, with several mini-cycles which are often loosely grouped together and in two cases explicitly titled. These are four 'Linguistic Sonnets', each exploring the cross-linguistic sound symbolism of a single word such as 'Star' or 'Water', somewhat in the spirit of Velimir Khlebnikov, and five 'Dilijan Sonnets', vignettes from the poet's visit to this small resort town in Armenia. A number of other poems are also devoted to places visited, notably Crimea, Thailand, Moscow and Leningrad. There are sonnets about common objects (a shirt, a suitcase, a manuscript); anonymous characters on the margins of society (a homeless man in 'Sleeper', a mentally ill boy in 'Love', a female labour camp inmate in 'Urals in the Winter of 1950'); history ('Boris Godunov', 'Fire'); departed friends ('The Fearless'); and so on. Several are responses to classical texts: Petrarch, Dante and the Bible. Some are lyrical accounts of personal life events: being in a hospital or sanatorium, childhood memories, romantic encounters and everyday scenes. Ironic or satirical commentary on Soviet life shows up in many sonnets, notably 'Sonnet on Things Gone Missing' and 'Newspaper Editorial Sonnet'. Taken together, the *Sonnets on Shirts* can be read as a broad panorama of the poet's personal experiences, philosophical musings and commentary on life, firmly situated in his geographical setting and the society of the time.

What unites them into a cohesive whole is a very distinct authorial voice. Sapgir's style is choppy, telegraphic and elliptical, because he writes in tightly packed sequences of images, skimping on connective tissue, both in grammar and in logic. As he progresses towards the 1989 sonnets, this tendency becomes more pronounced, leading to poems that are outright cryptic and need to be carefully deciphered.

Several of the sonnets stand out as particularly extreme experiments in concrete poetry. 'Newspaper Editorial Sonnet', for instance, is ostensibly just that, an *objet trouvé* picked up from official Soviet media which Sapgir has transformed into a poem by breaking it into verses.

A pairing of 'New Year's Sonnet' and 'Commentary Sonnet' forms a striking conceptual piece. The first one has no text at all, only fourteen placeholder lines marked up with double dashes. The commentary starts off by explaining, line by line, the images that should be read from those empty lines: white emptiness, someone's tracks obliterated by the new snow, something that is no longer there, clear winter air – all iconically represented by empty lines on white paper. The sonnet ends with a statement that the 'concept', as in a piece of conceptual art, is silent music, the auditory equivalent of an empty page, and poetry 'is just a commentary'. It can be read as an invitation for the reader to look past the texts in the collection and try to envision or experience the state of mind that brought them to life. It can also be interpreted as a Zen Buddhist gesture towards an ultimate emptiness.

A note on the translation

In these translations, I want to render Sapgir's voice by imitating his characteristic choppy, elliptical syntax and easy, conversational tone. By the same token, I wish to reproduce rhyme patterns and metrical structure. From my personal experience there is little difference in the difficulty of rhyming well between English and Russian ('well' is the operative word here). One often hears that Russian is extremely easy to rhyme because of grammatical endings. Indeed, it is easy to chain multiple nouns in the same case or verbs in the same tense. However, such rhymes are not worth using. The whole point of an effective rhyme is that it brings words together in unexpected ways. Avoiding grammatical rhymes makes rhyming in Russian much harder and more interesting. On the other hand, English is often said to be rhyme-poor. There is some truth in that. Although Russian has more consonant phonemes than English (thirty-four as opposed to twenty-five), English has far more vowel sounds: over fifteen by any count, versus only five in Russian. This makes for a much larger potential variety of syllables, so many words have few or no *exact* rhymes. In addition, the strict word order in English makes it harder to place the rhyming word at the end of the line. However, because Sapgir makes liberal use of modern, approximate rhymes, I can do the same with rhymes like 'wisdom/socialism/reason/prison' and avoid hackneyed, overused rhymes. In addition, it is only hard to get the right word at the line end when lines must correspond to syntactically closed units. But contemporary poetry often embraces enjambment, and so is largely free from this limitation. This makes it much easier to end lines with rhyming words while keeping the syntax natural.

A difficult issue with any translation is conveying time- and place-specific notions. This is especially salient when it comes to texts that are as deeply rooted in their environment as *Sonnets on Shirts*. A Soviet *militsioner* is not at all like an American or British policeman. A newspaper editorial in *Pravda* sounds nothing like its counterpart in the *New York Times*. A small-town café in the Russian North shares little but its name with a café in Minnesota. When faced with such difficulties, I often resort to an inline gloss. On the other hand, love and death, joy and suffering are readily understandable for readers across time and space. And what a joy it is for a translator when a light-hearted sonnet composed entirely of synonyms for 'drunk' in Russian comes out in English without much difficulty either.

A selection of sonnets

ТЕЛО

*"Здесь только оболочка. Слезы вытри," –
сказал отец Димитрий.*

Продуто солнцем – всё в огромных дырах
И время водопадом – сквозь меня
Но стыну гипсом видимость храня
В метро в такси на улицах в квартирах

Меня легко представить как коня:
Храп трепет плоть. Но вообще я сыро:
Вспотевший вкус черствеющего сыра
В рогоже скользких мускулов возня

Чудовищный костюм – мильоны клеток
Дворец из тканей радужных расцветок
Пожалуй скиньте если надоест

Я многим тесно… А иным просторно…
Но вчуже видеть просто смехотворно
Как это решето спит! любит! ест!

BODY

*"'Tis but a shell. So wipe your tears" –
said Father Demetrious.*

I'm blown through by the sun – riddled with gaps
Time gushing in and out – like waterfalls
But I freeze plaster-like when playing roles
In beds in tubs on subways on the steps

Imagine me a horse – you'll be enthralled:
Rush snortle flesh. In fact I'm cheesy crap
The taste of staling cheese's sweaty sap
A burlap sack with slithering muscle rolls

A monstrous costume – scores of tiny cells
An iridescent palace rainbow shell
Try not to wear me if I weary you

For some I am too loose… For some too tight…
But it's absurd for an impartial sight
To see this goddamn sieve sleep! love! and chew!

ДУХ

Звезда ребенок бык сердечко птичье –
Все вздыблено и все летит – люблю –
И налету из хаоса леплю
Огонь цветок – все – новые обличья

Мое существованье фантастично
Разматываясь космос шевелю
И самого себя хочу настичь я
Стремясь из бесконечности к нулю

Есть! пойман!.. Нет! Еще ты дремлешь в стебле
Но как я одинок на самом деле
Ведь это я всё я – жасмин и моль и солнца свет

В башке поэта шалого от пьянства
Ни времени не знаю ни пространства
И изнутри трясу его сонет

SPIRIT

A star a child a bull a sparrow's heart –
I love it! – everything flies bulges folds
And from this chaos I pick out and mold
Now fire now flower – a mask for every part

I am impossible I'm off the charts
I stir the cosmos like a tightly coiled
Spring – in a quest to reach myself I dart
To zero from infinity – I hold

It! gotcha!.. No! You're still a dormant seed
I'm desperately lonely for indeed
It's only me all me: jasmine a moth an ocean tide

And in the dizzy brain of this drunk poet
Oblivious to time and space I throw it
Awry and shake his sonnet from inside.

ВОДА

Речь как река. Во всем – свои истоки
Индусское уда течет в воде
И мной разгадан смысл ее глубокий
В – влажность. О – овал. Движенье – Д.

Оудакам ю аква вато вотэ
…И выжимая влагу из волос
Как много дней и солнца пролилось
В небытие пустое как зевота

Я пить хочу. Горит моя гортань
В ней – скорпионы мерзостная дрянь!
Язык мой – враг мой вытянут как жало…

И – разрешилось! Ливнем снизошло
Все мокрое: асфальт кирпич стекло
Ты льешься в горло – мало! мало! мало!

WATER

Speech like a stream starts from a spring or seep
Sanskrit *Udá* flows in the water's sound
I found its meaning that was hidden deep
W is wet. T travels. R is round.

Voda – hiu – watō – aqua – udakam
... How many days and how much sun have flown
Into the void as empty as a yawn
While wringing wet hair in the morning calm

I am in thirst. My throat is dry and burning
It teams with scorpions the vicious vermin
My sting-like tongue – my foe – is strained and sore ...

And then – relief! It's raining waterfalls
Everything's drenched: pavement and glass and walls
You're pouring down my throat: more! more! more! more!

СОНЕТ О ТОМ ЧЕГО НЕТ

Яну Сатуновскому

То мяса нет – то колбасы то сыра
То шапок нет куда я ни зайду
Но я встречал и большую беду
Нет близких. Нет здоровья. Нет квартиры

Нет радости нет совести нет мира
Нет уваженья к своему труду
Нет на деревне теплого сортира
Нет урожая в будущем году

Но есть консервы РЫБНЫЕ ТЕФТЕЛИ
Расплывчатость и фантастичность цели
Есть подлость водка скука и балет –

Леса и степи, стройки и ракеты
Есть даже люди в захолустье где-то
И видит Бог! – хоть Бога тоже нет

SONNET OF THINGS GONE MISSING

For Yan Satunovsky

At times there is – no beef or ham or cheese
Now hats are gone from store shelves everywhere
But I have known calamities to spare
No place to live. No health. No relatives

No happiness no moral sense no peace
For one's own labor no respect nor care
No warm and comfy place to take a piss
No prospects for a harvest come next year

But there are FISH-BASED MEATBALLS in a can
And goals – both hazy and utopian
Betrayal cosmos vodka boredom missiles

There's forest, steppe, construction and ballet[4]
And even people – somewhere far away
And God's my witness! – though God's also missing

ПЬЯНЫЙ СОНЕТ

Навеселе под мухой под хмельком
За друга для сугрева для настроя
У магазина вздрогнули – нас трое
А кто-то в одиночку и молчком –

Наклюкался надрызгался надрался
Как зюзя назюзюкался раскис
Набрался налакался настебался
До чертиков! до положенья риз!

Нарезался. Распался по-российски
Пьян в дребодан! в дым! в сиську и в сосиску!
– Поколбасись еще! похулигань

Спой песню нам про цветики-цветочки
Нафиздипупился. Дошел до точки
Пьянь распьянющая! Распьянь и перепьянь

DRUNKEN SONNET

Inebriated plastered loaded stoned
To beat the chills to toast friends to cheer up
We split a bottle by the liquor shop
But some get soaked in silence and alone –

Got mighty buzzed all bibulous befuddled
Under the influence drunk like a brute
Got three sheets to the wind sloshed woozy muddled
Out of his gourd! As sozzled as a newt!

All sewed up. Fell to pieces à la Russe
Bombed, blasted! Stewed and pickled! Juiced and sluiced!
– Well, go ahead! become a total swine

Sing violets are blue asses are pink
Completely schnockered. Teetering on the brink
Outdrank the drinkdom's drunkest Drankenstein!

НЕЧТО – НИЧТО

Метафизический сонет

Качается шар. Навстречу шару
Качается шар. Один в один
Влетают шары: один – пара, один – пара, один – пара
Из сферы зеркальной за ними следим

Все отраженье. Предмет или дым
Шар или призрак. Подобно кошмару
Шар вырастает…Но вместо удара вместо удара вместо удара
Шар исчезает проглочен другим

Несутся – слоятся шары пропадая
В третьем – в десятом – целая стая
В лжебесконечность уходят шары шары шары шары шары шары шары шары шары шары шары и т.д.*

Стойте! Довольно! Не вынесу пытки!
Маленький шарик повисший на нитке –
Детский предлог для вселенской игры

* Строка уходит в бесконечность, ложно понимаемую.

SOMETHING – NOTHING

A metaphysical sonnet

A sphere swings. Towards the sphere
A sphere swings. Where they meet, they all
Collapse: one – a pair, one – a pair, one – a pair
We watch from a spherical mirror hall

Everything's a reflection. A ball or a troll
A thing or a cloud. It swells like a nightmare
Then without a crash… a ball disappears a ball disappears a ball disappears
Gobbled up by a ball

Streaking and splitting they fold and go –
In the third – in the tenth – all the host to the faux
Infinity: one after the next the next the next the next the next the next the next the next the next etc.*

Stop it! Enough! I can't stand this ordeal!
A ball on a thread in an infinite reel,
A universal game on a childish pretext

----

*The line stretches to a misconceived infinity. (*Author's note*)

СОНЕТ-СТАТЬЯ

"Большая роль в насыщении рынка товарами принадлежит торговле. Она необычный посредник между производством и покупателями: руково-

дители торговли отвечают за то, чтобы растущие потребности населения удовлетворялись полнее, для этого надо развивать гото-

вые связи, успешно улучшать проблемы улучшения качества работы, особенно в отношении сферы услуг, проводить курс на укрепле-

ние материально-технической базы, активно внедрять достижения техники, прогрессивные формы и методы организации труда на селе"

NEWSPAPER EDITORIAL SONNET

'An important role in saturating the market belongs to the points of sale. They are an unusual intermediary between the production industry and consumers: the trade admin-

istration is responsible for meeting the burgeoning demand for consumer goods by the Soviet people more comprehensively, and so we must keep developing the cur-

rently established channels, successfully improve the issues of work quality improvement, and especially as concerns services, stay the course of reinfor-

cing material and technical foundations, actively introduce technical advancements, progressive forms and methods of efficacious agricultural labor.'

Посвящается Герловиным

1. НОВОГОДНИЙ СОНЕТ

=
=
=
=

=
=
=
=

=
=
=

=
=

2. СОНЕТ-КОММЕНТАРИЙ

На первой строчке пусто и бело
Вторая – чей-то след порошей стертый
На третьей – то что было и прошло
И зимний чистый воздух на четвертой

На пятой – вздох: "как поздно рассвело"
Шестая – фортепьянные аккорды
Седьмая – ваше белое письмо
Восьмая – мысль: "здесь нечто от кроссворда"

И две терцины: все что вам придет
На ум когда наступит Новый Год
И все о чем вы здесь не прочитали

И основное: то что мой концепт
Из белых звуков сотканный концерт
Поэзия же – просто комментарий

To the Gerlovins

1. NEW YEAR'S SONNET

=
=
=
=

=
=
=
=

=
=
=

=
=
=

2. COMMENTARY SONNET

The first line: white and void and free of clutter
The second: tracks wiped from the snowy slate
The third: the crisp and frosty air of winter
And on the fourth are things that were but ain't

The fifth: piano chords roll off and flutter
The sixth: 'even the dawn today is late'
The seventh is your blank page of a letter
'Bit like a crossword puzzle' – on the eighth

Then two tercets: for everything that goes
Across your mind when it's New Year's and snows
And everything that's missing from my tally

And then the main point, which is that my concept
Is sounds of whiteness weaved into a concert
While poetry is just a commentary

Notes

1. The apartment shows that flourished during the following few years used the private apartments of the artists and their friends as exhibition spaces.
2. Translation is mine. In the original, Sapgir plays on the term *veschism*, derived from *vesch*: 'thing, material object', but also 'a piece (of art)'. The word already exists in Russian with a meaning close to 'consumerism, materialism'.
3. Dolnik is a metre that allows for one or two unstressed syllables between consecutive stresses, similar to the English ballad metre.
4. Cosmos, large construction projects, missiles and ballet were among the most iconic tokens of the official Soviet patriotism.

Works cited

Brodsky, Joseph. *Collected Poems in English*. Farrar, Straus & Giroux, 2000.

Khotimsky, Maria. 'Children's Poetry and Translation in the Soviet Era: Strategies of Rewriting, Transformation and Adaptation'. *A Companion to Soviet Children's Literature and Film*. Edited by Olga Voronina. Brill, 2019, pp. 341–388.

Olesha, Yuri. *No Day Without a Line: From Notebooks*. Translated by J. Rosengrant. Northwestern University Press, 1998.

Orlitsky, Yuri. 'Традиции русского и европейского авангарда в сонетном творчестве Генриха Сапгира'/ 'Traditions of Russian and Soviet Avant-Garde in Sonnet Oeuvres of Genrikh Sapgir'. *A Crown of Sonnetologists and Sonneteers, Proceedings of the 7th International Seminar 'The Sonnet School'*. Russkoe Slovo, 2016, pp. 331–344. (In Russian).

Ostashevsky, Eugene, ed. *OBERIU: An Anthology of Russian Absurdism* Evanston, IL Northwestern University Press, 2006.

Probstein, Ian. 'Генрих Сапгир: "Форма голоса" и голос формы'/ 'Genrikh Sapgir: "The Form of the Voice" and the Voice of the Form'. *Novyj Mir*, no. 6, 2019. http://www.nm1925.ru/Archive/Journal6_2019_6/Content/Publication6_7209/Default.asp. Accessed 17 August 2022. (In Russian).

Sapgir, Genrikh. *Сонеты на рубашках / Sonnets on Shirts*. Tret'ia volna, 1978. (In Russian).

Shrayer-Petrov, David and Maxim Shrayer, eds. *Генрих Сапгир. Стихотворения и поэмы/Genrikh Sapgir. Poems and Long Poems*. Akademicheskij Proekt, 2004. (In Russian).

Sovalin, Vladimir, ed. *The Russian Sonnet*. Moskovskij Rabochij, 1983. (In Russian).

Von Zitzewitz, Josephine. *The Culture of Samizdat: Literature and Underground Networks in the Late Soviet Union*. Bloomsbury Publishing, 2020.

14

The vulgar eloquence of Singaporean sonnets

Tse Hao Guang

The history of the sonnet is the history of eloquence, and of the languages powerful enough to be fit for eloquent utterance. Invented and circulated by notaries and civil servants at the court of Holy Roman Emperor Frederick II, the sonnet's emergence in Italian dialect pre-empted Dante's later defence of the dignity and legitimacy of the vernacular in *De Vulgari Eloquentia* (Spiller 13, 70). The spread of the sonnet from Italian to numerous European languages seems to be a logical development of this urge to make the vernacular eloquent. The rise of English as a global language through first British colonization and later Americanization and the internet has spawned many vernaculars of English – several, too, seeking recognition. African-American and postcolonial sonneteers in particular have often adopted double-voiced strategies to gain credibility with both general ('white' or 'colonial') audiences and specific ones at once (Kennedy; Grant 8).

In search of vulgar eloquence closer to home, I look at two contemporary books of sonnets by Singaporeans, the only published examples to my knowledge:[1] *Payday Loans* by Jee Leong Koh (2007, reprint 2014), an émigré to New York City, and *Sonnets from the Singlish* by Joshua Ip (2012), a public servant. Both books employ relatively traditional sonnet forms, but a closer look reveals innovative engagements with Singapore's postcolonial culture. If the sonnet engenders creativity through formal constraint, Singapore might also have blessed Koh's and Ip's poems with its own peculiar limitations. First, recognizing that the audience for poetry here is tiny (but growing) results in poetic personae being aware of themselves as speakers in need of readers and attempting to win them over rhetorically. Second, the lack of time to write amidst the pervasive demands of remunerative work manifests in uses of the sonnet and sonnet sequence as a means of ordering time. Both books were produced by writing a sonnet a day for a month, demonstrating how capitalistic productivity might be harnessed for artistic ends. Third, in Ip's work particularly, Singaporean culture is playfully integrated into the sonnet form.

The sonnet's spread has always crossed cultures and languages. What makes the sonnet in English postcolonial does not therefore depend simply on contextual translation, but also on its emergence as an aspirational form through colonial education. In nineteenth-century British India, Thomas Babington Macaulay argued for diverting money from Sanskrit and Persian to English-language publications and teaching:

> Whether we look at the intrinsic value of our literature, or at the particular situation of [India], we shall see the strongest reason to think that, of all foreign tongues, the English tongue is that which would be the most useful to our native subjects.

English literature in the empire was funded so the natives might internalize Britain's inherent superiority. In Macaulay's time, Shakespeare and his sonnets were re-evaluated by scholars and poets, despite a well-documented critical dislike of them throughout the eighteenth century (Sanderlin 464). This may explain why I read Shakespeare's and not Milton's sonnets in class, and highlights the enduring effect of colonial education policies on Singapore's literary culture.

Extending Michael Spiller's argument, Marya Grant claims that poets in Italy, Britain and India first began writing sonnets to increase their status during a period of national formation and development; the sonnet's traditional theme of desire for a beloved doubled as a desire for political favour (2). Post-independence, Indian sonneteers became more formally experimental, investigating 'notions of history, heritage, culture, and self to fit with contemporary global concerns' (43). This shift from formal conservatism to experiment implies a distinction between a traditional sonnet embodying 'Western' power and values, and a deconstructed one questioning both. The nascent Singaporean sonnet tradition, however, emerges in the 2000s, when Singapore's independence is well- and possibly over-established.

In the Singaporean postcolonial sonnet, therefore, innovation does not equal formal disruption, and traditional form signifies tradition's destabilization. Instead of writing their sonnets to a political elite, Koh and Ip appeal to the middle-class, mass-educated reader of English who is not necessarily conversant in literary history or theory, but who has some idea of sonnet structure. The sonnet becomes simply a short, humorous, melodious form that accommodates readers of varying levels of poetic literacy, while remaining familiar from the fallout of Shakespeare's continuing but diminished presence in Singapore's English Literature classrooms. Writing sonnets is no longer primarily an issue of appealing to canonicity. Instead, it is a novel act in a literary scene where, apart from figures such as Robert Yeo, Shirley Lim,

Gwee Li Sui and Toh Hsien Min, Anglophone poets had preferred writing free verse. The postcolonial sonnet here, its history no longer a defining factor, can represent culturally specific, everyday issues in a seemingly universal form while also questioning the assumptions undergirding this universality.

At this moment I would like to sketch out why a perceived lack of and a corresponding desire for mass readership should imprint itself so strongly on our Anglophone poetry. The introduction to *Writing Singapore* claims English-language literature is burgeoning:

> In the last forty years, a secondary consequence of government policies that established English as the medium of instruction in all schools has seen a growth in writing in English and indeed an audience for such writing. (Poon, Holden and Lim xxi)

Singapore has exchanged colonial education's fixation on Britain's inherent goodness with a pragmatic promotion of English as a bridge between cultures and to the wider world. Unsurprisingly, the *National Literary Reading and Writing Survey 2015* discovered that while 91 per cent of readers read in English, only 44 per cent of respondents had read a literary book within the past twelve months; of these, 4.5 per cent read poetry. Readers of Singapore poetry, while not measured specifically, are doubtless fewer. Considering the absolute size of Singapore's population and the fact that the reading public has been *growing*, English-language poets write to a minuscule audience. Instead of embracing the elitism of the medium, most Singapore writers and literary activists support efforts to encourage more people to read Singapore poetry. Koh and Ip, for example, established Singapore Unbound and Sing Lit Station respectively, two organizations that promote Singapore writing, including poetry, to a local and global audience.

To that end, Koh's and Ip's poetic personae speak as everymen even as they do so in sonnets. Their speakers address those interested in Singapore poetry (and also presumably more familiar with the 'Western' canon) and the wider English-speaking world, even though *both* groups are privileged by their proficiency in this global, elite language. Koh and Ip develop interrelated but distinct voicing strategies to convince this 'general' audience of poetry's worth. Ip's, I argue, is akin to seduction, while Koh's is more confrontational. Both strategies emerge from the sonnet's history as a status symbol, but where status is no longer measured by official approval. Instead, status accrues to a mass readership seemingly unattainable in poetry writing. In order to claim eloquence, therefore, it is this mass audience that Singaporean sonnets have to please.

Seduction and confrontation

To please his public, Ip is willing even to satirize the poetic vocation. In 'k ge zhi wang attends a poetry reading', the titular Karaoke King finds fault with poetry's drive to make it new: 'in karaoke, in his element, / originals are shunned' (23).[2] Instead, artistry is about earning the respect of 'k gods' by 'perform[ing] the standards before vent- / uring into new tunes'. In using the sonnet, however, Ip performs tradition *and* creates new poetry, poking fun at both Karaoke King and poets who perform *'what [they] just wrote'*. The poem asserts that art can participate in tradition without sacrificing inventive newness, as long as the audience is willing to step out of its comfort zone, avoiding both the Karaoke King's knee-jerk dislike of the new and the thin instantness of some kinds of poetry.

The first move Ip makes, then, is to ease the reader out of said comfort zone. I look closely at 'entry', the first poem in *Sonnets*; it demonstrates both his strategy of winning over the reader and the collection's humour and interpretive possibility:

entry

this poem comes with intentions and directions clearly labeled.
this poem has been vetted, cleared, and given the once-over
twice-over, overlooked with oversight. it has been tabled
ably to all appropriate approving fora.

this poem solemnly declares and swears it does not keep
in its possession any media. this poem is free
of any image-capturing device. it does not beep
a beep. this poem has surrendered its identity.

this poem is tucked-in, clean-shaved, and iron-creased, each last
cock-hair shaved off and burnt and tweezed with a mother's pride,
screaming 'inspect me' from each seam, no dirt, no dust –
this poem is so shiny you can see your face inside.

submitted, for approval, please – i'm willing to refine it.
or let me write it in your book-in book, and maybe sign it. (15)

The poem describes itself as a recruit, with readers being military inspectors. It has 'surrendered its identity', offered itself up to literal change – 'i'm willing to refine it'. However, the poem subverts its seeming submission.

Its unruly metre is hardly 'clean-shaved', its ostentatious internal rhyme far from '[solemn] declar[ation]', protestations of transparency finally undercut by its humour. Readers realize the poem's attempts at seduction, Ip's primary strategy of pleasure. Writing and signing the poem in a 'book-in book', readers allow it access to the highly controlled army camp of their minds.

In 'entry', infelicities in discourse shape reader-speaker relations. The first stanza uses labels to reassure *and* confuse readers, alluding to its 'intentions and directions' without naming them. The deitic function of the label goes unfulfilled; what it points to is too vague to be meaningful. The poem performs and parodies discourse claiming to be clear but harbouring complex or contradictory intentions and directions.

In the second, the poem continues to play recruit. Declaring 'it does not keep / in its possession any media', the language parallels the oath taken by Singaporean soldiers who cannot possess rounds after live firing exercises. Yet poetry *is* mediated meaning – the poem cannot take its oath truthfully without denying its existence. That the poem 'is free / of any image-capturing device' again both echoes the camera ban in army camps and shows the impossibility of excluding images and imagery from poetry. These paradoxes show that the relationship between text and reader is nothing like that of recruit and state. Singapore may discipline its citizen army, but a poem by definition resists any vacation of meaning or critical closure.

By the third stanza, the reader knows not to take the poem at face value. The focus is on good form: the poem presents itself 'tucked-in, clean-shaved, and iron-creased', every stray thread ('cock-hair') removed. As a sonnet, however, it wears its uniform slant: the metre varies from five to seven beats a line, takes frequent excursions out of the iamb, uses half rhymes like 'last'/'dust', and insists on lower case. Of course, poetic form is not uniform; 'rules' in verse are modified almost as a rule. A poem 'so shiny you can see your face inside' suggests technical polish revealing, finally, the reader's own image. Ip chooses the extended army metaphor to surface the fundamental incommensurability of poetic and military power. Where the latter can coerce, the former can only persuade.

In the final couplet text and reader relations are complicated and clarified by the speaker's appearance. Readers have been led to assume that speaker *is* poem, an independent consciousness. Now, the 'I', separate from poem, reveals itself as the poet ('i'm willing to refine it'). Unable to get the poem approved through force or self-contradictory obsequiousness, poet pleads with reader. No more need for the text to erase its distinctiveness: written down, autographed, it assumes a marked and material presence in its mediated, imagistic, metrically disobedient glory.

If sonnets are typically love poems, this one seduces. It gains acceptance by pretending to be transparent. When this is shown to be both impossible and a ruse, the poet steps in, desirous to work with the reader to revise the poem. Again, the poem having already been printed, this too is impossible; the poet finally admits the reader must 'take it or leave it'. Every line, even and especially the impossible or contradictory, points to an overwhelming need for poetry to be validated and accepted.

The poem is also a gift that binds the recipient. Its title refers both to an entry in the book-in book and the poem-soldier's entry into the reader's mind-camp. The reader owns the book-in book, may accept or reject the poem. Insofar as the reader's mind is an army camp, we can assume that speaker sees reader as discriminating, wary of letting in unwanted, unverified personnel for fear of security breaches. Poems are not passive; once in camp, they sneak around, interacting with other agents. In accepting the poem, the reader also bears responsibility for consequences that arise.

No surprise that Ip compares state with poetic power, investigating the correspondences but also the limits of such a comparison. Both public servant and poet, Ip embodies this tension between pragmatism and aestheticism, coercive and persuasive force. His arguments for poetry, that which exceeds purely communicative concerns, are disguised as pragmatism. Ip's work succeeds in maintaining an illusion of accessibility to the general public precisely because of this. Writing about everyday issues in sonnets ('the shitty carparking in orchard road', 38), he demonstrates the seductive power of poetry to give pleasure, while claiming that such pedestrian themes are fit to be verse.

Koh's poetic strategy of pleasure is also inflected by his relationship to the Singaporean public. A former evangelical Christian teaching at a public school, he moved to New York, coming out as both gay and a poet (Koh 65–66). For him writing poetry is inextricable from homosexuality. He exchanges Singapore for a new geographical, vocational and sexual landscape – pragmatism for pleasure. This conversion narrative, however, is problematic. In *Loans* are speakers debating with the past, the pragmatist, the straight man – symbols seemingly contrary to Koh's newfound identities. These quarrels show that 'gay' and 'poet' cannot fully represent Koh and his concerns. His strategy of pleasure confronts both his speakers' inconsistencies and an imagined reader embodying the largely conservative socio-political structures Koh left behind.

In 'April 14, Thursday', the speaker compares his former life to a 'low fever' brought about by church and state, announcing that in this new one, 'Poetry is my chosen course, the lever / for straightening dislocations in my bed' (27). Poetry is a course of action and a course of medication. Yet the 'you' is critical: 'You read my work for indiscretions, claim / them yours, to be used only with permission'. The reader inserts their own intentions and injunctions, limiting the speaker's supposed freedom. Crucially, 'you' personifies both constraint and love – 'Love, are you Priest or Law, another name / for Censor?'. The speaker recognizes a love motivating the restrictions of church and state, and a love *for* both, re-coding the fever of youth as passion: 'Or is *my* love in remission?'. He confesses his ambivalence to Singapore, a Singapore in which state, church and public are imaginatively blurred.

In 'April 13, Wednesday', confrontation extends beyond poem into real life. A John Donne-esque carpe diem love poem, it announces: 'Come on, straight boy, and make gay love with me' (25). As the straight boy gets an unwanted advance, the authorities banned its performance at a local gay pride reading (75). In light of difficulties facing the reception of both poetry and homosexuality in Singapore, the appeal for sex can also be understood as an appeal to be read, another conflation of orientation, vocation and freedom. Making love with women constrains – 'Why, in an oven she loves regulating, / you stick in your tray of cookie dough, and wait?' (25). With men, however, there is pleasure – 'they know well how to give / each other head'.

Koh advocates poetry as art for art's sake, sex for sex's sake. However, the speaker appeals to pragmatism in the form of farcical insistence on the inconsequentiality of gay sex. 'One night of loving will not turn you queer', the gay man assures the straight boy: 'What have you got to lose? Leap, acrobat! / You can always fall back on pussycat'. As in 'entry', the sceptic is addressed. However, where Ip's speaker warns of poetry's transformative power, Koh's speaker downplays the importance of sex acts to one's identity, by extension downplaying the effect of reading poetry on one's worldview.

Clearly, Koh does not believe this. His speaker has strong desires but weak justifications for them. The speaker wants instant gratification – woman's 'oven' needs waiting for, man gives 'straightforward relief'. Pleasure is good because it is inconsequential and immediate, yet poetry is rarely instant; desiring quick, painless fun is precisely the stand of a pragmatist. Using poetry to praise the instant seems contradictory. The confrontation with the straight man and regulatory authority only exists on the page. Readers realize that these forceful displays of rhetoric are knowingly impotent. The ban on the poem, the book's author page declares, 'made Koh Jee Leong out to be more dangerous than he is' (75).

In 'April 16, Saturday', the conflict between speaker's and reader's desires again leaves the poet helpless. 'You', both lover and reader, searches for the speaker's old poems, enjoying one 'in a style so jeweled / I blushed and stripped it down to a bright nude' (31). The beloved loves 'the body shod and gloved', loves intricate writing; Proust is mentioned. Yet this reader knows little of the power of words; he derives pleasure more from superficial attraction to the overwrought than from any real engagement – 'vaguely, vastly, you were moved'. In contrast, the speaker desires plain honesty, 'bright nude' style, bare emotion.

At a poetry reading, the speaker 'strip[s] before a cheering crowd', baring his soul to an audience while desiring acceptance only from his beloved. Heartbreakingly, the beloved replies with 'faint praise'. Yet, Koh does not intend to confuse his speaker's early style with Proust's – rather, he suggests that the reader/beloved cannot distinguish lushness from pretension. Conversely, the confessional is not necessarily an indicator of good writing. There is 'pulchritude / [in] blurry windows', beauty in veiling things that cannot be fully exposed. The reader's love for the speaker's older poems and Proust stems from a beauty he senses but cannot fully articulate.

This explains why the speaker craves the reader's acceptance; although perhaps naïve, the reader still intuitively discerns beauty. Although the speaker gains a larger audience, he has lost the one reader he cares for to his evolving aesthetic. Without going so far as to claim that this particular reader/beloved represents a Singaporean audience, I suggest the speaker is torn between past and present. The lover senses something deeper about the speaker's early work ('you saw more than I did'), and now he runs a crowd-pleasing stripper act.

In these three poems, Koh's strategy of pleasure surfaces through ambivalence underlying every confrontation between speaker and reader. Each works through the love – hate relationship between 'I' and 'you'. Every criticism of Singapore is enriched by the affection the speaker still feels towards it, every brash assertion of homosexuality or a new, naked style of writing undercut by doubt over the subject's ability to effect change, and mourning for what was lost on the path of change. Insofar as these poems end without resolution or with an admission of impotence, Koh, like Ip, realizes that poetry cannot force engagement. Surfacing these conflicts on the page is vulnerability, a way through which Koh shows he wants his beloveds – whomever they may be – to reciprocate his love despite every disagreement.

Ip's and Koh's speakers know their voices may not be heard or accepted. While Ip's charm themselves into readers' minds, Koh's argue with them in a way that admits desire. Both strategies are a result of a shift in attitudes towards poetry after empire, where power appears to reside in the average person, in appeals to democracy, even as poetry remains a niche production. The paradox of tiny actual audience versus desired mass readership, of elite poets and readers versus an aversion to elitism, reflects a bigger problem of whether Singapore writing should aim for a local or a global readership. Knowing that the local audience is limited rubs up against the desire to speak to local culture rather than merely write to the 'West', driving these poems to cater to both groups at once. The success of Koh's and Ip's poetry, therefore, depends on whether they succumb to this dilemma or productively stand in the gap not just between high and low art but between 'East' and 'West'.

Productivity and glocalization

Although pragmatism and pleasure have been placed in opposition thus far, it is through the 'productivity' alluded to above that poetry aligns with Singapore's results-oriented, even workaholic culture. Productivity is applied to composition methods; both *Sonnets* and *Loans* were birthed from attempts to write a poem a day for a month. This self-enforced union of poetic pleasure and pragmatic effort creates a better poet. Ip writes, in his preface to the second edition of *Loans*:

> A constraint, like the onerous sonnet form, like the twenty-four hours Jee Leong set himself to complete each poem, seems an unnecessary set of weights for a young poet to carry. But there are three benefits of constrained writing that surface upon closer examination – discipline, focus, and challenge. (xvii)

Poetic practice becomes entangled with an almost neoliberal work ethic, one familiar to Singaporeans brought up on a narrative of the nation's development from the third world to the first through hard work.

Of course, this method is not unique to Ip or Koh, or indeed Singaporean poets. In April 2003, Maureen Thorson announced the first ever National Poetry Writing Month (NaPoWriMo). Participants wrote one poem each day, and were encouraged to link up online. Koh wrote most of *Loans* during NaPoWriMo 2005 (73). Ip posted his sonnets on a blog as he wrote them (joshuaip.com). He later declared April 2014 Singapore Poetry Writing Month (SingPoWriMo), challenging local writers to write a poem a day on Facebook for the entire month. SingPoWriMo grows out of and shapes contemporary network culture, both indebted to the global and adapting it. Roland Robertson's 'glocalisation' captures this concept: 'the simultaneity – the co-presence – of both universalizing and particularizing tendencies' (2001). Likewise, the sonnet's recognizable, authoritative form and online composition constitutes the universalizing tendency, while the particularizing tendency drives both poets towards cultural specificity and the quotidian.

The production and medium of Ip's and Koh's work is an extension of their concern with speaker-reader relations. Following Marshall McLuhan, it is widely recognized that media is not transparent; form and content cannot be separated except theoretically. In this case, the authors' productive choices are also part of the message. Online readers watched these collections take shape before their very eyes; these readers could give praise or suggestions practically instantaneously. They might even have acted out the speaker – reader dynamics Ip and Koh embed in their poems. That the first audiences of these poems were online ones reinforces their concealed eliteness – it appears as if any person may now read them, but internet connectivity and familiarity with English are not defining features of most audiences.

Of course, speaker-reader relations are written into the sonnet form as well. The sonnet's relative brevity, rigidity and rhetorical structure provide Ip with a template through which thought might flow easily under time constraints:

> under the time pressure, every single poem that emerged turned out to be a sonnet. short and somewhat formulaic, the sonnet form was perfect for bashing out thoughts and organising them in a very short germination period. (joshuaip.com)

Ip's readers also benefit from these characteristics of the sonnet – busy readers, who do not otherwise have time for poetry, can now consume these bite-sized poems on the go. The familiar structure and deployment of the sonnet serves as a soft landing, assuring readers they need not encounter obscurity or difficulty. The sonnet, unburdened from being read primarily as contributing to or desiring colonial power, takes on the role of mediator between poet and reader as a form easy to both write and read.

Working within this framework, Ip imbues his sonnets with languages, cultures and experiences familiar to modern Singaporeans. More than simply filling 'Western' form with 'Eastern' content, or 'old' with 'new', local context structures his poetry. Treating localness as a fertile source rather than a barrier against understanding, Ip innovates by writing what he knows. His Singlish sonnets with hybrid DNA speak to both the postcolonial consciousness of Singapore and the wider Anglophone world.

'Chope' shows how postcolonial glocalization is mapped onto reader – speaker relations. It means 'to book, or reserve a place, such as a seat in a fast food restaurant, sometimes by placing a packet of tissue paper on it' (Ip 63). The poem uses this culturally specific expression to comment on increasingly expensive and outrageous wedding proposals – will 'you' say yes if 'i, / while at a hawker stall, drop to a knee, / and place a tissue packet on your thigh?'

(42). Unable and/or unwilling to give 'you' 'flash mobs and fireworks and fighter rides', the speaker turns away from the materialistic one-upmanship of the wedding proposal, inviting her to consider 'the prospect of a hdb', of co-owning a government flat. The abrupt suggestion to 'chope' her makes a Singlish term a means of imagining an alternative wedding culture, unspectacular but certainly inventive.

This marriage of the 'you' and the 'I' occurs in a sweet spot of pragmatism and pleasure – the commitment of buying a house together, the surprise of co-opting 'chope'. This productive proposal also makes use of sonnet form. The octet sets up a problem (too-flashy proposals); the sestet solves it by invoking 'HDB' and 'chope', not as dispensable local colour but as integral elements of the poem's argument (simple proposals are better). Clearly this proposal is also for readers. The persona asks, 'is there an issue of sincerity…?', and 'would it be disrespectful if…?' – also questions of a speaker trying to persuade a reader to engage with his work. Lacking either coercive power or capital, the poet uses the sonnet argument to make a case for his poetry.

'Rag and Bone' further illustrates the use of the postcolonial sonnet to relate global and local concerns. The problem of worldwide ecological disaster is laid out in the octet:

> we ate and shat, and ate, and shat, and shat
> ………………………………………………………………..
> evolving from our brittle forms
> to that which lasts forever – planet styrofoam. (50)

The repetition of 'ate and shat' underlies a hysterical cycle of consumption and waste. This dystopian vision is the result of pragmatism and pleasure taken to extremes, all natural resources depleted to 'feed the grow- / ing appetite of mankind and machines'. Evolution as survival of the fittest becomes, ironically, regression – to survive, man becomes plastic. The sterility of a plastic earth, however, is made fertile again in the sestet.

Two forces contribute to this reinvigoration. First, the karang guni or rag-and-bone man quite literally makes a living off all the world's junk; typically of low social standing, he becomes the last man standing, 'lord of all he sees'. He invests worthless objects with purpose and value, a symbol of productivity. This is the triumph of simple man over worldwide disaster, meaning over meaninglessness, and productivity over either pleasure or pragmatism.

Secondly, Ip incorporates the karang guni man's distinctive cry – "'poh chuah gu sar kor pai dian see kee": hokkien for "newspapers, old clothes, broken televisions"' – into the final couplet (64). He reinterprets worldwide destruction through the lens of a specific aspect of Singaporean culture.

Again, this is more than a superficial act; Ip's adaptation[3] of the karang guni call respects the sonnet's iambic pentameter and rhyme. Just as the sonnet is infused with hokkien, the karang guni cry also changes. Ip takes two traditions and creates something unmistakably related to both, but also different, new, demonstrating the regenerative power of the postcolonial situation. His poems on Disney characters, Michael Jackson and the Defense of the Ancients computer game sit alongside those on local TV show *The Unbeatables* and local restaurant chain Al Azhar, and those using (in 'conversaytion') thick, unapologetic Singlish dialogue. In *Sonnets*, the global and local interpenetrate, both reflecting contemporary Singapore culture and making a case for the representation of cultural specifics to the wider world.

In Koh's collection, postcoloniality manifests in the use of time. The thirty poems in *Loans* are named after April's thirty days. A draft manuscript of its second edition includes a diagram showing the shape of the moon daily for a month, arranged in a circle. Each poem or 'day' is prefaced by another diagram of the moon on that particular day. The text accompanying the diagram states, 'A month is a unit of time, used with calendars, as a natural period related to the motion of the Moon'. Although this text was eventually removed, the associations with the Chinese lunar calendar are suggestive of time being configured to operate across cultures. The 'natural period' of a synodic month proceeds alongside the artificial ordering of time by the sonnet sequence. The circular arrangement of days on the diagram concurrent with the titling of poems by chronological date shows how time in this collection is both cyclical and linear.

In 'April 1, Friday', the speaker is anxious, uncertain, writing with one eye on the ticking clock, afraid of poverty and potential death. He implores 'Mr Certain Death' to lend him thirty – dollars, days, sonnets – promising repayment 'on my payday / [...] with the surety of breath' (Koh 1). Writing sonnets means living off borrowed time; NaPoWriMo production takes on a sinister, urgent tone in light of this. The speaker '[needs] a loan right now' to sort out the many problems in his life – 'My boyfriend doesn't want me to move in / yet. I'm leaving school without a job. / My visa is expiring'. The flip side to the speaker's new sexual, vocational and geographical freedoms is that his new immigrant status renders them fragile. His response – 'I begin / again a sonnet when the brain's a throb' – suggests literary production as a way to stave off this uncertainty, a way of disciplining chaos into the order of the sonnet's iambic pentameter and rhyme.

The attempt, however, is and must be imperfect. Just as the sestet's 'Coke-drinking economist' finally remarks that 'it's irrational / to borrow from [Death] to subsist', Koh's minor deviations from the sonnet form suggest that the speaker's poems cannot be a perfect substitute for facing up to and living out his future. Adhering too strictly to form is imitation, not art. Koh rhymes 'economist' slant with 'pissed' and 'subsist'; the octet sets up an expectation of Shakespearean sonnet structure with its ABABCDCD rhyme scheme, but the sestet uses a more conventionally Petrarchan EFEFFE. The metre varies from six stresses in a line:

/　　/　^　/　^　/^　/　^　/
Please lend me thirty, Mr Certain Death.

to four:

^　　/^　^　^　/　^　/　^　/
My visa is expiring. I begin

Time, although regularly marked in the titles of each sonnet, escapes patterning upon closer inspection. With this not-quite-certain sonnet, Koh both suggests and subverts the poetic solution to his speaker's problems. Verse can only offer a semblance of hope, and time borrowed from Death will have to be paid with '[jacked] up [...] interest'.

Just as Ip's sonnets reveal the postcolonial stakes of his complex speaker-reader relationships, Koh's obsession with time reveals another dimension of the interplay between 'I' and 'you'. The reader is Death, the figure with whom the speaker pleads to both literally and idiomatically buy his poetry. The speaker needs acceptance and money 'right now' in order to both shore up his shaken sense of self and survive. When the economist says that this act is irrational, he also suggests that one cannot subsist on poetry. This anxiety inflects Koh's poem-a-day practice. More than just an artistic challenge, it is also a way to produce poetry quickly enough to assemble a collection, get sales and readership, and somehow prove the pragmatic economist wrong.

In 'April 19, Tuesday', Koh's handling of time describes this anxiety behind poetic production, while suggesting a way out of worrying about the future through the quotidian present:

April 19, Tuesday

This is not a lunch poem. It's an after
lunch poem. I can write this cuz I'm jobless.
I've got the afternoon to sit and stare.
This morning I rode the 6 train to Lex

> to interview with the School Head. She said
> she could sponsor me for an American
> visa. I don't remember what my head
> said but my heart flew to my stomach. Then
> I had a turkey sandwich with grilled
> turkey and American cheese, and made eyes
> at the huge, blond Latino behind the till.
> He looked away. I cruised the park to say HI!
> to the gulls. Call coming in. [stops writing]…
> It was the Head. I've got a job waiting. (37)

The speaker appears to compose his 'after / lunch poem' in real time. 'I can write this cuz I'm jobless', he says; 'I've got the afternoon to sit and stare'. Koh wants readers to believe that the poem is the fruit of his speaker's inability to find more productive ways of spending time. It consists largely of blow-by-blow descriptions of the day: morning commute, job interview, lunch, indifferent flirting, wandering, nothing particularly momentous. Most of Koh's poems are conversational – this speaker goes further, using 'cuz' (because), suggesting he is composing on a mobile phone in real time.

The tension between the 'liveness' of the speaker and the always-already belated written word also reflects the tension between poetic vocation and 'real' job, between quotidian moments and time paid by monthly salary. Of course 'liveness' is constructed. The poem fits the sonnet's rules, even as the speaker recalls his day seemingly off the cuff. When he is interrupted by a prospective employer's phone call, the poem gives 'stage directions' – '[stops writing]' – to suggest immediate response. Yet these directions are not external to the poem; they are part of the final rhyming couplet. The call is the sonnet's volta, turning from description to metafictional awareness, from anxiety to anticipation. The offer of employment and the wandering moment, structure and free-flow, are parts of the same equation. The sonnet set-up and ending turn are appropriate to this tension.

Conclusion

Ip's and Koh's poems question both the universality of the sonnet form and the specificity of the Singaporean subject, or the everyday moment. These sonnets emerge from a specifically Singaporean milieu; yet, Ip's Singlish and Koh's speakers' experiences remain largely translatable, relatable. Relevant Singaporean references in *Sonnets* are helpfully decoded in end notes. Both collections construct speakers who, self-reflexively, broadcast a desire for readers and for understanding. On one hand, this situation can be traced to the specific difficulties of poets and poetry in and from Singapore. On the other, this follows from a long tradition of the sonnet as a means to please powerful rulers, patrons and beloveds, with today's patrons only rather more democratically located in the English-educated, digitally connected global middle class.

Both collections also argue for granting dignity and legitimacy to Anglophone literature produced at the margins of the Anglosphere. Rajeev Patke provides a wider definition of postcolonial poetry than discussed thus far:

> In a more dynamic sense, postcolonial poetry shows awareness of what it means to write from a place and in a language shaped by colonial history, at a time that is not yet free from the force of that shaping. (Patke 2006, 4)

To the extent that their sonnets largely adhere to formal constraints in the context of Singapore literature's free verse culture, Koh's and Ip's poems make readers aware of how colonial history shapes their language. Refraining from radical deviation reflects how English language and culture, for good or ill, influences and constitutes significant aspects of Singaporean identity. Yet to the extent that these same sonnets celebrate local variation, Koh and Ip suggest that postcolonial literatures are vitalized, not paralyzed, by their histories, and indeed that they make valuable contributions to the wider Anglophone literary world.

Ultimately, however, *Sonnets* and *Loans* do not seem confident that their readers will accept these claims. Both books conclude with an incomplete bridging of the gap between speaker and reader, local and global. Ip's last poem, "'we spoke'", invests this interaction with vague and immense historical significance:

> we spoke: treaties were signed, lords overthrown,
> children conceived, put through the rise and fall
> of states and syllabi, of texts and thrones,
> because two people spoke…. (57)

The poem ends, however, in the 'awkward room' of the present where 'co-workers who once spoke twiddle thumbs / while wondering how to revert to one another'. 'Revert', commonly misused in Singaporean offices to mean 'reply', underlines the gap between speaker and spoken to who desire reversion to oneness but do not quite know how to achieve it.

The final poem of *Loans*, 'April 30, Saturday', sums up Koh's meditation on time and money, relating both to each through sex: 'a coin is dropped / into a bottle each time a couple fuck' (59). These moments, crystallized into coin, are spent as lovers spend time: 'They take the rest of their lives, seconds copped, / to empty the decanter'. The coin stands for the everyday moment Koh values throughout, spent in 'exact cash for food / I enjoyed as more than friend and less than spouse', self and other at last in a relation of more than goodwill but less than commitment. In the multiply ironic final line, 'I read on a dime *e pluribus unum*'. The American promise of synthesis, rendered in that rarified language, inscribed on coin, mapped onto time, remains unfulfilled.

This chapter argues that Singaporean sonnets participate in a current of the sonnet tradition, one which seeks to elevate vernacular languages and cultures by skilfully employing both in sonnet form. No longer signifying cultural elitism while remaining familiar to elite Anglophones, the Singaporean sonnet playfully performs tensions between 'high' and 'low' culture, between elite readership versus a desire for wider appeal. With some willed distance from its Western origins, the sonnet's rhetorical and metrical properties can be exploited to embody vexed speaker-reader relations, cultural hybridity and artistic production under the demands of 'real' work. These issues are the mark of a specifically Singaporean character in Koh's and Ip's works. Yet, they also resonate with the five tendencies of contemporary sonnets identified by Stephanie Burt: 'formal play, a sense of history, a commitment to dailiness, use within sequences, and tension between vatic ambition and ordinary experience' (246).

That sonnet collections from Singaporeans have emerged in the past few years suggests that at least some poets here feel confident in owning the form and using it to participate in global and historical artistic conversations. Indeed, Koh's and Ip's debuts may prefigure a renewed interest in Singaporean formal poetry. *Sonnets* co-won the Singapore Literature Prize in 2014. Since then, SingPoWriMo has included daily prompts augmented with restrictive 'bonuses' that young poets productively fetter themselves with. The platform has also led to several invented or rediscovered forms entering circulation, as well as Southeast Asia-wide spinoff SEAPoWriMo. The 2017 poetry anthology *UnFree Verse*, gathering formal work from the 1930s to the present day, may present further opportunities to re-evaluate the historical role of formal poetry in Singapore literature. Even as these collective claims of vulgar eloquence are made, the larger question remains as to when or whether they will be accepted by the Singaporean public, let alone a regional or global readership. If the history of the sonnet is anything to go by, however, we can be certain that Singaporean and other poets writing in the vernacular will continue to exploit its seemingly endless flexibility.

Notes

1 Toh Hsien Min has a collection of sonnets in manuscript.
2 The full text of poems in *Sonnets* can be found at http://www.joshuaip.com/sonnets-from-the-singlish.html.
3 The full version translates to 'Rag and bone, newspapers and old clothes, broken *radios*, televisions …'.

Works cited

Burt, Stephanie. 'The Contemporary Sonnet'. *The Cambridge Companion to the Sonnet*. Edited by A. D. Cousins and Peter Howarth. Cambridge University Press, 2011, pp. 245–266.

Dante, Alighieri. *De Vulgari Eloquentia*. Translated by Steven Botterill. Cambridge University Press, 1996.

Grant, Marya. '*A Scanty Plot of Ground*': *Navigating Identity and the Archive in English Indian Sonnets*. Concordia University Montreal, 2008. Spectrum Research Repository. https://spectrum.library.concordia.ca/975662/. Accessed 30 December 2020.

Ip, Joshua. 'Preface'. *Payday Loans*. Koh Jee Leong. Math Paper Press, 2014. xvii–xxiii.

Ip, Joshua. *Sonnets from the Singlish*. Math Paper Press, 2012.

Ip, Joshua. 'sonnets from the singlish – origins'. joshuaip.com, 2012. http://www.joshuaip.com/2/post/2012/07/sonnets-from-the-singlish-origins.html. Accessed 30 December 2020.

Kennedy, Karen C. 'Unfettered Genius: The African American Sonnet'. *Yale National Initiative*, 2011. https://teachers.yale.edu/curriculum/viewer/initiative_11.02.01_u. Accessed 28 December 2020.

Koh, Jee Leong. *Payday Loans*. Math Paper Press, 2014.

Macaulay, Thomas B. 'Minute by the Hon'ble T. B. Macaulay, dated the 2nd February 1835'. *columbia.edu*, website of Frances W. Pritchett. http://www.columbia.edu/itc/mealac/pritchett/00generallinks/macaulay/txt_minute_education_1835.html. Accessed 30 December 2020.

McLuhan, Marshall. *Understanding Media: The Extensions of Man*. McGraw-Hill, 1964.

National Literary Reading and Writing Survey 2015, National Arts Council Singapore. https://www.nac.gov.sg/dam/jcr:72e71144-91c4-430c-bbe0-8d7a3ec358e4. Accessed 30 December 2020.

Patke, Rajeev. *Postcolonial Poetry in English*. Oxford University Press, 2006.

Poon, Angelia, Phillip Holden and Shirley Lim, eds. *Writing Singapore: An Historical Anthology of Singapore Literature*. NUS Press, 2009.

Robertson, Roland. 'Comments on the "Global Triad" and "Glocalization."' Kokugajuin University Institute for Japanese Culture and Classics, 2001. http://www2.kokugakuin.ac.jp/ijcc/wp/global/15robertson.html. Accessed 25 December 2020.

Sanderlin, George. 'The Repute of Shakespeare's Sonnets in the Early Nineteenth Century'. *Modern Language Notes*, vol. 54, no. 6, 1939: pp. 462–466.

'SingPoWriMo'. *Facebook*, 2014. https://www.facebook.com/groups/singpowrimo. Accessed 30 December 2020.

Spiller, Michael R. G. *The Development of the Sonnet: An Introduction*. Routledge, 1992.

Thorson, Maureen. 'Announcing NaPoWriMo'. *versAtile*, 2003. http://www.reenhead.com/varchives/2003_03_16_varchives.php#90858622#90858622. Accessed 30 December 2020.

Part Four

Cross-media adaptations and beyond

15

On the theatricality of the *Canzoniere*, from medieval to modern times

Jean-Luc Nardone

Whether complete or partial, the countless translations of Petrarch's *Canzoniere* have adopted various approaches, but today's trends amongst French translators are at odds with prose translations like those of Ferdinand de Gramont, a writer and (Petrarchan) poet of the nineteenth century, which Gallimard republished in 1983 with a preface by Jean-Michel Gardair (Petrarch 1983).[1] Wisely abstaining from commenting on the translator's formal choices, Gardair nonetheless remarks that the collection tells the story of Laura, or what he calls '[le] roman de Laure' (Petrarch 1983, 10). The idea that the *Canzoniere* can be read as a protean novel was recently defended again by Anna Dolfi, in her volume on twentieth-century Petrarchism and anti-Petrarchism. It is true that there are arguments galore for reading the collection as a narrative with main characters – the poet, Laura, Love – and secondary ones – the Colonnas, Petrarch's friends (see Nardone 2006) – along with a structuring chronology, peripeteiae and drama. One might do as Queneau does in his *Exercises in Style*: cut the blanks between Gramont's prose translations and title the collection *Novel*. But, then, could another exercise not bear the title *Theatre*? For the collection can be read as a powerful drama in two major acts, with nature and solitude as its setting and a long monologue following the exposition contained in the introductory sonnet, in which the poet addresses his audience to inform them of the torments with which they are about to be presented. In the case of lyric verse, the conjunction between poetry and theatre was not thoroughly developed by Aristotle. Indeed, as Joseph Hardy puts it, 'Neither Aristotle nor Plato dealt with lyrical poetry in their literary doctrines',[2] and, accordingly, 'our literary historians study theatre and poetry separately' (Aristotle 11).[3] Yet it is precisely to that end that a cross-pollination of the two genres can be envisaged.

Medieval Italian poetry indisputably had a theatrical dimension, which was necessary in a time when theatre had disappeared (Ubersfeld 39 ff.,

136 ff., 168). After Aeschylus, Sophocles, Euripides, Plautus, Terence, Seneca and the like had achieved their immense glory, the theatrical tradition did not leave any apparent trace in medieval Italy, and it was only with the poetry of the Franciscan Jacopone da Todi (1230–1306) that the so-called *Laude drammatiche*, or dialogic lauds, emerged as one of the most common forms of medieval Italian theatre. Lauds are series of stanzas dedicated to a character (Mary, the People, Christ and so on) and declaimed in front of an audience of believers. The revival of theatre therefore came about through religious poetry, and in the fifteenth century the first plays written in Italian were *Sacre rappresentazioni*. A generation after Dante and Jacopone, Petrarch apparently wanted to reconnect with Roman theatre, for he is known to be the author of *Philologia Philostrati*, a play he probably wrote during the Avignon decade (1326–1336) before destroying it – his letter VII, 16, to Lapo di Castiglionchio, explicitly refers to it.[4]

For all these reasons, the theatricality of the *Canzoniere* and the forms it can take are worth examining, and are discussed here through three kinds of diachronic reading. The first is concerned with the intrinsically dialogic dimension and the dramatic themes (pain, madness, passion, anger, despair, hope, illusion, remorse, etc.) at work in the *Canzoniere*. The second studies the ways in which these sonnets have been used on stage, with examples from Shakespeare, Molière and Goldoni.[5] The third, and last, shows how theatre – from Fabre d'Églantine's comic opera titled *Laure et Pétrarque* to François Vaucienne's tragedy in five acts, *Pétrarque et Laure*, produced in 1927 in Avignon – has recycled not only Petrarch's poetry, but also the figure of the poet as a dramatic stereotype.

First of all, let us observe how the *Canzoniere* and, more precisely, the sonnets collected in it rely on a great variety of dialogues which feed the poet's monologue and make it dynamic. Three rather significant examples must be observed: the introductory sonnet, which works as an expository scene, the extraordinary *Occhi piangete* (LXXXIV) and the famous *S' amor non è* (CXXXII), with its indirect interrogations. The introductory sonnet begins:

> Voi ch'ascolate in rime sparse il suono
> Di quei sospiri ond'io nudriva 'l core
> In sul mio primo giovenile errore
> Quand'era in parte altr'uom da quel ch'i' sono
>
> Del vario stile in ch'io piango et ragiono
> Fra le vane speranze e 'l van dolore
> Ove sia chi per prova intenda amore,
> Spero trovar pietà, nonché perdono.[6]

Addressing the audience is a naturally theatrical device. At the start of the *Canzoniere*, the 'you' is a rhetorical imperative leading to an anacoluthon ('Voi ch' ascolate [...] Spero trovar pietà') that is both subtle and unexpected in a sonnet that Petrarch reworked so many times. It should therefore be given a strongly symbolic meaning: that of a complex link between the readers as ringside spectators and the author who, standing in the wings, is actually the subject of the main clause – and of the work. Preferring qualities of speech to grammatical correctness, Petrarch places this sonnet – and therefore the entire collection – under the sign of the orality of a poetry now deprived of any extrinsic musical accompaniment, which de facto gives a new eloquence to both poetic writing and its enunciation. Here, again, interpretative declamation must convey the text's power, while the sonnet's rhythm, its subtle and compact writing and its clear sonorities must contain their own poetic musicality. It was precisely this dichotomy between text and music that fostered innovation.

Petrarch's monologue exploring the poet's inner tensions has often been said to be static: the story does not develop. The poet's first meeting with Laura may be followed by his passion, Laura's death, his exacerbated feelings and so on, and comparing Sonnet LXII (the famous *Padre del ciel*, ending on the ternary rhythm of a supplication) to the last three lines in the final song *Vergine bella* (CCCLXVI) is enough to demonstrate that Petrarch, as in his *Secretum*, is completely locked within his contradictory passions. At the same time, the dialogic form appears as a rhetorical solution to these inner torments and revives the sonnets' discourse. The most striking example is the *Occhi piangete* (LXXXIV), where the poet and his eyes engage in a dialogue in which he blames them for being the cause of his woe, since they let Love penetrate his heart. Each quatrain falls into a pair of two-line cues, and each of the characters playing in this short scene has a final tercet:

– Occhi, piangete : accompagnate il core
che di vostro fallir morte sostene.
– Così sempre facciamo; et ne convene
lamentar più l'altrui, che 'l nostro errore.

– Già prima ebbe per voi l'entrata Amore,
là onde anchor come in suo albergo vène.
– Noi gli aprimmo la via per quella spene
che mosse d'entro da colui che more.

– Non son, come a voi par, le ragion' pari:
ché pur voi foste ne la prima vista,
del vostro et del suo mal cotanto avari.

> – Or questo è quel che più ch' altro n' atrista,
> che' perfetti giudicii son sì rari,
> et d'altrui colpa altrui biasmo s'acquista.[7]

Such an elaborate dialogue is an exception in the *Canzoniere* and in the whole of medieval Italian poetry. The sonnet sounds like a secular version of Jacopone's theatrical strategy in his *Laude drammatiche*. It is a lively, quick and striking exchange that explores, within the fixed form of the sonnet, the valences of its textual restructuring at the risk of chipping the poetic edifice – a risk which becomes quite clear in this case. For it is honestly hard to deem this sonnet poetical. It is altogether different, and no doubt theatrical. No comedy, tragedy or melodrama can do without these moments of acceleration through dialogue. It is Petrarch's way of preventing speech from petering out. In the quatrains, as in the tercets, the intertwining of the rhymes illustrates the dialogic interpenetration of the cues in a wonderfully efficient way. This device is therefore no doubt an experimental solution which Petrarch had potentially put to good use in his *Philologia Philostrati*.

A third and final example of theatrical dialogism is Sonnet CXXXII, *S'amor non è, che dunque è quel ch'io sento?*, in which the quatrains are a series of seven direct questions:

> S'amor non è, che dunque è quel ch'io sento?
>   Ma s' egli è amor, perdio, che cosa et quale?
>   Se bona, onde l'efffecto aspro mortale?
>   Se ria, onde sì dolce ogni tormento?
>
>   S'a mia voglia ardo, onde 'l pianto e lamento?
>   S'al mal mio grado, il lamentar che vale?
>   O viva morte, o dilectoso male,
>   Come puoi tanto in me, s'io no 'l consento?[8]

Petrarch is again experimenting with one of the devices typically used on stage: expressing one's contradictory feelings. This is anything but realistic – who questions themselves out loud? – but it belongs in the fictional space of theatre, where characters must share with the audience ambivalent feelings of all kinds (love, envy, anger, vengeance, etc.). To be more precise, Petrarch is staging in this text his own version of a commonplace theatrical character: the lover grappling with a nascent feeling that shakes and upsets him so much that deep down, he starts doubting his own existential integrity. The device is all the more efficient as it is versatile; Mozart, for instance, turned it into a kind of dialogic monologue when, in *The Marriage of Figaro*, Cherubino tries to have the Countess answer the questions he is asking himself. Diction, rhythm and everything else in these lines recall Sonnet CXXXII:

> Voi che sapete
> Che cosa è amor,
> Donne, vedete,
> S'io l'ho nel cor,
> Donne, vedete,
> S'io l'ho nel cor.
> Quello ch'io provo,
> Vi ridirò,
> È per me nuovo
> Capir nol so.
> Sento un affetto
> Pien di desir,
> Ch' ora è diletto,
> Ch' ora è martir.
> Gelo e poi sento
> L'alma avvampar,
> E in un momento
> Torno a gelar.[9]

Taking an example from this Mozart opera – a musical form of theatre – rather than from a strictly theatrical work provides an opportunity to demonstrate the flexibility of Petrarch's classical hendecasyllables: with their regular caesurae and musical rhythms, they paved the way for all kinds of imitations in plays, of course, but also of performing arts, including opera.[10]

In short, it seems rather obvious that the *Canzoniere* includes more than one sonnet displaying a form which, in some respects, distances itself from lyrical poetry as it existed in Italy in the fourteenth century, thus opening up a new oratory space which brings the poems significantly closer to the rhetorical devices used on stage.

What did theatre do, then, with the possibilities offered by poetry? The *general* scheme is of course well known: theatre took up the metrical form and (nearly) everywhere, the poet's line became the playwright's – as with the case of Petrarch's hendecasyllable in Italy. As a consequence, theatre inherited the Petrarchan line's measured combinations of nouns and epithets, fixed phrases turned commonplace, oxymorons, repetitions, anaphoras, enjambments, *rejets* and *contre-rejets*, interjections – in short, all the poetic devices producing the formal power of discourse, especially the lover's discourse. Tracking all the resurgences of poetic language in theatrical language is probably not very interesting. What seems more relevant is to study how playwrights enjoyed staging the sonnet itself, often in its entirety, be it *by* Petrarch or *à la* Petrarch. Canonical plays by illustrious authors quickly come to mind: in Shakespeare, the sonnet written as a prologue to *Romeo and Juliet*, and above all the four sonnets from *Love's Labour's Lost*; Oronte's sonnet in Molière's *The Misanthrope* and Trissotin's to Princess Urania in his *The Learned Women*; and, later, the imbroglio caused by Florindo's sonnet in Goldoni's *Liar* (II, 4).[11] Whether these authors, like Shakespeare, also wrote (Petrarchan or anti-Petrarchan) sonnets or did not care about writing poetry, the lyrical sonnet was evidently deployed in their plays as an emblem of the transfixed lover or ridiculous pedant. Mercutio jibes at Romeo: 'Now is he for the numbers that Petrarch flowed in. Laura to his lady was a kitchen wench – marry, she had a better love to be-rhyme her' (42). In the comedy *Love's Labour's Lost*, each of the four lovers writes a poem to his beloved lady. Since three of these compositions are sonnets, the scene is a kind of paroxysmal use of the sonnet on stage. The three sonnets, as well as Dumaine's slightly less canonical play, all naturally display the clichés of the lyrical poetry of the time, without great originality but in the direct lineage of Petrarchism. Berowne's poem exclaims:

> If love make me forsworn, how shall I swear to love?
> O never faith could hold, if not to beauty vowed! (43)

And Longaville's:

> If broken, then, it is no fault of mine.
> If by me broke, what fool is not so wise
> To lose an oath to win a paradise? (48)

In Berowne's first two lines, one quickly picks up the jibe at Petrarch's Sonnet CXXXII, *S'amor non è, che dunque è quel ch'io sento?*, already mentioned above. What's more, both Berowne's and Longaville's compositions take the form of the English sonnet, with three quatrains followed by a distich. As for the king's composition, it is a caudate sonnet which, ending on a double distich, sounds more majestic. The gentleness, the eyes, the tears, the lover's grief, the metaphor of the bright lady and the analogy with nature (trees, flowers, water etc.) – everything in this sonnet is profoundly Petrarchan. However, two remarks must be made at this point. The first is that the sonnets are not simply mentioned on stage: they are spoken and, as it were, turned into a theatrical moment.[12] The second is that the language contained in the sonnets spills over and feeds the characters' cues, whether they be glossing the text or simply talking about love – and the seepage of poetic language into theatrical speech thus becomes even more obvious. It is the case when Berowne confides in the King:

> My eyes are then no eyes, nor I Berowne:
> Oh! but for my love, day would turn to night.
> Of all complexions the cull'd sovereignty
> Do meet, as at a fair, in her fair cheek;
> Where several worthies make one dignity,
> Where nothing wants that want itself doth seek. (54)

All of this can also be found in Molière or Goldoni, notably the reciting of an entire sonnet, although obviously with modalities and perspectives that are specific to each play. Thus, in his preface to *The Liar*, Goldoni signals that the sonnet may be the most ridiculous moment in the play.[13] Florindo nevertheless composes a perfect sonnet for his Rosaura, alternating rhymes to echo paronyms in the quatrains:

> Idolo del mio cor, nume adorato
> Per voi peno tacendo, e v'amo tanto
> Che temendo d'altrui vi voglia il fato
> M'esce dagli occhi, e più dal cuore il pianto.
>
> Io non son cavalier, nè titolato,
> Nè ricchezze o tesori aver mi vanto
> A me diede il destin mediocre stato,
> Ed è l'industria mia tutto il mio vanto.
>
> Io nacqui in Lombardia sott'altro cielo.
> Mi vedete sovente a voi d'intorno.
> Tacqui un tempo in mio danno, ed or mi svelo.
>
> Sol per vostra cagion fo qui soggiorno.
> A voi, Rosaura mia, noto è il mio zelo,
> E il nome mio vi farò noto un giorno.[14] (Goldoni 1909, 360)

The whole lexicon of Italian Petrarchism can be perceived in the first quatrain: address to the loved one ('Idolo mio'), tears in the eyes as well as in the heart (line 4), the oxymoronic silent pain ('peno tacendo'), the lover's fear ('temo'). But what follows is nothing more than a letter in the shape of a sonnet, in which Florindo hopes to be identified without saying his name by alluding to his social rank, his small fortune and his Lombard origins – nothing very poetical, on the whole. And it is precisely because Lelio, the 'liar', believes all sonnets are the same that he later tries to claim authorship of the text, as flatly biographical as it may be. It is therefore clear why Goldoni, a skilful sonnet writer, signals from the start (in his prologue) that the text is ridiculous: it is not a lover's sonnet. Lelio nonetheless makes sure to feed his discourse with the archaizing terminology of genre poetry ('cordoglio', 'desiri', 'spero') and reminds the audience that 'poets usually speak in a figurative language' (Goldoni 1909, 365).[15] Having assimilated this coded lexicon to a greater degree than Florindo, he declares to Rosaura, 'Ardo per voi, né trovo pace senza la speranza di conseguirvi' (Goldoni 1909, 365), which is very close to Petrarch's Sonnet CXXXIV:

Pace non trovo et non ho da far guerra
E temo e spero; et ardo, et son un ghiaccio.[16]

This striking example shows that while the sonnet is not *necessarily* the locus of Petrarchan language, it does seem to be highlighted within Lelio's prose. This implies there is only one language for love, in poems as on the stage, and that the sonnet either expresses it or calls for it. This language is undeniably perverted here, since it is the liar who is using it. This is indeed a conspicuous constant: the transfixed lover's sonnet is sometimes mocked and sometimes twisted to disparage an apparently pedantic fashion. The two aspects were already present in Shakespeare. Indeed, in *Love's Labour's Lost* a certain Don Adriano de Armado, 'a fantastical Spaniard', states his intention to fashion a sonnet from two quatrains his page Moth has clumsily composed in imitation of traditionally Petrarchan descriptions of a woman's red and white complexion. There is also a scene in which the paired characters Nathaniel and Holofernes comment on Berowne's love sonnet (mistakenly placed in their hands) in a jargon dappled with Latin words. Holofernes finally concludes: 'I will prove those verses to be very unlearned, neither savouring of poetry, wit, nor invention' (45).

Thus, theatre's treatment of Petrarchan sonnets never consists of delivering them raw to the audience, but of staging them. The characters who read them or to whom they are read decipher and deconstruct their language, properly or not. The most notorious case of such poetic decomposition or chopping is that of Trissotin's sonnet in *The Learned Women* (31–35), savoured *ad libitum* by Armande, Bélise and Philaminte, the 'ridiculous précieuses'. And this sonnet, like the epigram quoted afterwards, is a text by Charles Cotin, the abbot Molière used as a model for the pedant he scathingly portrays in Trissotin. In *The Misanthrope*, Oronte's performance of his octosyllabic sonnet is similarly interrupted by Alceste, while Molière's fatal rhyming of 'sonnet' with 'cabinet' (toilet) leaves no room for ambiguity. Alceste actually adds:

> Ce style figuré dont on fait vanité
> Sort du bon caractère et de la vérité:
> Ce n'est que jeu de mots, qu'affectation pure
> Et ce n'est point ainsi que parle la nature.
> Le méchant goût du siècle, en cela, me fait peur.[17] (Molière 1872, 23)

This merely rephrases the harsh criticism the Pléiade poets levelled at Petrarch's forms and ideas. One needs only to recall 'J'ai oublié l'art de pétrarquiser', in which Du Bellay says that he wants to 'converse frankly / without flatteries or costumery' (70–71).[18] It is true that flattery had become one of the most widespread ills of the seventeenth century. That being said, it is nevertheless obvious that in *The Learned Women*, when Trissotin or Philaminte is speaking without commenting on the sonnet, syntagms typical of Petrarch's poetry and Petrarchism are back at work, as with the invocations of a 'thousand gentle shivers' ('mille doux frissons', 33) or a 'thousand gentle attentions' ('mille doux soins', 57). From Shakespeare to Goldoni, the theatrical language of love – in spontaneous surges as in mocking imitations – is always that of Petrarchan poetry.

The ultimate piece of evidence could be sought in works by playwrights who, instead of merely staging fashionable lines and sonnets by Petrarch or in his style, decided to stage the figure of the poet himself along with his verses. In the field of French literature,[19] the material available is a small corpus of three main plays that can be briefly presented: a comic opera in one act, *Laure et Pétrarque*,[20] Fabre d'Églantine's very first work, produced in Maastricht in 1780,[21] when he had also been playing *The Misanthrope* as well as Léandre in Regnard's *Distrait* for a year;[22] an opera in five acts, *Pétrarque*, produced in 1873 by an author from Toulon, Hyppolite Duprat; and *Pétrarque et Laure*, a play by François Vaucienne (an alias for Jeanne Battesti), which is a verse tragedy in five acts, produced in front of the Palais des Papes in Avignon in 1927. It is quite obvious we are not dealing with masterpieces. Fabre d'Églantine's comic opera has not left many traces except the earworm 'Il pleut il pleut, bergère', which is very typical of eighteenth-century pastoral literature, but it seems Petrarch's Provençal love stories inspired this native of Carcassonne exiled in Maastricht. It is possible that *The Misanthrope*'s sonnet or *The Distrait*'s jibes ('The [weaker] sex likes lines', 57)[23] were the reasons d'Églantine got absorbed again in the works of the canonical Tuscan.

More is known about Hippolyte Duprat's *Pétrarque*, since it survived through the ages. However, in their *Dictionnaire* Clément and Larousse are merciless about it:

> It is hard to understand why someone would conceive of doing violence to a story in both its historical and legendary dimensions, in a country so close to where Petrarch and Laura lived. [...]
> No doubt was it unnecessary to try and draw the audience's attention by turning the beautiful Laura de Noves, a virtuous mother and *crebris partubus fessa* (in Petrarch's own words), into a plain mistress. In doing so, the authors deprived themselves of what is most needed to make a lyrical or dramatic work powerful: character. If this passion hadn't had anything characteristic, Petrarch wouldn't have dedicated his 318 sonnets and 88 songs to Laura's immortality. (871)[24]

Colonna plays a major part in the opera. In the overture of Act I, he is already answering the 'chorus of the exiled',[25] for 'the Italian lords who took refuge in Avignon mysteriously meet on the banks of the Rhône at Colonna's invitation, the latter joining them a moment later to give them news from their homeland' (Duprat 6).[26] Petrarch intervenes in the second scene, with the romance of the 'fearful dove' noted by Clément:

> La colombe craintive
> Au déclin d'un beau jour
> Vient d'une voix plaintive
> Exhaler son amour
> Sur le rameau fidèle
> On n'entend qu'un soupir
> Et moi je veux comme elle,
> Je veux chanter, gémir.[27] (29–30)

The text is rather poor, and it is only in the next scene, when Petrarch sees Laura, that the audience will enjoy a few lines clearly but freely inspired by the *Vergine bella canzone* at the end of the *Canzoniere*:

> Reine éternelle
> Du haut des cieux
> Du cœur fidèle
> Comble les vœux
> Vierge Marie
> Entends nos voix

> Et pour nous prie
> Le Roi des Rois.[28] (35–36)

It is therefore obvious that the librettists, Duprat and Dharmenon, knew the *Canzoniere,* maybe through Joseph Poulenc's bilingual edition in four volumes, *Rimes de Pétrarque, traduites en vers, texte en regard,* first published in Paris in 1865 and republished several times (by La Librairie Internationale and A. Lacroix, Verboeckhoven and Cie), or through Emma Mahul's no less famous translation, which Firmin-Didot Frères published in 1869, this time in a monolingual edition.

Back in Avignon after his coronation in Rome, Petrarch is welcomed with a dire procession. It is Laura's funeral. And when Colonna invites him to pray, Petrarch exclaims:

> Qui moi ? J'invoquerais ce Dieu dont la colère
> De l'innocence a voulu le trépas
> Non ! Il fut sans pitié, je serai sans prière.[29] (377)

The romance follows:

> L'amour me ramenait vers toi
> Mon cœur s' enivrait d'espérance
> Ton image malgré l'absence
> De loin rayonnait devant moi
> Viens rendre à mon cœur qui t'implore
> L'ivresse d'un rêve si beau
> Réveille-toi ! Sors du tombeau
> Je veux te voir, te voir encore !
> O Laure, quelle horrible souffrance !
> Cruelle mort tu déchires mon cœur,
> Et tu n'es plus. Ton œil glacé
> Me laisse errant dans ma nuit sombre
> Ton front pâli jette son ombre
> Sur l'avenir et le passé.
> Idole à jamais envolée
> Partout je vais portant ton deuil
> Laisse la mort sur ton cercueil
> Prendre mon âme désolée
> Vous n'emporterez pas, moi vivant, cette femme,
> C'est mon cœur qu'on arrache, et ma vie et mon âme.[30] (378–385)

This excerpt is completely different from Petrarch's poetry and, ultimately, from its very form. The 'violence' discussed by Clément and Larousse in their analysis of the work is not only that of a great narrative departure from history, but also from the Tuscan poet's coy eroticism. In a way, as time passed, the continuous landslide that constituted the history of Petrarchism met its end in the degradation of both content (the purity of the poet's feelings) and form (the lines being once more subjected to music).

In François Vaucienne's *Pétrarque et Laure*, a verse tragedy in five acts, Laura, Petrarch's passionate lover, is once again the victim of a jealous rival, the terrible Isoarde de Pierrefeu. In the preface, the author deems it necessary to explain: 'It is therefore the story of the two lovers that I tried to revive on stage. [...] The whole story fits in the *Canzoniere*' (Vaucienne 29).[31]

At the beginning of Act V, twenty years have passed since Petrarch and Laura's first meeting, and Petrarch returns to Avignon. This is how his lifelong friend, Philippe de Cabassole, sums it all up:

> Vingt années ont passé de leur belle jeunesse,
> Et Pétrarque ébloui chante encor sa maîtresse,
> Vingt ans qu'il la louange, et l'adore et lui rend
> Cet immortel honneur qui, lui, l'aura fait grand.
> La gloire, les faveurs, l'amitié des monarques,
> Les voyages, Vaucluse, en l'âme de Pétrarque
> N'ont pas pu ralentir l'élan prédestiné
> D'un désir qui ne vit que d'espoirs condamnés.[32] (210)

It is their anniversary day and Laura is getting ready to receive him. Poisoned by Isoarde, she is at death's door when he arrives. Phanette de Gantelme, Laura's cousin, gives another summary compiling many echoes of the *Canzoniere*:

> Se sont joués, brillants comme ceux d'une aurore,
> À vos changeants reflets, je la demande encore
> Avec son cou de neige et ses cheveux de lin.[33] (223)

This is actually a rather free rewriting of the very famous song CXXVI, *Chiare, fresche et dolci acque*. Phanette goes on:

> À Lyon, ce sonnet écrit devant le Rhône
> Et dans ses eaux jeté, frémissante couronne :
> Beau fleuve impatient qui dévore tes bords
> Pour courir vers la mer où ton destin te mène

> Comme toi je voudrais, rapide et sans effort,
> Gagner presque d'un bond la soleilleuse plaine!³⁴ (224)

A few scenes later, this free rewriting of Sonnet CCVIII, *Rapido fiume che d'alpestra vena*, is followed by another sonnet, which Petrarch declaims in front of Laura. The stage direction indicates that 'in a kind of mystical and religious invocation, [he] salutes the young lady with this excerpt from the *Canzonere*', which is the famous Sonnet LXI itself, *Benedetto sia 'l giorno, e 'l mese, e 'l anno*:

> Béni soit donc le jour, et le mois et l'année
> Béni soit le pays... l'heure... l'instant... le lieu
> Où mon âme et ma chair à ton amour sont nées,
> Où je vis se lever ma chère destinée
> Portant le poids divin de ses joies condamnées
> Au ciel brûlant de tes beaux yeux!³⁵ (234)

These lines constitute a single exception: the sonnet is no longer announced and recited as such but is declaimed as a cue. In this regard, the differences between the text and its translation include the use of ellipses apparently giving the lines a rhythm more appropriate to the present scene:³⁶ they condense the enumeration that takes place in the second line of the first quatrain and give free rein to the actor's expression. Then, working like a kind of rhythmic compensation, the introduction of a second anaphora ('Où mon âme [...] Où je vis') feeds the music of the tirade by forming a symmetry with the first two lines. This is what we were looking for: a Petrarch sonnet reshaped for the stage.

To conclude this foray into what should be called the theatricality of Petrarch's *Canzoniere*, and more specifically his sonnets, one can observe it relies on a kind of circular argumentation: the idea that Petrarch's writing has a theatrical dimension is intrinsic, since the Tuscan wanted to sever poetry from musical accompaniment, postulating in his introductory sonnet that this music must be contained in the lines themselves. In doing so, he paved the way for a new poetic rhetoric, notably one of elocution. Relating this requirement to the emergence of a Renaissance theatre which progressively aspired to the rhythm of verse, one will naturally notice a tendency, in the tight prosodic composition of long lines, to borrow a theatrical diction from Petrarch and the Petrarchan writers – a diction which was, as one can imagine, particularly tied up with the lover's discourse. Hence, from this perspective, the intrusion of the sonnet into scenes involving lovers is a striking metatheatrical device which essentially parodies a language that is exasperating in both its formalism and its content: with Goldoni's liar, who believes one can say anything with a sonnet – including a sonnet as unpoetical and as explicit as Florindo's – the target shifts from the lover to the manipulator, the pedant, the forger. The way opera got hold of Petrarch's poetry (as well as, for instance, the writing of music for madrigals in the sixteenth and seventeenth centuries) must therefore be seen as an attempt to reconnect poetry with music, as if it should return to its primitive form: poems to be sung. This vein hasn't been exhausted yet, and one can listen indefinitely to Verde Lauro,[37] a metal rock band who have nearly exclusively been dedicating themselves to this task with a flabbergasting Petrarchism.

Fundamentally speaking, Petrarch is therefore more than the master of the sonnet. It is precisely because he was the first to fix its form in a monumental way, with more than three hundred pieces, that he could explore its *varietas* in new poetic adventures. Critics were right to focus on the poems' content. But in his attempt to exhaust the form, the poet quickly welcomed all the declamatory potential of a text stripped of – one could even say liberated from – any ornamental music: this is how he also paved the way for the theatrical recitation of his poetry. It may also be the reason why, before the term *dramaturge* appeared in the eighteenth century, playwrights were called 'poets'.

Translated from the French by Fanny Quément
with the editors of the volume

Notes

1. See, for instance, de Gramont's epilogue, *Vous qui lirez un jour ces rimes détachées*, which patently echoes Petrarch's introductory sonnet.
2. 'Aristote pas plus que Platon n'a fait rentrer la poésie lyrique dans le cadre de sa doctrine littéraire.' All unattributed translations have been produced by Fanny Quément for the purpose of this article.
3. To quote more extensively: 'We are still living under the sign of Romanticism: the lyrical poet is considered as the poet *par excellence*. We see Racine as a playwright who *also* was a poet. Our literary historians study poetry and theatre separately. We no longer speak the language of Corneille, in which tragedies were called "dramatic poems"; we no longer share Montesquieu's idea that "dramatic poets are the poets *par excellence*."' ('Nous vivons encore sous le signe du Romantisme: le poète lyrique est pour nous le poète par excellence. Racine est à nos yeux un dramaturge qui par surcroît est poète. Nos historiens de la littérature étudient séparément le théâtre et la poésie. Nous ne parlons plus la langue de Corneille qui désigne la tragédie sous le nom de "poème dramatique"; nous ne pensons

plus, comme Montesquieu, que "les poètes dramatiques sont les poètes par excellence"') (Aristotle p. 11).

4 'Comediam, quam petis, me admodum tenera etate dictasse non infitior sub Philologie nomine' ('As for the comedy you ask of me, I don't deny having written it when I was very young, under the title of *Philology*') (2002b, VII, 16). See also II, 7: 'Meministi, credo, in Philologia nostras, quam ob id solum ut curas tibi iocis excuterem scripsi, qui Tranquillinus noster ait' ('Tranquillinus [...] was one of the characters') (Petrarch 2002a, 406).

5 This approach leaves aside contemporary productions in which sonnets are read on stage, for they are extraneous to theatrical practices from the centuries under study.

6 'You who hear the sound, in scattered rhymes, / of those sighs on which I fed my heart, / in my first vagrant youthfulness, / when I was partly other than I am, // I hope to find pity, and forgiveness, / for all the modes in which I talk and weep, / between vain hope and vain sadness, / in those who understand love through its trials' (Petrarch 2001, 18).

7 'Weep, eyes: accompany the heart /that is about to die for your failings./ 'So we are, always weeping: we must mourn/ for another's fault rather than our own.' //Yet it was through you that Love first entered, / where he still lives as though it were his home. / 'We opened the way because of that hope that came from within that heart that is to die.' //These claims are not, as they may seem, equal: /for it was you, so eager at first sight, /who did harm to yourself, and to that one.// 'Now that is what saddens us more than anything,/that perfect judgement is so rare, /and we are blamed for another's fault' (Petrarch 2001, 145).

8 'What do I feel if this is not love? / But if it is love, God, what thing is this? / If good, why this effect: bitter, mortal? / If bad, then why is every suffering sweet? // If I desire to burn, why tears and grief? / If my state's evil, what's the use of grieving? / O living death, O delightful evil, / how can you be in me so, if I do not consent?' (Petrarch 2001, 219).

9 'You indeed know what love is. / Look ladies, if I have it in my heart. / I'll tell you what I feel. / It's all new to me. I don't understand it. / I feel a passion that is full of desire, / at times I feel torment, at times delight. / And then I feel frozen, then on fire, / and in an instant, frozen again' (Mozart 61).

10 Of the three canonical forms the Italian hendecasyllable took, the two *a minore* require a secondary stress on the fourth syllable. It was this pattern that informed the pentasyllabic scheme in Mozart's opera.

11 Regarding the link between Corneille's *Liar* and Goldoni's, see Goldoni's *Memoirs*, Part II, Chapter VIII.

12 Shakespeare aligns the poetic with the theatrical and the performative in his own sonnets as well as on the stage; for discussion of this dimension of his sonnets, see Schalkwyk (1998) and Cheney (2001).

13 'Il sonetto è forse la parte più ridicola della commedia' (Goldoni 1909, 303).
14 'Heart's idol, O my most adored fate, / For thee I suffer silently and long, / Fearing the gods have picked another mate / To pair with thee and cause th' eternal wrong. // [...] I am no knight, no title can I claim, / Gold have I none and riches little store, / A middle station and a modest name, / And honest toil and there is nothing more. // Lombard am I and bred to other skies, / Oft in thy sight I lurk and at thy hand – / Silence I've nourisht, now I raise my eyes, // For thee an exile in a foreign land. / Rosaura, goddess, know at length my zeal – / Soon, soon, shall I my name and heart reveal' (Goldoni 1922, 62).
15 'I poeti sogliono servirsi del parlar figurato.'
16 'I find no peace, and yet I make no war: / and fear, and hope: and burn, and I am ice' (Petrarch 2001, 221).
17 'This style, full of conceits, that we're so vain of, / Is far from truth to life and genuineness; / 'Tis merely play on words, sheer affectation, / And nature speaks far otherwise than so. / The wretched taste of this age makes me shudder' (Molière 1908, 312).
18 'franchement deviser / Sans vous flatter et sans me déguiser.'
19 In my preliminary researches, I also identified an Italian melodrama in five acts by Alberto Nota, which premiered in Turin in 1832, as well as a German opera with music by Kienlen, performed in Carlsruhe in 1820 (*Laure et Pétrarque*, mentioned in Clément and Larousse 640). This opera by J.-Ch. Kienlen (1783–1929) may have been created in 1816 in Bratislava.
20 Strangely enough, this work does not feature in Clément and Larousse, even though it claims to be an inventory of 'all operas, comic operas, operettas and lyrical dramas that have been performed in France and abroad from the birth of these genres to the present' ('tous les opéras, opéras-comiques, opérettes et drames lyriques représentés en France et à l'étranger depuis l'origine de ces genres d'ouvrages jusqu'à nos jours', subtitle of the *Dictionnaire*).
21 With music by François-Léonard Rouwijzer (1737–1827), a native from Maastricht. See Jan Fransen, *Les comédiens français en Hollande: au XVIIe et au XVIIIe siècles*, Genève, Éditions Slatkine, 1978.
22 As in Molière, poetic writing is disparaged in *The Distrait*, a comedy (1697) by Jean-Louis Regnard. See IV, 9.
23 'Le sexe aime les vers'.
24 'Il est difficile de comprendre qu'on ait eu la pensée de violenter aussi bien l'histoire que la légende dans un pays si voisin des lieux habités par Pétrarque et par Laure. [...] Sans doute n'était-il pas nécessaire, pour exciter l'intérêt, de transformer en une maîtresse ordinaire la belle Laure de Noves, cette vertueuse mère de famille, *crebris partubus fessa*, a dit d'elle Pétrarque lui-même. Les auteurs se sont ainsi privés de l'élément qui donne le plus de force à une œuvre lyrique ou dramatique, le caractère. Sans le caractère

spécial de cette passion, Pétrarque n'aurait pas consacré à l'immortalité de Laure ses 318 sonnets et 88 chansons: "*Qui riposan quei caste et felici ossa / Di quell'alma gentile et sola in terra*".

25 'Chœur d'exilés'.
26 'Les Seigneurs Italiens réfugiés à Avignon se réunissent mystérieusement sur les bords du Rhône conviés par COLONNA qui arrive un peu après pour leur donner des nouvelles de la patrie.'
27 'The fearful dove / At the close of a beautiful day / Comes in a plaintive way / Voicing her love / On the faithful bough / She can but sigh and groan / And I, like her right now, / I want to sing and moan.'
28 Eternal Queen / Of highest skies / Of faithful hearts / Grant the wishes / Virgin Mary / Hear our voices / And for us pray / The King of Kings.
29 'Shall *I* implore this wrathful God, / The murderer of innocence? / No mercy did he show, no prayer shall I say.'
30 'My love was so that I came back / My heart was drunk with hope / Your image in your absence / Was shining in the distance / Return to my imploring heart / The beauty of this drunken dream / Wake up! Raise from the dead / I want to see you, yes, once more! / Oh Laura, what a horrid grief! / Oh cruel death, you're tearing up my heart, / And you, you are no more. Your icy eye / Drove me astray in my dark night / Your pallid brow its shadow casts / On the future and the past.'
31 Vaucienne 29.
32 'Two decades have passed in their fair youth / And still his dazzling mistress Petrarch sings, / Two decades of praise and love / And endless honour that also credited him. / Glory, favours and the friendship of monarchs, / Journeys and Vaucluse, in Petrarch's soul / Could not slow down the fated rush / Of a desire feeding on wrecked hopes.'
33 'As shining as dawn's / to your shifting reflects, I ask for it again / With her snowy neck and linen hair.'
34 'This sonnet writ as Petrarch faced the Rhône / And thrown in water like a shiv'ring wreath: / O fair impatient river that consumes its sides / To rush towards the sea you're destined to / I wish I could be quick and swift like you / And in a single leap thus reach the sunny plains!'
35 'Blessed be the day and the month and the year / Blessed be the land … the hour … the second … the place / Where my soul and flesh were born from your love, / Where I could see my dearest fate ascend / Raising the godly burden of its wrecked joys / To the burning sky that shines in your fair eyes!'
36 Let us recall the first quatrain of Petrarch's sonnet can be translated thus: 'Blessed be the day, and the month, and the year, / and the season, and the time, and the hour, and the moment, / and the beautiful country, and the place where I was joined / to the two beautiful eyes that have bound me' (Petrarch 2001, 109).
37 I particularly recommend the track based on *Son animali*, 'Sono Animali al Mondo'.

Works cited

Aristotle. *Poétique*, translated by Joseph Hardy. Les Belles Lettres, 1979 (1932).

Cheney, Patrick. "'O, Let My Books Be... Dumb Presagers': Poetry and Theater in Shakespeare's Sonnets". *Shakespeare Quarterly*, vol. 52, no. 2, 2001: pp. 222–245.

Clément, Félix and Pierre Larousse. *Dictionnaire des operas*. Librairie Larousse, 1869.

Dolfi, Anna. 'Petrarca, Ungaretti e il romanzo del *Canzoniere*'. *Leopardi e il Novecento. Sul leopardismo dei poeti*, edited by Anna Dolfi. Le Lettere, 2009, pp. 193–207.

Du Bellay, Joachim. *Divers jeux rustiques*, edited by Verdun L. Saulnier. Droz, 1965.

Duprat, Hippolyte. *Pétrarque: opéra en cinq actes*. Brandus, 1880.

Goldoni, Carlo. *The Liar*, translated by Grace Lovat Fraser. Alfred A. Knopf, 1922.

Goldoni, Carlo. *Memoirs of Goldoni*, translated by John Black. 2 vols. Henry Colborn, 1814.

Goldoni, Carlo. *Opere complete di Carlo Goldoni – Volume IV*, edite dal *Municipio di Venezia nel II centenario della nascita*. Municipio di Venezia, 1909.

Molière. *Les Femmes Savantes*. Chez Devers, 1803.

Molière. *Le Misanthrope*. Holt & Williams, 1872.

Molière. *The Misanthrope*, translated by Curtis Hidden Page. *French Classics for English Readers: Molière*, edited by Adolphe Cohn and Curtis Hidden Page, vol. 1. The Nickerbocker Press, 1908.

Mozart, Wolfgang Amadeus. *The Marriage of Figaro: Opera Classics Library*, edited by Burton D. Fisher. Opera Journeys Publishing, 2001.

Nardone, Jean-Luc. 'Pétrarque dans la poésie de ses contemporains: études sur les valences d'un pré-pétrarquisme'. *Sul* Canzoniere *di Francesco Petrarca: atti della giornata di studi del 25 nov. 2005*, edited by Paolo Grossi and Frank La Brasca. Istituto Italiano di Cultura, 2006, pp. 87–100. (Also in 'Actes du colloque sur Pétrarque des 24–27 nov. 2004 de Sfax-Gafsa'. Faculté de Lettres et Sciences Humaines de l'Université de Sfax, 2008, pp. 21–32.)

Petrarch. *Canzoniere*. Gallimard, 1983.

Petrarch. *The Complete Canzoniere*, translated by A. S. Kline. Poetry in Translation, 2001.

Petrarch. *Lettres familières. Tome I: Livres I–III*, edited by Ugo Dotti and translated by Frank La Brasca. Les Belles Lettres, 2002a.

Petrarch. *Lettres familières. Tome II: Livres IV–VII*, edited by Ugo Dotti and translated by Christophe Carraud, Frank La Brasca and André Longpré. Les Belles Lettres, 2002b.

Regnard, Jean-François. *Le distrait*. Compagnie des Imprimeurs-Libraires, 1773.

Schalkwyk, David. 'What May Words Do? The Performative of Praise in Shakespeare's Sonnets'. *Shakespeare Quarterly*, vol. 49, no. 3, 1998, pp. 251–268.
Shakespeare, William. *Love's Labour's Lost*, edited by John Dover Wilson. Cambridge University Press, 1969a.
Shakespeare, William. *Romeo and Juliet*, edited by John Dover Wilson. Cambridge University Press, 1969b.
Ubersfeld, Anne. *Lire le théâtre*. Éditions sociales, 1997.
Vaucienne, François. *Pétrarque et Laure. Tragédie en cinq actes en vers*. Éditions Macabet Frères, 1942.
Verde Lauro. 'VERDE LAURO – SONO ANIMALI AL MONDO'. YouTube. https://www.youtube.com/watch?v=j75oFvJ6S8. Accessed 21 November 2021.

16

Raymond Queneau's *Cent mille milliards de poèmes*: An attempt to exhaust the sonnet*

Natalie Berkman

Introduction

Jean Molinet's fifteenth-century *Sept rondeaux sur un rondeau* is an interesting take on fixed-form poetry. While the group of poets, the *Grands Rhétoriqueurs*, with which he was associated was known for its word games and playful experimentation, Molinet's 'rondeau' is blatantly mathematical. Beginning with a few instructional verses, Molinet alludes to the mathematical potential of his system: 'Sept rondeaux en ce rondeau / Sont tissus et cordellés, / Il ne fault claux ne cordeaux / Mettés sus, se rondellés' (16).[1] The following poem, through its internal rhymes and specific syntactic structure, can be read as seven different poems, all of which conform to the specifications of a rondeau.[2]

Souffrons a point	Soyons bons	Compaignons
Bourgois loyaux	Serviteurs	De noblesse
Barons en point	Prosperons	Besoingnons
Souffrons a point	Soyons bons	Compaignons
Vuidons s'on point	Conquerons	Esperons
François loyaulx	Soyons seurs	Gentillesse
Souffrons a point	Soyons bons	Compaignons
Bourgois leaulx	Serviteurs	De noblesse.

Not only is the poem in its entirety technically a rondeau (in that it satisfies all the constraints of the fixed form), but each column is also a coherent rondeau. Furthermore, any two columns read together (1&2, 2&3 and 1&3) conform to the rules of the rondeau. This is not only a

---

* This chapter was originally published in chapters 3 and 4 of Natalie Berkman's *OuLiPo and the Mathematics of Literature* (Oxford: Peter Lang, 2022), pp. 119–32, 180–2, 205–7, 221. Reproduced with permission from Peter Lang Group AG.

particularly impressive feat, but also a mathematical one. Indeed, by recognizing the combinatorial potential of the rondeau form, Molinet is able to write poetry mathematically through its paratextual instructions (the preliminary verses) and its typography (the way it is printed in columns). Such a text sets the stage for a far more ambitious experimental volume, one that makes use of an even more famous type of fixed-form poetry – the sonnet.

In 1960 Paris, Raymond Queneau (former member of André Breton's Surrealist movement, writer, publisher and amateur mathematician) and François Le Lionnais (chemical engineer, chess expert and radio personality) created a writing group whose membership included writers, mathematicians and scientists. They called this group Ouvroir de Littérature Potentielle (OuLiPo). Etymologically related to *œuvrer* ('to work') and *œuvre* ('a work') and closely resembling the verb *ouvrir* ('to open'), the term *Ouvroir* designates a sewing circle, where religious women share patterns. Rather than dealing with just literature, Oulipo adds the adjectival modifier 'potential', an appropriately ambiguous word that could mean 'not yet existing' but can also be used as the adjectival form of *puissance*, or an exponential power. It is therefore unsurprising that Oulipo proposed mathematics to produce 'potential literature', theorizing the basic principle of constraint (a rigorously defined rule for composition). The first of their experimental texts was Queneau's *Cent mille milliards de poèmes* (1961). With a few additional rules, Queneau permutes the verses of ten original sonnets, creating an exponential number of potential poems that are impossible to read in a human lifetime. Like Molinet, Queneau begins his collection with instructions and redesigns the physical space of the poems to accommodate this potential literature.

This article considers *Cent mille milliards de poèmes* as a case study in Oulipo's greater history of algorithmic production. First, I examine the text's paratextual elements through the theoretical lens of Gérard Genette while also illuminating its historical relation to André Breton's Surrealism as well as the collective mathematician Nicolas Bourbaki. Then, I attempt to read the volume: first by doing a close reading of Queneau's ten base poems and then by performing a mathematically motivated 'distant reading' of the poems produced by the combinatorial machine. Finally, I discuss some of Oulipo's prototypical work in electronic literature and digital humanities. This chapter suggests the importance of the sonnet to Oulipo's overall mathematical project and elucidates the mathematical possibilities afforded by this poetic form.

Paratext

Cent mille milliards de poèmes, the first published Oulipian text, is considered by scholars and Oulipians alike to be of great importance in the definition of the group's aesthetics.³ It is also one of the few documents that Oulipo released in its first decade of existence apart from the *Dossier 17: Exercices de littérature potentielle*, published in the same year in the *Cahiers du Collège de 'Pataphysique*. Since the genesis of *Cent mille milliards de poèmes* predates Oulipo's creation,⁴ standard Oulipian vocabulary such as *potential* or *constraint* as well as the group's name is noticeably absent from the text. Queneau's text consists of an epigraph by Alan Turing, a curious preface by Queneau (called a *mode d'emploi*), ten sonnets with the verses printed on individual strips of paper so the main body of poetry looks as if it exploded, and Le Lionnais's post-scriptum, 'À propos de la littérature expérimentale.'⁵

Although *Cent mille milliards de poèmes* illustrates the potential contribution of mathematics to literature through its combinatorial constraint, the epigraph is a direct reference to computers: '*Seule une machine peut apprécier un sonnet écrit par une autre machine.* – Turing' (Queneau 1961 331).⁶ Gérard Genette signals four main uses of the epigraph: as commentary on the title; as commentary on the text itself; as commentary on the identity of the author; and as commentary on the intellectual or cultural nature of the work (145–149). Queneau's epigraph fulfills all of these uses, commenting on the exponential nature of the title and the poems contained within, and indicating an intellectual alliance with the logical, mathematical and scientific work of Alan Turing. It also serves an additional purpose that is not theorized by Genette: it is a warning, for the reader is not a machine and will therefore be incapable of *appreciating* this volume.

Alan Turing (1912–1954) was a British mathematician and one of the founders of computer science. In addition to his technical work, his theoretical understanding of computers and their capacities was ahead of his time, as he demonstrated in a London *Times* interview, stating a slightly different version of Queneau's epigraph:

> I do not see why [a computer] should not enter any one of the fields normally covered by the human intellect, and eventually compete on equal terms. I do not think you can even draw the line about sonnets, though the comparison is perhaps a little bit unfair because a sonnet written by a machine will be better appreciated by another machine. (Quoted in Hodges 420)

Queneau was an experienced English translator at Gallimard and is clearly not translating Turing directly, but paraphrasing his *Times* interview in a tongue-in-cheek manner. Turing's original statement can be interpreted as a criticism of his contemporaries who maintained that computers would never be able to replicate human creativity. However, Queneau's misquoting takes this to its logical extreme: not only can a machine produce a sonnet, but *only* a machine can appreciate a sonnet written by another machine. This interesting conflation of *reading* and *appreciation* is indicative of Queneau's aesthetic goals. While it is true that a human reader would be unable to *read* all the potential poems, he or she would certainly be able to *appreciate* a certain subset and the potentiality of the collection. Indeed, the mere suggestion that machines are better able to appreciate a canonical Western poetic form can also be understood as a provocative commentary on the nature of poetry itself.

Cent mille milliards de poèmes begins with a preface, unconventionally called a *mode d'emploi*.[7] Genette's theorization acknowledges that a preface can function as a user's manual, though he avoids reducing the nature of this paratext to a set of instructions: "'La préface, disait Novalis, fournit le mode d'emploi du livre.' La formule est juste, mais brutale. Guider la lecture, chercher à obtenir une bonne lecture, ne passe pas seulement par des consignes directes' (194).[8] Queneau's gesture indicates that he considers his volume requires a new intellectual effort on the part of the reader. His use of the term *mode d'emploi* is therefore a provocative continuation of the epigraph's mention of computers, as a *mode d'emploi* is a technical guide that traditionally accompanies a machine and teaches the user how to operate it. The implication is that Queneau's text is mechanical as well and the reader needs specific instructions on how to use it.

The use of this term is reminiscent of Nicolas Bourbaki's textbook, *Éléments de mathématique* (1939), which also began with a *mode d'emploi* that was more concerned with the theoretical conception of the volume than with providing the reader with specific instructions.[9] Likewise, Queneau's user's manual does not begin with rules for the reader to follow, but recounts the genesis of his text, claiming that it is inspired more by a children's game called *têtes folles* than Surrealist games such as *cadavre exquis*. The *cadavre exquis* was a collective game practised by André Breton's Surrealist group that assembled either words or images through the collective work of three authors or artists, each of whom would compose the next grammatical part of the sentence or draw the next anatomical part of the image beginning with the end of a previous participant's contribution. No single member would look at what had been written or drawn before, yet they knew what part of speech or body part their contribution was supposed to be.

The children's game, *têtes folles*, is similar in scope but mathematically regulated (Kummer). It offers a child a booklet divided into three parts: head, torso and legs. The child can flip the pages and create a complete body from a finite number of provided parts (Kummer). Immediately the reader is confronted with two models of collective production: the set theoretical rigor of Bourbaki and the counter-example of Surrealism.

Queneau's mention of such games inscribes his volume in a larger history of ludic literature, which has been defined and theorized by Warren Motte and Kimberly Bohman-Kalaja as 'Play-Texts'.[10] Bohman-Kalaja defines 'Play-Texts' as those in which 'the formal devices involved in the process of literary creation are foregrounded as aesthetic issues, especially as they complicate questions of reception and interpretation' (7). Queneau's text as explained in the *mode d'emploi* operates through a formal device in the process of literary creation, or in the author's words, it is a 'machine à fabriquer des poèmes, mais en nombre limité; il est vrai que ce nombre, quoique limité, fournit de la lecture pour près de deux cent millions d'années (en lisant vingt-quatre heures sur vingt-quatre)' (Queneau 1961 333).[11] By creating a formal device to produce more poems than can be read in a human lifetime, Queneau complicates issues of reception and interpretation, rendering any formal analysis of the volume in its entirety impossible.

The sonnet is a poetic form that depends upon a series of rules that determine the number of verses and stanzas, the types of rhymes and the versification. The rest of Queneau's *mode d'emploi* explains how he produced so many sonnets by adding a few new rules: first, he added a new level of difficulty concerning the diction, specifying that the rhymes could not be too banal and that there be at least forty different words in each quatrain and twenty in each tercet; second, each poem had to have a thematic continuity, while the poems formed by the combinatorial machine 'n'auraient pas eu le même charme';[12] finally, the grammatical structure of the verses had to remain constant, which allowed for their permutation:

> La structure grammaticale, enfin, devait être la même et demeurer invariante pour chaque substitution de vers. Une solution simple aurait été que chaque vers formât une proposition principale. Je ne me suis permis cette facilité que dans le sonnet n° 10 (le dernier !). J'ai veillé également à ce qu'il n'y eût pas de désaccord de féminin à masculin, ou de singulier à pluriel, d'un vers à l'autre dans les différents sonnets. (333–334)[13]

This final constraint is the hardest given the grammatical structure of the French language. The fact that any verse in any sonnet rhymes with the corresponding verse in any other, coupled with these grammatical considerations, allows Queneau to interchange the verses, producing 10^{14} potential sonnets. Queneau then invites the reader to create, and not to read poetry: 'il est facile de voir que le lecteur peut composer 10^{14} sonnets différents, soit cent mille milliards' (334).[14]

Contrary to Queneau's earlier insistence that this volume was inspired more by a children's game than by Surrealist practices, the effect of his poetic machine does indeed seem Surrealist. However, the combinatorial principle rejects the role of chance, which is central to a *cadavre exquis*. Despite the aleatory nature of such Surrealist practices, it is useful to note that practitioners of Surrealism were similarly concerned with preserving grammar: 'But as Aragon admits, Surrealism is not a refuge against style. On the contrary, in the best of their works the Surrealists' grammar is impeccable. The most incomprehensible sentence could be parsed, for it is not the structure that is ambiguous but [...] the mating of words and the incongruous image that results' (Balakian 164). Indeed, a text such as a *cadavre exquis* only functions because it is grammatical. Queneau's insistence on preserving the grammatical structure in his sonnets and then shuffling the verses can be understood as an answer to Surrealism using its own tools, as Queneau is able to produce incongruous poetry *automatically*, but through a mechanical process that was produced by an initial *conscious* reflection.

Reading the volume

After reading the paratextual material, the reader opens the volume and observes its unorthodox physical conception, which goes against the traditional reading protocol of books in general. Designed by Robert Massin, the physical object itself is a visualization of the combinatorial possibility of the collection:[15] the sonnets are printed on only one side of each page, then cut above and below each verse, producing a set of strips. Such a design touches upon what Queneau is doing to the sonnet. It is only by ignoring the integrity of each of the original ten sonnets and chopping them up that the collection functions as intended.

Queneau's *mode d'emploi* does not advise the reader on how to read the sonnets and can be best described as an attempt by the author to recount the genesis of his text *a posteriori*. In doing so, Queneau privileges the system he created above the content of the poems, which has had unfortunate consequences for the text's critical reception. Most literary critics do not discuss the content of the ten poems or any of their potential recombinations, but focus – like Queneau – on the physical conception of the volume and its implications. The conspicuous lack of more 'traditional' forms of literary

Raymond Queneau's Cent mille milliards de poèmes   289

Figure 16.1 Maxime Fournier – Livre-objet Queneau.

analysis such as close readings has two explanations: first, Queneau's volume resists traditional literary analysis, as it is impossible to read in its entirety; second, the original volume as designed by Massin makes reconstructing Queneau's original sonnets tedious.[16]

A closer look at Queneau's original ten poems reveals certain commonalities. Each exhibits the distinguishing features of Queneau's writing: a sense of humor and an oddly antiquated (and sometimes foreign) vocabulary. Furthermore, more than half of them deal with themes relating to a particular part of the world, which results in individual verses that contain culturally specific vocabulary: the first recounts a trip to South America (using words like *pampa, taureaux, gauchos, L'Amérique du Sud*); the second talks about Greece and London (*Parthénon, lord Elgin, climat londonien, la Tamise, Platon, Socrate, marbre*); the third has a maritime feel (*marin, poissons, requin, port, homards*, etc.); the fourth is about colonial India (*cinq o'clock, indigène, Du Gange au Malabar, Chandernagor, les Indes*); the fifth moves from Italy to Avignon; and the sixth has a metropolitan setting (Queneau 1961 335–340). The final four poems speak more generally about poetic themes: the eighth deals self-referentially with poetry and language while the tenth is a reflection on endings and death (344–342). The verses of these poems are thus *tagged* with specific terms, facilitating their identification as belonging to a particular poem.

The final poem speaks directly to the reader, who has been agonizing to finish these poems:

Cela considérant ô lecteur tu suffoques
Comptant tes abattis lecteur tu te disloques
Toute chose pourtant doit avoir une fin. (344)[17]

This exhausted reader breaks to pieces (*disloquer*), counts his limbs and resigns himself to the fact that everything must come to an end. However, Queneau's poems do not end here. The reader can dislocate (*disloquer*) the individual verses from their respective poems, breaking the volume to pieces to have enough poetry to read forever.

When shuffled, this specific vocabulary produces odd juxtapositions, for instance, resulting in a poem that includes gauchos and the leaning tower of Pisa with no logical continuity between them. While in the *mode d'emploi*, Queneau had facetiously claimed that the recombined poems do not have the 'charm' of the originals, they are *intentionally* nonsensical due to this specific vocabulary. While Queneau might have conceivably defined an additional constraint, forcing him to write each poem about the same theme, he intentionally chose not to do so. I do not consider Queneau's insistence on the grammatical and poetic rules of sonnets rather than on the content a mere oversight. Indeed, his choice of extremely specific subject matter for each poem demonstrates a desire to produce humorous, logically impossible and geographically destabilizing results.

The fact that the potential poems exhibit a lack of meaning that is antithetical to traditional poetry risks alienating the reader who, according to the paratextual material, makes the entire process possible. However, Queneau's insistence on the impossibility of reading the volume in its entirety problematizes any notion of interpretation.[18] Without being able to read all the poems, it is impossible to make a claim that no worthwhile poetry exists in the volume. Furthermore, a close reading of a single poem produced in this manner seems impossible, as one cannot speak of authorial intent or coherent themes. However, the fact that Queneau's *Cent mille milliards de poèmes* resists traditional analysis can be understood as a commentary on the methods themselves, which might indeed blind readers to certain aspects of the text by focusing on others.

It must be mentioned that *Cent mille milliards de poèmes* is not a perfect system. In the *mode d'emploi*, Queneau mentions that he had taken the repetition of rhyming words into consideration when writing his base poems: 'Il eût été, d'ailleurs, sans importance que de mêmes mots se trouvassent à la rime au même vers puisqu'on ne les lit pas en même temps; je ne me suis permis cette licence que pour "beaux" (substantif et anglicisme) et "beaux" (adjectif)' (Queneau 1961 333).[19] In addition to the two rhyming words that Queneau allowed himself to include in corresponding verses (the B-rhyme, *beaux*), there are actually two other cases: the A-rhyme, *marchandise* (repeated in poem 3, line 7 and poem 10, line 5) and the E-rhyme, *destin* (repeated in poem 2, line 10 and poem 7, line 10). At these three places where the possible rhymes are identical, *beaux* and *destin* repeat in the same verse, meaning that if substituted, they would not be identical to any other rhyme in the new poem. The rhyme *marchandise*, however, repeats in two separate verses, creating one instance where the new sonnet would have the same rhyme twice. Keeping those two verses constant and allowing for the permutation of the other verses creates 10^{12} 'potential poems' that are not sonnets in the strict sense, as one rhyme repeats twice. The glitch is not particularly disruptive for two reasons: first, this only constitutes 1 per cent of the collection; second, the title (*Cent mille milliards de poèmes*) still holds, given that these invalid sonnets are still poems. Given the relatively small percentage of invalid sonnets, a reader of a digital edition would be statistically unlikely to encounter a poem that did not conform to the rules of a sonnet.

Rather than a failure, this glitch is indicative of a possible strategy for reading a volume that Queneau maintains is impossible to read. In the physical book, once the reader is aware of which rhyme disrupts the system, he or she can immediately see all the potential disruptions by purposefully choosing both *marchandise* verses. Like a machine, this critical attitude towards a glitch allows the reader to acknowledge the brilliance of the programme while potentially improving it. Such a reader would have succeeded in reading like a machine, appreciating this collection for the technical capacity of the system.

Bohman-Kalaja comments on Oulipo's obsession with machine production: 'The fundamentally ludic nature of Oulipian formal experimentation flirts with the mechanization of creative production. In an age of artificial intelligence and cybernetics, the group's efforts and successes have pressing ethical implications concerning the production, reception, and interpretation of literary texts' (24). In the specific case of Queneau's *Cent mille milliards de poèmes*, this mechanization of creative production can be understood as a commentary on three different types of automatism: computers, Surrealist automatic writing and mass production. The Turing epigraph, the volume's design and the glitch produced by the repetition of the rhyme *marchandise* imply a certain sensitivity to computers. In the 1960s, as the personal computer was being developed, this new type of *automatism* had begun to supersede the Surrealist use of the term *automatic writing* as an expression of the unconscious mind. By creating a formal system reminiscent of computers to produce sonnets *automatically*, Queneau's system produces poems that sound as though they could have been produced by Surrealist *automatic* techniques. Indeed, some even reference Surrealist work, including the first line of poem 4 (C'était à cinq o'clock qu'il sortait la marquise), which is an allusion to the first *Manifeste du surréalisme*, a phrase that Breton attributes to Paul Valéry (15). In this sense, the semantic dissonance created by the intentional shuffling of specific references is not only a joking critique of Surrealist practices, but rivals them. Queneau's recombined poems sound remarkably like Surrealist writing without making claims about the nature of the unconscious or art itself. Through mathematical permutations, he proves that there is no need for recourse to the unconscious or dreams or collective writing to produce Surrealist imagery, but that it can be reproduced *mechanically* through craft and cleverness. Furthermore, Queneau's machine is far more efficient than Surrealist practices, producing an *exponential* quantity of poems from a limited number of originals.

The efficiency of Queneau's system brings to mind mass production, a highly politicized concept in post-war France, where American consumerist culture was proposed as a way to combat communism, ironically capitalizing on the same tools used in Nazi death camps for mass murder. While the ubiquitous nature of American products after the Second World War is not thematized in *Cent mille milliards de poèmes*, it could not have been far from Queneau's mind after the recent publication and success of *Zazie dans le métro* (1959), in which the title character is obsessed with 'bloudjinnzes' and 'cacocalo'. Queneau's sonnet-producing machine is also reminiscent of mass production, devaluing the worth of the poetic form and reducing it to a set of arbitrary rules that, when manipulated correctly, can be exhausted. When faced with the volume, the reader has the impression that the combinatorial results are cheapened poetry, uninteresting and nonsensical. This notion seems to have been predicted by Queneau as well, who used the rhyme *marchandise* not once, but twice,[20] ironically creating a glitch in the collection and perhaps a critique of the great mass of actual second-rate sonnets written throughout history, rehashing the same themes, tropes and rhymes.

Queneau 1961 and computer experiments

In addition to the creative attempts of individual members of Oulipo to use algorithmic procedures as a generative force for potential literature, the group organized several collaborations with computer scientists throughout the 1960s and 1970s. Given the logical, mathematical basis of computer programming and the fact that several of Oulipo's founding members were mathematicians who were also getting involved in computers in the 1960s, the topic was mentioned often in early Oulipo meetings. This developmental stage coincided with a partnership with a computer programmer from IBM. A second collaboration at the Centre Pompidou in the 1970s further nuanced the group's understanding of constraint, automatic procedures and the role of the reader.

Oulipo's practical engagement with computers was one of the earliest explicit projects cited in the group's meeting minutes. Indeed, the first mention of computers occurs in an annex to the minutes of the second meeting (19 December 1960), under the title 'TOP SECRET':

> Deux de nos membres les plus dévoués se sont donné pour tâche d'intéresser les sociétés IBM et BULL à nos travaux. Leur but est de tenter d'utiliser des machines électroniques pour différents travaux d'analyse littéraire, dans le cadre des activités de l'OLiPo. Nous souhaitons à ces vaillants tractateurs le plus grand succès dans leurs entreprises. (Bens, *Genèse* 32)[21]

The decision to seek out computer scientists occurred at a critical juncture, in the same meeting in which the group officially adopted its new acronym, *Ouvroir de Littérature Potentielle* instead of the previous *Séminaire de Littérature Expérimentale*, though they only adopted the acronym OuLiPo in the following meeting. The group's new name represents a pronounced shift from discussion to action. It is even more telling that at the same meeting, the members decided to seek out new tools for the analysis and creation of potential literature.

By August 1961, the group had set up a partnership with Dmitri Starynkevitch, a Russian-born computer programmer at IBM-Bull Computers, who worked on the SEA CAB 500 computer.[22] Using this computer, Starynkevitch had generated excerpts from *Cent mille milliards de poèmes*. While there is no surviving record of either Starynkevitch's code or the excerpts he sent to Queneau, it is not difficult to infer how he accomplished this. In computer science terms, a sonnet is an *array* of fourteen verses that can each be attributed a numbered index (the first verse, the fourteenth verse, and everything in between). Queneau's data structure of *Cent mille milliards de poèmes* is slightly more complicated, an array of arrays: ten sonnets of fourteen lines each. Each individual verse for Queneau's text can thus be attributed two indices: the first indicating in which poem the verse can be found; the second indicating which numbered line it occupies in that sonnet. To generate random sonnets using the PAF language, Starynkevitch would have input these verses into the computer's memory and constructed a data structure within which they could be swapped. The distinguishing feature of Starynkevitch's programme would have come from the pseudo-random number generator (PRNG), of which the answer was lost with the code.[23]

The reaction of Oulipo members to these computer-generated excerpts was not very enthusiastic: 'On souhaita que M. Starynkevitch nous précise la méthode utilisée; on espéra que le choix des vers ne fut pas laissé au hasard' (Bens, *Genèse* 79).[24] While Starynkevitch's method could not have been random given the incapacity of computers to generate true random numbers, it would have been entirely invisible when members were confronted with just the excerpts. However, there was something disconcerting for the early Oulipo about the appearance of randomness in the computer-generated poems, resulting in the members' insistence on seeing the underlying *method*, rather than just the *results*, in an attempt to avoid chance or *le hasard* (the first appearance of this key concept in Oulipian aesthetics). At this stage, the members realized that Starynkevitch's computer-generated poems prevented a potential reader from engaging properly with the text.

While the early Oulipians considered themselves opposed to randomness, which they understood as a central facet of Surrealist writing, computers represented a different, yet equally problematic type of randomness. *Cent mille milliards de poèmes* parodies Surrealist automatic writing, but is produced by a different, combinatorial process. However, generating poems using an actual computer presented a real danger: this new *automatism* had to avoid letting chance play a role in the selection. While Oulipo had originally been drawn to computer science due to its rigorous, mathematical nature, it is clear that the group was still sceptical about the aleatory nature of computer-assisted literature, as Mark Wolff notes: 'they sought to avoid chance and automatisms over which the computer user had no control' (5). Indeed, even in its first year, the group was more concerned with the computer *user* than the computer itself.

While the determinism of computers appealed to the early Oulipo, the members experienced first-hand the technological limitations of the time, which in turn influenced the group's future production and aesthetics. Indeed, they saw through Starynkevitch's work that computers at best only facilitate generating texts to read given a set of basic elements. Nevertheless, this collaboration produced important results on both sides: for Oulipo, although the practical results were underwhelming, the group refined its core terminology of *potential* and *chance* and began to conceptualize the role of the reader, developing fewer procedural constraints and more structural ones; for Starynkevitch, who was doing mostly mathematical work at IBM at the time, this was a rare occasion to understand the potential of computing for natural language.

A decade after this initial collaboration, Oulipo participated in a research group at the Centre Pompidou known as the *Atelier de Recherches et*

Techniques Avancées (ARTA), directed by computer scientist Paul Braffort, who had joined the group too late to participate in its first collaboration with Starynkevitch. The goal was to create a foundation for 'un possible accord entre l'informatique et la création littéraire' (Fournel 298).[25]

The first experimental text treated by Braffort's project was Queneau's *Cent mille milliards de poèmes*, ostensibly due to the physical volume, which complicates the selection of which verses to read: 'Le recueil imprimé est très joliment conçu mais la manipulation des languettes sur lesquelles chaque vers est imprimé est parfois délicate' (299).[26] While it is true that certain manipulations of the set of poems are cumbersome, the physical design of the volume is visually compelling and informative regarding the combinatorial aspects of the text and one risk of programming it on a computer is to lose this original object. Nevertheless, in a conference presentation on this initiative, Oulipian Paul Fournel claimed that a computer facilitates the reading process: 'L'ordinateur, lui, opère une sélection dans le corpus à partir de la longueur du nom du "lecteur" et du temps qu'il met à le dactylographier sur le terminal puis édite le sonnet qui porte la double signature de Queneau et de son lecteur' (299).[27] This method responds to the earlier question to Starynkevitch regarding the selection of the poems, determining the poem based on the reader's name and typing speed and therefore according the reader a limited role in the selection of the sonnets while also bestowing on this reader the title of co-author.

Wolff comments on this increased role of the reader:

> The program's algorithm provides a certain degree of interaction between the user and the machine, and the results of running the program are theoretically reproducible if a user types the same name in the same amount of time. The algorithm therefore has potential, but only insofar that it accelerates the production of poems... The original algorithm preserves an active role for the user, even if that role requires the minimal engagement of typing one's name in order to sustain the creative process. (6)

While the ARTA programme has more potential than Starynkevitch's, which generated sonnets without any reader involvement, it is still restrictive. The physical edition affords the reader endless possibilities to read in different ways, but the ARTA programme only produces a single poem using a method that is never explained to the reader. Even though the programme does require some form of reader involvement, it is doubtful that a willing reader would find any amusement in reading more than one or two poems produced in this manner. Furthermore, as the reader is not privy to the selection process, he or she has little to no conscious control over the results.

Ironically, programming a computer-inspired text deprives the reader of an essential part of the reading experience – manipulating the physical object.

Like Starynkevitch's programme, the ARTA programme for *Cent mille milliards de poèmes* is not accessible today, and likely obsolete given the nature of programming languages. That said, Fournel did propose an interpretive use for the programme that has more creative potential than the reading experience: 'L'auteur lui-même peut faire son profit d'une telle édition: lorsque les combinaisons sont aussi nombreuses, il peut procéder à des contrôles par sondage. L'ordinateur joue dans ce cas un rôle d'assistant à la mise au point définitive du texte' (299).[28] The thought that the author could use a computer as a computational tool to organize an exponential quantity of poems could be viewed as contrary to the Oulipian project, as it represents simple calculations instead of a creative, generative device. However, this sampling idea could be viewed as an important precursor to digital humanities work, proposing an authorial equivalent to Franco Moretti's distant reading that would enable an author to deal with the exponential results of combinatorial literature.[29] In humanities scholarship today, this method could help literary scholars approach Queneau's text by allowing for educated statistical inferences about a body of poetry that the author has designed to be impossible to read in a human lifetime.

Conclusion

Queneau's *Cent mille milliards de poèmes* is truly an inexhaustible text,[30] despite the fact that it contains only a finite number of poems. While the text was inspired by computers and algorithmic procedures, programming it on a computer ironically forced Oulipo to bring it back to a human domain. For constrained literature, they found – mathematically or otherwise – the reader is key and must be willing to engage with the text based on the instructions (implicit or explicit) of the author. This is why, at every turn, *Cent mille milliards de poèmes* subverts the reader's expectations, all the while playfully mocking Surrealistic and machine-based production. Furthermore, Oulipo's work on this text with computers represents some of the first digital humanities work, falling under the category of exploratory programming and producing electronic literature. Understanding why the group abandoned these computer efforts is key to looking critically at the potential of digital humanities scholarship today, and more importantly to understanding its limitations.

Oulipo ultimately abandoned computers in favour of greater reader involvement and a renewed interest in pure mathematics as opposed to applied. This is due to the fact that abstract mathematical reasoning is much more human than computer programmes and algorithms. If the group ultimately abandoned the idea of computers, it is because it failed to align the methodical nature of programming with the axiomatic method the members wished to create for literature. Programming greatly appealed to Oulipo for its highly formalized nature; however, algorithms are designed to solve specific problems, whereas Oulipo considers the creation of constraints to be an end in itself.

Oulipo's predilection for abstract mathematics and its effects is illustrative of a possible strategy to bridge the two-culture divide in our scholarship, pedagogy and literary production. Therefore, rather than read them as unsatisfying experiments, I choose to understand these computer afterlives of *Cent mille milliards de poèmes* as indicative of the inexhaustible nature of Queneau's original text. Furthermore, this text says something about the nature of both literature and mathematics. By beginning with a highly constrained and prestigious literary form, the sonnet, Queneau constrains it further, unleashing the *potential* of the form itself. Governed by mathematical rules, sonnets – and, indeed, all types of fixed-form poetry – lend themselves to such a mechanical creation. In turn, this teaches us about the value of literature, a medium in which one can continue to find meaning forever.

Notes

1 Translation: 'Seven rondeaux in this rondeau / are woven and corded, / there are no strings nor cords / put together, they are rounded' (this and all subsequent translations are my own).
2 A mediaeval/Renaissance style of fixed-form poetry, often set to music, consisting of three isometric stanzas constructed around two rhymes, with certain mandatory repetitions, including an obligation to end with a reiteration of the first couplet. For a detailed explanation of the way this structure evolved throughout its history and has been misunderstood by scholars, please see Calvez (full reference in bibliography).
3 Warren Motte claimed that it is the 'seminal Oulipian text' (p. 47) while Jacques Roubaud emphasized that it represents the first public display of the power of constraint (Roubaud 2004, p. 101).
4 In an interview with Georges Charbonnier, Queneau acknowledges this timeline while also confirming the importance of this text within the genesis of Oulipo (Queneau 1962, p. 116).
5 This title indicates that the volume had gone to print while the group still referred to itself as the *Séminaire de Littérature Expérimentale* (*Sélitex*), before December 1960 (Bens p. 28).
6 Translation: 'Only a machine can appreciate a sonnet written by another machine.'
7 Queneau's use of the term *mode d'emploi* sets a precedent for future Oulipians and has been used most notably by Jacques Roubaud and most famously by Georges Perec in the title of his magnum opus, *La vie mode d'emploi*.

8   Translation: '"The preface," said Novalis, "provides the user's manual of the book." The turn of phrase is correct, but brutal. To guide the reading, to attempt to obtain a good reading, is not only accomplished by explicit directions.'

9   Nicolas Bourbaki is the pseudonym of a group of French mathematicians at the École Normale Supérieure, founded in the 1930s. The group published a series of mathematical textbooks as well as popular articles, promoting the conception of mathematics as an architecture, with a foundation grounded in the field of set theory. Oulipo was particularly influenced by Bourbaki's theoretical conception of mathematics, as well as its peculiar group culture.

10 See *Playtexts* by Warren Motte (1995) and *Reading Games* by Kimberly Bohman-Kalaja (2007).

11 Translation: 'machine for fabricating poetry, but in reduced quantities; it is true that this number, however limited, provides enough reading material for close to two hundred million years (reading 24/7).'

12 Translation: 'would not have had the same charm'.

13 Translation: 'Finally, the grammatical structure needed to be the same and remain invariable for each line substitution. A simple solution would have been to have each line form an independent clause. I only allowed myself this easy option in the tenth sonnet (the last one!). I also ensured that there would not be any disagreement between feminine and masculine, or singular and plural, from one line to another in the different sonnets.'

14 Translation: 'it is easy to see that the reader can produce 10^{14} different sonnets, otherwise one hundred thousand billion.'

15 The image below was taken by the Program Coordinator of the Film Department at SAE Institute Paris, Maxime Fournier, and reproduced with his permission.

16 In printing Queneau's original ten poems and not cutting between the verses, the Pléiade edition facilitates such a reading today. However, by printing each page recto verso, the editors have also prevented readers (even those who would consider taking scissors to a Pléiade edition) from producing their own recombined poems.

17 Translation: 'All things considered, oh reader, you are suffocating / counting your limbs, reader, you dislocate yourself / However, all things must come to an end'.

18 That said, although it is indeed impossible to read all the potential poems, reading the original ten and a few additional combinations gives the reader a fairly good idea of what the others look like, and it's unlikely that there are some that are especially brilliant or meaningful sonnets in the collection.

19 Translation: 'It would have been irrelevant if the same rhyming words occurred in the same line since they are not read at the same time; I only allowed myself this license for "beautiful" (noun and anglicism) and "beautiful" (adjective).'

20 Indeed, one of those merchandise verses reads 'on vous fait devenir une orde merchandise,' implying that death – like life – is simply a commodity, and a particularly disgusting one at that.
21 Translation: 'Two of our most devoted members gave themselves the task to interest IBM and BULL in our work. Their goal is to try to use electronic machines for different tasks in literary analysis, in the context of the OLiPo's activities. We wish these valiant *tractators* [*sic*] the greatest success in their endeavors.'
22 Developed by the French company SEA (Société d'Electronique et d'Automatisme) in 1956 and launched in 1960, the CAB (Calculatrice Arithmétique Binaire) 500 was designed to be a low-cost, easy-to-use computer for primarily scientific calculations. In an article, Starynkevitch notes that it could be viewed as a forerunner to the personal computer (p. 23).
23 In my personal correspondence with Starynkevitch's son, Basile, he claimed that his father was no expert in random number generators and would have simply used a rudimentary one.
24 Translation: 'We wish that Mr. Starynkevitch would tell us the method he used; we hope that the choice of lines was not left to chance.'
25 Translation: 'a possible agreement between computer science and literary creation.'
26 Translation: 'The printed volume is very nicely designed, but the manipulation of the strips on which each line is printed is sometimes delicate.'
27 Translation: 'The computer makes a selection from the corpus based on the length of the name of the "reader" and the time it takes to type it on the terminal, then publishes the sonnet which bears the double signature of Queneau and his reader.'
28 Translation: 'The author himself can profit from such an edition: when the combinations are so numerous, he can carry out random checks. In this case, the computer plays an assistant role in finalizing the text.'
29 In his award-winning essay collection of the same name, Moretti outlines his vision of 'distant reading', or a professional reading method that relies heavily on computer programmes.
30 Indeed, in addition to Oulipo's own efforts to programme *Cent mille milliards de poèmes*, there are a number of more recent amateur editions that can be found online, including those by Bev Rowe, Gordon Dow and myself (see Bibliography for full citations).

Works cited

Balakian, Anna. *Surrealism: The Road to the Absolute*. The University of Chicago Press, 1959.
Bens, Jacques. *Genèse de l'Oulipo 1960–1963*. Le Castor Astral, 2005.

Berkman, Natalie. 'Princeton-CDH/Digital-Oulipo'. *GitHub*. https://github.com/Princeton-CDH/digital-oulipo. Accessed 24 November 2020.
Bohman-Kalaja, Kimberly. *Reading Games: An Aesthetics of Play in Flann O'Brien, Samuel Beckett & Georges Perec*. Dalkey Archive Press, 2007.
Bourbaki, Nicolas. 'L'architecture des mathématiques'. *Les Grands courants de la pensée mathématique*. Albert Blanchard, 1962, pp. 35–47.
Bourbaki, Nicolas. *Éléments de mathématique*, vol. 1. Éditions Hermann, 1939.
Breton, André. *Manifestes du surréalisme*. Gallimard, 1966.
Calvez, Daniel. 'La Structure Du Rondeau: Mise Au Point'. *The French Review*, vol. 55, no. 4, American Association of Teachers of French, 1982, pp. 461–470.
Dow, Gordon. *100,000,000,000,000 Sonnets by Raymond Queneau*. http://www.growndodo.com/wordplay/oulipo/10%5e14sonnets.html. Accessed 24 November 2020.
Fournel, Paul. 'Ordinateur et écrivain : l'expérience du Centre Pompidou'. *Atlas de littérature potentielle*, by Oulipo, Gallimard, 1981, pp. 298–302.
Gauthier, Joëlle. *Machines à écrire*. 11 February 2009. http://nt2.uqam.ca/en/repertoire/machines-ecrire-0. Accessed 23 August 2022.
Genette, Gérard. *Seuils*. Seuil, 1987.
Hodges, Andrew. *Alan Turing: The Enigma*. Princeton University Press, 2012.
Kummer, Pascal. 8192 'Têtes Folles'. http://www.legrenierdepascal.net/2015/10/8192-tetes-folles.html. Accessed 22 April 2020.
Molinet, Jean. 'Sept rondeaux sur un rondeau'. *Anthologie de la poésie française du XVIe siécle*. Rookwood Press, 1999, p. 16.
Moretti, Franco. *Distant Reading*. 1st edn. Verso, 2013.
Motte, Warren F. *Playtexts: Ludics in Contemporary Literature*. University of Nebraska Press, 1995.
Motte, Warren. 'Raymond Queneau and the Early Oulipo'. *French Forum*, vol. 31, no. 1, 2006, pp. 41–54.
Queneau, Raymond. *Cent mille milliards de poèmes*. Gallimard, 1961.
Queneau, Raymond. *Entretiens avec Georges Charbonnier*. Gallimard, 1962.
Roubaud, Jacques. 'L'auteur oulipien'. *L'Auteur et le manuscrit*. PUF, 1991.
Roubaud, Jacques. 'Perecquian OULIPO'. *Yale French Studies*, vol. 105, 2004: pp. 99–109.
Rowe, Bev. *Queneau Sonnets*. http://www.bevrowe.info/Queneau/QueneauRandom_v4.html. Accessed 24 November 2020.
Starynkevitch, Dmitri. 'The SEA CAB 500 Computer'. *Annals of the History of Computing (American Federation of Information Processing Societies) 12*, vol. 12, no. 1, 1990, pp. 23–29.
Wolff, Mark. 'Reading Potential: The Oulipo and the Meaning of Algorithms'. *Digital Humanities Quarterly*, vol. 1, no. 1, 2007. http://digitalhumanities.org/dhq/vol/1/1/000005/000005.html. Accessed 23 August 2022.

17

The Four Seasons in flux: Translating the sonnets from Vivaldi's score in relation to performances by Nigel Kennedy

Paul Munden and Anouska Zummo

Introduction

In 2015, twenty-six years after his first, groundbreaking recording of Vivaldi's *The Four Seasons,* British violinist Nigel Kennedy released a radically new version. Early performances included singers, drawing attention to the texts that feature in the score: Italian phrases, which, when extracted, assemble into sonnets, one for each season. Having followed Kennedy's career and being engaged in a creative–critical interpretation of his work, I became intrigued by the sonnets, their origin and their relationship to the music. It struck me that the process of translating them afresh might provide a means of understanding Kennedy's own process as a musician.

I was already convinced that any writing about Kennedy should follow his own example: that 'interpretation' should be deeply attuned to the source material; that knowledge and disciplined technique should underpin departures from artistic convention; but that creative expression and, most importantly, the power to communicate should hold sway. To this end, addressing the Four Seasons sonnets as a poet and musician but with little knowledge of Italian, I recruited the expertise of Anouska Zummo, with whom this chapter is co-written.

In addition to the newly translated sonnets, my Kennedy study intends to incorporate other new poems of my own, linking the prose chapters with poetic *transitoires* – Kennedy's own term for the newly composed sections that link the movements of his *New Four Seasons* recording. The *transitoires* give Kennedy scope to dwell further on the sonnets, which he considers 'very important' (Kennedy 2012, 6). They also complicate the three-movement structure of each concerto, which, in the baroque period, was typically quick/slow/quick. Vivaldi was already moving in this direction: in 'Summer', for instance, the movements are remarkably unpredictable in their changes of tempo; it is the single structure of the sonnet, with all its shifts of mood, that governs. Kennedy's addition of *transitoires* should perhaps be viewed as a logical development of the original music's fluidity – and contemplative relationship with the text.

I find these complicating freedoms compelling. I approach my larger subject not as traditional biographer or critic but as a poet, creating a hybrid work, and I have approached translation in a similarly unorthodox way. The translations are not based solely on the Italian text: they take account of its unusual context; they are refracted through the music – specifically as reconceived in Kennedy's latest performances, with a wilfully contemporary idiom in the mix.

As Homi Bhabha states, 'hybridity is precisely about the fact that when a new situation, a new alliance formulates itself, it may demand that you should translate your principles, rethink them, extend them' (216). This definition of hybridity captures well my own personal approach to the interpretative task here discussed; I suggest that it applies to Kennedy's impulse too, and perhaps even Vivaldi's.

Music, poetry and intersemiotic translation

Vivaldi's concertos commonly referred to as *The Four Seasons* are part of *Il cimento dell'armonia e dell'inventione* (The contest between harmony and invention), a set of twelve concertos published in 1725. They are distinguished, musically, above the other eight works, but also on account of the sonnets included in the score. 'The poems are generally thought to be written by Vivaldi himself – based on comments he made in the margins of his sheet music, but there is some question over the attribution' (Spanoudis 1).

The inclusion of the poems makes clear the music's deliberate depiction of particular scenes. If attributed to Vivaldi, it would mark a significant, early instance of intersemiotic translation (the act of re-creation across different sign systems), a notion that is further enriched by the work's ekphrastic origins, being 'based on four paintings of the seasons by Marco Ricci' (Spanoudis 1).

The literary merit of the sonnets is insubstantial compared to the stature of the music, and translations tend to reflect their archaic language. Not even those (unattributed) translations in the booklet accompanying Kennedy's new recording rise above the banal. Here is the first stanza of 'Spring' together with the original Italian:

Giunt' è la Primavera e festosetti	Spring has arrived and festively
La Salutan gl' Augei con lieto canto,	the birds greet it with happy song,
E i fonti allo Spirar de' Zeffiretti	and the streams, blown by the West Wind,
Con dolce mormorio Scorrono intanto	flow past with gentle murmur. (Kennedy 2015)

There is little, poetically, to champion here, certainly in the English version. The original is at least prettified (and dignified) by the easy Italian rhymes, and some might claim that the Italian language is more intrinsically musical. The line 'Con dolce mormorio Scorrono intanto' has a rhythmic sonority that achieves a delightful onomatopoeic effect even for those with no grasp of Italian. The flow of soft, open vowel sounds corresponds to Vivaldi's groups of semi-quavers alternating between two notes (see C in Figure 17.1).

Whatever their poetic merits, the place of the poems in the broader history of art is of considerable significance, yet translations that do them justice are few. Those by W. D. Snodgrass are notable exceptions, accomplished sonnets in their own right, and Snodgrass is at pains to match the original segmentation, so that 'the English phrases could be inserted into the score at the same place as their Italian counterparts' (70). By contrast, our translation resisted such a linear approach, as we wanted the music to be present in the transaction; even the physical attributes of performance were to be brought into play – Kennedy in his customary Aston Villa football shirt, bumping fists with his fellow musicians.

So although I was provided with literal translations, following the Italian syntax, it was the notion of *The Four Seasons* as an existing work of intersemiotic translation that took precedence in the further drafting. The overall, multidimensional quality of what we engage with, witnessing a Kennedy/Vivaldi performance, mattered as much as the Italian words on the page. This approach is perhaps endorsed by Michael Edwards, who remarks of the translator:

> he can and should be concerned for what we call, out of sad necessity, poetry's aesthetic element, for what the Anglo-Saxons called *songcræft*, a term which expresses the work and study of poetry more strikingly than *poetics* or *the art of poetry*, which underlines the relation between poetry and the voice, and which affirms jubilantly the poem's desire to be fully achieved in all dimensions. (17)

A further underlying principle – close to Kennedy's heart – was already prevalent during the baroque period: the practice of treating scores as the

Figure 17.1 Score by Vivaldi. Every effort has been made to trace the copyright holder.

basis for improvisation. Such practice is less common in poetry, though Liam Guilar describes his approach to Old English poems varying 'from literal translation, via adaptation, to appropriation, to something more like a musical improvisation on a theme' (30). He also mentions Carol Braun Pasternack's claim 'that the Old English poems we know are made up of "movements" and that these movements were interchangeable between poems' (63).

> [T]he movement structure means a text is open 'to a certain amount of play, giving the reader the choice of leaving the ambiguities open, at

play, or resolving them through interpretation' (p. 23). [...] Pasternack's point is that, in use, any Old English text could have been reassembled to produce a very different 'poem'. (63)

'The poem' is thus made manifest by performance – and with considerable scope for variety. Paul Muldoon takes this notion further when he writes of translation that 'both original poem and poetic translation are manifestations of some ur-poem' (195). It is fascinating to relate such comment to *The Four Seasons*, of which we simply do not know whether the poems or the music came first. Future scholarship may yet establish the chronology but we are currently presented with two parallel attempts at the very same task; each addresses the same fundamental source of inspiration with a matching – or at least intimately related – creative and communicative purpose. And as readers or listeners, we too have a sense of the elemental seasons that speak to us each year in a sequence that is both repetitive and endlessly varied.

At this point, one might wonder that Kennedy has not taken even greater liberties in presenting the multiple movements of *The Four Seasons*. In an era when climate change seems to have run amok with our seasonal expectations, one might reasonably be confronted with some radical re-ordering. Kennedy has indeed occasionally broken off mid-sequence, to perform something else, and his 1989 release was promoted with CD singles, 'Summer' with Gershwin's 'Summertime' as a bonus track. Compilation albums present isolated seasons, though it is interesting that on Kennedy's own *Greatest Hits* CD (2002) 'Spring' and 'Summer' bookend the first disc – in the 'correct' order. Kennedy is remarkably faithful to structural imperatives, however much he stretches their compass. In *The New Four Seasons*, his introduction of jazz trumpet in 'Autumn' may seem radical, but it opens up the party atmosphere of the harvest celebrations precisely in accordance with the accompanying poem, without distorting Vivaldi's musical progression, further evidence that the sonnets are crucial to Kennedy's overall interpretation.

Kennedy's approach, from which I take my own cue, shares much with Walter Benjamin's concept of translation as a balancing act between capturing the original spirit and making it new. Kennedy is outspoken about so-called 'authentic', 'historical' performances, going so far as to accuse the classical musical establishment of turning 'philosophical masterpieces' into 'shallow showpieces' (Alberge n.p.). In his view, such performances are fundamentally misconceived, a view that chimes with Benjamin when he states:

> no translation would be possible if in its ultimate essence it strove for likeness to the original. For in its afterlife – which could not be called

that if it were not a transformation and a renewal of something living – the original undergoes a change. (73)

Transcreation

A useful term for the 'transformation and renewal' involved in both literary translation and musical performance is 'transcreation', made popular by Brazilian poet Haroldo de Campos, who considered that 'every translation of a creative text will always be a "re-creation", a parallel and autonomous, although reciprocal, translation – "transcreation"' (315). For me, the 'transcreation' of the Four Seasons sonnets was in part a means to understanding something of Kennedy's own processes. Bringing my own creativity to the task of 'interpretation' was fundamental. I was already involved in a sonnet-writing project with Paul Hetherington at the University of Canberra, exploring how the traditional form might be treated with a degree of freedom. That same spirit of experiment informed the Four Seasons writing more than any conscious engagement with translation theory, though it is interesting, in retrospect, to consider how the instinctive experiments fit with such theory, and where the poems sit on the spectrum between 'translations' and 'versions' (Reynolds 29). In terms of Roman Jakobson's tripartite distinction – between '*intralinguistic* (rewording), *interlinguistic* (translation proper) and *intersemiotic* (transmutation)' (quoted in Eco 65) – the *intersemiotic* or *transmutation* category clearly applies best.

Perhaps most relevant, though, is Eugene Nida's distinction between *formal* and *dynamic* equivalence: 'A translation of dynamic equivalence aims at complete naturalness of expression, and tries to relate the receptor to modes of behavior relevant within the context of his own culture' (1964, 159). Considering various degrees of equivalence within translation, Nida's *dynamic* equivalence hints at a transference of the spirit or sense of the original, whilst accepting that this may retain faithfulness beyond literal transfer. 'Thus a translation can express an evident "deep" sense of a text even by violating both lexical and referential faithfulness' (Eco 14).

In these new Four Seasons sonnets, the *culture* (to use Nida's term) is partly that of baroque concertos, partly that of the Munden and Hetherington 'untidy sonnets' project (2017), and partly that of maverick musician, Nigel Kennedy. The new sonnets aim to include all key images from the originals, while adhering more insistently to the vitality of Vivaldi's music – and Kennedy's rendition. Where he (Kennedy) takes the greatest liberties – as with a crushing electric violin in the summer storm – so do the new sonnets.

The original Four Seasons sonnets, once the individual lines are gathered from their positions in the score, are habitually presented in stanzas corresponding to the three movements of each concerto, rather than a more traditional sonnet form. My new poems follow suit, though varying the allocation of lines. The middle stanza/movement (typically a slow movement, adagio or largo) is indented, to accentuate the shift; sometimes, however, the syntax straddles the divide, reflecting the fluidity between movements mentioned earlier. There is a flexible rhyme scheme (including half-rhyme), typical of my rhyming poetry generally. Some rhymes operate at a distance across stanzas, not an unusual poetic strategy, but relating here to Kennedy's tendency to echo ideas between movements. A ten-syllable line (the typical English equivalent of the longer Italian line) is maintained throughout.

Each sonnet is titled like its equivalent concerto (e.g. 'Sonnet in E major'), signalling the intersemiotic nature of the work. The titling (and reference to musical tempi, e.g. *allegro – largo – allegro*) is partly a conceit, a tribute to Vivaldi's own dual thinking, but it is also suggestive of how music and poetry, despite fundamental differences, can operate alike. As Burton Raffel states:

> Both music and poetry are, in a sense, languages within languages. Organized sound – perhaps the broadest definition of music – is scarcely ever a communication system in the way that words are: music speaks, to be sure, but if its message is to be translated into verbal terms only the most elementary expressions are recognizable. But in the manipulation of its proper component parts – pitch, rhythm, instrumental color, dynamics, and the like – music is closely analogous to speech. (453)

In 'Winter' there are some notable 'departures' from the original text that actually align the words even more closely with the music. The *brrrrr*, for instance, is nowhere in sight within the original text; it's taken from the shivering low trill on the solo violin at the related moment in the music; a direct if unusual form of onomatopoeia. Likewise, the 'pizzicato' rain mirrors the music as much as the Italian text, with the quality of verbal/musical sound the priority, yet with the 'introduced' word (pizzicato) acting as a bond with the original language.

I have reflected Kennedy's more extreme departures, building in some justification for us both: 'Jazz trumpet? It's a party!' Those who frown at Kennedy's liberties will no doubt disapprove of mine too, but I would nevertheless maintain the integrity of the approach. Vivaldi's *Four Seasons* exists as a rich set of printed instructions for performative interpretation, and the unusual addition of poetic text adds complexity to the interpretative task. It is perhaps unsurprising that performances vary so widely: two different semiotic systems are in play, making it doubly unlikely that any two performers will react in the same way. In writing my sonnets, I have in effect attempted an imaginative account of how Nigel Kennedy might be 'reading' the whole score – musical notation *and words* – when preparing a performance. He takes the dog mentioned in the second movement of 'Spring' and gives it a prominent role in the third, where the festivities start, with vocalized barks, or as I convey it, 'revelry that breaks into yelps and whoops'. 'The dogs are out', I continue, alluding to the deliberately 'uncouth' sonic intervention, the sense of mayhem. But it is not the case that 'anything goes'; on the contrary, it is a serious (though boisterous) re-imagining of Vivaldi's 'Spring' – just as my 'fly-infested lull, a fractious growl / itching for a livewire scare' and Kennedy's extended silences mixed with distorted electronica attempt to depict the oppressive reality of his Italian 'Summer'. And I have yet to encounter another recording that captures the 'gallop' of the hunt in 'Autumn' so vividly. It inspired me to transfer that rhythmic urgency to the carousing that kicks the whole thing off: 'they drink at the gallop, drink till they drop'.

There is a deliberate conflation here of music and poetry, which accords with what Ray Jackendoff has argued:

> poetry is the result of superimposing musical principles to some degree on linguistic utterances. Thus to the extent that poetic form conveys affect, it is precisely because it invokes principles of musical perception that are not normally associated with language. (198)

That music and poetry relate in this way holds particular significance for the translator and yet, as Şebnem Susam-Sarajeva comments, 'the topic of translation and music has remained on the periphery of translation studies' (190). She goes on to say:

> Few of us with a background in translation studies can effectively deal with meanings derived not only from text, but also from melody, pitch, duration, loudness, timbre, dynamics, rhythm, tempo, expression, harmony, pause, stress or articulation in music. If we consider that research in translation and music may also require a background in media studies, cultural studies and/or semiotics, we can begin to appreciate the difficulties encountered by anyone who ventures into this field. (190)

Conclusion

Throughout this chapter I have referred to 'my' poems, partly for convenience, but the work of translating the original sonnets was a collaborative undertaking – informed by our different but complementary backgrounds. In Susam-Sarajeva's words, we experienced how 'The intersection of translation and music [...] can enrich our understanding of what translation might entail, how far its boundaries can be extended and how it relates to other forms of expression' (191).

Translating the sonnets was not part of my original plan in writing about Kennedy, but the process has proved to be hugely informative. It has perhaps highlighted a general virtue of translation as a practice for writers. As Raffel comments:

> Surely no one will deny that the immense facility with which musicians can cross-fertilize each other is a blessing to the art. It would seem to be largely poets, however – and only a minority even among poets – who are aware of how much translation can do to cross-fertilize them. (456)

Our collaboration has served a valuable purpose not only in translating the sonnets but also in approaching my larger subject – a musician for whom collaboration is an essential, driving force. Unlike music, poetry is often viewed as a predominantly solitary art, and the viability of poetry in translation is ever questioned. Perhaps a model of collaborative, intersemiotic, poetic translation may usefully unsettle both views.

THE FOUR SEASONS
(Il Cimento dell' Armonia e dell' Inventione)
after Vivaldi, Nigel Kennedy and the Orchestra of Life

Sonnet in E Major (La Primavera/Spring)
allegro – largo – allegro

> Ushered in by a noodling guitarist,
> the birds are in full swing; for the soloist,
> with this music in his veins, it's a lark.
> In his Villa shirt he chirps and chirrups
> while tight, bright buds unfurl to improvise
> a canopy of leaves. His supple wrist
> whips up a storm then settles for reprise.

> A trance... he drifts off, sprawled under the trees
> among daisies and meadow buttercups,
> with a sampled, softly murmuring breeze
> and the viola's monotonous bark.

Bring on the cheerleaders, goat skins and pipes,
revelry that breaks into yelps and whoops...
The dogs are out – *Yeah!* A bump of the fist.

Sonnet in G Minor (L'Estate/Summer)
allegro non molto – adagio – presto

Scorched pines. A sweltering stasis. The heat
has pressed the air almost to silence. Note
follows note like stuttering beads of sweat
but there – in the bow's quick tilt – the cuckoo,
followed by a warbling dove and the trill
of the finch, those fingers thrillingly close.
Breezing triplets flutter against a beat
the north wind blasts to hell – and there'll be more.

> A fly-infested lull, a fractious growl
> itching for a livewire scare. So why not –
> with a stack of Marshalls to hand – let loose

the thunder and lightning for real?... *One... two
mississippi three mississippi four...*
The cornfields are all trashed by golf-ball hail.

Sonnet in F Major (L'Autunno/Autumn)
allegro – adagio molto – allegro

Jazz trumpet? It's a party! – the harvest
gathered in. The drinking is in earnest
with flagons of claret and ale on tap;
they drink at the gallop, drink till they drop,
nod off... only to get that second wind
and party on full pelt into the night.

> Passed out, they enter a parallel realm –
> a kaleidoscopic haze in which time
> is an elasticated, weightless dream
> in the autumnal cool – sleeping till dawn

when it's hip flask, hunting horn, horse and hound.
One poor terrified animal must run
for its life – their sport. It gives up the fight.
Job done, they saddle up and trot back home.

Sonnet in F Minor (L'Inverno/Winter)
allegro non molto – largo – allegro

Frost… snow… layers of ice. The wind has bite.
We're shivering in its grip, a cold snap
like nothing we've known… *brrrrrr*… We run, and thump
our numbed, gloved hands together, stop and stamp
our snow-deep frozen boots on frozen earth.

> Later, feet up, in a chair by the hearth,
> I hear the pizzicato rain outside,
> a soporific, intimate reprieve

before we're back on the shifting ice, slide
and slip with skittering strings that believe
they can negotiate the cracks. The slap-
stick of our fall is what hurries our flight,
and if the wind howls through the house despite
battening it down, it's a shrill delight.[1]

Note

1 Nigel Kennedy/Vivaldi: *The New Four Seasons* (2015) is available to preview on YouTube: https://www.youtube.com/watch?v=BzBGDYvJzlA. The original Italian sonnets can be found at: https://www.baroquemusic.org/vivaldiseasons.html.

Acknowledgements

'Summer' from Paul Munden's 'The Four Seasons' appeared in *Axon: Creative Explorations* (Capsule 2), and the full quartet in the ACT States of Poetry Anthology (Series Three), published by *Australian Book Review*.

A version of this chapter was published in *TEXT* Special Issue 51: Climates of Change, 2018.

Works cited

Alberge, Dalya. 'Nigel Kennedy Accuses Fellow Violinists of Destroying Bach's legacy'. *The Guardian*, 13 August 2011. https://www.theguardian.com/music/2011/aug/13/nigel-kennedy-violinists-bach. Accessed 26 February 2018.

Bassnett, Susan and Harish Trivedi, eds. *Post-colonial Translation*. Routledge, 1999.

Benjamin, Walter. 'The Task of the Translator'. *Illuminations*. Edited by Hannah Arendt. Translated by Harry Zohn. Harcourt Brace Jovanovich, 1968 [1923].

Bhabha, Homi. *Identity, Community, Culture, Difference*. Edited by Jonathan Rutherford. London: Lawrence & Wishart, 1990.

De Campos, Haroldo. 'Translation as Creation and Criticism'. *Novas: Selected Writings of Haroldo de Campos*. Edited by Antonio Sergio Bessa and Odile Cisneros. Translated by Diana Gibson and Haroldo de Campos. Northwestern University Press, [1963] 2007.

Eco, Umberto. *Experiences in Translation*. University of Toronto Press, 2001.

Edwards, Michael. 'Believing in Poetry'. *Literature and Theology*, vol. 25, no. 1, 2011: pp. 10–19.

Guilar, Liam. *Anhaga: An Exploration in Poetry of Narrative, Memory and Identity*. PhD thesis, Deakin University, 2017.

Jackendoff, Ray. 'Parallels and Nonparallels between Language and Music'. *Music Perception: An Interdisciplinary Journal*, vol. 26, no. 3, 2009: pp. 195–204.

Jakobson, Roman. 'On Linguistic Aspects of Translation'. *On Translation. Harvard Studies in Comparative Literature*. Edited by R. A. Brower. Harvard University Press, 1959, pp. 232–239.

Kennedy, Nigel. *Vivaldi. The Four Seasons*. CD, EMI, 1989.

Kennedy, Nigel. *Nigel Kennedy's Greatest Hits*. CD, EMI, 2002.

Kennedy, Nigel. *Official Tour Programme*. Claire Gibson, 2012.

Kennedy, Nigel. *Vivaldi: The New Four Seasons*. CD, Sony, 2015.

Muldoon, Paul. *The End of the Poem*. Faber and Faber, 2006.

Munden, Paul and Paul Hetherington. 'A Doubtful Freedom: Untidy Sonnets and a Contemporary Poetics'. *The Authorised Theft Papers: The Refereed*

Proceedings of the 21st Conference of the Australasian Association of Writing Programs, Canberra, 2017. https://www.aawp.org.au/wp-content/uploads/2017/03/Hetherington_Munden_AAWP_2016_A-doubtful-freedom-1.pdf. Accessed 18 August 2022.

Nida, Eugene A. *Towards a Science of Translating*. EJ Brill, 1964.

Pedersen, Daniel. 'Exploring the Concept of Transcreation: Transcreation as "More than Translation"?' *Cultus, Journal of Intercultural Mediation and Communication*, vol. 7, 2014: pp. 57–71.

Raffel, Burton. 'Music, Poetry, and Translation'. *The Antioch Review*, vol. 24, no. 4, Winter, 1964–65: pp. 453–461.

Reynolds, Matthew. *The Poetry of Translation from Chaucer & Petrarch to Homer & Logue*. Oxford University Press, 2011.

Snodgrass, W. D. 'The Four Seasons'. *Syracuse Scholar*, vol. 1, no. 2, 1980: pp. 70–71.

Spanoudis, S. L. 'Le Quattro Stagioni (The Four Seasons) by Antonio Vivaldi'. *Poets' Corner Scripting*, 2009. http://www.theotherpages.org/poems/part2/vivaldi01.html. Accessed 27 February 2018.

Susam-Sarajeva, Şebnem. 'Translation and Music'. *The Translator*, vol. 14, no. 2, 2014: pp. 187–200.

18

Debating sonnet translation in the Soviet and post-Soviet era: Rethinking and transforming the Russian sonnet

Alexander Markov

Introductory remarks

In 1969, several events took place in Russian literature, both in creative practice and in discussions about translation, which shifted the focus from the sonnet as a form of lyrical expression and transformed it into a way of studying the aesthetics of distant eras. For a long time, the sonnet had been understood in Russia firstly in terms of poetic rules, and secondarily as a love poem. For the Symbolists and their heirs, the erotic and the theoretical were intertwined. But in 1969, there arose a rejection of the sensual or neo-Romantic understanding of love, and the thematic content of the sonnet expanded. Discussions about translation contributed to the emergence of the postmodern sonnet, in which the conversation about poetic rules was accompanied by irony. This study follows three parts, organized chronologically. The first part examines sonnet controversies in Soviet times. The second one looks at postmodern sonnets, where creative method and love are presented as part of an experiment with language. Finally, in the third part, I show how the poet Olga Sedakova has combined the aesthetics of postmodernism with the study of the psychology of distant eras, using sonnet translation as a vehicle for understanding the history of emotions in old Europe.

Sonnet translation controversies in Soviet times: The Russian sonnet as narration or allegory of love?

In 1969, the journal *Voprosy literatury* published an article by Natalia Avtonomova and Mikhail Gasparov, 'Shakespeare's Sonnets in Marshak's Translations'. Samuil Marshak, who had begun as a Zionist poet and then become a leading children's poet in Soviet times, was perceived as a person with an impeccable moral reputation and a competent translator. His *Shakespeare's Sonnets* (1949) was evaluated by critics as one of the highest achievements of Soviet poetic translation and a work no less important than his own poems. Korney Chukovsky, for example, said that it would be more correct to consider Marshak as the author of these sonnets, given the work done: 'in Marshak's translations I don't feel anything translated' (Chukovsky 1971, 101).[1] But Marshak's excessive modern lyrical mood in the translated text was challenged by Avtonomova and Gasparov. These critics adhered to the method of criticism that Chukovsky himself espoused in his *Shelley's Defence*, which criticized Konstantin Balmont's translations from Shelley (Chukovsky 1907): Balmont, a Russian symbolist poet and an admirer of Edgar Allan Poe and Baudelaire, had translated the entire corpus of Shelley's writing, seeing him as an exemplary Romantic lyricist, while widely borrowing clichés and images from Russian Romanticism in his translation, which Chukovsky considered outdated. Chukovsky accused Balmont of not being able to grapple with a rigid form such as the sonnet. This criticism changed broader attitudes towards Balmont's translations: while intellectuals of the older generation, like the philosopher Vladimir Soloviev, had enthusiastically welcomed them, Vladimir Nabokov declared them to be associated with vulgar taste: 'Getting to know Shelley (at least through Balmont's nasty retelling) was somehow once a sign of elegance'. Marshak, on the other hand, was defined by Chukovsky as an 'expert wordsmith' (Chukovsky 1971, 103).

According to Avtonomova and Gasparov, by using Romantic clichés, Marshak had changed not only the mood but also the meaning of Shakespeare's sonnets: the parallels between human life and natural elements – typical early modern correspondences – were replaced with a sensual enthusiasm for natural phenomena. Therefore, their article, though carried out as an analysis of translation decisions, coincided with the desire of Samizdat poetry to appeal to early modern culture and the high modernism of Pound and Eliot and to religious and mystical ideas of universal correspondences, in order to oppose Soviet populism and atheism. Just as Chukovsky had accused Balmont of introducing excessive abstract nouns in his translations of Shelley, so Avtonomova and Gasparov reproached Marshak for replacing Shakespeare's dizzying early modern comparisons with the abstract metaphors of nineteenth-century poetry. At the same time, they condemned Marshak for domestication in his translations, observing, for example, that he had used the image of a 'pendulum', which was appropriate in nineteenth-century poetry as a symbol of life's uncertainties, whereas there was no pendulum clock in Shakespeare's time, when poetry was structured according to a stable perspective aligned with ideas of God and monarchy. The general conclusion of Avtonomova and Gasparov was that the 'definite character' (*konkretnost*) of such conventional post-Romanticist images was 'illusory'.

This conclusion was also important for Samizdat religious poetry: Leonid Aronzon, Viktor Krivulin, Elena Shvarts and Olga Sedakova all loved the baroque complexity of images, far removed from Romantic emotion, and simultaneously evoking the intellectuality of the early modern and the experimentation of modernism and the avant-garde. The latter had been interrupted, according to these authors, by the simplified canon of Soviet populist style. These authors considered their task to be the destruction of the official Soviet style and the rehabilitation of the old culture of deep intellectual contemplation of the religious experience.

The journal published the article without much eagerness: as Sedakova testifies, the editor suspected Avtonomova and Gasparov of a biased attitude and personal motives. Sedakova strictly rejects these suspicions (Sedakova 2019), arguing that the article adhered to all the usual rules of intellectual literary discussion, and hence that such suspicions attacked their intellectual and literary practice. But from the point of view of Soviet cultural and educational officials, the article called into question the recognized principles of translation and therefore partially disqualified the contributors: a ban on the profession of researcher had long weighed over Avtonomova. At the same time, the argument of this article became the common property of intellectuals who perceived the Soviet cultural canon critically and sought to understand the structures of different cultures.[2]

In their seminal article, Avtonomova and Gasparov (who were atheist scholars) had reproached Marshak with not retaining the epithet 'glorious' in reference to morning, thus misleading the reader: early modern culture represented the sun not as a simple source of light fit for Romantic exaltation, but as a person, an animated creation befitting meditations on God's glory. Echoing this discussion, the same line from Shakespeare – 'Full many a glorious morning have I seen' (Sonnet 33, line 1) – was quoted by Sergey Averintsev, the leading Soviet scholar of ancient culture, a clandestine Christian who was also known as 'Soviet Gilson', to explain how the biblical identification between 'glory' and a 'holy flash' had become a commonplace of Western theology and literature. Averintsev may have been partly arguing against his teacher Alexey Losev, who in his *The Dialectics of Myth* considered allegory, including early modern allegory, as only a special instrument of mnemonic association, indifferent to personalization or reification, while he himself saw in the symbol the only real source of the artistic image. Averintsev interpreted the allegoric use of the personalized Sun as positive in all Western cultures, unwittingly recalling the stern critics of Marshak's translations.

Such a keen critical perception is partly due to the fact that the sonnet in Russian poetry was considered less a means of expression than a form of reflection. The sonnet as a representative of Western poetry in Russia was not for the communication of love, but a means to demonstrate poetic mastery; the *sonnet on the sonnet*, a meditation on the structure of poetry, was thus a milestone for poets. Discussion of eminent sonnet translations also touched on the general design of modern poetry. The Russian philosopher Vladimir Bibikhin, translator of Petrarch's prose and long-term correspondent of Sedakova, argued that a model of the sonnet as a 'song', a reflection of poetic mood, had been created by the troubadours at the dawn of the genre:

> 'I will compose poems about nothing'; so the first troubadour Guillaume of Aquitaine [William IX, Duke of Aquitaine] (1071–1126) begins his *Song of Nothing*; a poet can do without a theme for poetry if he breathes it like air. In contrast to the Latin-language culture of saving a treasure, which in itself possesses the fullness of life and can never be grasped by a human word, Provencal poetry spoke of a reality that existed to the extent that it was realized (articulated, sung, acted out) in the dance of *courtoise* actions and gestures. (Bibikhin 1982, 16)

In Russia, this model was created (or renovated, if we trust Bibikhin) by Pushkin: his rewriting of Wordsworth's 'Scorn not the Sonnet', 'Surovyi Dant ne prezíral soneta' ('Severe Dante Did Not Scorn the Sonnet', 1830), was a short explanation of why the poets of the modern world, from Dante and Petrarch to Pushkin's Russian contemporaries, paid so much attention to the formal elaboration and thematic diversity of the sonnet. Thus, Pushkin achieved a double goal: he inscribed young Russian literature within a wider world literature and pointed to the sonnet as a genre requiring high skill. It should be recalled that Pushkin advocated a professional attitude towards literature in a largely feudal country, where the idea of a professional division of labour was still unfamiliar to the public.

From Pushkin, the writing of sonnets began to be considered the most important criterion of poetic skill: for such *maîtres* of Russian poetry of the early twentieth century as Valery Bryusov or Nikolai Gumilyov, writing a sonnet was the diploma of an accomplished professional poet. The second generation were imitators of these poets and were not themselves professionals; they included the translator and cultural historian Abram Efros, the philologist Leonid Grossman (brother of Vassily Grossman, author of *Life and Fate*) and the cellist Vadim Borisovsky (his sonnets were published after his death, with myself as one of the editors). They mainly wrote cycles of sonnets, in order to prove to readers the legitimacy of their literary ambitions. Leonid Grossman even composed a sonnet in 1919 which was a reworking of Pushkin's, listing other poets, from Pushkin and his predecessors to Grossman's own contemporaries and acquaintances, to prove the cogency of Pushkin's project. However, certain members of the Russian avant-garde had the opposite aspiration, seeking to separate form from content: for example, in 1922 Ilya Selvinsky used a crown of sonnets to retell a historical anecdote about the Bar Kokhba uprising, fit for prose much more than for poetry. This tradition of the narrative and dramaturgic sonnet was partly picked up by Joseph Brodsky in his 'Twenty Sonnets to Mary Queen of Scots' (1974).

From allegory to postmodern irony

Gasparov and Avtonomova (who, as a translator, became an apostle of Foucault and Derrida for Soviet and post-Soviet readers) were very authoritative for the Samizdat poets, who focused on the reception of the Western literary tradition from antiquity to modernism. Thus, the idea of the 'semantic halo of the metre', coined by Gasparov on the basis of the arguments of Russian formalists, determined a reflective attitude to the instruments of verse, and a corresponding deepening of cultural allusions in lyric poetry. As Sedakova testifies in the essay 'In Praise of Poetry' (1982), the approach of the Russian formalists seemed too mechanistic to her circle, while the philosophical analysis of the boundaries of poetic utterance, taking into account the cultural variability of the meaning of the techniques, was closer to her mind. So, from the 1960s onwards, Samizdat and later poets – whether religious, secular or conceptualist – used the sonnet to probe and experiment with the mechanics of this poetic structure and use it for deeper self-knowledge.

In 1969, Leonid Aronzon wrote 'Pustoi sonet' ('Empty Sonnet'). This is a sonnet constructed according to all the usual rules, but also representing a graphic work. It was typewritten in a spiral along the edges of the sheet, while the middle remained empty.[3]

> Who loved you more enthusiastically than me?
> God bless you, God bless you, God bless you.
> There are gardens, there are gardens, they are standing at night.
> And you are in the gardens, and you are standing in the gardens too.
>
> I wish, I wish I had my sorrow
> To inspire you so, to inspire you so, without disturbing

Your sight of the grass of the night, your sight of its stream,
so that that sorrow, so that that grass becomes a bed for us.

Infiltrate the night, infiltrate the garden, infiltrate you,
raise your eyes, raise your eyes to heaven
compare the night in the garden, and the garden in the night, and the garden,
that is full of your nightly voices.

I go to them. The face is full of eyes...
For you to stand in them, the gardens are.

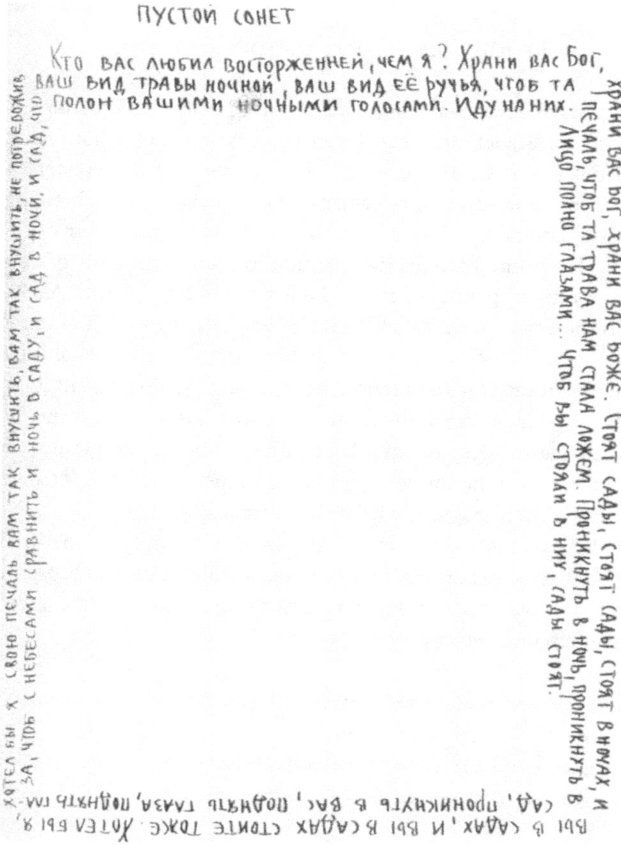

ПУСТОЙ СОНЕТ

Кто вас любил восторженней, чем я? Храни вас Бог,
ваш вид травы ночной, ваш вид её ручья, чтоб та
полон вашими ночными голосами. Иду на них.

Храни вас Бог, храни вас боже. Стоят сады, стоят сады, стоят в ночах,
печаль, чтоб та трава нам стала ложем. Проникнуть в ночь, проникнуть в
лицо полно глазами... Чтоб вы стояли в них, сады стоят.

Хотел бы я свою печаль вам так внушить, вам так внушить, не потревожить,
за, чтоб с небесами сравнить и ночь в саду, и сад в ночи, и сад, что
вы в садах, и вы в садах стоите тоже. Хотел бы я,
сад, проникнуть в вас, поднять глаза, поднять гла-

Figure 18.1 Empty Sonnet – Aronzon. Reproduced by permission of Felix Yacubson.

Although this is a love poem from the era of the sexual revolution, it mostly explores the possibilities of poetic sound, and how simple repetitions can create the poetic quality of an utterance. Other poets followed the path of Aronzon, for whom the sonnet combined the study of particular poetic devices and an act of deep self-knowledge. In 1972 – preceding the book *Voskresnye oblaka* (*Sunday/Resurrection Day Clouds*), in which he abandoned Soviet populism and reconciliation with the crowd in favour of a special form of self-knowledge – Viktor Krivulin wrote 'Udlinennyi sonet' ('Elongated Sonnet'):

A bundle of human brushwood. I have to go
long ago to make peace with the crowd
and push and crowd within himself,
and the soul is ripe for a fire.

But a face will meet not like a face.
Face will move that in the lake of morning
all the silvery fish a game of love,
all the sun wheels are sparkling spokes.

Then you will see yourself, but together:
a bright house flows over the lake,
his mirror brother on the circle froze unsteadily…

One in many and many in one
as two lonelinesses, two forces are driving us.
Between the sky in the lake and the sky in the sky

there is, as it were, a human opening.

This poem intertwines motifs from Russian religious and philosophical lyrics of the early twentieth century, predominantly Vyacheslav Ivanov's crown of sonnets 'My – dva grozoi zazhzhennye stvola' ('We Are Two Lighted Trunks by a Thunderstorm', 1902), in which the recognition of otherness in another person is identified with the mystical Christian way of life. Formal innovation in Krivulin's sonnet consists of only one additional line: Krivulin did not want to deviate far from the traditions of the Russian poetry of the early twentieth century, where the form of the sonnet was strictly observed. But the theme of the face was developed by Krivulin not in the mood of the Russian Symbolist poets, but of Leonid Aronzon, who understood the face not as a subjective proof of the existence of God, like Vyacheslav Ivanov did, but as an objective sign of the presence of God in the affairs of the world, as in this keystone stanza:

> All is face: face is face
> dust is face, word is face,
> everything is face. Of Him. Of the Creator.
> Only He Himself is without a face.

Although the religious Samizdat poets appreciated the heritage of Russian Symbolism, they adhered not to subjective but to objective idealism, denying the position of the Russian Symbolists as influenced by Nietzsche, *fin de siècle* rhetorical manipulations and the technocentrism of the *belle époque*. This criticism was summed up by the above-mentioned philosopher Bibikhin:

> In the end, it turns out that the more pious and sacred the symbols of [Viacheslav] Ivanov are, the less pious is his intimate attitude towards them – the attitude of a juggler and a magician, turning the latent levers of a complex mechanism. And from my heart I want to abandon all this symbolism as far as possible, none of its deepest understanding and possession of it seduces me. The scenery is boring – although I do want to see how the levers are arranged under the stage, that's interesting. It is clear that it is hardly possible to discredit a symbol and a myth worse [than symbolists like Ivanov do]. (Bibikhin 1998)

Aronzon, affirming objective idealism, wrote the poem 'Two Identical Sonnets' (1969) as if postulating the independent existence of poetry from our will, and the autonomy of the 'person'. This is a repeated text outlining a love appeal, in which the speaker demands immediate sexual relations with the addressee:

> My love, sleep, my sweetheart
> all dressed in satin skin.
> It seems to me that we met somewhere:
> I am so familiar with your nipples and underwear.
>
> Oh, how to face! oh, how are you! oh, how it goes!
> all this day, all this Bach, this whole body!
> and this day, and this Bach, and the plane,
> flying there, flying here, flying somewhere!

> And in this garden, and in this Bach, and in this moment
> sleep, my love, sleep without hiding:
> and face and backside, and backside and groin, and groin and face –
>
> let everything fall asleep, let everything fall asleep, my living!
> Without approaching one *iota*, not one step,
> surrender yourself to me in all gardens and cases.

The poem, as I have stated, belongs to the era of the sexual revolution, but the large number of repetitions in the text itself makes us look not at the predictable plotting of the sonnet as a genre of love lyrics, but at its formal structure, and how emotions can be located within this structure.

Aronzon's poem exemplifies the Russian sonnet as a masculine genre: women poets, including such recognized figures as Elena Shvarts and Olga Sedakova, did not write sonnets. At the same time, women experimented with such complex forms as the canzone, the elegy and the eclogue, often abandoning metrical fidelity for the sake of compositional and thematic adherence to ancient or medieval tradition. The pressure of Petrarch's masculinity and man-centred ethics (Laura for Petrarch as addressee of his sonnets was a metaphor of his masculine glory, of *laurus*) was made virtually synonymous with the sonnet form, symbolically barring women from its use. This may partly explain why Russian women poets did not often write sonnets: if in calling a work an *elegy* you should not permit an elegiac distich, given that in Russian Romanticism elegies were written in iambic, then you cannot call a poem a sonnet without observing its rigid form. The first notable cycle of sonnets written by a woman in post-Soviet times is arguably *Twenty Sonnets to M* by Maria Stepanova (1996), a polemical statement in response to the above-mentioned cycle by Brodsky.

The male Samizdat poets, on the other hand, necessarily wrote sonnets, but for them this was not so much a test of poetic professionalism as a sign of loyalty to the achievements of the old poetic tradition, which was, as stated above, opposed to Soviet popular poetry. These achievements can be summed up as meditation combined with analysis of heterogeneous phenomena, as opposed to the simplistic poster aesthetics of the official Soviet poetry. This older tradition was also characterized by unexpected plot twists which gave way to the final, most important questions of life, as opposed to the moralism and requisite atheism of Soviet poetry. This concluding statement, or *pointe*, presumably further explains why the named women poets did not write sonnets: poets such as Shvarts and Sedakova preferred an initial *pointe*, at the poem's first line or lines. An example of a sonnet with a concluding *pointe* is the 'Sentiabr'skii sonet' ('September Sonnet') by Alexander Mironov (1974):

> There's a draft inside me
> September with a ripe apple in the palms,
> and time bears fruit as a fool,
> and everyone will speak and touch me.
>
> After eating tea, I go to watch
> like, having dreamed of a samovar,
> overseas creatures are pacing,
> everything is new to them, as to an idiot named death.
>
> I'm going to myself, gnawing harsh apples,
> but the good God is packing the cloud,
> and the grey rain is slightly mad,
>
> but it's good that I understood today,
> how to do without the grace of the Lord
> and run away from the evil call.

At the same time, conceptualists began to write sonnets. In one of the early sonnets by Dmitry Alexandrovich Prigov, written in 1963, 'Vsia mestnost' slovno chudilas' v dymu' ('The whole area seemed to be in smoke…'), the simple plot of a meeting with a stray dog in the then new districts of Moscow allows one to deconstruct the epithet in traditional Russian poetry. Under the influence of the Greek language and Church Slavonic liturgy, cumbersome, complex epithets increasingly appeared in Russian-language literature (e.g. in Chekhov's short story 'Easter Eve', 1886). It is difficult to say whether these came from Church tradition or were invented by modern poets. But Prigov constructed a *pastiche* from these sublime epithets, describing the unfavourable scene of his poem. Combining everyday language and ways of understanding things with the sonnet form as a means of telling an overarching story of experiences and changes, he observes the composition and themes of Petrarch's sonnets here, turning the classic form into an empty container through which to narrate ordinary life.

The outcome of Viktor Krivulin's experiments with the sonnet was 'Sonet s obratnoi perspektivoi' ('Sonnet with Reverse Perspective', 2000):

> Aivazovsky before the sea of covetousness
> with brushes of different thickness
> and wool

P. Filonov from *The Youth Union*
at the feast of the fathers an official guest
but no space without a device

his Malevich on the table of Saint Kazimir
with a howl-creak on the chains, Kandinsky crawled
a new chandelier rose
in the drum of the old Byzantine church

and of course we are without a name without a kind
unknown whether I am or not
it sees from the crowd at the entrance
out of lack of existence

The poem depicts the movement from realistic painting (that of the Russian–Armenian marine painter Ivan Aivazovsky, whose work is here compared with the social paintings of the Russian *Itinerants* [Russian: *Peredvizhniki*]) to the avant-garde of Malevich and Kandinsky as a reverse perspective; a movement from modernity to medieval symbolism and folk mythological ideas. The artist must return to archaic impersonality in order to create a complex composition, working not with images, but with light, form and colours. This corresponds to the ideas of Pavel Florensky's article 'Reverse Perspective', which sees in the plane perspective of the medieval icon the premodern state of society that seems to Florensky more harmonious than the modern one, and takes into account the experiments of the avant-garde with space. The sonnet encrypts Pavel Filonov's painting *Feast of Kings* (1913), depicting the afterlife feast of chthonic kings as a demand for the death of representative art in favour of the avant-garde. Thus, the sonnet describes the disintegration of the institutions of modern art, which do not know how to work with the fact of death, and the assertion of the new church religious art as a communication of existential experience.

For poets of the *Sots-Art* Moscow underground, such as Genrikh Sapgir, the sonnet became a means of countercultural expression, undermining culture from within. The sonnet form briefly represented the historical high culture, while experimentation with it showed the crisis and non-modernity of this culture. So, Sapgir's 'New Year's Sonnet' is composed of just fourteen dashes, while another sonnet, 'Sonnet-paragraph', is a report by a Soviet bureaucrat broken into lines, which is necessarily formal and boring. Sapgir also wrote two parodies, 'Sonnets in Petrarch's Mood', where the style of Petrarch's sublime contrasts and antinomies is brought to the point of absurdity. Especially noteworthy is Alexander Eremenko's 'Non-Crown of Sonnets', satirical poems that combine childhood impressions and standard childhood experiences with the reproduction of marginal registers of speech (the speech of the lower urban strata – criminals, soldiers, sailors, prison wardens – but also of kindergarten teachers and school teachers, who in the spirit of Foucault's thought are considered kinds of warden), creating a general effect of artificiality and contravening any regular poetic form.

In general, the conceptualists turned out to be leaders in writing sonnets, publishing books including *Sonnets on Shirts* (1978, published in Samizdat and in Paris) by Sapgir (and translated into English by Dmitri Manin in this volume) and *Twenty Sonnets to Sasha Zapoyeva* (1995) by Timur Kibirov. The latter contains sentimental observations of the birth and growth of a daughter, representing direct experience independent of both cultural patterns and countercultural strategies. One product of the *Sots-Art* tradition today is *500 Sonnets to Leroy Merlin* (2019) by Vadim Mesiats, in which the sonnet form and the number 500 are not in fact observed (even the title parodies the German Nazi-era song 'Lili Marlene', translated into Russian by Brodsky, while 'Leroy Merlin' is a French home decoration retailer): many regular poetic traditions are thus declared optional. Sometimes today's sonnets express private and cultural nostalgia, again as optional, not standardized, feelings. For example, Danila Davydov (who claims to be the spiritual heir of Sapgir), Andrey Polonsky, Anastasia Romanova and Alexei Yakovlev published the book *Crimean Sonnets* (2014), which reflected impressions of the free life of Crimea a year before the Russian annexation, where the traditions of hippies and other subcultural groups were still preserved. We can read these examples as a negotiation of the boundaries of creativity and of the legacies of creative traditions and rules through the form of the sonnet.

Translation as the study of love narratives

Although Russian women poets have tended to eschew the sonnet, Olga Sedakova has written what readers have found to be exemplary translations of the sonnets of Petrarch and Rilke. In her translation of 'Delfica' (1854) by Gérard de Nerval,[4] we can observe clear features of Nerval's semiotic perception. So, '*Cette chanson d'amour qui toujours recommence*' (line 4) is translated as 'Tu pesniu, chto liubov' nachnet neschetnyi raz' ('That song that love will begin countless times'). This accurate translation contains a subtle bias, however. Nerval's version gives the sense of a song that is always renewed, sung by any lover. In Sedakova's version love appears a fatal force that can dispose of any number of listeners. The Romantic idea of elective affinities is replaced here by the idea of contemplation and the religious perception of time. In her translation, Sedakova incorporates Virgil's *Fourth Eclogue*, translating the return of *l'ordre des anciens jours*, the *novus ordo saeclorum* (Latin: 'new order of ages') in Virgil, as a 'turn of the centuries' and 'holy times', remaking Nerval's nostalgic love of ancient Greece as a religious sentiment, understood through reference to ancient Rome.[5]

It is worth analyzing in detail the technique of Sedakova's translation of the *Canzoniere*, to examine how her understanding of Petrarch both echoes and negotiates with the poetics of Pushkin. Sonnet 62 exemplifies a characteristic statement by Petrarch, who was constantly looking back and realizing the whole experience of love as captivity, as oppression. A poet can contemplate different time intervals, and therefore experiences of different duration, but in comparison with the light of God, these all have no value and turn out to be painful – instances of unjustified languor. Sedakova characterized this Petrarchan mood as *amechania* (stupor or helplessness), taking this Greek term from philosophical works by Bibikhin and contrasting it with Dante's energy in his adventures across three worlds:

> Life with Laura in the soul is a *tetanus*, in which an enchanted person, captured by *amechania*, sees especially clearly how *il tempo fugge*, time flies. Or it is moving immobility, wandering (*il mio vaneggiar*), walking in a circle (366 parts of *Canzoniere* seem to inscribe 21 years of service to Laura in the rotation of one leap year). (Sedakova 1995)

A number of images appear in the translation which shift the images of Petrarch's original sonnet. First of all, the Petrarchan image of nights 'spent on pompous speeches' (*notti vaneggiando spese*) turns into the image of a candle: instead of writing letters or dreamy reflections, we are presented with this candle as a general symbol of a burnt life. Such a transition from a night vigil to its atmospheric conditions corresponds to Pushkin's poem 'Night' (Moi golos dlia tebia i laskovyi i stroinyi, 'My voice is both gentle and languid for you'), in which the beloved is reading the poet's letter and verses and a lonely candle in the longing poet's room merges with the delight of his reader's loving eyes.

In Pushkin, the alluring flame turns out to be part of the general theme of female infidelity, while in Sedavoka's Petrarch it is a symbol of *amechania*: the candle burns out, and does not flash. There are no insatiable groans in the Petrarch sonnet; it speaks of 'a desire ignited in the heart' (*desio ch'al cor s'accese*). Likewise, the broken snare, a somewhat grotesque image conveying the 'stretched nets' (*le reti indarno tese*) of Petrarch, also resembles Pushkin's images. His early poem 'I breathe sweet baby hope' (1823) states 'I would crush life, an ugly idol' – you cannot escape captivity, but can only break the conditions of captivity themselves.

It is emphasized in the translation that Petrarch is oppressed not by his thoughts (which could be understood in a Romantic mood), but by love as such. But the ending, which mentions a book in translation (the 'good book' – of course, the Book of Life (*Rev.* 20:12)), does not correspond to Petrarch's *miglior luogo* ('better place'), which denotes meditation before the Cross, but does fully correspond to the image of the book in Pushkin's *The Wanderer* (1835, a lyrical response to *Pilgrim's Progress* by John Bunyan), where the only way to escape from the profane world is involved reading. For Pushkin, the situation of love turns out to be inescapable, and the light of reason – for example, in the poem 'From Pindemonti' – is identified with the search for wonderful impressions in this life. Likewise, in Sedakova's translation, Petrarch is immersed in reflections on this present life and not on the future, as in the original text, but this life also requires an excess of divine light, otherwise the poetic speech of the subject remains confused. It turns out in translation that love for God can differ from love for a woman only in the intensity of mercy and the power of theophany, and not in the peculiarities of thinking, as in the original.

Sonnet 189 tells a story about the experiences of a lover, where Love (*Amore* is masculine in Italian, but feminine in Russian: *Ljubov'*) turns out to be 'lord and enemy' (*siede 'l signore, anzi' l nimico mio*). In this case, bodily life is compared with a ship, and emotional life with a storm. The metaphor has since become a tired trope, but Petrarch invented this image of torn ropes.

The phrase 'amusing himself with death and a storm on the way' in translation (for *che la tempesta e 'l fin par ch'abbi a scherno*) resembles the stormy imagery of subsequent Romantic poetry more than it does that of Petrarch, for whom romantic thoughts are so lively and diverting that they do not apprehend the storm. Petrarch explores his own carelessness and regrets it, while Sedakova has in mind the perspective of Pushkin's Romantic 'To the Sea' (1824), where the sea has become an object of imagination in village life, and this imaginary is historically situated: excitement regarding the sea was identified by Pushkin with Napoleon's old age, which is imagined through the image of Napoleon looking at the sea.

This corresponds to the concept of love as transitioning between the imaginary and the real in all of Pushkin's love lyrics. Where in Petrarch's work to love is to be blinded and bewitched, Pushkin sometimes admits to being blind, but never to being bewitched, and Sedakova similarly replaces 'charms' with 'amusement'. Therefore, if Petrarch considers the cause of amatory troubles to be *error con ignorantia* ('error paired with ignorance' – in other words, ignorance of the consequences of falling in love), then in translation the ship is crushed first by madness, and afterwards by a storm. In the original it is not foolishness that brings the ship into the storm as much as the storm itself, but this is more complicated in the translation: here, the foolishness is what breaks the ship no less than the storm. Sedakova replaces Petrarch's fatalism with a theological understanding of foolishness and ignorance as a sin. Her emphasis on reality links medieval theology and Pushkin's imagination to restore the consistency of Petrarch's imagery.

The next sonnet, Sonnet 190, is a description of an (imaginary) encounter with a sacred animal, *Una candida cerva sopra l'erba*, which immediately introduces love into the context of mythologizing descriptions. In fact, the poem speaks of a meeting with the visualization of one's own love, pure, impetuous and unattainable, but this meeting turns out to be not desirable, but terrible: the doe belongs to its Lord, Love, which has power over Petrarch's lyrical speaker. Therefore, if we speak in the language of psychoanalysis, the lyric narrator sees in this doe a visualized projection of himself and his attitude to Love, which thereby awakens in him a forever unquenchable desire that exhausts him. Sedakova's use of 'meekness' (*krotosti*) and 'pride' (*gordyni*) in the translation, instead of Petrarch's 'sweetly arrogant look' (*vista si dolce superba*), to describe this doe immediately resembles Pushkin's moral epithets about art. The added words 'alive' (*zhivoy*) and 'sleepy' (*sonnoy*) reassemble Petrarch's conventional image as an allegory of *amechania*, connecting the story of the doe to the enchanted gardens of classical mythology and their fantastic Renaissance variations: Circea or Armida.

In the translation, the image of a 'mirror of the living' (*zerkalo zhivovo*) appears, which is frequent in the original lyrics of Sedakova herself, while Petrarch simply says that Laura alone is a light and a view (*lume et speglio*) for him – that is, that it is only gratifying to look at her. Of course, superficially, this means that Laura is understood as a mirror of the proud Petrarch, who wanted to be crowned with a laurel of poetic fame thanks to his love lyrics. But in fact, the appearance of such epithets as 'sparkling' in Sedakova's translation, and the general maritime theme, refers to Pushkin's tales, primarily to the 'Tale of Tsar Saltan' (1831), written almost immediately after Pushkin's marriage. The story describes the kingdom of Guidon, where everything sparkles and boats fly easily across the sea when the wind urges. In Sedakova's translation, instead of 'waiting for good fresh news' (*d'aspettato ben fresche novelle*), we read '*otradnoi vest'iu, izdali zovushchei*' ('for good news, calling from afar') – with the addition of distance suggesting a fantastic or religious call. The fairy tale style consists of a plot destroyed by rhetoric, the plot of life as a test. Therefore, Sedakova returns to Petrarch's sonnets their integrity, broken by their own content.

This is how the translated sonnet achieves what Avtonomova and Gasparov demanded – historical fidelity – through taking into account medieval or later ideas key for translating poetic imagery without adding romantic ideology and its verbal expressions (the Russian idiom 'inertia of style', *inertsia stilia*, fits here). But the means of this achievement were, for example, Pushkin's Romanticism, which expressed admiration for Petrarch's experience, and medieval theology, which condemned *amechania* as *acedia* (torpor), from which Petrarch, as a critic of scholasticism, departed.

Conclusion

In the USSR, translation of older European literature was often understood by leading cultural theorists of the late Soviet era, such as Averintsev and Gasparov, as a way to study and understand the values of a foreign culture, such as love and poetic skill. It turned out that in older European cultures, these concepts functioned differently to how they did in the modern era and so, like literary criticism, sonnet translation was used to ascertain that emotions worked differently centuries ago. Simultaneously, the literature of Samizdat turned to those emotions that were undesirable in Soviet official culture, such as religiosity and pessimism. This cultural movement, for example, allowed Bibikhin to discover *amechania* as the basic emotion of Petrarch's lyrics, which had been considered optimistic by official Soviet critics. The next step was taken by Olga Sedakova, a practitioner of sonnet translation, who reconstructed Petrarch as a Christian poet, pointing not only to his despair but also to his desire for salvation as an effect of the sonnet form.

Thus, the Symbolists understood the sonnet as a means of creative inspiration, legitimizing the erotic and allowing experiments in the emotions of love. These concerns had been weakened in Soviet poetry – Marshak, in his translation of Shakespeare's sonnets, conveyed only the 'high' and decent sides of love. Avtonomova and Gasparov opposed this simplistic Romanticism to the allegorical content of sonnets from Petrarch to Shakespeare, pointing out that bold allegories could well build a life. Symbolist life-creation (life as work of art) returned to a new level, both in Samizdat poetry and in translation practices. At the same time, the desire to understand the emotions of a foreign culture made it possible to move away from neo-Romanticism and accept the Christian programme of salvation, which was fundamental for Petrarch.

Notes

1 All translations from Russian are mine.
2 Averintsev also developed the idea of strict rationality of scholasticism as deductive and performative metaphysics, inspiring for art, drawing on Auerbach and Curtius to develop the concept of the unity of Western culture in his seminal 1971 article 'Greek Literature and Near Eastern Writing' (p. 50). For the first time since Lev Shestov, he contrasted the intellectual principles of ancient Greek classics with those of the Hebrew Bible as expressed in the core structure of the texts, rather than in particular ideas. Comparing the aesthetic autonomy of Western *literature* and the practical goals of biblical *wisdom*, Averintsev pointed to the same example with which Avtonomova and Gasparov had started their analysis.
3 See the reproduction of the manuscript here: https://arzamas.academy/micro/visual/15, and typescript here: http://ruthenia.ru/60s/aronzon/sonet.htm. Accessed 27 August 2020.
4 Sedakova's poems and translations can be accessed on her official website: www.olgasedakova.com. Accessed 24 August 2022.
5 Another translation of this sonnet was proposed by Vadim Kozovoy (1937–99) (p. 38), a Russian–French poet who was the son-in-law of Pasternak's mistress Olga Ivinskaya and a pupil of Henri Michaux. Kozovoy proceeded from the generally Symbolist idea of a parallel between the impressions formed by nature and art. The music for Daphne (personification of Petrarch's *Laurus-Laura* and spring), *ancienne romance*, is therefore named in translation 'love romance', but the Russian word romance (*romans*) means not the song in general, but a particular genre close to love stories with simple expressions and 'Gipsy' incendiary rhythms (Russian: *tsygantschyna*, 'Gipsy Wave'). This is quite in the spirit of Symbolism – the name of a particular genre grows to designate an artistic principle – and it was intended as a homage to Petrarch. If Sedakova's translation is theological, Kozovoy's translation is melodramatic: the lonely tear of the translation is more philistine than the original *tu pleures toujours*, while the 'sadness of the gods', absent in the original, is more novelistic than it is typical of ancient Greek or Nervalian phrasing. These and other decisions say a lot more about the poetics of Kozovoy himself than about those of Petrarch or Nerval.

Works cited

Auerbach, Erich *Mimesis: The Representation of Reality in Western Literature*. Princeton, 2013.
Averintsev, Sergei 'Grecheskaya literatura i blizhnevostochnaya slovesnost': Dva tvorcheskikh printsipa'. Voprosy literatury, vol. 8, 1971, pp. 40–68. (in Russian)

Avtonomova, Natalia and Mikhail Gasparov. 'Sonety Shekspira – Perevody Marshaka'. [Shakespeare's Sonnets in Marshak's Translations]. *Voprosy Literatury*, vol. 2, 1969, 100–112. (in Russian)

Barthes, Roland. *Fragments d'un discours amoureux*. Paris: Éditions du Seuil, 1977.

Bibikhin, Vladimir. 'Slovo Petrarki' [Petrarch's Publicity]. *Petrarch's Aesthetical Mixture*. Moscow: Iskusstvo Publishing, 1982, pp. 7–37. (in Russian)

Bibikhin, Vladimir. Uznaj sebja [To the Self-knowledge]. Nauka Publ, St. Petersburg, 1998. E-source. http://www.bibikhin.ru/uznay_sebya (official site). Accessed 31 August 2020. (in Russian)

Borisovsky, Vadim. *Zerkal volshebnyj krug* [Magic Cycle of Mirrors: A Collection of Poetry]. Reka Vremen Publ., 2012. (in Russian)

Chukovsky, Korney. 'Marshak'. *Ya dumal, chustvoval, ya zhil* [My Thoughts, Senses, and Life]. Sovetsky Pisatel Publ., 1971, pp. 97–116. (in Russian)

Chukovsky, Korney. 'V zaschitu Shelli' [In defence of Shelley]. *Vesy*, vol. 3, 1907, pp. 61–68. (in Russian)

Curtius, Ernst Robert. *European Literature and the Latin Middle Ages*. Princeton, 1953.

Efros, Abram. *Jeroticheskie sonety* [Erotic Sonnets]. Moscow 7th typography, 1922. (in Russian)

Florensky, Pavel. 'Reverse Perspective' (1919–1922). *Beyond Vision: Essays on the Perception of Art*. Reaction Books, 2002, pp. 197–272.

Grossman, Leonid. *Plejada* [Pleias: A poetry]. Odessa, 1919. (in Russian)

Kozovoy, Vadim. trans., notes. *Frantsuzkaya Poesia* [French Poetry: An Anthology in Translation]. Dom Intellectualnoj Knigi Publ, 2001. (in Russian)

Losev, Aleksei Fyodorovich. *The Dialectics of Myth*. Routledge, 2003.

Nabokov, Vladimir. 'O vosstavshikh angelakh'. *Rul'* (newspaper), 15 October 1930. (in Russian)

Ober, Kenneth H. and W. U. Ober. '"Scorn Not the Sonnet": Pushkin and Wordsworth'. *The Wordsworth Circle*, vol. 34, no. 2, 2003, pp. 119–126.

Sapgir, Genrikh and O. Sedakova. *Beatrice, Laura, Lara: Proshanie s provodnitsei*. [Speech at the International Symposium 'Sophia: Russian Idea, Idea of Europe' (Rome, 1995).] E-source: http://www.olgasedakova.com/Poetica/231 (official site). Accessed 27 August 2020. (in Russian)

Sedakova, Olga. Facebook post, 29 December 2019. https://www.facebook.com/osedakova/posts/2267105336655671. Accessed 31 August 2020. (in Russian)

Sedakova, Olga. 'Gerard de Nerval, Delfica'. https://www.olgasedakova.com/113

Shestov, Lev. *Athens and Jerusalem*. Ohio University Press, 1966.

Bibliography

General bibliography

Aroui, Jean-Louis and Andy Arleo, eds. 'Metrical Structure of the European Sonnet'. *Towards a Typology of Poetic Forms. From Language to Metrics and Beyond*. Benjamins, 2009, pp. 385–401.

Backès, Jean-Louis. 'Poétique de la traduction'. *Revue d'Histoire Littéraire de la France*, vol. 97, no. 3, May–June 1997, pp. 437–447.

Berman, Antoine. *Pour une critique des traductions: John Donne*. Gallimard, 1995.

Birkan-Berz, Carole, Guillaume Coatalen and Thomas Vuong, eds. *Translating Petrarch's Poetry: L'Aura Del Petrarca from the Quattrocento to the 21st Century*. NED-New edition, vol. 8. Modern Humanities Research Association, 2020. https://doi.org/10.2307/j.ctv16kkxw0

Braden, Gordon, Robert Cummings and Stuart Gillespie, eds. *The Oxford History of Literary Translation in English, Volume 2: 1550–1660*. Oxford University Press, 2010.

Burt, Stephanie and David Mikics. *The Art of the Sonnet*. Harvard University Press, 2010.

Caplan, David. *Questions of Possibility: Contemporary Poetry and Poetic Form*. Oxford University Press, 2005.

Caplan, David. 'What Was New Formalism?'. *A Companion to Poetic Genre*, edited by Erik Martiny. Wiley-Blackwell, 2011, pp. 18–33.

Chivers, Tom, ed. *Adventures in Form: A Compendium of Poetic Forms, Rules and Constraints*. Penned in the Margins, 2012.

Cohen, Walter. *A History of European Literature: The West and the World from Antiquity to the Present*. Oxford University Press, 2017.

Cousins, A. D. and Peter Howarth, eds. *The Cambridge Companion to the Sonnet*. Cambridge University Press, 2011.

Degott, Bertrand and Pierre Garrigues, eds. *Le Sonnet au risque du sonnet*. L'Harmattan, 2006, pp. 263–278.

DellaNeva, JoAnn. *Unlikely Exemplars: Reading and Imitating beyond the Italian Canon in French Renaissance Poetry*. University of Delaware Press, 2009.

Distiller, Natasha. *Desire and Gender in the Sonnet Tradition*. Palgrave Macmillan UK, 2008.

Dubrow, Heather. *Echoes of Desire: English Petrarchism and Its Counterdiscourses*. Cornell University Press, 1995.

Duché, Véronique, ed. *Histoire des traductions en langue française, sous la direction de Jean-Yves Masson et Yves Chevrel, XV et XVIème siècles, 1470–1610*. Verdier, 2015.

Etkind, Efim. *Un art en crise: essai de poétique sur la traduction poétique*. L'Âge d'homme, 1982.

Felch, Susan M. "'Halff a Scrypture Woman": Heteroglossia and Female Authorial Agency in Prayers by Lady Elizabeth Tyrwhit, Anne Lock, and Anne Wheathill'. *English Women, Religion, and Textual Production, 1500–1625*, edited by Micheline White. Ashgate, 2011, pp. 147–166

Felch, Susan M. 'The Public Life of Anne Vaughan Lock: Her Reception in England and Scotland'. *Early Modern Women and Transnational Communities of Letters*, edited by Julie D. Campbell and Anne R. Larsen. Ashgate Publishing, Ltd., 2009, pp. 137–158.

Folkart, Barbara. *Second Finding. A Poetics of Translation*. University of Ottawa Press, 2007.

France, Peter. *The Oxford Guide to Literature in English Translation*. Oxford University Press, 2000.

France, Peter, ed. *The Oxford History of Literary Translation in English*. Oxford University Press, 2008.

Francisci, Enza De and Chris Stamatakis. *Shakespeare, Italy, and Transnational Exchange: Early Modern to Present*. Routledge, 2017.

Gillespie, Stuart and David Hopkins. *The Oxford History of Literary Translation in English*. Oxford University Press, 2005.

Greene, Roland. *Post-Petrarchism: Origins and Innovations of the Western Lyric Sequence*. Princeton University Press, 1991.

Martiny, Erik, ed. *A Companion to Poetic Genre*. Wiley-Blackwell, 2011.

Métayer, Guillaume. *A Comme Babel: traduction, poétique*. Éditions La Rumeur libre, 2020.

Pujante, Angel-Luis and Ton Hoenselaars, eds. *Four Hundred Years of Shakespeare in Europe*. University of Delaware Press, 2003.

Ramazani, Jahan. *The Hybrid Muse: Postcolonial Poetry in English*. University of Chicago Press, 2001.

Ramazani, Jahan. *Poetry in a Global Age*. University of Chicago Press, 2020.

Ramazani, Jahan. *A Transnational Poetics*. University of Chicago Press, 2009.

Regan, Stephen. *The Sonnet*. Oxford University Press, 2019.

Reynolds, Matthew. *The Poetry of Translation: From Chaucer & Petrarch to Homer & Logue*. Oxford University Press, 2011.

Robinson, Peter. *Poetry & Translation: The Art of the Impossible*. Liverpool University Press, 2010.

Spiller, Michael R. G. *The Development of the Sonnet: An Introduction*. Routledge, 1992.

Ughetto, André. *Le Sonnet: une forme européenne de poésie: étude, suivie d'un choix de sonnets italiens, espagnols, anglais, allemands, russes et français*. Ellipses, 2005.

Venuti, Laurence. *The Translator's Invisibility: A History of Translation*. Routledge, 2008.

Sonnet anthologies

Bromwich, David. *American Sonnets: An Anthology*. Library of America, 2007. Print. American Poets Project; 25.
Crawforth, Hannah and Elizabeth Scott-Baumann, eds. *On Shakespeare's Sonnets: A Poets' Celebration*. Bloomsbury, 2016.
Hilson, Jeff. *The Reality Street Book of Sonnets*. Reality Street, 2008.
Boland, Eavan and Edward Hirsch, eds. *The Making of a Sonnet: A Norton Anthology*. First edition. W. W. Norton & Company, 2008.
Howard, Henry, Earl of Surrey, Sir Thomas Wyatt, the Elder, Nicholas Grimald, and Uncertain Authors. *Tottel's Miscellany: Songes and Sonettes*. London, 1557.
Levin, Phillis. *The Penguin Book of the Sonnet: 500 Years of a Classic Tradition in English*. Penguin, 2001.
Lofft, Capel. *Laura: Or, An Anthology of Sonnets, (on the Petrarcan Model,) and Elegiac Quatuorzains: English, Italian, Spanish, Portuguese, French, and German; Original and Translated; Great Part Never before Published*. Printed by R. Taylor for B. and R. Crosby, 1813–14, 1813. https://babel.hathitrust.org/cgi/pt?id=ucl.b3137335&view=1up&seq=7
Malech, Dora and Laura T. Smith, eds. *Sonnets from the American: An Anthology of Poems and Essays*. University of Iowa Press, forthcoming.
Nardone, Jean-Luc. *Pétrarque et la poésie européenne: Anthologie pétrarquiste bilingue*. Jérôme Millon, 2021.
Roche, Thomas. *Petrarch in English*. Penguin, 2005.
Roubaud, Jacques. *Quasi-Cristaux*. Yves Lambert & Martine Aboucaya, 2013.
Russell, Matthew. *Sonnets on the Sonnet: An Anthology*. London, 1898.
Smith, Christopher. *Thrice Fourteen: An Anthology of Sonnets Mainly in French*. Solen, 1994.
Tomlinson, Charles. *The Sonnet; Its Origin, Structure, and Place in Poetry. With Original Translations from the Sonnets of Dante, Petrarch, Etc., and Remarks on the Art of Translating*. J. Murray, 1874.

Early modern studies

Alduy, Cécile. *Politique des 'Amours': Poétique et genèse d'un genre français nouveau (1544–1560)*. Droz, 2007.
Alexander, Gavin. *Writing after Sidney: The Literary Response to Sir Philip Sidney, 1586–1640*. Clarendon Press, 2006.
Balsamo, Jean. *Les Poètes français de la Renaissance et Pétrarque*. Droz, 2004.
Barker, S. K. and Brenda M. Hosington, eds. *Renaissance Cultural Crossroads: Translation, Print and Culture in Britain, 1473–1640*. Brill, 2013.
Bates, Catherine. *Masculinity, Gender and Identity in the English Renaissance Lyric*. Cambridge University Press, 2007.

Bates, Catherine. *The Rhetoric of Courtship in Elizabethan Language and Literature*. Cambridge University Press, 1992.

Belle, Marie-Alice. 'Elizabethan Defences of Translation, from Rhetoric to Poetics: Harington's and Chapman's "Brief Apologies"'. *Elizabethan Translation and Literary Culture*, edited by Gabriela Schmidt. De Gruyter, 2013, pp. 43–80.

Belle, Marie-Alice and Brenda Hosington. *Thresholds of Translation: Paratexts, Print, and Cultural Exchange in Early Modern Britain (1473-1660)*. Palgrave Macmillan, 2018.

Berensmeyer, Ingo, ed. *Handbook of English Renaissance Literature*. De Gruyter, 2019.

Budini, Paolo. 'Le Sonnet italien de Louise Labé'. *Francofonia*, vol. 20, 1991. Spring, pp. 47–59.

Burrow, Colin. *Imitating Authors: Plato to Futurity*. Oxford University Press, 2019.

Burton, Ben and Elizabeth Scott-Baumann. *The Work of Form: Poetics and Materiality in Early Modern Culture*. Oxford University Press, 2014.

Coatalen, Guillaume. 'An English Translation of Desportes' Christian Sonnets Presented to John Scudamour by Edward Ski[...]'. *The Review of English Studies*, vol. 65, no. 271, Oxford University Press, 2014, pp. 619–646.

Coatalen, Guillaume. 'Unpublished Elizabethan Sonnets in a Legal Manuscript from the Cambridge University Library'. *Review of English Studies: The Leading Journal of English Literature and the English Language*, vol. 54, no. 217, 2003, pp. 552–565.

Coldiron, A. E. B. 'How Spenser Excavates Du Bellay's Antiquitez: Or, the Role of the Poet, Lyric Historiography, and the English Sonnet'. *Journal of English and Germanic Philology*, vol. 101, no. 1, 2002, pp. 41–67.

Coles, Kimberly Anne. *Religion, Reform, and Women's Writing in Early Modern England*. Cambridge University Press, 2008.

Colie, Rosalie L. *The Resources of Kind: Genre-Theory in the Renaissance*. University of California Press, 1973.

Dasenbrock, Reed Way. *Imitating the Italians: Wyatt, Spenser, Synge, Pound, Joyce*. Johns Hopkins University Press, 1991.

Dasenbrock, Reed Way. 'The Petrarchan Context of Spenser's Amoretti'. *PMLA*, vol. 100, no. 1, January 1985, pp. 38–50.

Dasenbrock, Reed Way. 'Wyatt's Transformation of Petrarch'. *Comparative Literature*, vol. 40, no. 2, Duke University Press, University of Oregon, 1988, pp. 122–133.

Duncan-Jones, Katherine. 'Bess Carey's Petrarch: Newly Discovered Elizabethan Sonnets'. *Review of English Studies: A Quarterly Journal of English Literature and the English Language*, vol. 50, no. 199, 1999, pp. 304–319.

Engelking, Tama Lea. 'Genre and the Mark of Gender: Renée Vivien's "Sonnet féminin"'. *Modern Language Studies*, vol. 23, no. 4, Fall 1993, pp. 79–92.

Eschrich, Gabriella Scarlatta. 'Reading Philippe Desportes In Le Rencontre Des Muses De France Et D'italie'. *Renaissance Studies: Journal of the Society for Renaissance Studies*, vol. 26, no. 3, 2012, pp. 385-398.

Ferry, Anne. *The 'Inward' Language: Sonnets of Wyatt, Sidney, Shakespeare, Donne*. University of Chicago Press, 1983.

Fuzier, Jean. 'Spenser, traducteur du Songe de du Bellay: regards sur la problématique de la traduction poétique au XVIe siècle'. *Bulletin de l'Association d'étude sur l'humanisme, la réforme et la renaissance*, n°15, 1982. Les rapports entre les langues au XVIème siècle. *Actes du colloque de Sommières*, 14-17 septembre 1981. Tome I. pp. 96-101.

Gettzler, Pierre et Jacques Roubaud. *Le sonnet en France des origines à 1630: matériaux pour une base de données du sonnet français*. Inalco, 1999.

Glaser, Joe. 'Wyatt, Petrarch, and the Uses of Mistranslation'. *College Literature*, vol. 11, no. 3, Johns Hopkins University Press, 1984, pp. 214-222.

Greene, Thomas L. *The Light in Troy: Imitation and Discovery in Renaissance Poetry*. Yale University Press, 1982.

Hadfield, Andrew. 'Edmund Spenser's Translations of Du Bellay in Jan Van Der Noot's A Theatre For Voluptuous Worldlings'. *Tudor Translation*. Palgrave Macmillan, 2011, pp. 143-160.

Haldane, Michael G. 'The Open Valley: Translation, Transmission and Transfiguration of the Sonnet in Sixteenth-Century England, and the Triumph of Form'. *Dissertation Abstracts International*, Section C: Worldwide 66.3, 2005, p. 564.

Holton, Amanda. 'An Obscured Tradition: The Sonnet and Its Fourteen-Line Predecessors'. *The Review of English Studies*, vol. 62, no. 255, 2011, pp. 373-392.

Lewalski, Barbara. *Protestant Poetics and the Seventeenth-Century Religious Lyric*. Princeton University Press, 1979.

Melehy, Hassan. *The Poetics of Literary Transfer in Early Modern France and England*. Ashgate, 2010.

Morini, Massimiliano. *Tudor Translation in Theory and Practice*. Ashgate Pub, 2006.

Prescott, Anne Lake. 'King David as a "Right Poet": Sidney and the Psalmist'. *English Literary Renaissance*, vol. 19, no. 2, 1989, pp. 131-151.

Prescott, Anne Lake. 'The Reputation of Clément Marot in Renaissance England'. *Studies in the Renaissance*, vol. 18, 1971, pp. 173-202.

Prescott, Anne Lake. 'Sibling Harps: The Sidneys and the Chérons Translate the Psalms'. *Psalms in the Early Modern World*, edited by Linda Phyllis Austern, Kari Boyd McBride and David L. Orvis. Routledge, 2011, pp. 235-256.

Prescott, Anne Lake. 'Two Annes, Two Davids'. *Tradition, Heterodoxy and Religious Culture*, edited by Chanita Goodblatt and Howard Kreisel. Ben Guiron University of the Negev Press, 2007, pp. 311-330.

Reid, Joshua S. 'The Enchantments of Circe: Translation Studies and the English Renaissance'. *The Spenser Review*, vol. 44, no. 1, 2014.

Serjeantson, Deirdre. 'Anne Lock's Anonymous Friend: "A Meditation of a Penitent Sinner" and the Problem of Ascription'. *Enigma and Revelation in Renaissance Literature*, edited by Helen Cooney and Mark S. Sweetnam. Four Courts, 2012, pp. 51–68.

Serjeantson, Deirdre. 'The Book of Psalms and the Early Modern Sonnet'. *Renaissance Studies*, vol. 29, no. 4, 2015, pp. 632–649.

Roche, Thomas. *Petrarch and the English Sonnet Sequences*. AMS Press, 1989.

Roubaud, Jacques. *La Forme du sonnet français de Marot à Malherbe*. Publications Langues'O, 1990.

Spiller, Michael R. G. *Early Modern Sonneteers: From Wyatt to Milton*. Northcote House in association with the British Council, 2001.

Spiller, Michael R. G. 'A Literary "First": The Sonnet Sequence of Anne Locke (1560) an Appreciation of Anne Locke's Sonnet Sequence: A Meditation of a Penitent Sinner... with Locke's Epistle to the... Duchesse of Suffolke'. *Renaissance Studies*, vol. 11, no. 1, 1997, pp. 41–55.

Schurink, Fred. *Tudor Translation*. Edited by Fred Schurink. Palgrave Macmillan Ltd, 2012.

Stapleton, M. L. 'Spenser, The Antiquitez De Rome, and the Development of the English Sonnet Form'. *Comparative Literature Studies*, vol. 27, no. 4, 1990, pp. 259–274.

Steinberg, Justin. *Accounting for Dante: Urban Readers and Writers in Late Medieval Italy*. University of Notre Dame Press, 2007.

Stillman, Robert E. *Philip Sidney and the Poetics of Renaissance Cosmopolitanism*. Ashgate Publishing Company, 2008.

Verweij, Sebastiaan. *The Literary Culture of Early Modern Scotland: Manuscript Production and Transmission, 1560–1625*. Oxford University Press, 2016, pp. 78–79.

Vuillemin, Rémi, Laetitia Sansonetti and Enrica Zanin, eds. *The Early Modern English Sonnet*. Manchester University Press, 2020.

18th–19th century

Cohen, Ralph. 'The Return to the Ode'. *The Cambridge Companion to Eighteenth-Century Poetry*, edited by John Sitter. Cambridge University Press, 2001, pp. 203–224. Cambridge Companions to Literature.

Curran, Stuart. *Poetic Form and British Romanticism*. Oxford University Press, 1986.

Duff, David. *Romanticism and the Uses of Genre*. Oxford University Press, 2009.

Feldman, Paula R. and Daniel Robinson, eds. *A Century of Sonnets: The Romantic-Era Revival 1750–1850*. Oxford University Press, 1999.

Ferber, Michael. 'Sainte-Beuve's "Imitations" of Two Sonnets by Wordsworth'. *Wordsworth Circle*, vol. 38, no. 4, 2007, pp. 215–217.
Going, William T. 'John Addington Symonds and the Victorian Sonnet Sequence'. *Victorian Poetry*, vol. 8, no. 1, pp. 25–38.
Johnson, Anthony L. 'Formal Messages in Keats's Sonnets'. *The Challenge of Keats: Bicentenary Essays 1795–1995*, edited by Allan C. Christensen, Lilla Maria Crisafulli Jones, Giuseppe Galigani and Anthony L. Johnson. Rodopi, 2000.
Phelan, Joseph. *The Nineteenth-Century Sonnet*. Palgrave Macmillan, 2005.
Pollack-Pelzner, Daniel. 'Revisionary Company: Keats, Homer, and Dante in the Chapman Sonnet'. *Keats-Shelley Journal*, vol. 56, 2007, pp. 39–49.
Raymond, Mark. 'The Romantic Sonnet Revival: Opening the Sonnet's Crypt'. *Literature Compass*, vol. 4, no. 3, 2007, pp. 721–736.
Regan, Stephen. 'The Victorian Sonnet, from George Meredith to Gerard Manley Hopkins'. *Yearbook of English Studies*, vol. 36, no. 2, 2006, pp. 17–34.
Robinson, Daniel. 'Reviving the Sonnet: Women Romantic Poets and the Sonnet Claim'. *European Romantic Review*, vol. 6, 1995, pp. 98–127.
Robinson, Philip. 'Traduction ou Trahison de "Paul et Virginie"? L'exemple de Helen Maria Williams'. *Revue d'Histoire Littéraire de La France*, vol. 89, no. 5, 1989, pp. 843–855.
Van Remoortel, Marianne. *Lives of the Sonnet, 1787–1895: Genre, Gender and Criticism*. Ashgate, 2011.
Wagner, Jennifer Ann. *A Moment's Monument: Revisionary Poetics and the Nineteenth-Century English Sonnet*. Fairleigh Dickinson University Press, 1996.
Wolfson, Susan. *Formal Charges: The Shaping of Poetry in British Romanticism*. Stanford University Press, 1997.
Zuccato, Edoardo. *Petrarch in Romantic England*. Palgrave Macmillan UK, 2008.

Contemporary

Adames, John. 'The Frontiers of the Psyche and the Limits of Form in Auden's 'Quest' Sonnets'. *Modern Language Review*, vol. 92, 1997, pp. 573–580.
Anderson, David. 'A Language to Translate into: The Pre-Elizabethan Idiom of Pound's Later Cavalcanti Translations'. *Studies in Medievalism*, vol. 2, no. 1, Fall 1982, pp. 9–18.
Birkan-Berz, Carole. 'Mapping the Contemporary Sonnet in Mainstream and Linguistically Innovative Late 20th and Early 21st Century British Poetry'. *Études britanniques contemporaines*, vol. 46, 2013.
Edwards, Michael. 'Yves Bonnefoy et les "Sonnets" de Shakespeare'. *Littérature*, vol. 2, no. 150, June 2008, pp. 25–39.

Gottlieb, Sidney. 'Milton's "On the Late Massacre in Piemont" and Eisenstein's "Potemkin"'. *Milton Quarterly*, vol. 19, no. 2, 1985, pp. 38–42.

Guissin-Stubbs, Tara. *The Modern Irish Sonnet*. Palgrave Macmillan, 2020.

Hsiao, Irene. 'Early William Carlos Williams: "Bad Keats"?'. *Cambridge Quarterly*, vol. 37, 2008, pp. 195–223.

Huang-Tiller, Gillian C. 'The Power of the Meta-Genre: Cultural, Sexual, and Racial Politics of the American Modernist Sonnet'. Unpublished Ph.D. thesis, University of Notre Dame, 2000.

Müller, Timo. *The African American Sonnet: A Literary History*. University Press of Mississippi, 2018.

Robbins, Hollis. *Forms of Contention: Influence and the African American Sonnet Tradition*. University of Georgia Press, 2020.

Robert-Foley, Lily. *Experimental Translation: The Work of Translation in the Age of Algorithmic Production*. Goldsmiths, 2022. (forthcoming)

Scotto, Fabio. 'Yves Bonnefoy traducteur de Leopardi et de Pétrarque'. *Littérature*, vol. 150, no. 2, 2008, pp. 70–82.

Sheppard, Robert. *The Meaning of Form: Forms and Forming in Contemporary Innovative Poetry*. Springer International Publishing AG, 2016.

Skoulding, Zoë. 'Poetry in Expanded Translation'. *English: Journal of the English Association*, vol. 69, no. 267, 2020, pp. 305–309.

Skoulding, Zoe. 'Poetry in Expanded Translation'. *Poetry in Expanded Translation*, special issue of *English: Journal of the English Association*, vol. 69, no. 267, Winter 2020, pp. 305–309.

Vendler, Helen. *Our Secret Discipline: Yeats and Lyric Form*. Oxford University Press, 2007.

Weissmann, Dirk and Vincent Broqua, directors. *Sound /Writing: traduire-écrire entre le son et le sens. Homophonic translation – traducson – Oberflächenübersetzung*. Éditions des archives contemporaines, Coll. 'Multilinguisme, traduction, création', 2019.

Index

Adès, Timothy (translator) 218, 225
Alighieri, Dante (see Dante)
Alter, Robert (translator) 117
Aragon, Louis 7, 218–222, 288; 'Imité de Camoëns' 222
Aristotle 263
Aronzon, Leonid 317, 321; 'Empty Sonnet' 319–320; 'Two Identical Sonnets' 322–323
Atkins, Tim 4
Auden, Wystan Hugh 209–210, 215–216
Averintsev, Sergey 31, 330
Averly, François and George (d') 77–78

Bacon, Francis 53–54
Bacon, Philip 54
Baldassarre Olimpo degli Alessandri, Caio: *La Camilla* 55, 61
Baldensperger, Fernand 212
Balmont, Konstantin (translator) 316
Barnes, Barnabe 62
Barnstone, Willis (translator) 117–118, 122, 124–127
Barrows, Anita (translator) 117, 119, 127
Baudelaire, Charles 5 196–198, 316
Bellay, Joachim du (see Du Bellay)
Bellivier, André (translator) 116, 215
Bembo, Cardinal 71
Benjamin, Walter 108, 305
Berni, Francesco 42, 47
Berrigan, Ted 7, 166–168
Betz, Maurice (translator) 116
Beza, Theodore: 'Abraham sacrifiant' 64
Bhabha, Homi 302
Bibikhin, Vladimir 318, 322, 327, 330

Bible 63, 212, 232; Matthew 8 24, 62
Billias, Nancy (translator) 119–120, 123–127
Blanchard, Maurice 211–212
Blaser, Robin (translator) 107
Bocage, Manuel Maria Barbosa du 222–223
Bök, Christian 4
Bonnefoy, Yves 100
Bonney, Sean 5
Borges, Jorges Luis 117
Borisovsky, Vadim 318
Borkovec, Petr 202
Boscán, Juan 2, 53
Bourbaki, Nicolas 284, 286–287
Bourbon-Montpensier, Charlotte (de) 77
Breton, André: *Manifeste du surréalisme* 284, 286, 292
Breton, Nicholas: 'A Most Excellent Passion'; *The Phoenix Nest* 62
Brodsky, Joseph 202, 326; *Twenty Sonnets to Mary Stuart* 231, 319, 323
Browning, Elizabeth Barrett 7; *Sonnets from the Portuguese* 115, 144–146; 'Catarina to Camoens' 144; *The Poetical Works of Elizabeth B. Browning* 144
Burrows, Mark (translator) 117
Burt, Stephanie 167, 178, 189, 258
Burt, Stephen (see Stephanie)

Caeiro, Alberto (heteronym) 8
Camões, Luís de 2, 140–4; 'Alma minha gentil, que te partiste' 140–41; *The Lusiads* 141, 221–223

Campbell, Roy 8, 222–223
Campos, Álvaro de (heteronym) 8, 131, 133, 139–140, 142–143; 'Ha quanto tempo não escrevo um soneto' ('So long I haven't written a sonnet') 140; 'Meu coração, o almirante errado' ('My heart, the erroneous admiral') 140
Campos, Haroldo de 306
Carew, Thomas: 'The Spring' 61; 'Prayer to the Wind' 61
Carson, Ciaran 7, 193, 198
Cassou, Jean 8, 217–219, 221; 'Traduit de Hofmannsthal' 218
Cavalcanti, Guido 201
Chapman, George 6, 18, 91–94
Chekhov, Anton 202; *Easter Eve* 324
Chukovsky, Korney 229, 316
Clément, Nicolas 77–78
Cohn, Stephen (translator) 117, 119, 121, 125, 127
Coldiron, Anne 2, 35–36
Colonna, Vittoria 71
Cook, David (translator) 117, 119, 124, 127
Crucefix, Martyn (translator) 122–125

Daniel, Samuel 35, 41
Dante 92, 94, 99, 100, 178, 201, 232, 264, 318, 327; *De Vulgari Eloquentia* 243
Darmangeat, Pierre 220–221
Davydov, Danila (et al.): *Crimean Sonnets* 326
Denaisius, Peter 70, 71, 75, 78–79
Desnos, Robert 175, 221; 'Le Paysage' 186–187
Desportes, Philippe 2, 35, 45–47, 64
Dionísio, João 136
Dolfi, Anna 263
Donne, John 61, 249; 'A Valediction: Forbidding Mourning' 61

Drayton, Michael: *Endimion and Phœbe* 63
Drummond, William 53; *Poems* 61, 63
Dryden 113
Du Bartas 3, 19–20, 25–29, 53
Du Bellay, Joachim 2, 5, 17–33, 35–49, 64–65, 73–74, 271; *La Deffence, et illustration de la langue françoyse* 19, 24, 47; 'Le premier livre des antiquitez de Rome' 17, 35–37, 73; 'Les Regrets' 25, 35–38, 42; *L'Olive* 35, 38, 40, 44; 'Divins Esprits, dont la poudreuse cendre' 21
Ducellier, Claude (translator) 116
Duncan, Robert (translator) 107
Du Nesme, Jean 5, 19, 21, 25–27, 29; 'Le Miracle de la paix en France' 17, 20, 25; 'Mais quel autre Soleil nos campagnes decore' 28; 'Fille du Tout-puissant, alme, riche, feconde' 28
Duprat, Hippolyte 272–273
Dutilleux, Henri 219
d'Heere, Lucas 73

Eco, Umberto 306
Edwards, Michael 303
Efros, Abram 318
Eliot, T.S. 118, 316
Elizabeth I 26, 29–30, 78
Eremenko, Alexander: 'Non-Crown of Sonnets' 326
Etkind, Efim 3, 4, 9

Fabre d'Églantine, Philippe-François 264, 271
Fairfax, Edward: translation of Tasso 63
Farnaby, Thomas 54
Filonov, Pavel 325

Fischart, Johann 70–71, 75–76, 79; 'Solchs that er / weil er sich befahrt' 75–76
Florensky, Pavel (Paul) 325
Fowler, Alastair 30
Frederick II 243
Frederick IV (Elector Palatine) 78
Froe, Balthasar 73–75, 79; 'Zv zeitten wann Gott kompt zu vnserm lohne' 74

Garcia Lorca, Frederico 221
Garcilaso de la Vega 2, 220
Gardair, Jean-Michel 263
Gascoyne, David 213–214
Gasparov, Mikhail 315–317, 319, 330
Genette, Gérard 19, 284–286
Golding, Arthur 62–63
Goldoni, Carlo 264, 268–271, 276; *The Liar* 268
Góngora, Luis de 156, 162, 171, 220–221
Good, Graham (translator) 124, 125
Gorges, Sir Arthur 35, 38–39, 41
Gramont, Ferdinand de 263
Grossman, Leonid 318–319
Grossman, Vassily 318

Heaney, Seamus 7, 193, 197, 200–201
Herbert, George 55, 61–63; *The Temple* 55; 'The Search' 61
Hill, Geoffrey 1, 219, 215
Hilský, Martin 203–205
Hilson, Jeff 1, 4–5
Hofmannsthal, Hugo von 217–218
Holding, Aidan C. (translator) 119, 122, 124–125, 127
Holland, Hugh: *Pancharis* 54
Homer 18, 25, 53, 91–94, 109
Hopkins, Gerard Manley 7, 163–164, 231
Horace 37

Ip, Joshua 5, 8, 243–260; *Sonnets from the Singlish* 243; 'chope' 252–253; 'conversaytion' 254; 'entry' 246–248, 249; 'k ge zhi wang attends a poetry reading' 246; 'rag and bone' 253; 'the shitty carparking in orchard road' 248; 'we spoke' 257
Ivanov, Vyacheslav 321–322; 'We are two lighted trunks by a thunderstorm' 321

Jaccottet, Philippe 216
Jackendoff, Ray 308
Jacopone da Todi 264, 266
Jakobson, Roman 8, 306
James VI of Scotland 2, 71, 78
Jennings, Hubert D. 138, 145
Jobin, Bernhard 75
Jonson, Ben 54, 65; 'Ode on Himself' 54; *The New Inn* 54
Jouve, Pierre Jean (translator) 162, 163, 213–214

Keats, John 6, 89–104; 'On sitting down to read King Lear once again' 98, 99; 'If by dull rhymes our English must be chain'd' 89; 'On first looking into Chapman's Homer' 6, 90–94, 98, 99; 'To Homer' 93–94; 'This pleasant tale is like a little copse' 99; 'Translated from Ronsard' ('Nature ornant Cassandre') 95–98; 'As Hermes once took to his feathers light' 99–100
Kennedy, Nigel 301–313
Khlebnikov, Velimir 232
Kibirov, Timur: *Twenty Sonnets to Sasha Zapoyeva* 326
Kippenberg, Anton 116–117
Kochnitzky, Léon (Giraud d'Uccle) 210–212

Koh, Jee Leong 243–260; *Payday Loans* 248; 'April 1, Friday' 254; 'April 13, Wednesday' 249; 'April 14, Thursday' 248; 'April 16, Saturday' 249; 'April 19, Tuesday' 255; 'April 30, Saturday' 258
Kovozoy, Vadim 331n
Krivulin, Viktor 317; 'Elongated Sonnet' 321; 'Sonnet with Reverse Perspective' 324

Labé, Louise 117
Lança, Eduardo (fictional author): 'Sonetos d'Amor' 144
Leishman, James Blair (translator) 115, 116, 122
Lightman, Ira (translator) 118
Lima, Ângelo de 132–34; 'Edd'ora Addio ... —Mia Soave! ... ' 133
Lock, Anne 62
Lodge, Thomas 18, 63
Lok, Henry 62
Lombez, Christine 209–210, 217, 220
Lorenz, Eleonore 8, 223–224
Losev, Alexey Fedorovich 317
Lowell, Robert (translator) 4, 118

Macauley, Thomas Babington 244
Machado, Antonio 7, 175, 177, 180–184, 220–221; 'Otras canciones a Guiomar' 183; 'Profesion de fe' 181–182
MacIntyre, C.F. (translator) 122
Mac Low, Jackson 7, 166
Macy, Joanna (translator) 117, 119, 124, 127
Mahon, Derek 7, 199–200
Maldeghem, Philippe de 59, 63–65
Malevich, Kazimir 325
Mallarmé, Stéphane 115, 198
Marot, Clément 19, 29, 73, 75; Marotic Rhyme 63

Marshak, Samuil 9, 229, 231, 315–317; 'Translation of Shakespeare's *Sonnets*' 9, 330
Mason, Eudo Colecestra (translator) 116
Melehy, Hassan 2, 35–36, 47, 49
Mesiats (Mesyats), Vadim *500 Sonnets to Leroy Merlin* 326
Meter (discussion of): caesura/césure 74, 78, 109, 119, 128, 267; iambic pentameter 3, 120–121, 213, 231, 254; hendecasyllable 267, 277; octave/sestet 2, 26, 75, 81, 105, 163, 179–181, 213–214, 23; rhyming couplet 2, 26, 40–41, 62–63, 75, 78, 89, 105–106, 134, 163–170, 182, 189, 247, 253, 297; rhyme scheme 3, 24, 26, 63, 71, 79, 105, 122, 157, 165, 179, 199, 201, 307
Metre journal (and translation) 195–196
Mhac an tSaoi, Maire 7, 205–206
Michelangelo 7, 200, 214
Middleton, Thomas: *The Wisdome of Salomon Paraphrased* 62, 63
Miltonian tradition 138
Mironov, Alexander: 'September Sonnet' 324
Molière 264, 268, 269, 270–271
Moniz, Dr. Egas (psychiatrist) 133
Monteiro, George 141–142, 144
Montgomerie, Alexander 63, 78
Mozart, Wolfgang Amadeus 202; *The Marriage of Figaro* 266–267; *Voi che sapete* (air) 267
Mulcaster, Richard 73
Muldoon, Paul 193, 305

Nabokov, Vladimir 316
Nerval, Gérard de 6, 105–113; 'Delphica' 106; 'Le Christ aux Oliviers' 105; 'El Desdichado' 108; *Les Illuminés* 106, 107

Neruda, Jan 202
Nesme (see Du Nesme)
Nida, Eugene 306
Nietzsche, Friedrich 322
North, Dudley, third Baron North: *A Forest of Varieties* 53

Ochino, Bernardino 71–72
Opitz, Martin 6, 69–71; *Poemata* 69, 71
Orpheus 108, 112, 118–121; '*Die Sonette an Orpheus*' 6, 115–130, 175–184, 214–216
Otto, Carlos (fictional author) 137; 'Sonho de Gorgias' ('Dream of Gorgias') 137
Oulipo 4, 9, 158–159, 211, 284–285, 291–294, 296–297
Ovid 37, 53; *Fasti* 24; *Metamorphoses* 62, 63, 124

Palacky, František 204
Pasternak, Boris 1, 229, 231
Paterson, Don 3, 4, 7, 118–120, 124, 125, 127, 175–190; 'America' 180; 'Incunabula' 179–180; 'Miguel' 186; 'Poetry' 183; 'The Landscape' 186–187; 'The Light' 177–178; 'The Spin' 184; 'Waking with Russell' 178, 183
Peletier du Mans, Jacques: 'Art poétique' 2, 17
Pessoa, Fernando 131–153; 'Antígona' 144–45; 'Como te amo? Não sei de quantos modos varios' 144; *Fausto* 138; heteronyms 131–32; 'How many masks wear we, and undermasks' 136–37; intersectionism 133; Jorge (brother) 145; 'Joseph Chamberlain' 138–39; 'Kitchener' 138–39; Madalena Henriqueta (sister) 145, Maria Clara (sister) 145; *Mensagem* 131, 141; 'Oft in the great void silence of the night' 148; 'Oh gentle spirit mine that didst depart' (translation) 142–43; orthonym 131–32, 138; "O poeta é um fingidor' ('The poet is a forger') 133; pseudonym 138; semi-heteronym 131; 'Sometimes a softness steals into my heart' 146–47; 'Tell me again that story of the Prince' 134–35; 'The night holds things more curious than the day' 149; *35 Sonnets* 135–36, 146; Supra-Camões (prophecy) 141; syntax 135
Petrarch (Petrarca, Francesco) 2, 4, 5, 8, 9, 38, 73, 115, 53–68, 140–43, 175, 199–200, 202–204, 232, 263–28, 318, 323–330
RVF (see *Rerum Vulgarium Fragmenta*)
Petrarchism 2, 35–36, 38–39, 42, 44, 47, 263, 268–269, 271
Philieul, Vasquin (translator) 2, 59, 64–65
Pizarro, Jerónimo 133, 136; anxiety of unity (theory) 136
Plath, Sylvia: 'Edge' 180
Plato 18, 26; *Ion* 18, 26; *Symposium* 39, 48, 61, 94, 179
Platonism (and Neo-Platonism) 17–19, 24, 26–30, 46–49, 61, 141, 178, 179
Pléiade poets 35, 72, 80, 271
Poe, Edgar Allen 316; 'Annabel Lee' 166
Poetic form: Cadavre exquis (Play-Text) 286–288; canzone 272, 323; eclogue 29, 323, 327; elegy 186, 323; haiku 1, 207n; madrigal 3, 55, 276; ode 20, 89; psalm 3, 19, 29, 31, 54,

55, 61–65; rondeau 283–284; sestina 164–165
Polikoff, Daniel Joseph (translator) 119, 123–125, 127
Pollock, Estill (translator) 117
Poulin, Alfred A. (translator) 116
Prescott, Ann Lake 2–3, 35–37, 53
Prudhommeaux, André 211–212
Pushkin, Alexander 9, 318–319, 327–330; 'To the Sea' 328; 'Severe Dante did not scorn the sonnet' 318; 'Tale of Tsar Saltan' 329; 'The Wanderer' 328; 'From Pindemonti' 328
Puttenham, George 18

Quarles, Francis 62
Queneau, Raymond: *Cent mille milliards de poèmes* (*CMMP*) 283–300; First ten sonnets of *CMMP* 289–290
Quinn, Justin 7, 194–198, 202–206

Raimondo, Riccardo 4, 19
Ramazani, Jahan 1, 3, 4
Regan, Stephen 4, 193, 194, 200
Reis, Ricardo (heteronym) 131, 138
Rerum Vulgarium Fragmenta (*RVF*, *Canzoniere*): *RVF* 1: 'Voi ch'ascoltate in rime sparse' 264; *RVF* 31: 'Quest' anima gentil, che si diparte'; *RVF* 48: 'Se mai foco per foco non si spense' 59; *RVF* 61: 'Benedetto sia 'l giorno, e 'l mese et l'anno' 275; *RVF* 62 : 'Padre del Ciel' 265; *RVF* 84: '– Occhi piangete' 264–265; *RVF* 126: 'Chiare, fresche et dolci acque' 274; *RVF* 132: 'S'amor non è' 264, 266, 268; *RVF* 134: 'Pace non trovo' 270; *RVF* 189: 'Passa la nave mia colma d'oblio' 57; *RVF* 366: 'Vergine bella' 265, 272–273

Reynolds, Matthew 4, 6, 306
Rilke, Rainer Maria 6, 7, 8, 115–130, 180, 181, 184–186, 202, 205, 209, 213–217, 326; '*Die Sonette an Orpheus*' 6, 115–130, 175–184, 214–216; 'Da stieg ein Baum. O reine Übersteigung' 127; 'Spiegel: nor nie hat man wissen beschrieben' 120; 'Tänzerin: o du Verlegung' 184
Robertson, Roland (glocalisation) 251
Rodin, Auguste 115
Ronsard, Pierre de 18, 53, 64, 69, 72, 75, 80, 94, 95–98, 100, 195
Rossetti, Dante Gabriel 202
Roubaud, Jacques 7, 155–173; *Churchill 40* 155–173; 'Ma nouvelle casquette' 158–159; 'Camden Lock' 160; 'Hotel Boulderado' 163, 166; 'Winston Churchill à Carcassonne, octobre 1940' 168; 'Constable country' 170–171

San Gimignano, Folgore da 7, 202
Sapgir, Genrich 229–243, 325–326; *Sonnets on Shirts* 229–242; 'Body' 230, 234; 'Spirit' 230, 235; 'Water' 232, 236; 'Sonnet of Things Gone Missing' 232, 236; 'Drunken Sonnet' 237; 'Something – Nothing' 231, 238; 'Newspaper Editorial Sonnet 232, 239'; 'New Year's Sonnet '232, 241; 'Commentary Sonnet' 232, 241
Scève, Maurice 38
Schede Melissus, Paul 71, 76; 'Was im Weltkreise rund allenthalb lebt vnd schwebet' 78
Schwabe von der Heyde, Ernst 80
Scott, Clive 3

Search, Alexander (fictional author) 137–39
Sedakova, Olga 9, 315, 317–319, 323, 326–330
Sena, Jorge de 136, 146
Seneca 55, 264
Shakespeare, William 1, 4, 5, 7, 8, 9, 35–52, 57, 61–62, 63, 65, 93, 99, 146, 162, 163, 164, 175, 176, 193, 203–205, 210–212, 220, 224, 231, 264, 268, 270–271, 315–317, 330; *As You Like It* 43; *A Midsummer Night's Dream* 203; *Love's Labour's Lost* 268–270; *Twelfth Night* 43; *Romeo and Juliet* 43, 268; *Venus and Adonis* 63; *The Sonnets*: 'Sonnet 51' 61; 'Sonnet 116' 57, 62; 'Sonnet 66' 1; 'Sonnet 12' 211; 'Sonnet 119' 211; 134, 137, 48
Shvarts, Elena 317
Sidney, Sir Philip 18, 65; *Apology for Poetry (Defence of Poesy)* 30, 61; *Astrophel and Stella* 11; 'Sonnet 76' 61.
Snodgrass, W.D.: 'The Four Seasons' 303
Soares, Bernardo (semi-heteronym) 131; *Livro do Desassossego (The Book of Disquiet)* 131
Sonnet: Berrigan-sonnet 7, 167–168; caesura/césure (see metre); caudate sonnet 268; crypto-sonnet 155, curtal sonnet 163–164, 179; decasyllable (see metre); double sonnet 155, fragment 167, 179–180, hendecasyllable (see metre), iambic pentameter (see metre), Lichtenberg's knife (to describe the sonnet) 165, octave/sestet (see metre), parts vs whole (in sonnet sequence) 46, 70, 117–119, 232, 274, Petrarchan/ Italian sonnet 2, 7, 89, 105–112, 134, 163, 196, 198, 255, postcolonial sonnet 193–194, 243–257, prose sonnet (or prose translations of sonnets) 3, 162–164, 188n, 211, 212, 263, rhyme scheme (see metre), Ronsardian sonnet 78; 105–106, Shakespearean sonnet 1, 63, 89, 97, 137, 178, 195, 202, 255, sonnet sequence 2, 17, 24, 30, 33–39, 47–51, 105–109, 115–125, 157, 188, 204, 207, 215, 243, 253, Spenserian sonnet 78–79, visual effects 119, 157–162, 172, 230, 288, visual sonnet 5, volta 40, 42, 177, 185, 204, 215, 256
Southwell, Robert 19
Speirs, Ruth (translator) 116
Spenser, Edmund 2, 5, 17–33, 35–37, 44–47, 49, 65, 73–75, 193; *Amoretti* 45, 46, 57, 62; *Epithalamion* 44, 45; 'The Shepheardes Calendar' 18; *Complaints* 20, 30, 35, 49, 73; *Amoretti*, 'Sonnet 34' 57, 62; *Faerie Queene* 62, (2.2.208) 22; 'Ruines of Rome: by Bellay' 17, 19, 20, 24, 30, 35, 37; 'Ye heavenly spirites, whose ashie cinders lie' 21–22; 'Bellay, first garland of free Poësie' 35
Spiller, Michael R.G. 2, 3, 243, 244
Stampa, Gaspara 221, 223–224
Starynkevitch, Dmitri 293–296
Stepanova, Maria: *Twenty Sonnets to M* 323
Surrey, Henry Howard, Earl of: 'The louer describes his restlesse state' 59
Sylvester, Josuah 5, 17, 19, 25–30; 'The Miracle of the Peace in

Fraunce' 17, 26, 30; 'But what new Sunne doth now adorne our Land' 28; 'Faire fruitfull daughter of th'Omnipotent' 28

Tomlinson, Charles (translator) 122

Tottel's Miscellany: Songs and Sonnettes 54, 59

Translation: and creativity 3, 5, 118, 123, 243, 286, 306, 326; as imitation 2, 4–6, 18, 26, 30–31, 35–36, 39, 45–49, 53–55, 61–65, 69–70, 76–77, 140, 201, 209, 210–227, 255, 267; as response 5, 8, 36, 54, 89, 98–100, 177, 180, 187, 232, 257; author or translator's preface 3, 94, 100, 113, 117, 181, 188, 251, 269, 274, 285, 298; transposition 6, 76, 120, 201–202; translating sound 3, 6, 21, 105, 109, 118, 121, 158–159, 162, 182–183, 231–233, 303, 307

Trediakovsky 231

Turing, Alan 285–286, 291

Utenhove, Charles 73

Valéry, Paul 115, 196, 214, 216, 292

Vallejo, Cesar, 'A mi hermano Miguel' 186

Van der Noot, Jan 2, 35, 70, 71–72, 73–76, 79, 80; *Extasis* 74; 'T'was inden tijd als Gods ghift' t'onsen loone' 74

Vaucienne, François 264, 271, 274

Vendler, Helen 193, 195

Vinclair, Pierre 5

Virgil 23–24; *Aeneid* 94, 21–22; *Fourth Eclogue* 325

Vivaldi, Antonio: *The Four Seasons* 9, 301–313

Wheatley, David 7, 195–197

William IX Duke of Aquitaine (troubadour) 318

Wirsung, Christoph 70, 71–72, 73, 75, 79

Wyatt, Frederick (fictional author) 137, 139

Wyatt, Sir Thomas 2, 54, 62; 'My galley, chargèd with forgetfulness' 54

Yeats, William Butler 193, 195, 205–206

Zábrana, Jan 203

www.ingramcontent.com/pod-product-compliance
Lightning Source LLC
Chambersburg PA
CBHW052141300426
44115CB00011B/1464